American Literary Scholarship
1967

American Literary Scholarship

An Annual / 1967

Edited by James Woodress

Essays by John C. Broderick, Hyatt H. Waggoner, Merton M. Sealts, Jr., Edward F. Grier, John C. Gerber, William T. Stafford, Robert A. Wiggins, William White, Richard Beale Davis, Joseph V. Ridgely, J. Albert Robbins, Warren French, Richard D. Lehan, Brom Weber, Oliver Evans, Walter Meserve, John T. Flanagan, Harry Finestone.

Indexed by Joseph M. Flora

Duke University Press, Durham, North Carolina, 1969

Foreword

With this volume *American Literary Scholarship* completes its first half decade. It now is well established as one of the standard tools for the study of American literature. A considerable part of the success of this enterprise has resulted from the continuity of contributors. Four of the present list of contributors have appeared in every volume of this series, while seven others have written for *ALS* four times, and another five, three times. Thus 63 out of a total of 88 essays appearing here in the five years since this work was inaugurated have been written by scholars whose dedication to this project and to the service of other scholars has been remarkably generous. Those who have appeared here five times are Richard Beale Davis, Oliver Evans, John C. Gerber, and J. Albert Robbins; four times: Louis J. Budd, Harry Finestone, Edward F. Grier, Frederick J. Hoffman, B. R. McElderry, Jr., William T. Stafford, and Willard Thorp; three times: John T. Flanagan, Malcolm Goldstein, Walter Harding, C. Hugh Holman, and Robert A. Wiggins.

The format and coverage remain about the same in this volume as in the previous one. The only significant change shifts Emily Dickinson from the general chapter on 19th-Century poetry to the chapter on Whitman. The form of the bibliographical notation continues to follow the style used in the MLA International Bibliography prior to the 1967 compilation. In general the articles reviewed give the author, the title, the journal, the volume, and the pages. It may be assumed that in every case, unless otherwise stated, the year is 1967. When articles are cited from journals that page each number separately, the number of the issue is included. The periodicals in which the articles appear are listed by abbreviation or acronym, and a key to the periodicals may be found in the pages immediately following the Table of Contents. Books cited are listed with author, title, place of publication, and publisher. The dates, as with journal citations, are 1967 unless otherwise specified. In the case of *Festschriften* or other collections of essays short titles have been used in the text and the full bibliographical data given in the "Key to Abbreviations."

James Woodress

University of California at Davis

Table of Contents

Key to Abbreviations

ABC   *American Book Collector*
AI   *American Imago*
AION-SG   *Annali Istituto Universitario Orientale, Napoli, Sezione Germanica*
AL   *American Literature*
All These to Teach   Robert A. Bryan, *et al.*, eds., *All These To Teach, A Symposium: Essays in Honor of C. A. Robertson* (Gainesville, Univ. of Fla. Press)
ALR   *American Literary Realism*
ALS   *American Literary Scholarship: An Annual*
AmA   *American Archivist*
The American Theater Today   Alan S. Downer, ed., *The American Theater Today* (New York, Basic Books)
AN&Q   *American Notes and Queries*
Approdo   *L'Approdo Letterario* (Rome)
AQ   *American Quarterly*
AR   *Antioch Review*
Archiv   *Archiv für das Studium der Neueren Sprachen und Literaturen*
ArQ   *Arizona Quarterly*
AS   *American Speech*
ASch   *American Scholar*
ATR   *Anglican Theological Review*
AW   *American West*
BB   *Bulletin of Bibliography*
BBr   *Books at Brown*
BI   *Books at Iowa*
BNYPL   *Bulletin of the New York Public Library*
BSUF   *Ball State University Forum*
BuR   *Bucknell Review*
BYUS   *Brigham Young University Studies*

CE   *College English*
CentR   *The Centennial Review*
CH   *Church History*
ChiR   *Chicago Review*
Cithera   (St. Bonaventure University)
CJF   *Chicago Jewish Forum*
CL   *Comparative Literature*
CLAJ   *College Language Association Journal*
CLJ   *Cornell Library Journal*
CLQ   *Colby Library Quarterly*
CLS   *Comparative Literature Studies* (University of Illinois)
CM   *The Carlton Miscellany*
ConnR   *Connecticut Review*
CQ   *Cambridge Quarterly*
CR   *Critical Review* (Melbourne)
Crit   *Critique: Studies in Modern Fiction*
Criticism   (Wayne State)
CritQ   *Critical Quarterly*
CUF   *Columbia University Forum*
DA   *Dissertation Abstracts*
DC   *Drama Critique*
Discourse   (Concordia College)
DLit   *Doshisha Literature* (Japan)
DR   *Dalhousie Review*
DramS   *Drama Survey* (Minneapolis)
EA   *Etudes Anglaises*
EALN   *Early American Literature Newsletter*
EIC   *Essays in Criticism*
EIHC   *Essex Institute Historical Collections*
ELH   *Journal of English Literary History*
ELN   *English Language Notes*
ER   *English Record* (N.Y. State English Council)
ES   **English Studies**

ESQ	*Emerson Society Quarterly*
Essays on American Literature	Clarence Gohdes, ed., *Essays on American Literature in Honor of Jay B. Hubbell* (Durham, N.C., Duke Univ. Press)
Essays in American and English Literature	Max Schulz, ed., *Essays in American and English Literature Presented to Bruce Robert McElderry, Jr.,* (Athens, Ohio Univ. Press)
Essays on History and Literature	Bremmer, Robert H., ed., *Essays on History and Literature* [in honor of Foster Rhea Dulles] (Columbus, Ohio State Univ. Press, 1966)
Expl	*Explicator*
Explorations of Literature	Rima D. Reck, ed., *Explorations of Literature* (La. State Univ. Stud., Humanistic Series, Baton Rouge, La. State Univ. Press, 1966)
FFMA	*Folklore and Folkmusic Archivist* (Indiana University)
FitzN	*Fitzgerald Newsletter* (London)
Folklore International	D. K. Wilgus, ed., *Folklore International: Essays . . . in Honor of Wayland Debs Hand . . .* (Hatboro, Pa., Folklore Associates)
Folklore Studies	*Folklore Studies in Honor of Arthur Palmer Hudson* (*N.C. Folklore*, XIII [1965], i–ii, Chapel Hill, N.C. Folklore Society)
ForumH	*Forum* (Houston)
The Frontier Reexamined	John F. McDermott, ed., *The Frontier Reexamined* (Urbana, Univ. of Ill. Press)
FuS	*Furman Studies*
GaR	*Georgia Review*
HAB	*Humanities Association Bulletin* (Canada)
HC	*The Hollins Critic*
HLB	*Harvard Library Bulletin*
HMPEC	*Historical Magazine of the Protestant Episcopal Church*
HSE	*Hungarian Studies in English*
HTR	*Harvard Theological Review*
HudR	*Hudson Review*
IAC	*Indo-Asian Culture*
IEY	*Iowa English Yearbook*
In Defense of Historical Literature	David Levin, *In Defense of Historical Literature: Essays on American History, Autobiography, Drama, and Fiction* (New York, Hill and Wang)
JA	*Jahrbuch für Amerikastudien*
JAF	*Journal of American Folklore*
JAmS	*Journal of American Studies*
JFI	*Journal of the Folklore Institute*
JGE	*Journal of General Education*
JHI	*Journal of the History of Ideas*
JJQ	*James Joyce Quarterly*
JNH	*Journal of Negro History*
JPC	*Journal of Popular Culture*
JPH	*Journal of Presbyterian History*
JQ	*Journalism Quarterly*
KBAA	*Kieler Beiträge für Anglistik und Americanistik*
KFLQ	*Kentucky Foreign Language Quarterly*
KFQ	*Keystone Folklore Quarterly*
KFR	*Kentucky Folklore Record*
KN	*Kwartalnik Neofilologiczny* (Warsaw)
KR	*Kenyon Review*
LaS	*Louisiana Studies*
LangQ	*Language Quarterly* (Univ. of South Fla.)
LC	*Library Chronicle* (Univ. of Pa.)
LCrit	*Literary Criterion* (Univ. of Mysore, India)
LHY	*The Literary Half-Yearly*
LitR	*Literary Review* (Fairleigh Dickinson Univ.)
L&P	*Literature and Psychology*
Man's Changing Mask	Charles C. Walcutt, *Man's Changing Mask: Modes and Methods of*

	Characterization in Fiction (Minneapolis, Univ. of Minn. Press, 1966)	PLL	Papers on Language and Literature
MASJ	Midcontinent American Studies Journal	PMASAL	Papers of the Michigan Academy of Science, Arts, and Letters
McNR	McNeese Review	PMLA	Publications of the Modern Language Association
MD	Modern Drama		
MFS	Modern Fiction Studies	PQ	Philological Quarterly
MH	Minnesota History	QJLC	Quarterly Journal of the Library of Congress
MinnR	Minnesota Review		
MissQ	Mississippi Quarterly	QJS	Quarterly Journal of Speech
MLN	Modern Language Notes		
MLQ	Modern Language Quarterly	RLC	Revue de Littérature Comparée
MQ	Midwest Quarterly		
MQR	Michigan Quarterly Review	RLV	Revue des Langues Vivantes
MR	Massachusetts Review	RS	Research Studies (Washington State Univ.)
MRR	Mad River Review (Dayton, Ohio)	SA	Studi Americani
MSS	Manuscripts	SAB	South Atlantic Bulletin
MTJ	Mark Twain Journal	Salmagundi	(Flushing, New York)
NAR	North American Review	SAQ	South Atlantic Quarterly
NCF	Nineteenth Century Fiction	SatR	The Saturday Review
		SB	Studies in Bibliography
NoCF	North Carolina Folklore	S&C	Studies and Critiques (Univ. of Tex., Arlington)
NEQ	New England Quarterly		
NH	Nebraska History		
N&Q	Notes and Queries	SCN	Seventeenth Century News
NRF	Nouvelle Revue Française		
NS	Die Neueren Sprachen	SELit	Studies in English Literature (Univ. of Tokyo)
NTM	New Theater Magazine (Bristol)		
		Serif	The Serif (Kent, Ohio)
NYFQ	New York Folklore Quarterly	Seven Contemporary Authors	Thomas B. Whitbread, ed., Seven Contemporary Authors: Essays on Cozzens, Miller, West, Golding, Heller, Albee, and Powers (Austin, Univ. of Tex. Press)
NYTM	New York Times Magazine		
PAPS	Proceedings of the American Philosophical Society		
Patterns of Commitment	Marston LaFrance, ed., Patterns of Commitment in American Literature (Toronto, Univ. of Toronto Press)	SFQ	Southern Folklore Quarterly
		SF&R	Scholars Facsimiles and Reprints (Gainesville, Fla.)
PBSA	Papers of the Bibliographical Society of America	ShawR	Shaw Review
		SHR	Southern Humanities Review
PFL	Pennsylvania Folk Life	SIR	Studies in Romanticism
PH	Pennsylvania History	SNL	Satire Newsletter
Phoenix	(Seoul: English Lit. Soc., Korea Univ.)	SoQ	The Southern Quarterly (Univ. of So. Miss.)
PICLA	Francois Jost, ed., Proceedings of the Fourth Congress of the International Comparative Literature Association (The Hague, Mouton, 1966)	SoR	Southern Review
		SPHQ	Swedish Pioneer Historical Quarterly
		SR	Sewanee Review
		SSF	Studies in Short Fiction (Newberry College, Newberry, S. C.)

SSL	*Studies in Scottish Literature*
SWS	Southwestern Writers Series (Austin, Tex., Steck-Vaughan)
Sunny Slopes	Wilson M. Hunt and Allen Maxwell, eds., *The Sunny Slopes of Long Ago* (Dallas, So. Methodist Univ. Press, 1966)
TCL	*Twentieth Century Literature*
TDR	*Tulane Drama Review*
TFSB	*Tennessee Folklore Society Bulletin*
The Thirties	Warren French, ed., *The Thirties: Fiction, Poetry, Drama* (Deland, Fla., Everett Edwards)
Topic	(Washington and Jefferson College)
TQ	*Texas Quarterly*
Tradition and Tolerance	David Howard, John Lucas, and John Goode, eds., *Tradition and Tolerance in Nineteenth-Century Fiction: Critical Essays on Some English and American Novels* (London and New York, Routledge and K. Paul, Barnes and Noble, 1966)
TransR	*Transatlantic Review*
TriQ	*Tri-Quarterly* (Evanston, Ill.)
TSB	*Thoreau Society Bulletin*
TSE	*Tulane Studies in English*
TSL	*Tennessee Studies in Literature*
TSLL	*Texas Studies in Literature and Language*

TUSAS	Twayne United States Authors Series
Twelve Great American Novels	Arthur Mizener, *Twelve Great American Novels* (New York, New American Library)
UDQ	*University of Denver Quarterly*
UDR	*University of Dayton Review*
UMPAW	University of Minnesota Pamphlets on American Writers
UR	*University Review*
UTQ	*University of Toronto Quarterly*
UWR	*University of Windsor Review*
VLit	*Voprosy Literatury*
VMHB	*Virginia Magazine of History and Biography*
VQR	*Virginia Quarterly Review*
VS	*Victorian Studies*
WAL	*Western American Literature*
WascanaR	*Wascana Review* (Regina, Saskatchewan)
WF	*Western Folklore*
WHR	*Western Humanities Review*
WMQ	*William and Mary Quarterly*
WSCL	*Wisconsin Studies in Contemporary Literature*
WWR	*Walt Whitman Review*
XUS	*Xavier University Studies*
YCGL	*Yearbook of Comparative and General Literature*
YR	*Yale Review*
YULG	*Yale University Library Gazette*

Part I

1. Emerson, Thoreau, and Transcendentalism

John C. Broderick

If one measure of the vitality and relevance of literature of the past is its capacity to arouse and sustain sophisticated scholarly inquiry, the literature of New England Transcendentalism thrives. The scholarly output for 1967 was very large (at least 75 separate entries in the incomplete MLA International Bibliography) but not uniformly excellent. In the commentary that follows, I have slighted the seemingly inconsequential or merely corroborative in order to give more attention to important individual studies or trends in research.

i. Dissertations

Dissertation Abstracts includes nineteen relevant dissertations, all but two of which had been completed in 1966 or 1967, a statistical sign of vigor. Recurrent concerns in these studies are the artistry of Transcendental literature, especially that of Thoreau; the personal and literary relationship of Emerson and Thoreau; and the shifts in Emerson's thought and mood from the 1830's to the 1850's. None of these are new themes, of course, and published scholarship of the past 15 or 20 years has generally provided outlines which the dissertations validate in detail. Almost all interest at the doctoral level is in Emerson and Thoreau, with Jones Very a distant but strong third.

Emerson's aesthetic theory was the subject of two dissertations. Lawrence I. Buell in "Emerson: From Preacher to Poet" (*DA*, XXVIII, 189A) indicates the extent to which Dr. Channing and other Unitarians in their stress on the union of religion and art anticipated Emerson's aesthetic. For Emerson, art "came to be seen as the more natural expression of the religious spirit." A contrary view is expressed by Richard A. Yoder in "Emerson's Poetry: A Study of Form and Techniques" (*DA*, XXVIII, 1453A–1454A). Despite Emerson's bardic pronouncements, his own poetry is notable for skepticism, compression, and "the limited dramatic ego he employs." The reiterated confrontation of the poet and nature involves a "small protagonist" and an unknown, incomprehensible Not-Me.

The division in Emerson assumed by Yoder underlies two studies concerned with his social thought. In "Ralph Waldo Emerson: Self and Society, 1850–1870" (*DA*, XXVIII, 1428A) Herbert Bogart contrasts Emerson's "inner, divine self" and "the prudential, social self." In his later writings Emerson saw the spiritual self as no more than a social goal which the prudential self might attain if sufficiently transformed by a genteel culture. In "Emerson's *Eroica*: A Study of His Idea of Greatness" (*DA*, XXVIII, 246A–247A) Gustaaf Victor Van Cromphout contrasts the lecture series "Biography" (1835) and *Representative Men* (1850). The early lectures reveal Emerson's concern with his own personal greatness. The "representative men" were more objectively chosen, less critical in Emerson's own psychic history, and are therefore for the most part found wanting.

Emerson's transformation into a man of the world is a phenomenon also studied from the biographical point of view by Paul Hourihan in "The Inner Dynamics of the Emerson-Thoreau Relationship" (*DA*, XXVIII, 1787A–1788A). The relationship was one of "continuing *mutual* influence." Thoreau, initially attracted by Emerson's personality, nevertheless "is seen as the fulfillment of Emerson's principal ideas—the new type of scholar-hero." Richard Carl Tuerk, on the other hand, argues that Thoreau "is by no means a 'specific Emerson.'" Tuerk's approach in "Circle Imagery in the Prose of Emerson and Thoreau from *Nature* (1836) to *Walden* (1854)" (*DA*, XXVIII, 1798A) is through literary analysis. He finds that Emerson employs the circle as an adjunct to his philosophy whereas Thoreau uses it as an end in itself. Emerson perceives a circular order in the universe and occasionally reproduces it in his writing. Thoreau creates a self-contained universe in art, partly through images of circularity.

Thoreau is widely recognized as the prose artist of Transcendentalism. For that reason, among others, research topics which might otherwise lead toward intellectual history are now usually turned into commentary on his art. William W. Nichols entitled his study "Science and the Development of Thoreau's Art" (*DA*, XXVII, 3056A–3057A) and limits its interest to "the impact of his involvement in science on his development as a literary artist." Science enabled Thoreau to fuse actual and ideal with force. John Robert Burns's study, "Thoreau's Use of the Bible" (*DA*, XXVII, 3864A), is perhaps chiefly valuable for its Biblical glossary to Thoreau's writings. However, it too concerns itself with matters of style and revision. A comparable study of different materials is Lonnie Leon Willis, "Folklore in the Published Writings of Henry David Thoreau: A Study and a Compendium-Index" (*DA*, XXVIII, 1412A–1413A). A checklist of wordplays and commonplaces is also a part of Joseph J. Moldenhauer's 1964 dissertation "The Rhetoric of *Walden*," only recently abstracted (*DA*, XXVIII, 638A) but already the source of published articles. In "Thoreau's Shifting Stance Toward Nature: A Study in Romanticism" (*DA*, XXVIII, 236A), James Henry McIntosh detects Thoreau's sharing both Goethe's sensuous involvement with nature and a Wordsworthian mysticism, joined through Emersonian polarities and technical experimentation. To Leonard Nick Neufeldt in "The Wild Apple Tree: Possibilities of the Self in Thoreau" (*DA*, XXVII, 4261A), Thoreau seems an exemplary strategist for revealing in art the resources and energies of the self in the midst of circumstances. William D. Drake, on the other hand, regards Thoreau's central belief—in an "innocent, unconscious, and childlike existence of nature"—as a failure. In "The Depth of Walden: Thoreau's Symbolism of the Divine in Nature" (*DA*, XXVIII, 1393A–1394A), Drake argues from revisions of the *Walden* manuscript that Thoreau surrendered his early belief. Donovan LeRoy Welch also posits a loss of innocence in Thoreau, which affected both his theory and practice of poetry. In "A Chronological Study of the Poetry of Henry David Thoreau" (*DA*, XXVII, 3435A–3436A) Welch denies that Thoreau's verse reveals organic form, no matter how much Thoreau admired it. His verse also lacks beauty.

Jones Very's poetry was the subject of one dissertation and figured largely in another. Henry Lawrence Jones in "Symbolism in the Mystical Poetry of Jones Very" (*DA*, XXVIII, 2210A) regards Very's sonnets as an organized portrayal of a mystical journey and identifies twenty-four symbols. Very, along with Emerson and Thoreau, is discussed by Carl Edward Dennis in "The Poetry of Mind and Nature: A Study of the Idea of Nature in American Transcendental Poetry" (*DA*, XXVII, 2496A), in which the Americans are distinguished from the English Romantics through their emphasis on the theory of correspondence, rather than through their viewing nature as either active force or passive matter, as the British inconsistently did. There was also a study of "Charles Lane and the Fruitlands Utopia" by Robert Howard Walker (*DA*, XXVII, 4232A).

Finally, lest literary scholars grow complacent in admiration of Transcendental paradoxes, there is Irving Joseph Rein, "The New England Transcendentalists: Rhetoric of Paradox" (*DA*, XXVII, 3149A). Rein regards Transcendental rhetoric as a failure, unlike that of European anarchists, because its intended audience rejected it.

ii. Texts, Editions, Bibliographies

There was less editorial activity than usual in 1967, especially with respect to Emerson studies. The text of a single manuscript leaf recently acquired by Stanford University Library and apparently related to *English Traits* is printed by David M. Stevens (*ESQ*, No. 47, pp. 103–105), and George Monteiro supplements Rusk in "Bibliographical Notes on Four Emerson Letters" (*ibid.*, pp. 15–16). Two of the notes are based on discovery of the manuscripts at the Houghton Library and in the Massachusetts Historical Society. In *PBSA* (LXI, 124–126) Jacob Blanck corrects the entry for *Letters and Social Aims* (Boston, 1876) in his *Bibliography of American Literature*. Four printings of the edition are now identifiable. Kenneth Cameron continued to produce results from his scrutiny of dealers' catalogs, reporting on manuscripts (*ESQ*, No. 47, pp. 125–126) and presentation copies (*ESQ*, No. 47, pp. 106–108).

A good deal of textual and bibliographical activity concerned the Orient. A bibliography published in a limited edition of 500 copies in Kyoto in 1947 is reprinted (*ESQ*, No. 46, pp. 53–89): Bunshō Jugaku, "A Bibliography of Ralph Waldo Emerson in Japan from 1878 to 1935." A brief introduction on Japanese interest in Emerson is followed by a well annotated checklist of 228 items—"far from being complete or exhaustive in any sense." William Bysshe Stein has selected and introduced *Two Brahman Sources of Emerson and Thoreau* (SF&R). The two are Rajah R. Roy's translation of . . . *Texts of the Veds* . . . (London, 1832), and William Ward's *A View of the History, Literature, and Mythology of the Hindoos*, vol. II (London, 1822). Stein has also listed approximately 75 Oriental texts, English and French translations of Veda, Epic, Purana,

Kanya, etc. in "A Bibliography of Hindu and Buddhist Literature Available to Thoreau Through 1854" (*ESQ*, No. 47, pp. 52–56).

Ten letters of Thoreau were edited in 1967, six from manuscripts found among his surveying papers in the Concord Free Public Library by Albert F. McLean, Jr. ("Addenda to the Thoreau Correspondence," *BNYPL*, LXXI, 265–267). The remaining four texts were based on facsimiles and excerpts in dealers' catalogs (*ESQ*, No. 48, pp. 73–81). All ten are minor and have to do with lecture appointments and surveying business. Under the title *The Variorum Civil Disobedience* (New York, Twayne), Walter Harding has reprinted, with annotations, the text of the essay found in *A Yankee in Canada* (1866), indicating 1849 variants. It is questionable whether the volume of commentary on "Civil Disobedience" or its textual history as yet justifies the designation "variorum" for any edition.

Russell E. Durning prints "Margaret Fuller's Translation of Goethe's 'Prometheus,'" found in an 1838 letter to Caroline S. Tappan in the Fuller papers at Houghton Library (*JA*, XII, 240–245). The translation and her comments about it reveal Margaret's "close temperamental kinship" with Goethe at the time.

The major bibliographical contribution of the year is undoubtedly *Emerson's Library*, a checklist compiled by Walter Harding (Charlottesville, Univ. Press of Va.). Based upon a card catalog of the library as preserved in the Concord Antiquarian Society, the checklist provides further evidence of the range of Emerson's interests and will be the basis for study of influences and literary associations affecting Emerson's work. There is, it should be added, no attempt to analyze the evidence in a brief preface, which is confined to methods of preparing and presenting the list.

The usual specialized checklists appear in *ESQ*, No. 48, and *TSB*, all issues.

iii. Studies Chiefly Biographical

Ellen Tucker Emerson has been a biographically shadowy figure, whose early death apparently did no more than free her husband simultaneously from orthodoxy and the usual financial exigencies. The publication of her letters in 1962 began the process of reconsideration. Now, based on her letters and other original sources,

Henry F. Pommer has made an admirable brief biographical study of *Emerson's First Marriage* (Carbondale, Southern Ill. Univ. Press). In an appendix, "A Touchstone for Biographers," the author somewhat dryly documents past neglect or over-simplification of the episode. Pommer's own study is remarkable no less for what it reveals of Ellen than for the changed view of Emerson necessitated by its evidence. In courtship and early marriage, he was notable for warmth and directness of affection; any intellectualization of his love came later. His mood following his wife's death approached suicidal apathy. He probably found it easier to resign his pastorate because he had lost interest in almost everything. It seems likely that Emerson's thought and writing concerning immortality and compensation were significantly influenced by Ellen's death and her own reliance on such supports. Pommer's study is an important corrective not only to Emerson's misrepresentation in retrospect of his own strong human feelings but to similar tendencies in literary scholarship.

There were no biographical studies of Thoreau worth mentioning, but the story of "Thoreau's Village Background" is charmingly told by Ruth R. Wheeler (*TSB*, No. 100, pp. 1–6).

A refrain of earlier issues of *ALS* has been the neglect of "minor" Transcendentalists. In 1967 three biographies were published, each one of which deserves attention. The briefest but most impressive is Frederick T. McGill, *Channing of Concord: A Life of William Ellery Channing II* (New Brunswick, Rutgers Univ. Press). In fewer than 200 pages of text McGill admirably distills extensive research in Massachusetts, New York City, and the Middle West. The result is a credible portrait of a young man with every seeming advantage, who cultivated irresponsibility as a matter of Emersonian principle and lived a long, substantially wasted life. McGill indicates several themes and poetic effects in which Channing anticipated Emerson, to the benefit of the latter's verse. Channing's eccentricities may also have served Thoreau as corrective to his own waywardness. He certainly served Thoreau well through his editorial labors and championing after the death of the poet-naturalist (as he happily designated his friend).

Charles Crowe's *George Ripley: Transcendentalist and Utopian Socialist* (Athens, Univ. of Ga. Press) is the first book-length study of Ripley since Frothingham's biography in 1882, an unaccountable neglect since Ripley was central to a great many Transcendental enterprises (Brook Farm, *The Dial, Specimens of Foreign Standard Literature*, etc.). Despite the emphasis indicated by the subtitle, Crowe's final chapter summarizing the 30 "New York years" seems relatively the most successful, partly, no doubt, because of the poignance and irony of Ripley's glorious but shrunken last phase. As a boy, Ripley is said to have found in Greenfield, Mass., an image of social harmony which he sought in middle life to reproduce at Brook Farm. His movement from docile social conservative to reformer and political activist is attributed in part to a rejection of the values of his father. Crowe assigns Ripley a momentous place in national reform activities of the 1840's and softens the eccentricities and failings of Brook Farm as seen by other commentators. He has made good use of unpublished materials in the Houghton Library and the Massachusetts Historical Society but overlooked potentially valuable material for the New York period in the Library of Congress (especially the Whitelaw Reid papers).

Edwin Gittleman's *Jones Very: The Effective Years 1833–1840* (New York, Columbia Univ. Press) was the most important of several publications about the Salem poet, a veritable revival. Unlike the two biographies just mentioned, Gittleman's is a combination inner life and *biographia literaria*. The major influences on Very were his mother Lydia, his strong but suppressed sexuality, the consequent inner warfare during his early Harvard years, and his contemporaries, particularly Emerson. Gittleman accepts the irregular or non-contractual marriage of Very's parents and attributes much in Very to his feelings of guilt, especially over the character his mother was forced to assume. The "period of grace" beginning in September, 1838, ended in the summer of 1839 when Very visited Concord and realized from his attraction toward Lidian Emerson that his love of beauty (his own momentous sacrifice) had not been quelled. Thereafter, his manner is interpreted as a pose seeking to perpetuate an earlier authentic change of heart. Except for the editorial insistence of Emerson, Very's published verse would have articulated a comprehensive Allegory of the Self, with the various way-stations toward spiritual awakening. Gittleman's biography is comprehensive, informed, and critically sophisticated. It provides close readings of verse and prose to substantiate its viewpoints. It seems, nevertheless, somewhat attenuated and occasionally cryptic in style. There is also some question whether the sequential writings and the commonplace books of anyone, even Very, present a movement susceptible to almost week-by-week analysis. Does reading largely in Wordsworth a few months later than in Byron necessarily betoken the growth of the mind?

(As a footnote, it is interesting that Emerson does not come off exceptionally well in these biographies of his contemporaries. Whether as unconscious exploiter of Channing and ultimately unfortunate influence, as the reluctant reformer unwilling to "participate," or as the slightly supercilious advocate of Very whose editorial efforts thwarted as much as served the poet, Emerson receives some low marks. Paradoxically, the portrayals, if anything, strengthen interest in Emerson as a man and as a force in his own times.)

The word "mystic" is conspicuous by its absence from the analytical vocabulary of Gittleman. However, it figures prominently in Harry L. Jones, "The Very Madness: A New Manuscript" (*CLAJ*, X, 196–200), in which is printed Very's letter to Bellows, Dec. 24, 1838, commenting on confinement at McLean Asylum following his "change of heart." Paschal Reeves briefly reviews Very's biographical history (*EIHC*, CIII, 3–30). The title of his essay indicates its special emphasis, "The Making of a Mystic: A Reconsideration of the Life of Jones Very." Gittleman was no doubt wise to seek to free his study of Very's psychic life and its literary consequences from the built-in associations of the terminology of mysticism. That traditional terminology nevertheless has an obviously strong hold upon students of Very. Very's role in Adelphoi Theologia is revealed in Kenneth W. Cameron's "Sophomore Thoreau and Religious Improvement" (*ESQ*, No. 48, pp. 82–85), which, despite its title, has more to tell us of Very than of Thoreau.

C. Carroll Hollis has brought together Orestes Brownson's commentary on New England in "Brownson on Native New England" (*NEQ*, XL, 212–226), revealing surprising appreciation for the values of the region, especially its independence, the strength of the old Puritan tradition, and the sturdiness of the native vernacular. William H. and Jane H. Pease summarize Samuel J. May's activities in support of civil liberties (*CLJ*, No. 3, pp. 7–25). In "Toward the Holy Land: Platonism in the Middle West" (*SAB*, XXXII, ii, 1–6) George M. Harper adds to our understanding of Alcott's relations with the Midwestern Hegelians. Margaret Fuller is among those discussed by Hilton Anderson in "Americans in Europe Before the Civil War" (*SoQ*, V, 273–294).

iv. Sources and Influence

An interesting source study is Sacvan Bercovitch, "The Philosophical Background to the Fable of Emerson's 'American Scholar'" (*JHI*, XXVIII, 123–128). The division of Man into men is traced to Empedocles, in whom Emerson was demonstrably interested. John B. Wilson comments on the curious loss of interest in Gérando after the early 1830's (*CL*, XIX, 334–340). Two scholars find minor Miltonic echoes in *Walden* (*ESQ*, No. 47, pp. 19–21 and 65–66). A 1965 article heretofore overlooked in *PMLA* and *ALS* is Alfred S. Reid, "Emerson and Bushnell as Forerunners of Jamesian Pragmatism" (*FuS*, XIII, i, 18–30). Reid contends that Bushnell was more the rudimentary pragmatist than Emerson.

In a general essay, "Time, Doubt and Vision: Notes on Emerson and T. S. Eliot" (*ASch*, XXXVI, 125–132), John Clendenning finds similarities where none had been thought to exist. Both writers shared a similar concept of time, an insistence on necessary skepticisms, and a religion based on faith, not reason. Many of Eliot's animadversions are interpreted as directed against lingering Emersonianism in Boston at the turn of the century.

In "Emerson and Indian Philosophy" (*JHI*, XXVIII, 115–122), Dale Riepe provides a resume of Emerson's philosophical and spiritual kinship with Oriental thought. B. Damodar Rao, on the other hand, eschews an "exclusively Indian approach." In *Indian Response to American Literature*, ed. C. D. Narasimhaiah (New Delhi, U. S. Educational Foundation), pp. 15–27, he demonstrates Emerson's prose artistry in "Self-Reliance," citing in particular the "dialectical progress, an arrival at and a departure from tentative positions." Sensitive literary analysis by foreign scholars may be the ultimate evidence of influence.

A special Thoreau issue of *Europe* (No. 459–460) provides comparable evidence of that writer's influence. In one of a dozen contributions, "Thoreau et les Français" (pp. 177–185), Micheline Flak notes but does not really account for the greater interest in Thoreau elsewhere in the world (Japan, for instance) than in France. There are apparently two classes of French Thoreauvians, the anarchist-individualists who espouse his political thought and the academics who are chiefly interested in the stylist. However, Mlle. Flak points out that the younger generation is thoroughly familiar with Thoreau's work, partly through excerpts in school textbooks, and she anticipates a new dialogue between "Chanteclair" and "notre vieux Coq gaulois." The remaining essays in the symposium serve almost to belie Mlle Flak's contention of relative neglect of Thoreau. Outstanding perhaps is Roger Asselineau, "Un narcisse puritain: Quelques réflexions sur la personnalité de Thoreau" (pp.149–157). Asselineau is intrigued by the strange contradictions in Thoreau, particularly that between the man of simplicity portrayed in *Walden* and the sensual and egotistic artist who emerges from study of his life and work. Of Thoreau he writes: "Il était le moins spontane des hommes." Another article concerned with psychological motives is "Les ironies de la solitude" (pp. 162–169), by Jean Normand, in which Thoreau and Hawthorne are considered. Less psychoanalytical in approach is Micheline Flak's second essay, "L'homme de Concord" (pp. 158–162), which seeks to analyze the spirit of place and its effect on Thoreau, stressing in particular Thoreau's mythic sense of the importance of the Westward movement.

Thoreau the advocate of political dissent figures in the symposium in translations of articles by Walter Harding and Henry Miller, in the translation of a number of passages from Thoreau's writing, in particular "A Plea for Captain John Brown," and in Louis Simon's "De désobéir au crime d'obéir" (pp. 210–219).

Leo Tolstoy, like some of the present-day French students, prefered "Civil Disobedience" to *Walden*, although he tried the latter a second time the year before he died. This fact, along with a summary of Tolstoy's fairly frequent references to Thoreau, appears in N. K. Gudzij, "Lev Tolstoj i Toro" in *Russko-europejskie literaturnye svjazi: Sbornik statej k 70-letiju so dnja roždenija akademika M. P. Alekseeva* (Moscow, Nanka, 1966), pp. 63–68. (I was unable to see the article on Thoreau and Bergson, *RLV*, XXXIII, 489–492.)

v. Studies Chiefly Critical

The principal non-biographical study of Emerson is Michael H. Cowan, *City of the West: Emerson, America, and Urban Metaphor*

(New York, Yale Univ. Press). It resembles the work of Sherman Paul and Jonathan Bishop in some respects. All provide the twentieth-century scholarly equivalent of an Emersonian essay, drawing images, phrases, and paragraphs from various writings by Emerson and weaving them into a complex, more or less individualized exposition. Cowan's interest is Emerson's literary fusion of several mythic themes—the Western spirit, the personal pilgrimage toward a moral ideal, the movement of human history, technological change, and the necessary reconciliation of man and nature. Cowan helpfully attaches his analysis to the actualities of Emerson's prose by including close readings of "Experience," "The Young American," *English Traits,* and the 1861 lecture "Boston." He concludes that Emerson was basically optimistic about urban civilization because it contains its own modes of self-criticism and organic growth. Although faintly pretentious in its dismissal of scholarship of all but the very recent past, Cowan's is a serious and erudite study, admirable in its own right as an intellectual construct and likely to contribute to better understanding of Emerson's writings.

The shifts in Emerson's thought explored by the late Stephen Whicher are substantiated anew in J. A. Ward's study of "Emerson and 'The Educated Will': Notes on the Process of Conversion" (*ELH,* XXXIV, 495–517). In the 1830's Emerson accepted Coleridge's view of faith as the synthesis of reason and will, which has only to be seized for conversion to occur. By the 1840's "faith" is no more than unauthenticated confidence or the will to believe. In *Essays: Second Series* Emerson is affirmative only from Olympian perspective. As private man, he is anxious and perplexed. There is, however, resolution in the late essays.

Carl Strauch continues to enlarge understanding and appreciation of Emerson's poetry. In "Emerson and the Doctrine of Sympathy" (*SIR,* VI, 152–174) he considers Emerson's treatment of sympathy in man's relations to nature.[1] The affinities between man and nature at every level of the Platonic scale inform many early poems, but *Poems* (1847) also confronts man's falling away from inherent cosmic harmony. "Woodnotes" is central to the theme, but "The Sphinx" depicts disjunction. Analysis of several short poems makes clear that the sympathetic victory in "Woodnotes" represents

1. A companion piece by Strauch, published in 1968, on sympathy in man's relations to individuals and society, will be discussed in the next issue of *ALS.*

no easy optimism but hard-won poetic affirmation of a living uni-
verse. A different group of poems comes under the scrutiny of
Richard Lee Francis in his "Archangel in the Pleached Garden:
Emerson's Poetry" (*ELH*, XXXIII [1966], 461–472). The two ar-
ticles are compatible though the vocabularies differ somewhat.
Francis admires Emerson's mythological/ontological poems which
delineate "the great Order" and reattach dismembered things to it.
Most admirable in this respect is "Two Rivers." Brief notes on
"Uriel," "Threnody," "The Snow-Storm," and a fragmentary quatrain
in the collected poems complete the year's work on Emerson's
poetry. See Hugh H. Witemeyer (*PMLA*, LXXXII, 98–103); John
M. Reilly (*ESQ*, No. 47, pp. 17–19); Jan B. Gordon (*ibid.*, pp. 42–
43); and Karl Keller (*AL*, XXXIX, 94–98).

Anthony Herbold's "Nature as Concept and Technique in the
Poetry of Jones Very" (*NEQ*, XL, 244–259), discerns the same double vision in Very's poems that Strauch and Francis find in Emerson.
Very's poetry is a dialectic between finite, contingent, imperfect
nature and infinite, self-generating, perfect Nature.

Recent analyses of Emerson's prose have sought the analogical
key which will disclose organic structure for all to see and admire.
For "Self-Reliance," one writer (Enno Klammer) offers a spiral
staircase (*ESQ*, No. 47, pp. 81–83). The structure of "Experience"
seems to George Sebouhian "a thought pattern in process" (*ESQ*,
No. 47, pp. 75–78). And Richard Lee Francis in "The Architectonics
of Emerson's *Nature*" (*AQ*, XIX, 39–52) discerns a dialectical and
forward movement ("definitional escalation"), of which "Prospects"
is the synthesis and capstone. The style is baroque as defined by
Morris Croll (and Cotton Mather) with alternating recitatives and
chorales.

Of all the analyses of Emerson's essays from the rhetorical point
of view, perhaps the most helpful is Mary Worden Edrich, "The
Rhetoric of Apostasy" (*TSLL*, VIII, 547–560), in which she accounts
for the vehemence of reaction to "The Divinity School Address" by
Emerson's rhetorical excesses. Doctrinally, the Address could not
have offended, nor was it merely a matter of auspices, but Emerson's
fluid symbolic language, his paradoxes, and his extremes of expression aroused hostility. The author concludes that Emerson could
legitimately be faulted for absence of logic, a not always suggestive
vagueness, and a certain testiness and irritability, including tasteless

allusions to his own ministerial history. A subject seemingly exhausted by the methods of literary and intellectual history quickens to literary analysis.

Two good discussions of Thoreau's artistry in *Walden* appeared in 1967. Joseph J. Moldenhauer treats "The Rhetorical Function of Proverbs in *Walden*" (*JAF*, LXXX, 151–159). Moldenhauer finds about 100 proverbs and aphorisms in *Walden* usually altered somewhat from the popular form or creatively "invented." By such linguistic means, Thoreau achieves a movement in *Walden* from early repudiation of the old society to the vision of a new community of moral interest. (See also p. 287.) Melvin E. Lyon in "Walden Pond as a Symbol" (*PMLA*, LXXXII, 289–300), substantiates the same movement (discussed earlier by a good many commentators, including Richard Adams and Lauriat Lane). By focusing on the Pond as a symbol, however, Lyon is able to distinguish Thoreau's "more limited romanticism" from that of Emerson and Whitman. In his emphasis on the purity and serenity, not the creativity, of the pond, Thoreau is conservative. Hence perhaps the admirable firmness and clarity of the book's structure.

In regard to Thoreau's political thought, Joseph DeFalco in *Topic* (XII, 43–49) interprets the movement from "Civil Disobedience" to "A Plea for Captain John Brown" as one toward moral action, justified by intensification of his legitimate moral outrage. Joseph Wood Krutch (*ASch*, XXXVII, 15–18), also examines Thoreau's behavior and pronouncements on civil disobedience as a preliminary to discussing dissent in the 1960's. Krutch concludes that Thoreau provides "no usable answer," but Krutch's own answer—distinguishing between disobedience as a "right" and disobedience as a moral duty with the necessary acceptance of its inseparable consequences—sounds strangely Thoreauvian to me. Not so strangely at that.

There was also considerable interest in Thoreau's doctrine of wildness and the writings in which it is an important theme. Lauriat Lane, Jr., identifies several dimensions—from the sensory to the moral and imaginative—inherent in "Thoreau's Response to the Maine Woods" (*ESQ*, No. 47, pp. 37–41). (Vesta M. Parsons also discusses *The Maine Woods* in *The Husson Review*, I, 17–27.) Richard J. Fein, in "*Walden* and the Village of the Mind" (*BSUF*, VIII, i, 55–61) locates the wildness within and celebrates Thoreau's ability to find in nature forms for "those ideas, inclinations, and fancies which he nurtured in himself." In *Wilderness and the American Mind* (New Haven, Yale Univ. Press), Roderick Nash considers the theme from a historical point of view. His chapter on Thoreau (pp. 84–95) explains the extent to which conceptions of wilderness converged in Transcendentalism and especially in Thoreau. Whereas earlier writers, however, had idealized the rural, agrarian condition, Thoreau "arrived at the middle by straddling," seeking the best of civilization and wildness. He thus led an intellectual revolution beginning to invest wilderness with attractive rather than repulsive qualities.

vi. Miscellaneous

A few reprints warrant brief mention. From various nineteenth-century sources Kenneth W. Cameron has reprinted a great many comments about Emerson (totalling 499 pages) in *Emerson Among His Contemporaries* (Hartford, Transcendental Books). Reginald L. Cook's 1948 volume *Passage to Walden* has been reprinted with citations identified. And ungathered essays by the late Perry Miller have been reprinted under the title of *Nature's Nation* (Cambridge, Harvard Univ. Press, Belknap). They include four essays on Transcendentalism.

To sum up. The life and work of Ralph Waldo Emerson continue to evoke exemplary scholarly contributions. By contrast, Thoreau's work is widely admired, but scholarship has not yet managed to cope with it nearly as well. Perhaps the most encouraging trend in 1967 was the evidence of greater interest in those Transcendentalists who, only by virtue of exacting literary standards or the bias of literary scholars, deserve the designation "minor."

Library of Congress

2. Hawthorne

Hyatt H. Waggoner[1]

The year 1967 brought more Hawthorne studies of lasting importance than the trend toward downgrading Hawthorne discussed in earlier reports in this volume might have led us to anticipate. Though serious students of Hawthorne will find little value in much of what was published, and though there were no new biographical studies, no book-length critical studies of real significance, and no new editions of the fiction, yet Hawthorne's early poems were searched out and handsomely printed for the first time, several of the tales and romances received definitive clarification, an important bibliographical aid appeared, and the level of the best writing was distinguished. All in all, it was a rather good Hawthorne year.

Since nearly all the more important items to be discussed, with the exception of the poems and the *ESQ* bibliography, take the form of articles in the journals, it has seemed convenient to organize the studies by the subjects treated—general topics, the romances, the tales and sketches—with the bibliography and the book of verse receiving separate mention outside that framework.[2]

ESQ, No. 47, in two parts, contained a much-needed annotated bibliography of secondary works and critical editions. The annotations tend to be non-evaluative factual summaries—precisely what is wanted in a work of this kind. A sampling of the listings suggests to this reviewer that the list is complete and the descriptive comments

1. I wish to thank John Patterson of the Pennsylvania State University, Capital Campus, for assistance in winnowing the grain from the chaff in the report that follows.

2. Omissions from the following discussion fall into three groups: (1) articles —some three or four of them, none of which appeared to be important—which were in the bindery when needed; (2) articles, introductions to editions, and so on that offered nothing fresh or interesting, in the judgment of this reviewer; and, (3) microfilmed dissertation abstracts, omitted on the ground that if anything in them is at all significant it will reach print—and very probably, heaven help us, will be printed even if it is *not* significant. It was the quality of the "DA's" on Hawthorne in 1967 that more than anything else seemed to this reviewer to confirm the earlier gloomy predictions.

judicious. This indispensable work is now available in hard covers: Buford Jones, ed., *A Checklist of Hawthorne Criticism: 1951–1966* (Hartford, Transcendental Books).

Serious students of Hawthorne will welcome Richard Peck's edition of Hawthorne's *Poems* (Charlottesville, Va., The Bibliographical Society of the Univ. of Va.), consisting of twenty-nine poems, most of them juvenilia, even though, as Hawthorne himself must have thought since he made no effort to preserve them, only two or three are at all impressive as poetry. Seven were printed during Hawthorne's lifetime, including one printed as early as 1825 in the Salem *Gazette* and two chosen by Rufus Griswold for inclusion in his *Scenes in the Life of the Saviour by the Poets and Painters* (1845). Hawthorne's biographers take note: these two poems, stylistically the most mature in the book and apparently written later than the others, should be noted in any discussion of the development of Hawthorne's religious attitudes.

i. General

Nelson F. Adkins in "Notes on the Hawthorne Canon" (*PBSA*, LX [1966], 364–367), produces no great surprises in his survey of works at one time or another attributed to Hawthorne but not originally printed under Hawthorne's signature. He finds, for example, that it is highly probable that Hawthorne did write "Sketches from Memory," first publicly attributed to him in the posthumously published *The Dolliver Romance and Other Pieces*, and almost certainly did not write a collection of tales called *The Flower Basket*. We are told that "a manuscript, not at the moment ready for release, presents in detail the reasons for these judgments."

One of the most important contributions of the year was David Levin's intelligent and persuasive chapter on Hawthorne in his *In Defense of Historical Literature* (pp. 98–117). Levin finds that "the value of Puritan history" for Hawthorne was that his close knowledge of it helped him to make *The Scarlet Letter* by far his greatest romance.

> "His greatest work combines an extremely skillful recreation of the Puritan past with a forceful statement on the central issues of nineteenth-century romanticism. *The Scarlet Letter* is not only allegory but historical romance. . . . I must insist on the

depth of Hawthorne's understanding of seventeenth-century New England, for recent attention to his guilt-feelings on the one hand and his religious allegiance on the other has naturally over-emphasized the powerful language in which he condemned his ancestors."

Though chiefly concerned with *The Scarlet Letter*, the essay also treats, more briefly, Hawthorne's use of history in the other romances. This piece should be compared with the Baughman article mentioned later. The two are complementary.

In an unusually interesting and convincing treatment of "The Head, the Heart, and the Unpardonable Sin" (*NEQ*, XL, 31–47), Nina Baym takes issue with the notion that Hawthorne's sinners "Can be arranged in a hierarchy depending on the preponderance of head or heart in their transgressions." She finds, rather, "Hawthorne's view of the dynamics of personality does not really permit the existence of a sin *committed* by the intellect. . . . Selfish passions produce sin. . . . The focus of Hawthorne's fiction is the heart, seen in its capacities for both good and evil." Correcting the present writer, among others, the author finds "no cases whatsoever" in Hawthorne of a "purely intellectual mania"—what I once referred to as *libido sciendi* or "lust for knowledge." The point is an important one, persuasively presented.

Disputing Hoeltje and Wagenknecht, who have emphasized Hawthorne's "serenity," his "lightness," and minimized what Melville, Levin, the present writer, and others have called his "blackness," Earle Hilton in "The Body in the Fountain" (*PMASAL*, LII, 383–389), concludes that "Whatever affirmations he may make, that man has more than a normal share of knowledge of blackness, who, when he gropes for an image, comes up again and again with a corpse decaying beneath the dark water." I should think so. Nevertheless, Seymour L. Gross in "Hawthorne versus Melville" (*BuR*, XIV, iii, 89–109) is certainly right when he reminds us that Hawthorne's "knowledge of blackness" is not nearly so much like Melville's as Melville seems to have thought when he wrote his famous review of *Mosses*. In a careful survey of all the evidence, Mr. Gross compares the themes and character types of the two men, particularly their treatment of alienation, concluding, in part, that with Melville, "it is the world from which the 'isolato' is alienated that is the villain. . . . [whereas] For Hawthorne, isolation is not an apotheosis but a dungeon. . . . [Hawthorne] always returns to a tragic acceptance of the difficult world men are born to live in." The author finds *Billy Budd* the most nearly "Hawthornesque" of Melville's fictions. This article contains few if any surprises but much good sense, and what it says needed to be said.

Just two more pieces seem to require extended comment in this "general" category. The first is Joseph C. Pattison's careful survey of Hawthorne's handling of "point of view" (*PMLA*, LXXXII, 363–369), which leads him to conclude that "From premise to plan to finished work, Hawthorne developed and maintained the stance of the artist as a conscious dreamer." Thus the "proper point of view" Hawthorne asked of readers of his work may be defined, we are told, as "one of dream." (This—probably more or less true—idea turned up a number of times in 1967.) The second is Leo B. Levy's "Hawthorne and the Idea of 'Bartleby'" (*ESQ*, No. 47, pp. 66–69), in which both external and internal evidence is presented tending to show that Melville's tale was inspired by Hawthorne's "The Old Apple Dealer." The evidence is persuasive, though Mr. Levy presses the similarities between the sketch and the tale harder than there was any need to.

Less significant than the pieces just discussed are several items that still seem to deserve brief mention. In *Hawthorne and the Modern Short Story: A Study in Genre* (The Hague, Mouton, 1966), Mary Rohrberger uses Hawthorne's tales as a starting point for a discussion aimed at clarifying the distinctions between simple narrative and the short story proper, finding, not surprisingly, that Hawthorne pioneered in the development of the form. David B. Kesterson ("Hawthorne and Nature: Thoreauvian Influence?" *ELN*, IV, 200–206), persuasively argues that "Hawthorne did not take nature lessons from Thoreau. Rather, he shared with him an interest already formed. . . ." Just as unsurprising is the conclusion reached by Robert Dusenberg in "Hawthorne's Merry Company: The Anatomy of Laughter in the Tales and Short Stories" (*PMLA*, LXXXII, 285–288), that "laughter is used as a dramatic device for revealing character in many of Hawthorne's stories" and that, with certain exceptions such as children, "laughter represents gradations of evil among men."

Students of Hawthorne will be interested and genuinely informed by two other pieces. Sidney E. Lind, in his "source-study" of Emily

Dickinson's "Further in Summer than the Birds" (*AL*, XXXIX, 163–169), finds the poem inspired by a passage in "The Old Manse" in which intimations of autumn occur to Hawthorne in mid-summer. It seems highly probable that many more examples of Dickinson's use of Hawthorne remain to be discovered. One example: "I Heard a Fly Buzz When I Died" and the "Governor Pyncheon" chapter of *Seven Gables*. Hawthorne meant much more to the poet than has been commonly realized. A very different sort of contribution, but equally important in the sense that we are grateful for it as a genuine "contribution to knowledge," is George Monteiro's note on "Maule's Curse and Julian Hawthorne" (*N&Q*, XIV, 62–63). Once again Julian Hawthorne is proved to have been an unreliable reporter of family traditions. It was not "Aunt Ebe," as Julian's account in *Hawthorne and His Wife* implies, who was responsible for the erroneous belief that Hawthorne's ancestor, John Hathorne, was cursed by one of the accused witches; it was Julian himself, with his unacknowledged omissions and alterations of family letters.

Apart from the Rohrberger study previously mentioned, the only whole book on Hawthorne in 1967 was one that in this reviewer's opinion should never have been published. The special merit claimed in jauntily ignorant prose, by the editor of the series, for Jac Tharpe's *Nathaniel Hawthorne: Identity and Knowledge* (Carbondale, Southern Ill. Univ. Press; one of a series called "Crosscurrents Modern Critiques") is that it relates Hawthorne to world literature in such a way as to show that he was not "provincial." In a prefatory statement the author confesses that "Most of the following material was composed when I had access to little more of pertinence than a copy of the Riverside Edition of Hawthorne's work." In the work itself it becomes clear that he lacked not only "access to" but any prior *acquaintance with* the whole body of Hawthorne scholarship, as well as any sense of the distinction between responsible and irresponsible speculation. Literary history *need* not be guesswork. Reading this book, we become "positivists": "What is the *evidence*?" seems the only question worth asking.

I shall conclude with two articles related only by contrast. One treats Hawthorne respectfully while the other comes close to writing him off. In the first, Christopher Lohman in "The Burden of the Past in Hawthorne's American Romances" (*SAQ*, LXVI, 92–104), believes that the present writer's remarks on his subject are true but insufficient, and that we ought to go further and say that "the past in Hawthorne's works often assumes a moral, ethical, or theological function, so that its treatment is frequently identical with his treatment of sin and guilt." In the second, G. D. Josipovici ("Hawthorne's Modernity," *CritQ*, VIII [1966], 351–360) concludes that at his very best Hawthorne was sufficiently "modern" for our tastes and that he was more consciously in control of his "logic of compulsion" themes than Crews has argued; but he also believes that there is not very much of this "best": "And yet, when all is said and done, there is much about Hawthorne that is unsatisfactory. . . . There remains *The Scarlet Letter* and a handful of stories. And there remains the question: why are they so good and the rest so bad?" To which some of us might like to reply by asking another question: Is it really so clear that "the rest" are "so bad"? The *tone* of this piece is very offensive to this reviewer.

ii. The Romances

For several years now *The Scarlet Letter* has been less frequently written about than the other romances, particularly than *Blithedale* and *The Marble Faun*. In 1967, this imbalance was partially righted. The year saw five published articles on *The Scarlet Letter* and five on *Blithedale*. The point here is not only numerical. At least two of the five on *The Scarlet Letter* are important contributions, not likely to be soon upset. Ernest W. Baughman in "Public Confession and *The Scarlet Letter*" (*NEQ*, XL, 532–550), has not "reinterpreted" *The Scarlet Letter*—a fact for which we ought to be grateful; rather, he has done a piece of "homework" one would think ought to have been done long ago. He has come up with good reasons for continuing to believe the received opinions that the novel is great and moves to its conclusion with an inevitableness having nothing essential to do with "the logic of compulsion." Mr. Baughman has surveyed all available evidence on the practice of public confession in the period represented by the story and concluded that the way Hawthorne worked out Dimmesdale's and Hester's problems was wholly consistent with contemporary Puritan practices. He finds the ending of the novel historically as well as aesthetically justified.

"The dark necessity that follows the first step awry flowers as it does because all of the major characters live outside the prescribed practices of the church, which are known to every church member. . . . He was on sure theological ground too when he refused to assure the reader of a happy reunion in heaven for Hester and Dimmesdale. . . . Hawthorne would not say that salvation is guaranteed even to truly repentant sinners; he knew Puritan doctrine too well to be definite."

This is a more important article, and covers more ground, than its title suggests. If one were to cavil, it would be only to suggest there were, after all, alternatives to the rigidity of Puritan doctrine and practice—alternatives available perhaps only at the price of exile to Rhode Island, but still available, as witness Ann Hutchinson and Roger Williams. Hawthorne does, after all, refer to the former as the "sainted" Ann Hutchinson. But these are minor quibbles. The article makes the strongest case for the novel's artistic validity I have seen for a long time.[3] This is also the effect of Nicholas Canaday, Jr.'s note on the rose blooming beside the prison ("'Some Sweet Moral Blossom'; A Note on Hawthorne's Rose," *PLL*, III, 186–187), which suggests that the rose symbolism at the end of Canto 29 of Dante's *Purgatorio* may have influenced Hawthorne at this point. For Hawthorne as for Dante the rose symbolizes "love" in its several meanings and dimensions, culminating in New Testament *caritas* or "charity."

Three other pieces on *The Scarlet Letter* deserve mention, for very different reasons. It is good to have Matthew J. Bruccoli's "Notes on the Destruction of *The Scarlet Letter* Manuscript" (*SB*, XX, 257–259). Although the question of whether Hawthorne himself (as Mrs. Field insists) or her husband's firm burned the manuscript of Hawthorne's greatest work cannot be resolved by this article, we do have here a piece of evidence—Mrs. Field's letter to Julian—which helps us to guess intelligently. . . . The other two articles on the romance are mentioned only because there *are* no others, and because it seems to this reviewer that any attention paid to *The Scarlet Letter* ought to be noted. Richard Coanda's "Hawthorne's Scarlet Alphabet" (*Renascence*, XIX, 161–166) speculates that Hawthorne "May have hinted through the initials of the names Hester, Arthur, Roger, and Pearl" at the heavenly *harp*. One doubts it. The study of the ways

---

3. This sentence was written before I had read David Levin's piece, mentioned earlier, on *The Scarlet Letter* and history. At present, I am uncertain which one is "most important."

of literary history and objective interpretation is a demanding intellectual discipline, not to be confused with the ability to spawn "novel ideas." Too much of what is published shows a complete failure to think logically and analytically. A specimen: Viola Sachs on "The Myth of America in Hawthorne's *The Scarlet Letter*" (*KN*, XIV, 245–267). One doubts that "the myth of America" is "the key" to the meaning of *The Scarlet Letter.*

As was the case with *The Scarlet Letter*, the most important article on *The Seven Gables* during 1967 was a defense of the novel's aesthetic validity, in particular a justification of its much-objected-to ending. In "*The House of the Seven Gables*: New Light on Old Problems" (*PMLA*, LXXXII, 579–590), Francis Joseph Battaglia argues persuasively that Hawthorne's plot is not incoherent, that the ending is "neither artificial nor forced" but carefully prepared for by early revelation of the developing love between Phoebe and Holgrave, and that the theme of the work is not, as has been said, in conflict with Hawthorne's "moral" as stated by him in the Preface. Neither are the main characters static pasteboard figures, as so many have alleged. To this reader the argument, based as it is on both a thorough reassessment of familiar objections to the work and a sensitive reading of passages too often overlooked, is wholly convincing.

Less important but worthy of notice are a short note and a portion of a lecture, both having the effect of tending to increase our respect for the work. John O. Rees, Jr., presents convincing evidence ("Elizabeth Peabody and 'The Very ABC': A Note on *The House of the Seven Gables*," *AL*, XXXVIII, 537–540), that Hawthorne's sister-in-law's cloudy linguistic theories and claims as expressed in her *First Nursery Reading Book* (1849) are being glanced at ironically in Hepzibah's recognition, early in the work, that now that even the "ABC's" have become a "science," she was not fit to teach. And Henry Nash Smith mingles praise for Crews's Freudian reading with observations on the significance of the Judge's business activities ("The Morals of Power: Business Enterprise as a Theme in Mid-Nineteenth-Century American Fiction," *Essays on American Literature*, pp. 90–107).

The year's work on *Blithedale* was at once greater in bulk and more mixed in character and quality. John Shroeder discovers in Spenser's *The Shepheards Calendar* what he believes we ought to consider *the* chief literary source of the novel ("Miles Coverdale's Calendar; or, A Major Literary Source for *The Blithedale Romance*," *EIHC*, CIII, 353–364). This reader finds the "a" of Mr. Shroeder's title more judicious than the later suggested "the," but the piece is a pleasure to read and seems not seriously open to question. In an article and a note that tend to overlap with each other and partially overlap with the article just mentioned, Buford Jones discusses other Spenserian sources of Hawthorne's romances, particularly *Blithedale*, finding the "Mutability" Canto echoed in that work. ("The *Faery Land* of Hawthorne's Romances," *ESQ*, No. 48, pp. 106–124; and "Hawthorne's Coverdale and Spenser's Allegory of Mutability," *AL*, XXXIX, 215–219.) Since it is clear that Hawthorne knew his Spenser very well indeed and drew upon him often, it is not difficult to believe that more than one passage in the work of his favorite poet came to mind as he worked on his novel.

The two treatments of *Blithedale* still to be mentioned are a very different kettle of fish. Each represents a facet of what might be called, drawing an analogy from public life, the "New Left" in literary scholarship; each exhibits much cleverness, but at Hawthorne's expense. David Howard follows his fellow Englishman Martin Greene's example and exhibits similar impatience with Hawthorne in "*The Blithedale Romance* and a Sense of Revolution" (*Tradition and Tolerance*, pp. 55–97). In a book described by the editors as "frankly intended as polemical," Mr. Howard finds Hawthorne guilty of a failure of intelligence and a lack of positive sympathy for social revolution. His "inclusiveness" of vision is illusory. Like his own Miles Coverdale, Mr. Howard believes, Hawthorne did not so much endorse old values as show himself "unable to cope" with social change. To like-minded readers this essay will no doubt *not* seem, as it does to this reader, irritatingly arrogant in its contemptuous dismissal of all past criticism of the novel. Though it makes some significant discriminations in the course of its argument, whether one finds it persuasive or not is likely to depend more on the reader's own point of view than on the author's logic.

Another controversial discussion of the work occurs in "Some Rents in the Veil: New Light on Priscilla and Zenobia in *The Blithedale Romance*" (*NCF*, XXI [1966], 263–275), by Allan and Barbara Lefcowitz. The authors find at the center of *Blithedale* "what amounts to a fascinating but elusive dream vision" which, when inspected closely, reveals "a sharp disjunction between the novel's realistic foundation and its symbolic patterns." In passing, the authors throw out suggestions that we ought to think of Priscilla as a prostitute, Old Moody as a pimp, and Coverdale as a client. Whether the "Freudianizing" of this article is critically helpful toward an understanding and judgment of Hawthorne's work is, clearly, a matter of opinion in which one's "point of view," once again, will be likely to play a decisive role. To this reader, the article seems an encumbrance, but there are, obviously, those who think otherwise.

When we turn to the year's work on *The Marble Faun* we encounter David Howard once again working at his self-appointed task of trying to obliterate Hawthorne's reputation. This time he tries to persuade us, in an essay that manages to convey the impression that everything written about the novel up to now is not worth so much as passing mention, that just as Hawthorne's characters get "out of their depth" in the work, so Hawthorne himself is "forced to desperate evasions of that depth." ("The Fortunate Fall and Hawthorne's *The Marble Faun*," in Ian Fletcher, ed., *Romantic Mythologies*, London, Routledge and K. Paul; New York, Barnes and Noble, pp. 97–136.) There is, I suspect, considerable justice in the charge, but Mr. Howard's brashness and arrogant condescension toward both Hawthorne and all other writers on Hawthorne will throw many readers off.

The remaining items are both less ambitious and less polemical in tone. In "The Theme of the Fortunate Fall in *The Marble Faun*" (*ESQ*, No. 47, pp. 56–62), Peter G. Beidler surveys existing opinion on the subject, finds that Austin Warren and the present writer too hastily concluded that the novel's structure rejects the idea of the fortunate fall, and tries to "clear Hawthorne of the charge of inconsistency . . . in his treatment of the theme." The author sees the work as Hawthorne's "most mature novel." Sheldon W. Liebman ("The Design of *The Marble Faun*, *NEQ*, XL, 61–68), on the other hand, believes that the theme of the fortunate fall is less crucial in the novel than it has often been considered to be. The several motifs—the fall, transformation, etc.—which have received so much critical attention seem to him not to "set the pace and frame the action of the novel as a whole." What does do so, he argues, is the recurrent image of a sarcophagus, which takes many shapes, from Rome itself with its catacombs to the hearts of men.

iii. The Tales and Sketches

Several of the tales were the subjects of unusually illuminating discussions in 1967. Sidney P. Moss's "The Mountain God of Hawthorne's 'The Ambitious Guest'" (*ESQ*, No. 47, pp. 74–75) persuasively interprets the tale as "a parable, Hawthorne's somber reminder that Providence, however dark and ominous it may appear at times, is at heart benign, so long as we have faith, and love and serve one another. The moment we lose this faith, we run 'into the pathway of destruction.'" The interpretation seems to account for several aspects of the story that readers have generally found puzzling. The same thing can be said of Edward R. Stephenson's explication of "The Wives of the Dead" (*Expl*, XXV, Item 63), a close reading of this puzzling early tale that is at once respectful, sensitive, and perspicacious. According to this reading, the tale is Hawthorne's answer to the hypothetical question, "What would happen to the 'wives' if the 'dead' were found living?" The differing responses of the two sisters to the events of the night take us to "the core of the meaning," which involves the idea of "the necessity of human solidarity."

Very helpful also is Sacvan Bercovitch's imaginative and interesting article, "Endicott's Breastplate: Symbolism and Typology in 'Endicott and the Red Cross'" (*SSF*, IV, 289–299). The author concludes that the tale "affords an important early demonstration of [Hawthorne's] symbolic method." In the breastplate Hawthorne created "an historically verifiable and imaginatively liberating 'metaphor' that opens into a consummate symbol of Puritanism."

"My Kinsman" was the subject of a brief note and a short article. Marilyn G. Rose suggests (*ESQ*, No. 47, pp. 21–23) that Robin's journey parallels certain episodes in the Theseus legend, particularly "the father search and the minotaur combat" in the labyrinth. John Russell, writing on "Allegory and 'My Kinsman, Major Molineux'" (*NEQ*, XL, 432–440), treats the tale as a political allegory in which Robin "represents the six governors of Massachusetts Bay Colony between the years 1686 and 1729." According to this reading, "woods

represent England" and "the 'country' Robin is from . . . is England."
Perhaps. But if so, the story seems much less interesting than we
have thought it.

Three other tales received attention. Nicholas Canaday, Jr.,
treats "The Minister's Black Veil" ("Hawthorne's Minister and the
Veiling Deception of Self," SSF, IV, 135–142), concluding that the
minister is guilty of pride in his attempt to "gain an absolute perspective on life" and that "The final irony is Hawthorne's, for whom
the veil must symbolize the imperfect human vision, which, because
of the finiteness of the human condition, sees only darkly." G. T. Mc-
Cullen, Jr., argues plausibly, though without greatly illuminating
the tale, that Hawthorne's knowledge of Greek and Roman burial
rites is reflected in "Roger Malvin's Burial" ("Ancient Rites for the
Dead and Hawthorne's 'Roger Malvin's Burial,'" SFQ, XXX, 313–
322). Morton L. Ross ("Hawthorne's Bosom Serpent and Mather's
Magnalia," ESQ, No. 47, p. 13), "Without quarreling with Shroeder
by denying Stewart's suggestion" (that Hawthorne found his bosom
serpent in The Fairie Queen), points out that Hawthorne could have
read about a similar serpent in Mather. He not only could have, he
probably did, but Elliston's exclamation, "It gnaws," seems more
like an echo of Spenser's "sting" than it does of anything in the
passage quoted from Mather's work, in which, also, the serpent is
described as being located "in the left ventricle" of the victim's
"heart," not in his stomach as in Hawthorne's tale. (Hawthorne's
"bosom" also seems an echo of Spenser's "bosome.") I conclude that
though Hawthorne might have remembered the passage in Mather,
the evidence presented does not compel assent to the author's conclusion that "Mather's borrowed anecdote may be as legitimate
a source for Hawthorne's bosom serpent as Spenser's lines."

Brown University

3. Melville

Merton M. Sealts, Jr.

Much of the best work on Melville in 1967 concentrated on *Moby-Dick* and the writing that came after it, especially *The Confidence-Man* and *Billy Budd, Sailor*; there was relatively little study of the earlier books. Quantity continued to increase: exclusive of dissertations, I have counted 86 items either appearing during the year or not previously listed in annual MLA bibliographies. Of these books and articles, 56 are noticed here. The 10 other essays (especially some from abroad) that I have not been able to track down will have to be considered for the 1968 survey.

i. Books

Klaus Ensslen, *Melvilles Erzählungen: Stil- und strukturanalytische Untersuchungen* (Heidelberg, Carl Winter, 1966) is a commendable 220-page examination of sixteen prose pieces, beginning with "Bartleby" and including *Billy Budd, Sailor*. Particularly notable is Ensslen's sensitivity to recurrent thematic, rhetorical, and structural patterns. The author is abreast of current scholarship and criticism, including unpublished doctoral dissertations written in the United States; his own analysis is enlightening and his inferences are consistently temperate and sound. A more speculative book is James Guetti, *The Limits of Metaphor: A Study of Melville, Conrad and Faulkner* (Ithaca, Cornell Univ. Press), an outgrowth of the dissertation briefly noticed two years ago by Professor Thorp (*ALS*, 1965, pp. 42–43); since Guetti treats Melville primarily in terms of *Moby-Dick*, his approach will be considered with other work on *Moby-Dick* in Section *vi* below.

Three paperback texts of 1967 afford an interesting comparison. *White-Jacket* as edited by Hennig Cohen (New York, Holt, Rinehart and Winston) offers an excellent editor's introduction of thirty pages, a chronology, and a selected bibliography; there are minimal textual

notes but no explanatory annotation. *The Confidence-Man* as edited
by H. Bruce Franklin (Indianapolis, Bobbs-Merrill) includes similar
apparatus plus extensive explanatory notes that offer new interpretations as well as a digest of previous scholarship and criticism.
Moby-Dick as edited by Harrison Hayford and Hershel Parker (New
York, W. W. Norton) is lightly annotated in comparison with Franklin's volume or with earlier editions of *Moby-Dick* itself by Mansfield
and Vincent (1952) and Feidelson (1964), but there is helpful supporting material on whales and whaling (prepared by John B. Putnam) together with maps, extracts from sources and analogues, over
a hundred pages of selected criticism 1851–1962, and a full bibliography. Scholars will especially welcome both the carefully established critical text that Hayford and Parker provide, incorporating
corrections and revisions made by Melville himself for the first English edition of *Moby-Dick*, and the accompanying textual apparatus
and discussion, in which the editors take soundings for their further
treatment of the text in the forthcoming Northwestern-Newberry
edition.

In *The Recognition of Herman Melville: Selected Criticism Since
1846* (Ann Arbor, The Univ. of Mich. Press) Hershel Parker has
assembled a well-proportioned and revealing cross-section of critical
commentary, prefaced by a brief but sharply focused survey of the
reversals in Melville's fame. The selections are presented in four
groups: contemporary reviews and appraisals through 1876, interim
observations of 1884–1912, voices of revival to 1932, and samples of
"academic recognition," 1938–1967. The first three sections are admirably representative, apart from the conspicuous omission of D. H.
Lawrence, whose chapters on Melville in *Studies in Classic American Literature* are of course both well known and readily accessible
elsewhere. The final group of eleven selections drawn from various
phases and fashions of academic criticism is admittedly the least
comprehensive of the four, necessarily passing over much influential
work and omitting some familiar names. By way of compensation,
this group concludes with two previously unpublished studies of
conspicuous merit. One of these, Walker Cowen's survey of Melville's
marginalia (see pp. 44–45), the other, John D. Seelye's "The Ironic
Diagram" (pp. 347–364), is examined here as a touchstone for discussion of other recent criticism.

For Seelye, Melville regarded his own art as "a system of tensions produced by diagrammatic contrasts, a paradoxical structure which would accommodate his search for belief and express his capacity for doubt"; Seelye himself, though detecting "nihilistic" implications even in Melville's earliest work, gives more weight to the interaction between these opposing tendencies than do other critics whose principal emphasis falls on one side or the other. Melville's "diagram" is a recurrent thematic and structural pattern with two components:

> "a linear dimension, associated with the sequential or 'story' element, and given shape by the hero's absolutist quest; and a circular dimension, associated with the relativistic maze within which that quest founders. I say 'circle,' because of the importance to his diagram of the return trip of wisdom as opposed to the voyage out of initiation, a roundness of total experience which corresponds to the wholeness of matched contraries that is the world."

After *Pierre*, Seelye observes, "the dynamic quester" disappears, "the forward thrust loses its impetus, and the system of ironic contrasts becomes more important, but the strategic balance—with all that it implies—remains to the very end."

ii. *Typee* and *Omoo*

No articles were published on *Typee* during 1967; there was one study of *Omoo* by Edwin M. Eigner, "The Romantic Unity of Melville's *Omoo*" (*PQ*, XLVI, 95–108). If there is unity in the book, Eigner argues, it must be looked for in the psychological development of the narrator, an "alienated" figure whose supposed "regeneration and recovery of identity" at the end he finds contrived and unconvincing; the real "drift" of the narrative, he thinks, is "toward despair." Eigner's treatment of characterization in *Omoo*, his handling of incident and "the two major digressions" (on the cruise of the *Julia* and the condition of Tahitians), and his remarks on Melville's use of time-symbolism and costuming in this and other books are generally perceptive and certainly ingenious, though the repeated comparisons of *Omoo* with later works are a temptation into possible over-reading of Melville's second book. "The despair and alienation which have to some extent unified *Omoo*," Eigner concludes, "remain to provide thematic unity for the novels to come"; one's response to this statement is likely to depend on whether he too regards "despair and alienation" as dominant notes in Melville's writing as early as 1847.

iii. Mardi

Mildred K. Travis, "Melville's Furies: Technique in *Mardi* and *Moby-Dick*" (*ESQ*, No. 47, pp. 71–73), examines, as forerunners of the gams in *Moby-Dick*, the successive meetings in *Mardi* between Taji and both Hautia's heralds and the phantom avengers of the slain Aleema—a total of some thirteen to fifteen confrontations. The avengers, she thinks, are like the Furies in Greek myth; the gams, which "seem to evolve from the canoe encounters of *Mardi*," serve like the chorus in Greek drama. These points, if relatively minor, bear on the development of Melville as an artist; it might be added that in March of 1849 he bought a set of Harper's Classical Library which included the dramas of Aeschylus, Sophocles, and Euripides, and that a spate of classical allusions in *Redburn* suggests immediate use of his new purchase.

iv. Redburn

Reaction against interpretations of *Redburn* as an initiation-story is strong in two "revisionist" articles: James Schroeter, "*Redburn* and the Failure of Mythic Criticism" (*AL*, XXXIX, 279–297), and Terrence G. Lish, "Melville's *Redburn*: A Study in Dualism" (*ELN*, V, 113–120).

Lish's essay, which has both psychological and metaphysical overtones, sees young Redburn confronting in the *Highlander* a microcosm of "interwoven dualities"; his story as Melville tells it employs "the traditional structure of the young seeker tale while departing from its traditional application." Among other "twin" relationships, Harry Bolton appears as an "alter ego" whom young Redburn finally rejects (*vide* Bruce Franklin, "Redburn's Wicked End," *NCF*, XX [1965], 190–194), thus retaining his innocence while relinquishing his brotherhood with mankind. So Redburn, Lish concludes, never learns, "never reaches the baptismal font," and so "defeats his own purpose as a seeker and earns the reader's contempt."

Schroeter's article opens with an over-long polemical survey of both biographical and mythic readings of *Redburn* before offering his own analysis—comparable to Seelye's conception of balanced contraries in Melville. The book, he holds, has an "ironically comic tone"; Melville was writing neither "democratic romance" nor "bourgeois tragedy" but "tough-minded realism." *Redburn* as protagonist is carefully placed between two foils or counterparts, Harry Bolton and Jackson, who as models of contrasting experience, one aristocratic and the other plebeian, represent "certain attractions but also dangers" which Redburn himself must avoid. Redburn's two-fold rejection of Jackson as well as Bolton and Melville's own "rejection of the genteel and 'Jacksonian' viewpoints," Schroeter concludes, "seem both to derive from Melville-Redburn's striving for balance and independence." Here the book anticipates *Moby-Dick*, he feels; its various deliberate balances "represent a more nearly unique and independent artistic achievement" than other critics "have given Melville credit for."

v. White-Jacket

Charles L. Regan, "Melville's Horned Woman" (*ELN*, V, 34–39) deals with a specimen in Surgeon Cuticle's collection of morbid anatomy in Ch. 61: Melville may have known of the "horned woman" he describes there through Marston's play *The Malcontent*, though his account is detailed enough to suggest indebtedness to some more extensive account—perhaps an English pamphlet of 1588.

vi. Moby-Dick

In *The Limits of Metaphor*, James Guetti is concerned primarily with three works: *Moby-Dick*, Conrad's *Heart of Darkness*, and Faulkner's *Absalom, Absalom!* His overall thesis is that "the basic emphasis" of each author "is not upon some ultimate idea of truth or reality, or even upon some standard ideological dichotomy or paradox, but upon the unreality of imaginative structure of any sort and upon the radical linguistic nature . . . of the problem of order." With respect to *Moby-Dick*, which alone among the three books deals successfully with the "paradox within the idea of metaphor," according to Guetti, the analysis is concentrated in Chapters II and

V. In this reading, Ahab's struggle with the whale is subordinate; the major conflict is between two kinds of consciousness and two kinds of language, dramatized respectively in Ahab and Ishmael. Ahab is a "seer" with expectations of apprehending "the 'ineffable'"; Ishmael is a seeker believing that "only the seeking" can be known— before the ineffable the movement of his language, and perhaps all language, appears "inevitably circular." Toward Ahab, Melville himself is ambivalent; he both accepts and rejects him. Whatever the significance of Ahab's quest for the ultimate, his "tension" and "vitality" serve to quicken Ishmael's rhetoric. That Ahab fails has the effect of lending Melville's endorsement to Ishmael's antithetical position, thus closing "the imaginative gap between author and narrator"; Ahab's death "not only seems to deny that the ineffable can be perceived but also casts doubt upon whether it exists." Put another way, "Ahab's failure—the final possibility of knowing—is Melville's success." This is because "Ahab functions as the possibility of rendering the narrative finally coherent"—a possibility, says Guetti, that is shown to be "unreal." The result is that "the burden of incoherency rests in Ishmael's narrative consciousness." Melville's success, Guetti is saying, derives from the success of his narrator in carrying this burden, "preoccupation with imaginative failure," which in the books by Conrad and Faulkner he finds to be unsupportable.

This is not the place to examine Guetti's analysis of the other two authors or the linguistically oriented chapters with which his study concludes. On the "languages" of *Moby-Dick* and two of its principals he is rewarding, though his reading of the book seems remote indeed from the excitement of the chase which Melville depicts; Melville's own whale is both a whale and an idea, while Guetti's seems merely an abstraction. If I have followed Guetti's reasoning correctly, his incidental suggestion that "an artistic dichotomy"— Ahab and Ishmael—springs from a "kind of split vision" in Melville himself is in essential harmony with Seelye's conception of a recurrent "ironic diagram" in his writings; by creating both an absolutist and an opposing skeptic, in other words, Melville was successfully dramatizing his own intellectual tensions.

One of Guetti's points, that Ahab is not a tragic hero but "a kind of ritual sacrifice" to the gods of Ishmael-Melville's imagination, finds support in other commentary. Guetti thinks Ahab's death is not tragic; Betty C. Senescu, explicating the paragraph describing it, notes that he dies "a death neither of defiance nor of heroism" ("Melville's *Moby Dick*," *Expl*, XXV, Item 78). Milton R. Stern addresses a larger issue in "Melville's Tragic Imagination: The Hero Without a Home" (*Patterns of Commitment in American Literature*, pp. 39–52). Because Melville's vision, in Stern's view, "tends toward the naturalistic and the existential," it is "not tragic in a classic sense." What he offers instead, as in *Moby-Dick*, is an alternative conception of tragic heroism appropriate to a purely secular, relativistic universe: "an education into the astounding endurance of which man is capable." This, according to Stern, "is what *Moby-Dick* is all about and what Ishmael tries to tell us." In his reading not Ahab but Ishmael emerges as the book's "modern-romantic-naturalistic-existential hero."

Other critics do not confine their attention to Ahab and Ishmael either in looking for its hero or in attributing Melville's sympathies wholly to one or the other. Is Melville altogether "naturalistic"? Adducing a number of parallel passages suggesting affinities between Melville and Emerson, S. A. Cowan questions the view that in *Moby-Dick* Melville is satirizing Emersonian Transcendentalism. Cowan's article, "In Praise of Self-Reliance: The Role of Bulkington in *Moby-Dick*" (*AL*, XXXVIII, 547–556), argues that the book is no simple allegory cast in either/or terms. Ahab, out of harmony with nature, is scarcely Emersonian; Bulkington suggests Melville's own admiration of "virtuous self-reliance and the Transcendentalist's dedication to the solitary search for truth." Vincent Buckley, noting that the "logic" of *Moby-Dick* "tends to subvert an 'Either-Or' mentality in its critics," argues ingeniously for "The White Whale as Hero" (*CR*, Melbourne, No. 9 [1966], pp. 3–21). "Moby Dick *is*, in the most relevant sense, the book's protagonist," Buckley holds; "it is only to Ahab that he appears the enemy of life." What he "embodies and represents" is "certain awe-invoking forces of life which Ahab . . . denies and Ishmael . . . has not yet found, but in relation to which he feels guilt." Though these are "religious forces," Moby Dick "is not God; but he is not simply 'God's Whale' either; he is God's analogy." A section of Buckley's challenging article discusses the prose of *Moby-Dick*: its "prose rhythms have to accommodate two or more conflicting elements," both in Melville's temperament and in his themes, and sometimes there are resultant weaknesses and excesses.

Looking at the opening of *Moby-Dick*, Louis D. Rubin, Jr., attacks the pretense that it is "'impersonal,' the writing of an anonymous, effaced author who was content to let his story speak for itself and who never tried to introduce himself into his narrative" (*The Teller in the Tale* [Seattle, Univ. of Wash. Press], p. 212). Ishmael, Rubin asserts, "*is* Melville all the same," for besides being in the story he can also stand aside and tell us "what it means"; he is both a character and the author's surrogate. Rubin's point is neatly illustrated in a brief note by Heinz Kosok, "Ishmael's Audience in 'The Town-Ho's Story'" (*N&Q*, XIV, 54–56): Ishmael's narrative at Lima is "an abbreviated and simplified version" of the entire book (or perhaps of the hypothetical *Ur-Moby-Dick*); his superficial listeners constitute "an image of Melville's reading public"; their interruptions oblige Ishmael to justify his inclusion of factual detail, which—like Melville himself on a larger scale—he turns into "relevant subject matter." Remembering what Melville's Babbalanja is given to say about the writings of Lombardo, or Ishmael's own remarks on the painted whale at the Spouter Inn, I think Melville was quite capable of the gambit Kosok suggests: commenting through Ishmael on his own book and its potential readers.

Herbert C. Eldridge, "'Careful Disorder': The Structure of *Moby-Dick*" (*AL*, XXXIX, 145–162) rejects analogies drawn between the book and a tree, an epic poem, and a five-act tragedy; in composing it, he thinks, Melville had his own "overall strategy of composition." *Moby-Dick* is another of his fictional voyages, with its "major segments" the successive oceans sailed. Eldridge offers a six-part outline of the narrative structure reflecting "a reasonably proportionate allocation of chapters" and showing within each of the parts "a measured subdivision" at its numerical center so as to constitute a series of "balanced pairs." That Melville was "working mechanically within a measured spatial framework," as in *Redburn* and *White-Jacket*, seems further suggested, he believes, by the spacing of the nine gams, already remarked by other critics. Along with the work of Ensslen, Seelye, Miss Travis, and Schroeter noticed above, Eldridge's study contributes to a growing understanding of Melville's characteristic structural patterns.

vii. Pierre

R. K. Gupta, "Melville's Use of Non-Novelistic Conventions in *Pierre*" (*ESQ*, No. 48, pp. 141–145), studies invocation, apostrophe, and

Homeric simile, derived from the epic; and foreshadowing, dramatic irony, and soliloquy, derived from the drama. Taizo Tanimoto, "Pierre the Shepherd: The Meaning of Saddle Meadows in Melville's *Pierre*" (*DLit*, XXIV [1966], 23–40), argues that Melville deliberately balanced the "artificiality, the stylized conventionality of pastoral" in the early chapters dealing with the Glendinning estate against the urban "world of actual life" where Pierre, "the helpless shepherd of the pastoral world," is subsequently defeated. John Logan, "Psychological Motifs in Melville's *Pierre*" (*MinnR*, VII, 325–330), reads the book as more melodramatic than tragic because Pierre "undergoes no *anagnorisis*, no self-understanding." Although differing with Henry A. Murray on several points of interpretation, Logan too stresses autobiographical elements in Pierre's situation, viewing him primarily as a "self-damaging" artist seeking "atonement" for "his own actual superiority as a writer."

Taking his cue from a remark on the creative process by Washington Allston, C. W. Bush observes in "This Stupendous Fabric: The Metaphysics of Order in Melville's *Pierre* and Nathanael West's *Miss Lonelyhearts*" (*JAmS*, I, 269–274) that the two books illustrate a plot recurrent in American fiction. Their unlike heroes attempt a new synthesis when "their inherited visions of ideal Christian order fail"; in trying to imitate Christ they both confuse Christian charity and their own sexual preoccupations. The resulting visions of discontinuity, disorder, and death give "a nightmare quality" to each work that is reinforced by images drawn from pictorial art. Bush's juxtaposition of Melville with both Allston and West is illuminating.

viii. Tales

The growing interest in Melville's shorter prose has spread to Europe, as indicated by publication of Klaus Ensslen's *Melvilles Erzählungen* (see p. 29), which surveys all the work of the 1850's, and Augusto Guidi's "Di alcuni racconti di Melville" (*AION-SG*, IX [1966], 119–140), which concentrates on what the author takes to be less celebrated pieces: "The Lightning-Rod Man," "The Tartarus of Maids," "The Bell-Tower," and "The Encantadas." Guidi, impressed by the power of Melville's imagery in the tales, is convinced that nothing of his prodigious creativity was lost in the supposed "decline" after *Moby-Dick*.

"Bartleby" is the subject of two articles: Leo B. Levy, "Haw-

thorne and the Idea of 'Bartleby'" (*ESQ*, No. 47, pp. 66–69), and
Ray B. Browne, "The Affirmation of 'Bartleby'" (*Folklore International*, pp. 11–21). Both studies remark Melville's continuing interest
in the theme of "patient submission" (Levy) or "heroic endurance"
(Browne), shown in his "Agatha" correspondence with Hawthorne
and in his characterizations of Bartleby and of Hunilla in "The Encantadas." Levy points out elements in common between Melville's
story and Hawthorne's "The Old Apple Dealer"; Browne sees a line
of "savior-figures" running from Bartleby and Hunilla to their culmination in Billy Budd, who is termed a more successful embodiment than Bartleby of "the universal hero-savior of world folklore
and mythology."

Robert Ilson, "*Benito Cereno* from Melville to Lowell" (*Salmagundi*, I, 78–86) notes differences between Melville's story and Robert Lowell's recent play, examining the latter as a tract for the times
requiring certain changes in characterization and perspective.

H. Bruce Franklin, "The Island Worlds of Darwin and Melville"
(*CentR*, XI, 353–370), similarly contrasts two authors' handling of
common basic material: in "The Encantadas," he argues, Melville
"challenges and parodies" *The Voyage of the Beagle*, which he
owned and used, rejecting Darwin's "particular observations, his use
of these observations, and his metaphoric structure."

Malcolm O. Magaw, examining "Apocalyptic Imagery in Melville's 'The Apple-Tree Table'" (*MQ*, VIII, 357–369), finds Melville
introducing allusions to John's vision on Patmos in a story concerned
with contrasting views on the possibility of an after-life that "ends
without a formulation of conclusive judgment." "The ambiguities,"
he concludes, "are deliberate and meaningful; they reinforce the
relativism of Melville's metaphysics."

John Seelye's "The Ironic Diagram" (see pp. 30–31) includes a
comparative analysis of "The Piazza" and the second of Melville's
early "Fragments from a Writing Desk" (1839) in terms of the
quest-motif.

ix. Israel Potter

Raymona Hull, "London and Melville's *Israel Potter*" (*ESQ*, No. 47,
pp. 78–81), examines Melville's use of impressions recorded in his
journal during his visit to London in 1849; Bert C. Bach, "Melville's

Israel Potter: A Revelation of its Reputation and Meaning" (*Cithara*, VII, 39–50), is a more comprehensive study presumably based on his dissertation (see *ALS, 1966*, p. 37), which deals with "Narrative Point of View in the Fiction . . . after *Moby-Dick*." Certain scenes of *Israel Potter*, Bach concludes, "give intimations of a powerful novel which could have been written"; Melville's "failure" derives from faulty handling of point of view.

x. The Confidence-Man

Following a suggestion of Daniel Hoffman, Hans-Joachim Lang, "Ein Ärgerteufel bei Hawthorne und Melville: Quellenuntersuchung zu *The Confidence-Man*" (*JA*, XII, 246–251), explores structural parallels with "The Seven Vagabonds" and points to evident resemblances between Melville's title character and Hawthorne's "prophetic beggar": both share with "the Devil in popular stories," to borrow Hawthorne's words, "a love of deception for its own sake, a shrewd eye and keen relish for human weakness and ridiculous infirmity, and the talent of petty fraud."

A different approach to Melville's central figure is taken by Malcolm O. Magaw, "*The Confidence-Man* and Christian Deity: Melville's Imagery of Ambiguity" (*Explorations of Literature*, pp. 81–99). Like Guetti in *The Limits of Metaphor*, Magaw links the confidence-man and the White Whale: both are "masked images of an unknowable, ambiguous God," and the qualities man imputes to them are "merely projections of man's own love or hate, faith or fear." Like Magaw's article on "The Apple-Tree Table" (see p. 38), this essay evidently derives from his 1964 dissertation, "Melville and the Christian Myth: The Imagery of Ambiguity" (*ALS, 1965*, p. 42). His discussion here takes issue with interpretations of *The Confidence-Man* as Christian allegory; its frequent allusions to the Christian myth "merely lend suggestiveness to the many masks of a symbol so complex and comprehensive that it cannot be defined. . . . If God is unknowable, then the artist must make his imagery of Him ambiguous. And with ambiguity of meaning must come a corresponding ambiguity of tone— . . . a mingling of sympathy and censure . . . toward the illusioned passengers aboard the *Fidèle*."

Ernest Tuveson, "The Creed of the Confidence-Man" (*ELH*, XXXIII [1966], 247–270), is less concerned with who the central figure is than with what he preaches—what Tuveson terms "a new religion" like the eighteenth-century philosophy of "Tout est bien," and what Melville himself calls "Confidence." This optimistic creed the confidence-man promulgates "by insinuating that he is preaching straightforward Christian doctrine"; the new faith has also its "false prophet" (Winsome), its "backslider" (the barber), and in the final chapter, its "eschatology." The faith of Confidence, Tuveson observes, "appears to be in essence a confidence-game played on the human race and especially on the American segment of it . . . by mankind on itself." Even so, in Melville's reading of human nature, he concludes, though "absolute optimism is essentially a delusion," there still remains "a psychic need for confidence"; stripped of it, man "confronts the blank, terrible universe with no spiritual shield."

It is Melville addressing such a universe that Leon F. Seltzer depicts, in terms of affinities with *The Myth of Sisyphus*, in "Camus' Absurd and the World of Melville's *Confidence-Man*" (*PMLA*, LXXXII, 14–27). His book is to be read as absurd rather than satirical, in Seltzer's analysis, because "its final aim cannot legitimately be regarded as corrective." As the book itself is "nihilistic," or even an "*anti*-novel," so its "trickster-hero (or anti-hero)" is intended "to be taken as a nihilist of tremendous lucidity," a "natural successor" to Ahab and Pierre, who passes "beyond absurd reasoning to absurd action." Here Seltzer finds Melville himself, like Camus, in "perilous waters": though seeing only a world without values he nevertheless is moved to suggest indirectly the "essential immorality" of his confidence-man. Even while composing a "lament" for "the Christian ethic of charity," he has nevertheless declared, negatively and reluctantly, for ethical relativism; both the "openness" of the book's ending and Melville's withdrawal from fiction-writing, Seltzer thinks, may be signs of his defeated hope.

xi. *Clarel* and Other Poems

Commenting on a partial translation of *Clarel* into Italian by Elémire Zolla, Claudio Gorlier remarks that the "exhumed" poem is not well-known even to American readers ("Due classici dissepolti: Wieland e Clarel," *Approdo*, XII [1966], 3–8). In the words of Robert Penn Warren, *Clarel* in Melville's day was "a seismograph that nobody looked at"; now Warren himself finds it Jamesian in its concern with "the deep relation between personality and idea, and the mutual modification implicit in such a relation." These observations occur in "Melville's Poems" (*SR*, n.s. III, 799–855), a compressed but penetrating survey of Melville's best work in poetry from *Mardi* to *Billy Budd* that goes well beyond the brief treatment of "Melville the Poet" published by Warren more than twenty years ago (*KR*, VIII, Spring 1946). The finest of Melville's poetic achievements, he thinks, are "anecdotal or dramatic" pieces built upon "a 'prose' base. The lyric mood of unmoved emotion, or abstraction, was not for him," though Melville essayed it on occasion. As a poet he first came into his own in certain of the *Battle-Pieces* of 1866, which Warren treats brilliantly in terms both of poetic technique and of informing moral ideas, drawing a telling contrast with the war poetry of Whitman (admittedly "the greater poet"). Among the later verse discussed, "Billy in the Darbies" stands out as "Melville's most perfect poem— the poem in which he achieves complete mastery of style and, shall we say, of his life," since for Warren the two in Melville at his best are inseparable.

Warren's discussion examines at some length the "interpenetration" between "Billy in the Darbies" and *Billy Budd, Sailor*, which it concludes: he suggests that the death in 1886 of Melville's second son, Stanwix, influenced the change from his original conception of an older Billy to the young Billy presented in the finished poem and the story. Another approach to the novel by way of the late poetry is Robert Shulman, "Melville's 'Timoleon': From Plutarch to the Early Stages of *Billy Budd*" (*CL*, XIX, 351–361), which begins with a comparative examination of Melville's poem and its source in Plutarch's *Lives*. *Billy Budd*, Shulman thinks, works up themes from Plutarch not used in "Timoleon"; both show "how pervasively during the 1880's Melville was concerned with the figure of the suffering martyr, typically under the aspect of tragedy, not redemption."

xii. Billy Budd, Sailor

G. R. Wilson, Jr., "*Billy Budd* and Melville's Use of Dramatic Technique" (*SSF*, IX, 105–111) argues that Melville deliberately stopped short of exploiting the full possibilities for dramatizing his story, on the ground that its "ambiguity and inconsistency" are better presented through "a fallible human narrator" than in "the absolute

terms of dramatic action." Though Melville left *Billy Budd* unfinished, Wilson feels that the story is "a unified work of art"; his view
is not shared by Paul Brodtkorb, Jr., who argues that the several
compositional stages analyzed in the Hayford-Sealts edition (Chicago, 1962) may each define "a stage of Melville's changing intention" not entirely compatible with other stages ("The Definitive *Billy
Budd*: 'But aren't it all sham?'," *PMLA*, LXXXII, 602–612). Melville,
Brodtkorb thinks, "spent too long" on the story; "extreme divergence" among the critics may be the fault of resultant disunity. Moreover, the commentators are like the characters themselves: each tries
"to give form and thereby meaning to the incomprehensible by
translating it into something else, something morally conceptualiz-
able, something that he can understand and act upon." Each character and each critic has his own outlook, expressed in a special
language (the "lexicons" of the story) foreign to the others. This
being so, Brodtkorb argues, "the story escapes advocating either conservative or liberal moral choices" and likewise "eludes liberal or
conservative critical rhetoric." Whatever "moral forms we impose on
it do not, in the end, fit well."

Charles A. Reich, "The Tragedy of Justice in *Billy Budd*" (*YR*,
LVI, 368–389), sees in the action an encounter of natural forces of
good and evil, represented by Billy and Claggart, with society and
law, represented by Captain Vere. Billy is innocent in what he *is*,
says Reich, but not in what he *does*. Vere rightly sees in him a manifestation of Nature containing "both good and evil," but is nevertheless powerless to save him; indeed, Melville himself "allows Vere
no choice within the terms of the law itself." Society, then and now,
"has not learned how to deal with man as a flawed creature"; it views
men as "either good or evil," and therefore in a case such as Billy's
the law must either "condemn or let go." What "the novel ultimately
asks" its readers, in Reich's view, is not what is wrong with Vere or
his actions but what is wrong with the law and its progenitor, society.

Even Reich's thoughtful discussion, with its careful analysis of
the central moral and legal issues raised by the story, will scarcely
satisfy those who are more dubious than he about Melville's portrayal
of Vere. Ralph W. Willett, "Nelson and Vere: Hero and Victim in
Billy Budd, Sailor" (*PMLA*, LXXXII, 370–376), sees Melville drawing a deliberate contrast between Vere as an upholder of existing

laws, a victim of society, and Nelson, an heroic maker of new Order for society. Willett thinks that Melville showed "compassion and understanding" toward the captain while portraying him as less than heroic; Alice Chandler, however, is convinced that Melville, like herself, was strongly anti-Vere. In "The Name Symbolism of Captain Vere" (*NCF*, XXII, 86–89) she raises, but dismisses as "unlikely," the interesting possibility that Clement Markham's *The Fighting Veres*, published in March of 1888, suggested the name; emphasizing its "clearly aristocratic associations," she prefers to dwell upon pejorative connotations of both "Vere" and "Fairfax" in nineteenth-century literature, arguing that when Billy "is sent to his doom by a frightened aristocrat," an "order-threatening Christ" has once again been "crucified by a conservative Pilate." In "Captain Vere and the 'Tragedies of the Palace'" (*MFS*, XIII, 259–261) Miss Chandler holds that for Melville, Vere kills Billy just as Peter the Great kills his own son ("the palace tragedy" alluded to in the story); *Billy Budd*, she declares, "may well be" Melville's "bleakest statement" of "the way in which he saw injustice, tyranny, and hate at the heart of things," whether one reads it on the level of theology, of politics, or of psychology. So runs the continuing "ironist" analysis of *Billy Budd*; meanwhile, Robert Penn Warren in "Melville's Poetry" also reads the work as "a father-son story" but hardly as a piece of social criticism. Melville's chosen mode, he thinks, is not ironic but tragic, and it is "by the poem"—the concluding ballad—"that we know, in spite of whatever built-in ironies or ambiguities may be in the story, what the final meaning amounts to: reconciliation, or at least the possibility of reconciliation."

Like Warren, Reich too sees the ballad as an epitome of the book, but for him it raises the demanding social question of "the fate of the natural in man"; like both Willett and Miss Chandler, though on obviously different grounds, he finds in *Billy Budd* "a pessimistic view" of society and specifically of America's destiny. Brodtkorb, however, senses a kind of "serenity" or "acceptance" in the book deriving from Melville's contemplation of approaching death; at last he is "making up his mind to be annihilated." And so the debate goes on, despite recent hopes of a narrowed ground of disagreement among critics; a "mystery that is almost but not quite solvable" (Brodtkorb) continues to allure and elude its would-be intepreters.

xiii. Letters, Documents, and Miscellaneous

Five previously unpublished Melville letters appeared during 1967. Hennig Cohen (*AL*, XXXVIII, 556–559) prints four letters addressed to Julius Rockwell of Pittsfield: two of 1853 concerning a local Fourth of July celebration at which Melville had been invited to speak (he declined) and two of 1861 related to his unsuccessful attempts to secure a consular appointment abroad. G. Thomas Tanselle (*AL*, XXXIX, 391–392) prints a two-sentence letter of October, 1857, to William P. S. Cadwell accepting an invitation to lecture in New Bedford. A Melville document, his oath of allegiance as Inspector of Customs, dated December 5, 1866, is reproduced by Kenneth W. Cameron (*ESQ*, No. 47, p. 129). Morris Star, "A Checklist of Portraits of Herman Melville" (*BNYPL*, LXXI, 468–473), first quotes contemporary descriptions of Melville's personal appearance and then surveys chronologically the known paintings, photographs, and prints, briefly characterizing and locating each; his concise compilation is fascinating as well as useful.

Hennig Cohen (*PBSA*, LXI, 266–267) has added to the list of Melville association volumes given in my *Melville's Reading* (1966), as No. 87a, a book in the Columbia University library: Thomas Duer Broughton, *Selections from the Popular Poetry of the Hindoos* (London, 1814); it is both autographed ("H Melville") and marked. Tyrus Hillway, in "Two Books in Young Melville's Library" (*BNYPL*, LXXI, 474–476), discusses Levi W. Leonard's *The Literary and Scientific Class Book* (1826), a text assigned at the New-York Male High School when Melville was in attendance there (see *Melville's Reading*, p. 75: No. 325a), and *The Young Man's Own Book: A Manual of Politeness, Intellectual Improvement, and Moral Deportment* (1832), cited in Ch. 18 of *Typee*. Shigehesa Narita, "Melville on Arnold" (*SELit*, English No., 1966, pp. 41–53), surveys marking and annotation in Melville's copies of five works of Matthew Arnold (*Melville's Reading*, Nos. 16–20); there is unfortunately no reference in this discussion to Walter Bezanson's more penetrating analysis of 1954, "Melville's Reading of Arnold's Poetry" (*PMLA*, LXIX, 365–391, treating Nos. 20 and 21). Deserving of special notice and praise is a section from the Introduction of Walker Cowen's 1965 Harvard dissertation (which reproduces and analyzes all of Melville's known marginalia) printed as "Melville's 'Discoveries': A Dialogue of the Mind with Itself," in Parker's *The Recognition of Herman Melville* (pp. 333–346). A brief quotation will suggest the character and quality of Cowen's analysis: "The marginalia are the private journal of his discoveries, the documented history of Melville's half-century struggle with himself and his art. . . . Each of the markings and annotations is the product of an exercise in discrimination. They are moral actions in the intellectual life of an artist who seeks, in the end, to discover himself."

There have been two sequels (*BNYPL*, LXX [1966], 551–552, 552–553) to Heyward Ehrlich's discovery that Melville's "man who dives" was his friend Duyckinck rather than Emerson (see *ALS*, *1965*, pp. 40–41): in "Melville's 'Ducking' Duyckinck" James H. Pickering suggests as a source Irving's humorous allusion to the senior Evert Duyckinck in Knickerbocker's *History of New York*; in " 'Diving and Ducking Moralities': A Rejoinder" Ehrlich replies that more than humor is involved. Melville, he declares, was interested "in the meaning and not the sound" of the Duyckinck family name. His complimentary allusion of 1849 ("dive") reflects partiality to "the literary nationalism of 'Young America' " as represented by Duyckinck and Cornelius Mathews; later in *Pierre*, having renounced the movement, he satirized "diving and ducking moralities" (V, v)— and this "was enough to bring down the Duyckincks on the 'most immoral *moral*' of the book." Ehrlich has made a shrewd hit here; he is right too in calling for further study of the "Knickerbocker" element in Melville.

Another of Melville's friendships is considered by Seymour L. Gross, "Hawthorne versus Melville" (*BuR*, XIV [1966], iii, 89–109), which assesses "the differences of 'blackness' " in the two writers— primarily in terms of excellent comparative readings: "My Kinsman, Major Molineux" and *Redburn*, "Young Goodman Brown" and "Benito Cereno." The article is a fine essay in critical discrimination.

Briefly surveying Melville's portrayal of clergymen from *Typee* to *Billy Budd*, though passing over "The Two Temples" and *Clarel*, Neal B. Houston, "Silent Apostles: Melville's Animus against the Clergy" (*RS*, XXXIV [1966], 230–239), finds him voicing three major criticisms: "they possess a certain impracticability," they lack Father Mapple's "compulsion 'to preach the Truth in the face of False-

hood,'" and they are silent "when face to face with the tragedy of
life. Melville bears a grudge, and he includes an unflattering portrait
of a clergyman in most of his novels."

xiv. Dissertations

Dissertation Abstracts, 1967, includes fourteen items concerned with
Melville as against ten in 1966 and four in 1965; the MLA International Bibliography for 1967 lists thirteen dissertations that treat
Melville. In addition, another was completed in 1966 at Harvard,
which does not cooperate with *DA*: Helen P. Trimpi, "Romance
Structure and Melville's Use of Demonology and Witchcraft in
Moby-Dick." Seven of the dissertations listed in 1967 have already
been discussed by Professor Thorp (*ALS, 1966*); the paragraphs below survey nine dissertations abstracted through 1967 but not previously covered by him.

David G. Halliburton, "The Grotesque in American Literature:
Poe, Hawthorne and Melville" (*DA*, XXVII, 3840A–3841A), sees
the grotesque not as a genre but as "a way of creating and perceiv-
ing," heavily dependent on a sense of play—particularly in Melville,
for whom "the grotesque is a spatial configuration which must be
penetrated to its essence." Frank M. Davis, "Herman Melville and the
Nineteenth-Century Church Community" (*DA*, XXVII, 3866A–
3867A), organized chronologically, observes that Melville's treatment of churchmen "became increasingly hostile," with particular
emphasis on their indifference to "exploitation of the primitive and
the poor." Frustrated by the church's inconsistencies between its
ideals and its practices, he rejected the institution but not the ideals:
his own idealism "had to find realization in the historical."

Jane P. Tompkins, "Studies in Melville's Prose Style" (*DA*,
XXVIII, 246A), covering selected works and parts of works from
1838 to 1852, relates "facts of style" to Melville's "habits of thought,
thematic concerns, and larger structural patterns." Fern M. Eddy,
"A Dark Similitude: Melville and the Elizabethan-Jacobean Perspective" (*DA*, XXVIII, 626A), a study concentrated on *Moby-Dick,*
Pierre, and *The Confidence-Man,* investigates not only Melville's
reading in the English dramatists but also his familiarity with
nineteenth-century dramatic criticism and the New York stage of the
1840's. Marjorie C. Dew, "Herman Melville's Existential View of the

Universe: Essays in Phenomenological Interpretation" (*DA*, XXVIII, 672A), identifies Melville's "preoccupation with the existential theme" as the basis for his appeal to moderns. Never, writes Mrs. Dew, "did Melville's expressed view-of-the-universe brighten in the least; never did he bow his head in acceptance of this world." With his perceptive awareness, he lived "in continued torment."

Barbara H. Meldrum, "Melville's *Mardi, Moby-Dick*, and *Pierre*: Tragedy in Recoil" (*DA*, XXVIII, 686A), finds the idea of the hero as artist to be one of the common elements uniting the three works. In the first and third "the impersonality of the artist recoils and he destroys himself"; in *Moby-Dick*, however, Melville's own "achievement as impersonal artist is implicit in Ishmael's achievement." Daniel C. Noel, "The Portent Unwound: Religious and Psychological Development in the Imagery of Herman Melville 1819–1854" (*DA*, XXVIII, 1791A), traces Melville's "varying shapes of psycho-religious questing imagistically unfolded" until in 1851 his moment of "Hawthornian self-understanding" was over; emphasis is on the configurations of "circle," "line," and "spiral." Steven H. Faigelman, "The Development of Narrative Consciousness in *Moby-Dick*" (*DA*, XXVIII, 2243A–2244A), views as "the central story" Ishmael's "tale of how he came to assume his final narrative role." Ishmael learns to know himself through a series of confrontations and digressive evasions in which "The Try-Works" chapter is central; Melville both condemns the "Romantic Imagination" in Ahab's subjective idealism and tentatively affirms it through "Ishmael's final survival as a story-teller."

One dissertation, that by Robert C. Ryan, makes the first thorough analysis of the manuscript poems Melville left unpublished at his death: "*Weeds and Wildings Chiefly: With a Rose or Two* by Herman Melville: Reading Text and Genetic Text, Edited from the Manuscripts, with Introduction and Notes" (*DA*, XXVIII, 2262A). As the title suggests, Ryan's work follows the pattern of the 1962 edition of *Billy Budd, Sailor;* much of it will be incorporated in a volume of the forthcoming Northwestern-Newberry edition of Melville.

University of Wisconsin–Madison

4. Whitman and Dickinson[1]

Edward F. Grier

Whitman scholarship has been in the doldrums for the past two years, while the amount of scholarly attention given to Emily Dickinson continues to underscore her emergence as one of our major poets. There has been no important event in Whitman bibliography since the appearance of the Blodgett-Bradley edition of *Leaves of Grass* in 1965, though the annual gleanings in the MLA International Bibliography remain pretty constant: 36, 31, 37 items respectively during each of the past three years. The annual listings devoted to Emily Dickinson, however, while quantitively fewer than those dealing with Whitman, (23, 23, 22 between 1965 and 1967), contain a considerable amount of important scholarship. Since much of the significant work on Dickinson dates from the availability of the Johnson edition (1955), this is not surprising and justifies her removal from the general section on Nineteenth-Century poetry to twin billing with Whitman.

i. Whitman

a. **Texts and bibliography.** Only a few new bits of text have turned up. William White, "Author at Work, Whitman's *Specimen Days*," (*MSS*, XVIII [Summer, 1966], 26–28) reprints a rough draft of "The First Frost" (*Specimen Days*) to demonstrate Whitman's careful reworking of his prose before publication. In "Whitman to Grant: an Addendum" (*WWR*, XIII, 60–61) Mr. White prints the final draft of a letter of February 27, 1874, to Ulysses S. Grant (see *The Correspondence*, II, 280–281). Edwin Haviland Miller, "A New Whitman Letter to Josiah Child" (*WWR*, XIII, 32–33), prints the complete text of a letter of December 8, 1881, to his English agent (see *The Correspondence*, III, 255).

---

1. A number of items have been passed over. Others, which were not available when needed, will be considered for next year's report.

One might suppose that *Complete Leaves of Grass with Prose Essences and Annotations* by William L. Moore (Tokyo, Taibundo, 1966), was a text edition for Japanese students, did not the splendor of the book and its price ($35) indicate otherwise. To the 1892 text Mr. Moore has added his "essences," which are sensitive paraphrases which ought to be very helpful to a Japanese reader who is struggling to get beyond the problems of vocabulary and syntax. A good selection of critical essays has been appended, and recordings of the "essences" are available separately. The volume is a beautiful example of deluxe bookmaking and is evidently a labor of love by Mr. Moore. There must be a considerable number of wealthy Japanese bibliophiles with serious literary interests.

Walt Whitman: A Catalog Based on the Collections of the Library of Congress (Boston, J. S. Canner) is a reprint of the 1955 catalog. *WWR* continues to publish very full quarterly bibliographies and interesting photographs and manuscript fragments from the Feinberg collection.

b. **Biography.** Edwin Haviland Miller, in "Amy Dowe and Walt Whitman" (*WWR*, XIII, 73–99), prints the reminiscences, written in the 1930's, of Louisa Orr Whitman's niece, who visited in Camden at various times between 1879 and 1889. Pleasant trivia.

c. **General studies.** In "The Two Poets of *Leaves of Grass*" (*Patterns of Commitment*, pp. 53–72), Gay Wilson Allen points out that Whitman propagated from the beginning two images of himself: one of the patriotic prophet, the other of the mystic poet of the Self. Mr. Allen finds that his emphasis on nationalism increased between 1856 and 1860, probably, if the reviewer may interject a suggestion, because his personal problems of the period shook his faith in his personal Self and the drift toward dissolution of the Union raised a clear threat which had to be countered. Whitman's statements about his poetic technique show a split also between the image of the slapdash inspired rough and the careful reviser. The reviewer regrets that he was unable to read or find help to read Torben Boström's "Poesiens demokratisering" in his *Labyrint og Arabesk* (Copenhagen, Gyldendal, pp. 109–118), for Denmark has an honorable tradition in Whitman studies. David R. Weimer's important exploratory work, *The City as Metaphor* (New York, Random House,

Studies in Language and Literature No. 8, 1966) is not a study of
the sociological awareness of authors, but of how they perceived the
city, of how they used it for art rather than reportage. Naturally
Weimer begins with Whitman (pp. 14–33), who, with his contemporary, Baudelaire, was one of the first poets to recognize the
modern city. The fact that Whitman was dealing with the modern
city, the industrial city, the mass city is recognized by Mr. Weimer,
but insufficiently so; otherwise he might have tempered the tone of
his conclusion, which, although just in fact, is too severe in tone.
Robert Cushman Murphy's "The Poet Through a Naturalist's Eyes"
(*WWR*, XIII, 39–44) is a genial appreciation by a distinguished
naturalist who defends Whitman against charges of obscurantism
and attests to his familiarity with nature. Although Marian Stein, in
"Comrade or Camerado in *Leaves of Grass*" (*WWR*, XIII, 123–125),
can offer little to account for Whitman's misspelling of the Spanish,
she usefully points out that he used "comrade" generically or to refer
merely to the idea of close friendship but "camerado" to indicate
an immediate and close relationship. James McNally's "Varieties of
Alliteration in Whitman" (*WWR*, XIII, 28–32) is a brief but useful
demonstration of Whitman's control of sound patterns. V. K. Chari,
in "Poe and Whitman's Short-Poem Style" (*WWR*, XIII, 95–97),
proposes that Whitman took Poe's dictum seriously. Thomas L.
Brashear, in "A Modest Protest against Viewing Whitman as a
Pantheist and Reincarnationist" (*WWR*, XIII, 92–94), succinctly
says that whatever Whitman called himself he was a transcendentalist and that the "reincarnationist" passages in "Song of Myself,"
Sections 20, 27, 38, and 44, concern progressive evolution. Ida Fasel,
in "Whitman and Milton" (*WWR*, XIII, 79–87), gets off to a good
start by arguing that Whitman paid more careful attention to Milton
than his statements about him might suggest, but her attempts to
prove influences in specific passages are unconvincing.

d. **Individual poems.**   As usual, "Song of Myself" has attracted the
most attention. Griffith Dudding in "The Function of Whitman's
Imagery in 'Song of Myself'" (*WWR*, XIII, 3–11) covers fairly well-
trodden ground. T. J. Kallsen, in "The Improbabilities in Section 11
of 'Song of Myself'" (*WWR*, XIII, 87–92), despite the awkwardness
of his title, adds greatly to our understanding of the mysterious

episode of the twenty-nine bathers. In "'Song of Myself,' Section 21" (*WWR*, XIII, 98–99), Mary A. Neuman says that Section 21 is the climax of the theme of cosmic generation which is first stated in Section 5. In "The Sea-Fight Episode in 'Song of Myself'" (*WWR*, XIII, 16–21), Richard K. Adicks presents a fresh interpretation of the way in which Section 36 relates to the tone and structure of the entire poem and a good reading of ll. 959–965 of Section 38. In "Organic Language in 'Patrolling Barnegat'" (*WWR*, XIII, 125–127), Raymond G. Malbone shows Whitman's effective use of sounds to support his sense. Minor W. Major, in "A New Interpretation of Whitman's Calamus Poems" (*WWR*, XIII, 51–54), without denying the usual homosexual interpretation, suggests that, troubled by the nineteenth-century conflict between science and religion, Whitman was taking refuge in comradeship in this world. Mr. Major cites "Of the Terrible Doubt of Appearances," "I Saw in Louisiana a Live-Oak Growing," and "Full of Life Now" in support of his thesis. In "Some Traditional Poems from *Leaves of Grass*" (*WWR*, XIII, 44–51), J. R. Le Master shows Whitman's mastery of traditional forms in "Ethiopia Saluting the Colors" and "The Singer in Prison." Estelle W. Taylor, in "Analysis and Comparison of the 1855 and 1891 Versions of 'To Think of Time'" (*WWR*, XIII, 107–123), finds no change in Whitman's view of time, death and immortality but a sharpening of language. Although most readers have regretted Whitman's abandonment of the 1855 marks of suspension, Miss Taylor argues convincingly that in this poem at least, the substitution of conventional punctuation was an improvement.

e. **Reputation and influence.** Frederik L. Rusch, in "Of Eidólons and Orgone" (*WWR*, XIII, 11–15), finds striking similarities between Whitman's sense of cosmic energy and that of Wilhelm Reich. Ray Benoit, in "The Mind's Return: Whitman, Teilhard, and Jung" (*WWR*, XIII, 21–28), finds striking similarities between Whitman's ideas and those of the thinkers he mentions. A relationship more clearly demonstrable, between Whitman and Tagore, is pointed out by Harold M. Hurwitz in "Whitman, Tagore, and 'Passage to India'" (*WWR*, XIII, 56–60). Joseph Katz, in "Whitman, Crane, and the Odious Comparison" (*N&Q*, XIV, 66–67), reprints an 1885 review of Crane's *Black Riders* by Isaac Hull Platt, an early Whitmanite, in which, although he admired Crane's poems, he took exception to an unfavorable review which made a derogatory comparison with Whitman.

Since William Carlos Williams was one of the earliest major poets of the Twentieth Century to find nourishment in Whitman, two essays by James E. Breslin are important contributions. In "Whitman and the Early Development of William Carlos Williams" (*PMLA*, LXXXII, 613–621) Breslin traces Williams' growth from 1902 to 1914. It appears that although Williams was stimulated by Ezra Pound and was writing neo-Keatsian poetry, he was also jotting down spontaneous poems in the manner of Whitman as a result of his reading the *Leaves*. It was not, however, until 1914 that his real breakthrough came in "The Wanderer," partly as a result of rereading the *Leaves*. In "William Carlos Williams and the Whitman Tradition," in Phillip Damon, ed., *Literary Criticism and Historical Understanding: Selected Papers from the English Institute* [1966] (New York, Columbia Univ.), pp. 151–179, Mr. Breslin examines the relationship more closely. It is not based on a common manner but on Williams' discovery that the Self must be discovered by possessing the objective scene. He notes, of course, that Williams is assertive in his taking possession, whereas Whitman tends to be passive and receptive. Illustrative citations are from *Spring and All* (1923). Further interesting comparisons of the two poets are implied in Weimar's *The City as Metaphor* (see pp. 49–50).

Living writers are also responding to Whitman. As Peter Van Egmond points out in "Herzog's Quotation of Walt Whitman" (*WWR*, XIII, 54–56), Bellow quotes "in Paths Untrodden" to underline Herzog's loneliness. Didier T. Jaen, in "Borges y Whitman" (*Hispania*, L, 49–53), points out that the relationships between Borges and Whitman is closer that at first appears. He quotes Borges' translations of and comments on Whitman from *Discusiones, Poemas*, and from an unpublished lecture on Whitman at the University of Texas in 1961–1962.

f. **Theses.** The following completed doctoral theses have been reported. Hoople, Robin P., "*Leaves of Grass* (1860) as Opinion: A Study of Whitman's Understanding of the Major Problems of 1860 American Culture as Reflected in the Third Edition of *Leaves of Grass*" (*DA*, XXVII [1966], 1319A–1320A); Jones, Dan P., "Walt

Whitman's Perception of Time" (*DA*, XXVII, 3050A); Van Egmond, Peter G., "Walt Whitman's Study of Oratory and Uses of It in *Leaves of Grass*" (*DA*, XXVII, 2510A).

ii. Emily Dickinson

a. **Texts and bibliography.** Not every admirer of Emily Dickinson's poetry will jump to read R. W. Franklin's *The Editing of Emily Dickinson: A Reconsideration* (Madison, Univ. of Wis.), for textual problems have less audience appeal than any other form of literary scholarship. The book is, nevertheless, an important one. For one thing, it is a useful addition to the scant literature on the editing of modern literary manuscripts. Second, the serious Dickinson reader will want to consider Mr. Franklin's new readings and his arrangement of poems and perhaps annotate his own big or little Johnson. Third, the last section of the book deals wisely with the difficult problem of the much-needed Reader's Edition. Mr. Franklin's dictum is, "Start with the manuscripts." For the reader who involuntarily becomes an editor, as we all must when we use the Johnston texts, he shows quite conclusively that the capitals and dashes were a habit of handwriting and that Dickinson used them inconsistently in poems, letters, and recipes. One hopes that since Mr. Franklin is intimately familiar with the problems involved he will undertake the Reader's Edition.

Since, between the last revision of the Bibliography of the *Literary History of the United States* and the first volume of *ALS* there is a considerable time lapse, Susan Freis's "Emily Dickinson: A Check List of Criticism" (*PBSA*, LXI, 359–385) fills a need. There are 456 entries, comprising books, periodical articles, parts of books, and dissertations (including some of 1967). Reprinted excerpts of books, review articles and reprints of articles are noted.[1]

b. **General studies.** David Higgins' *Portrait of Emily Dickinson: The Poet and Her Prose* (New Brunswick, Rutgers Univ. Press) falls between a biography and a study of Emily Dickinson as a letter-writer. The organization is roughly chronological, but also topical,

---

1. A book-length bibliography (Sheila T. Clendenning, *Emily Dickinson, A Bibliography: 1850–1966*, Kent State Univ. Press, 1968), which appeared too late for inclusion in this essay, will be reviewed next year.

the thesis being that the style and manner of her correspondence varied not only with age but also with the recipient. Moreover, it is almost impossible to deal with the letters without some knowledge of the circumstances behind them and her relationship with the recipient, whereas the poems can stand alone. There are knotty problems in the letters, to be sure, quite aside from their cryptic and mannered style. Mr. Higgins is of the opinion that Samuel Bowles, editor of the Springfield *Republican*, was in some way involved with Emily Dickinson's emotional crisis of 1859–1861 or thereabouts and tentatively names Bowles as the person for whom the three "Master" drafts were intended. The Introduction was published in 1963 (see *ALS, 1963*, p. 126).

Ernest Sandeen, in "Delight Deferred by Retrospect: Emily Dickinson's Late-Summer Poems" (*NEQ*, XL, 483–500), modestly acknowledging previous studies of her use of the seasonal cycle, argues that the late-summer poems range more widely than any of the other seasonal groups through her concerns, bring into focus her conflicting reactions to life, and show very clearly her characteristic habit of cooly analyzing internalized experience of the most moving sort.

c. **Individual poems.** "I Heard a Fly Buzz When I Died" has attracted two critics. James T. Connelly in "Dickinson's 'I Heard a Fly Buzz When I Died'" (*Expl*, XXV [1966], Item 34) suggests that, since the color blue traditionally suggests evil, ghosts, and the prophecy of death [?], the fly is death. Ronald Beck, "Dickinson's 'I Heard a Fly Buzz When I Died'" (*Expl*, XXVI, Item 31) says, on the other hand, that despite the solemnity of the occasion King Death does not enter, only a fly—private death and decay. "Wild Nights" has been discussed in three notes. James L. Connelly, in "Dickinson's 'Wild Nights'" (*Expl*, XXV, Item 44), citing letter 332 in support, suggests that the poem is a glorification of and an apostrophe to death "whose presence and company are paradoxically exhilarating luxury." Paul Faris, in "Eroticism in Emily Dickinson's 'Wild Nights!'" (*NEQ*, XL, 269–274) denies the presence of erotic ecstasy in the poem and says that, rather, it is a cry for peace. Christof Wegelin, perhaps disturbed by this reading (no one has yet suggested that "thee . . . Thee" refers to God!), reads it as a Liebestod in which love is seen as being capable of fulfillment only on the other side of death ("Dickinson's 'Wild Nights,'" *Expl*, XXVI, Item 25). Robert L. Lair, in "Dickinson's 'As by the Dead We Love to Sit'" (*Expl*, XXV, Item 58), points out that the elliptical and convoluted syntax of the poem lifts it above the conventions of grief. Raymond G. Malbone, in "Dickinson's 'I Taste a Liquor Never Brewed'" (*Expl*, XXVI, Item 14), identifies "Tankards scooped in Pearl" as the swelling cumulous clouds of summer. Sidney E. Lind's "Emily Dickinson's 'Further in Summer than the Birds' and Nathaniel Hawthorne's 'The Old Manse'" (*AL*, XXXIX, 163–169) suggests that Hawthorne's essay, published in 1846 and which Dickinson may well have read, may have aroused in her a similar feeling of religious but pagan ecstacy at the declining summer (see Ernest Sandeen above). Hollis L. Cate, in "Emily Dickinson and 'The Prisoner of Chillon'" (*AN&Q*, VI, 6–7), points out that her four references in her letters to "The Prisoner" are her only references to Byron and that possibly she was identifying herself with the hero of the poem.

d. **Theses.** The following completed doctoral theses have been reported: Chaliff, Cynthia, "Emily Dickinson Against the World: An Interpretation of the Poet's Life and Work" (*DA*, XXVIII, 1070A); De Salvo, Leta P. "The Arrested Syllable: A Study of the Death Poetry of Emily Dickinson" (*DA*, XXVII [1966], 1916A); Frank, Bernhard, "The Wiles of Words: Ambiguity in Emily Dickinson's Poetry" (*DA*, XXVII [1966], 1784A); Kreisberg, Ruth M., "The Poetry of Emily Dickinson" (*DA*, XXVII, 3872–3873A); Lair, Robert L., "Emily Dickinson's Fracture of Grammar" (*DA*, XXVII, 3052A–3053A).

University of Kansas

5. Mark Twain

John C. Gerber

The year is one in which textual study and criticism predominate almost to the exclusion of biography. So far as I can recall, there has been no year within recent times in which so little on Mark Twain's life appeared. The central event of course was the publication of the first three volumes of the *Mark Twain Papers*. Not completely overshadowed, however, was the unabating flow of critical studies, mostly on *Huckleberry Finn*. Particularly, the number of studies on the last ten chapters continues to increase, most of them written by young critics determined to show that the ending if not a thing of beauty is at least a joy to be discussed forever. Uncle Silas never had it so good.

i. Texts and Editions

Undoubtedly the most important event of the year was the appearance of the first three of the fourteen projected volumes of the *Mark Twain Papers*. The *Papers* consist mainly of previously unpublished works and are produced under the direction of an editorial board composed of Walter Blair, Donald Coney, and Henry Nash Smith, with Frederick Anderson serving as Associate Editor. Since most of the Papers are in the General Library at the University of California at Berkeley, it is appropriate that the University of California Press should be the publisher. The books are extraordinarily handsome. What is more, their texts are eminently readable, for they are largely uncluttered by editorial paraphernalia. I would venture to guess that even that old curmudgeon, Samuel L. Clemens, would approve of the *Papers*, even though they contain works that he himself had rejected for publication.

The overall aim with each selection is to recover Mark Twain's last intention insofar as it can be determined. Where there has been only a single manuscript this has been easy. Where there have been both manuscripts and typescripts, the editors have had to determine which of the inevitable variants carry the final authority. Major variants that have been rejected, the editors tell us, are recorded in footnotes or appendixes. So are the author's cancellations and insertions that result in important changes in meaning, characterization, or action. What are clearly intentional misspellings are retained, and so are idiosyncratic spellings when they arc consistently used. The changes have been minor: the correction of unintentional misspellings, the substitution of "and" for the ampersand, the regularization of an occasional indecisive mark of punctuation, such as a dash at the end of a sentence. In short, if the editors have followed their own rules meticulously—and there is every reason to believe that they have—we have in these volumes the hitherto unpublished works as Mark Twain wanted them to be when he last worked on them. There will undoubtedly be purists who will regret that the volumes do not record every minor change or slip of the pen. But anyone interested in such minutiae would want to examine the manuscripts first-hand—or should want to. For the great majority of readers, these volumes will be quite satisfactory.

One volume was too far along in production to be examined by a representative of the Center for Editions of American Authors, and hence appears without the Center's seal. This was *Mark Twain's Satires and Burlesques*, edited with an introduction by Franklin R. Rogers. The editorial work, however, has been substantial and careful. The volume contains "Burlesque *Il Trovatore*," "A Novel: *Who Was He?*", "The Story of Mamie Grant, the Child-Missionary," "L'Homme Qui Rit," "Burlesque *Hamlet*," "1,002d Arabian Night," a sequence of three related pieces capped by "Hellfire Hotchkiss," and a series of four related pieces capped by the incomplete novel *Simon Wheeler, Detective*. In addition there are two appendixes containing incidental information, and eighteen pages of textual notes.

By any absolute standard these satires and burlesques are pretty bad. Nevertheless, they reveal a great deal about Mark Twain's methods of composition and the development of his thought. The first six, the latest of them written in 1883, show him using such obvious tricks of literary burlesque as exaggeration of action and style or the introduction of a new and incongruous character into a well-established text (a book-agent is introduced into *Hamlet*).

The two sequences of related selections are more interesting. Each sequence involves several tries with the same theme and, often, the same characters. The early tries in each sequence, written in the 1870's, are sheer buffoonery. The last ones, written in the 1890's, show him attempting to deal with more serious issues. Even if in these later works the edge of the satire is seldom felt because of the overlay of melodramatic claptrap, one becomes subtly conscious of a more troubled man behind the works. Biographers should be just as interested in these selections as critics. And the general reader will find much here that is hilariously funny.

Mark Twain's Which Was the Dream? and Other Symbolic Writings of the Later Years is edited with an introduction by John S. Tuckey and bears the seal of the Center for Editions of American Authors. It includes seven major texts: "Which Was the Dream?", "The Enchanted Sea-Wilderness," "An Adventure in Remote Seas," "The Great Dark," "Indiantown," "Which Was It?", and "Three Thousand Years Among the Microbes." All of these selections were written between 1896 and 1905. All are appearing in print for the first time except "The Great Dark," which Bernard DeVoto included in Letters from the Earth, and a part of "Three Thousand Years Among the Microbes," which A. B. Paine inserted into his biography of Mark Twain.

These are the texts into which Mark Twain poured so much of his remorse and frustration after the death of Susy and the collapse of his fortune in the early 1890's. One feels that it is almost an invasion of privacy to watch him speculating about the possibility that life is a dream—and hoping that it may be. Or in listening to his characters repeat over and over again that man is the slave of circumstance and therefore not responsible for what takes place. We enter here into fictive worlds which are the thinnest kind of disguise for the author's own inner world. Yet it would clearly be a mistake to conclude with Bernard DeVoto that these works show Mark Twain blocked creatively and on the edge of insanity. Far from being blocked, his imagination almost flourishes. Mr. Tuckey's quotations from letters tell us that he was often writing joyously. The forms of his narrative are ingenious, and the humor often as trenchant as ever. This is especially true in "Three Thousand Years Among the Microbes," a tale told by a cholera microbe named "Huck" (short for his middle name of Huxley). Ruled over by the

Pus dynasty, the microbes inhabit a tramp by the name of Blitzow-
ski. This selection and the others remain incomplete, it seems to
me, not so much because of any falling off of Twain's literary ingenuity but because the themes he is attempting to dramatize are
ones that he would have been incapable of dramatizing successfully
at *any* period of his creative career. The themes raise questions he
was never able to answer to his own satisfaction and hence to project
into works of art with a satisfactory beginning, middle, *and end.* Be
that as it may, these are texts that are invaluable for an understanding of Twain as thinker and writer. We can be grateful to
Mr. Tuckey for editing them so carefully and annotating them so
helpfully.

The third of the *Mark Twain Papers* to appear in 1967 was *Mark
Twain's Letters to His Publishers, 1867–1894.* The work is ably
edited with an introduction by Hamlin Hill, and carries the seal
of the Center for Editions of American Authors. Chiefly the letters
are to Elisha Bliss of the American Publishing Company, James R.
Osgood of James R. Osgood & Company, and Charles L. Webster
and Fred J. Hall of Twain's own firm, Charles L. Webster & Company. Covering the quarter century from 1867 to 1894, the letters
reveal Clemens at the time when as Mark Twain he was turning
out just about all of the works upon which his reputation rests. We
are dealing here, in short, with the man at the height of his powers.
The results in these letters are amusing, exciting, and sometimes
horrifying. One comes away from the book glad that he was not a
publisher that had to deal with the author. On the other hand, the
letters also make it clear that it was not simply a case of Mark Twain
against the good guys. With the possible exception of Osgood, the
publishers tended to be either crafty or inept, exasperating in either
case. Because of his splenetic correspondence Mark Twain probably
got a better deal from them than most. But we receive much more
than business detail here. As Mr. Hill points out, "Mark Twain reveals here a part of himself and a part of his life that was essential
both to his view of himself and to any reader's comprehension of
his complex personality." Mr. Hill's headnotes and footnotes are
so well articulated with the text that they make the book read
almost like a narrative.

In addition to what is contained in the three volumes of the
Papers, only a few other texts appear in print for the first time, or

are reprinted from hard-to-get-at sources. An early speech is presented with a detailed commentary by Edgar M. Branch in "Major
Perry and the Monitor *Comanche*: An Early Mark Twain Speech,"
(*AL*, XXXIX, 170–179). Delivered on June 12, 1864, the speech was
featured the next day on the front page of the San Francisco *Daily
Alta California*. As Branch points out, the speech is significant because it indicates that as early as 1864 Mark Twain was held in high
regard in San Francisco as a humorist—and speaker—and because
the memory of this earlier talk undoubtedly encouraged him to make
his more famous lecture on the Sandwich Islands in 1866. In "Samuel
Clemens and the Copperheads of 1864" (*MRR*, II, Winter-Spring,
3–20) Mr. Branch reprints three political reports he thinks were
written by Mark Twain. The reports appeared originally in the
San Francisco *Morning Call* on which Twain was a local reporter
for four months beginning June 6, 1864. They are headed "Democratic Meeting at Hayes' Park," "An Accumulation of Copperheads,"
and "Democratic Ratification Meeting." Mr. Branch speculates that
the *Call*, being Unionist and Republican in sympathy, used Twain
for such reports because of their hope that he would treat the
Democrats satirically. If this was really their hope, they were not
disappointed.

In "On Three Mark Twain Poems" (*MTJ*, XIII, iii, 10–11) Richard E. Peck corrects two texts in Arthur L. Scott's *On the Poetry of
Mark Twain* and adds a hitherto unpublished example of Twain's
verse. This last piece, untitled, ends with the chest-heaving question, "What most/Delicious is?"

Chester L. Davis continues to print letters written to A. B.
Paine that he has in his possession. They appear in all issues of the
Twainian for 1967. Those from Susan Crane and Fred J. Hall are
especially interesting. Hall, incidentally, says in one (*Twainian*,
XXVI, July–Aug., 3) that after he took over as head of Charles L.
Webster & Co., all decisions on what books to print were made by
Twain. In the Nov.–Dec. issue of the *Twainian* (p. 2) Mr. Davis
reprints a narrative entitled "All Right!" which appeared in *The
Carpet-Bag* June 14, 1851, and challenges Mark Twain scholars to
discover whether it was written by Mark Twain. He thinks it may
be the story Mark Twain claimed to have published in 1851. Both
"The Dandy Frightening the Squatter" and "Hannibal, Missouri"
(the latter published first in the *American Courier* [Philadelphia]

on May 1 or May 8, 1852) are reproduced in a folder produced by Roger Butterfield for the 18th annual meeting of the Antiquarian Booksellers' Association of America. William White in "Roger Butterfield and the Earliest Mark Twain" (*MTJ*, XIII, iv, 20) indicates that Butterfield is the first to identify the *Courier* article as Twain's.

Earl J. Dias in "Mark Twain in Fairhaven" (*MTJ*, XIII, iv, 11–15) provides the text of an amusing speech delivered by Twain in Fairhaven, February 22, 1894, on the occasion of the dedication of the town hall built by H. H. Rogers and presented to the town in his wife's name. Also reproduced is a letter Mark Twain wrote on the same day to the officers of the Millicent Library, a structure given the town by Rogers and named for his daughter who died at the age of eighteen. In his introduction of the texts Mr. Dias writes in interesting detail about Rogers and Fairhaven.

No new editions of major works, so far as I know, appeared in 1967. Two that did not get reported in 1966, however, are a Bantam Pathfinder edition of *Tom Sawyer* edited by Robert D. Spector, and a Heritage edition of *A Tramp Abroad* edited by Edward Wagenknecht.

Frederick Anderson, William M. Gibson, and Henry Nash Smith present in *Selected Mark Twain–Howells Letters: 1872–1910* (Cambridge, Harvard Univ. Press, Belknap) a one-volume version of their two-volume *Mark Twain–Howells Letters* published in 1960 by the Belknap Press. The letters selected for this edition appear without the cancelled words originally set off by angle brackets. In addition, many letters have been condensed by deleting passages the editors believe to be of small interest to those who are not specialists in American literature. Two letters that have come to light since 1960 have been added. The result is an attractive volume that page for page is more interesting and readable than its longer predecessor.

Coincidentally, the relationship between Mark Twain and William Dean Howells is the subject of another reprint: an edition of Howells' *My Mark Twain: Reminiscences and Criticisms* (Baton Rouge, La. State Univ. Press) edited by Marilyn Austin Baldwin. Like the original edition published by Harpers in 1910 this one reprints not only *My Mark Twain* but also a dozen essays that Howells wrote about Twain or about certain of Twain's major works. Topping off the collection is "The American Joke," a bit of high-class dog-

gerel that Howells read at the Clemens birthday dinner, December
5, 1905. The volume is a paperback with headnotes and footnotes
aimed at the non-specialist.

A rather ruthlessly abridged version of *My Mark Twain* appears
in *Mark Twain: A Profile* (New York, Hill and Wang). Edited by
Justin Kaplan, the book additionally contains essays by Dixon
Wecter, Van Wyck Brooks, Bernard DeVoto, Dwight MacDonald,
Kenneth S. Lynn, Leslie A. Fiedler, Winfield Townley Scott, Paul
Fatout, Henry Nash Smith, James M. Cox, and Mr. Kaplan himself.
The essays are good ones, but it is hard to see what they add up to.
Presumably they are to provide us with a "profile." If so, the camera
is out of adjustment. Possibly Mr. Kaplan is preparing us for this
in his introduction where he stresses the lack of unity in Twain's
personality. I am willing to concede that lack of focus here is not
necessarily a criticism of Mr. Kaplan because it is hard to see how
any combination of a dozen essays on Twain could result in a well
focused profile. Nevertheless, if an editor insists on collecting a
number of disparate essays and calling it a profile, he should at least
provide us with an introduction that indicates the unity and coherence he has in mind. Mr. Kaplan's introduction simply underlines
the diversity inherent in the essays.

ii. Biography

In few of the last twenty-five years has so little appeared on the
life of Mark Twain. Indeed, the only major work is not a new one
but the third edition of Edward's Wagenknecht's *Mark Twain: The
Man and His Work* (Norman, Univ. of Okla. Press). This edition
is the same as the second published in 1961 except that a section has
been added entitled "Commentary on Mark Twain Criticism and
Scholarship Since 1960." This section, unlike the bibliography in
the second edition, is put together in essay form much like that used
in *American Literary Scholarship*—though Mr. Wagenknecht engagingly asserts that he has "deliberately refrained" from reading
this section on Mark Twain in the annual *ALS*. The Commentary
is a useful reference work for the criticism and scholarship from
1960 to 1966. The book itself Mr. Wagenknecht calls a psychograph
to distinguish it from the conventional biography. Although other
studies have penetrated further into aspects of Mark Twain's per-

sonality, this one is still probably the best attempt at dealing with the totality of that personality. Young students of Mark Twain could do much worse than to start with this volume.

In "Mark Twain's Search for Identity" (*Essays in American and English Literature*, pp. 27–47) John C. Gerber suggests that if there is a deep centrality in Mark Twain, it probably lies in his persisting desire to learn his own identity, to define himself in terms of the contexts in which he existed. Unhappily, in no context could he define himself to his own satisfaction: religion, morality, manners, wealth, science, or art.

A brief impressionistic sketch of Clara Clemens by William Fifield appears in "Joyce's Brother, Lawrence's Wife, Wolfe's Mother, Twain's Daughter" (*TQ*, X, 69–87).

iii. General Criticism

Sydney J. Krause's *Mark Twain as Critic* (Baltimore, Johns Hopkins Press), the one major critical work of the year, is a book that is too slow in breaking free of the formulas imposed upon the material. It is divided into three parts: Twain's Early Criticism: The Critic as Muggins, Twain's Later Criticism: The Critic as Grumbler, and Twain's Appreciative Criticism: From History into Life. As these titles suggest, there is over-neatness about the way in which the first two sections divide Mark Twain's critical work, and there is a confusion about the relation of the third to the other two.

Mr. Krause argues in the first section that in his earlier years Mark Twain as critic played the role of a muggins, and that he did so because he needed the protection of the "ego-less muggins" for his ventures into the "ego-harrowing arena of criticism." In the second section Krause argues that as Twain gained a reputation and hence confidence, he shifted his critical role to that of the grumbler. In the one period, he hid behind the mask of the fool, in the second behind the mask of the curmudgeon. (There is something here that is analogous to the movement from tenderfoot to old-timer that some critics see in *Roughing It*.) The argument does point up a strong tendency, but it was only a tendency. Mark Twain played the role of grumbler early, and the role of fool in some of his latest critical works. Often he would play the two roles in the same work. And each of the roles is more complicated than Mr. Krause sug-

gests because Twain could play both the fool and the grumbler in
a variety of ways. Furthermore, one wonders why the arena of
criticism was so harrowing to him as a young critic when his main
targets of attack were the excesses of romanticism that most of the
humorists of the time were lampooning. One suspects that he really
adopted the role of muggins because it was the easiest and most
popular role to play and not from any psychological necessity. Furthermore, one wonders whether the role of grumbler was always a
role. Sam Clemens was no muggins but he *was* a grumbler. So when
is the grumbler a role and when is it the real Sam Clemens that is
standing up?

In the third section when he gets away from his formulas, Mr.
Krause's book is much more penetrating. The section on Macaulay
exhibits Twain as a critic of no little shrewdness. And those on
Howells, Howe and Zola, and Wilbrandt reinforce the impression
gained in the discussion of Macaulay that Mark Twain was considerably more than the simple-minded realist that many have portrayed
him. As Mr. Krause puts it, for Mark Twain "it was not history
alone, or fiction alone, but the two together that led to meaningful realism." It is a concept that illuminates not only the best criticism of Mark Twain but much of his best fiction too.

What is possibly the most penetrating article of the year is
Roger B. Salomon's "Mark Twain and Victorian Nostalgia" (*Patterns of Commitment*, pp. 73–91). Victorian nostalgia in the words
of Mr. Salomon, is "the repository of values of the intellectually
committed realist; it makes a place for the 'happier world' while
remaining fully conscious of its loss." Its chief literary strategy is
that of the double vision (e.g., the points of view of the fictional
"invader" and the world he invades, those of the author and his
characters, even his most sympathetic characters). Mr. Salomon
cites a number of examples but concentrates on the works of Mark
Twain, for in Twain's regional writing, especially, he finds the best
examples of this double vision at work: the fidelity to factual detail
countered by an emotional commitment to a lost wonderland full
of moral, spiritual, and imaginative possibilities for the hero. In
some detail Mr. Salomon shows how Mark Twain as a nostalgic
writer moves directly from *Tom Sawyer, The Prince and the Pauper,
Life on the Mississippi*, and *Huckleberry Finn* to *Pudd'nhead Wilson, Joan of Arc*, and *The Mysterious Stranger*, with only *A Con-*

necticut Yankee being an almost desperate attempt to "shatter the
nostalgic image and build a literature and a sustaining faith on the
present and the future." The article illuminates not only a major
tendency in Mark Twain but a central concern of Victorian writers
as a group. It may well be, as Mr. Salomon says, that a study of the
forms taken by Victorian nostalgia leads to the heart of the imagination of the period.

"Mark Twain and the Dark Angel" (*MQ*, VIII, 181–197) by
Larry R. Dennis sets forth the thesis that Mark Twain in his writings
is repeatedly attempting to place the fact of death in a tenable perspective. With Huck he succeeds best. Constantly having to con-
front death, Huck becomes aware not only that it destroys life but
also that it has life-giving possibilities. Death and life are not polar
opposites. In *Roughing It*, however, death is in opposition to life,
as it is in "Reflections on Religion." In *The Mysterious Stranger*
life and death are fruitlessly reconciled in a dream, and in "The
Great Dark" they are displayed as being equally horrible. In short,
Mr. Dennis believes that the only consciousness in Mark Twain's
fiction that was tough enough to come to terms with death was
Huck. The pathos of it all is that Huck's perspective is one Mark
Twain himself could not share. Despite the fact that this study
attributes many symbolic meanings to *Huckleberry Finn* that have
been attributed to it before, Mr. Dennis' focus on the theme of
death gives them a relevance they have not always had.

Like Walter Blair, E. Hudson Long, Gladys Bellamy, and other
scholars before him, D. S. Bertolotti, Jr., finds parallels between
Mark Twain and Carlyle: "Mark Twain Revisits the Tailor," (*MTJ*,
XIII, iv, 18–19). The chief difference between the two, he believes,
was that Twain was never able to follow Carlyle from the "Ever-
lasting No" through the "Centre of Indifference" to the "Everlast-
ing Yea."

Thomas O. Blues writes on "The Individual and the Community
in the Works of Mark Twain," (*DA*, XXVII, 3035A). Mr. Blues contends that to the mid-point of his literary career Mark Twain held
to a real if submerged faith in the community, and that the subsequent loss of this faith caused him to villify the community and to
seek alternatives for it. In "Mark Twain and the Bible: Characters
Who Use the Bible and Biblical Characters" (*DA*, XXVIII, 692A)
Robert A. Rees explores the various ways in which Mark Twain

made use of the Bible in writing his fiction, discovering among other things that his use of it for sustained fictional creation was largely limited to the first seven chapters of Genesis. Ben M. Vorpahl in "Such Stuff as Dreams Are Made On: History, Myth and the Comic Vision of Mark Twain and William Faulkner" (*DA*, XXVIII, 698A) finds that the comic as it occurs in Mark Twain and Faulkner involves not only similar assumptions about history and humanity, but also similar situations, such as the destruction of Edenic hopes through encounter with the circumstances of reality.

iv. Earlier Works

A really extraordinary amount of background material is brought together by Edgar M. Branch in " 'My voice is still for Setchell': A Background Study of 'Jim Smiley and His Jumping Frog'" (*PMLA*, LXXXII, 591–601). From Mark Twain's immediately prior experiences and his emotional conflicts of the period, Mr. Branch proposes a date of composition and a reading of the tale that emphasizes its personal meaning. I must confess I am not wholly convinced by Mr. Branch's contention that Twain is projecting into the story certain "tension-laden problems, closely connected with his need to find himself." But the evidence offered for Oct. 16–23, 1865, as the date of composition is most persuasive. And the article is well worth reading if only for the sources of characters, events, and names.

Colonel Sellers comes in for the bulk of a typically thoughtful discussion by Henry Nash Smith in "The Morals of Power: Business Enterprise as a Theme in Mid-Nineteenth-Century American Fiction" (*Essays on American Literature*, pp. 90–107). Mr. Smith finds that, on the whole, new captains of industry baffled the literary imagination in the middle of the last century. Emerson, however, visualized the entrepreneur as a self-made man, a Napoleon; Hawthorne through Jaffrey Pyncheon exhibits him as a power hostile to the plain people; and Mark Twain in Colonel Sellers shows him to be a creature of fantasy, indulging himself continually in ever more glittering dreams of the future. In an agrarian society he can remain the innocent, but once he moves into the politico-industrial world of Washington it is inevitable that he should lose his moral core and become the swindler.

Dennis Welland reports on two English reviews of *Tom Sawyer* in "A Note on Some Early Reviews of *Tom Sawyer*" (*JAmS*, I, 99–103). One appeared in the *Athaeneum* shortly after the publication of the English edition in June 1876. It was favorable but patronizing. A week before, a review in the *Examiner* was so knowledgeable and comprehensive that Mr. Welland thinks it was written by Moncure Conway, who had negotiated for Mark Twain with Chatto and Windus.

In "The Royal Image and the Theme of the Prince-Pauper Contrast in the Works of Mark Twain" (*DA*, XXVII, 2538A) Joseph W. Myers asserts that *The Prince and the Pauper* is a fable reflecting the extravagant economic hopes and the deep status anxieties of Mark Twain and of the America of his time.

"The Private History of a Campaign That Failed," according to Joanne Altieri, is a deceptive narrative since its apparent discursiveness obscures a structure so carefully built that it simultaneously achieves a narrative crisis and an affective climax: "The Structure of 'The Private History of a Campaign That Failed'" (*MTJ*, XIII, iii, 2–5).

v. Huckleberry Finn

One of the many articles on *Huckleberry Finn* deals with background material. In "Annie and Huck: A Note on *The Adventures of Huckleberry Finn*," (*AL*, XXXIX, 207–214) Horst H. Kruse calls attention to "A Complaint about Correspondents," an occasional piece by Twain that appeared in the San Francisco *Californian* on March 24, 1866. In it Twain demonstrates how much more colorful and informative a child's letter can be than a letter from an adult. His commentary also suggests that he saw the value in the child's perspective for exposing social and moral evil. Interestingly, the child's letter he quotes (and may have written) includes references to "Moses in the Bulrushers" and to a Mr. Sowerby (cf. Sowberry Hagan in the novel).

Three critical articles deal with the book as a whole. By all odds the most important of these is the psychoanalytic study written by Drs. Jose Barchilon and Joel S. Kovel, "*Huckleberry Finn*: A psychoanalytic Study" (*Journal of the American Psychoanalytic Association*, XIV [1966], 775–814). Their article makes previous Freudian interpretations of the novel look like childish dabbling. Many literary critics, especially the romantic "appreciators," will be annoyed by it, but anyone interested in seeing what trained psychoanalysts can do with a novel should attend to it with care. The authors assume that novels were the model for the modern case history (they have their medical students read novels). They try to determine the predominant affects of the characters as well as the one pervading the whole book. Using these affects as their first clues, they then look at the manifest content of the plot to discover what it might suitably symbolize, express, or defend against. Only material which recurs over and over (death is mentioned over 200 times in the first 100 pages of *Huckleberry Finn*) is used for basic interpretations. Resemblances to mythological heroes are noted (Huck partially echoes the Biblical Moses) and used to infer interpretations that can be validated with a high degree of probability. These and other steps in their method are listed by Drs. Barchilon and Kovel in a postscript to the article.

The article is so detailed that no summary can be completely adequate, and I shall not attempt a lengthy one here. Suffice it to say that the authors fiind deep and regressive layers of drive and defense in Huck's personality. He longs for his lost mother, but at the same time is enraged that she should have left him. This rage is turned against the self, and the result is a chronic state of passivity. Countering this passivity is a strong will to live; to the extent that he can, Huck must "abandon his archaic modes of regaining the nurturing mother and adapt to a reality of substitute objects." The authors spell out how he does this, especially through his associations with Jim (they do *not* see the boys as homosexuals) and through the fantasies of the last chapters where they "are caught and returned to the adult world through their very attempts to care for each other, for, in the terms of the novel and society such a mode of relationship—the community of childhood—is not compatible with an independent existence." In the end Huck finds in nature a substitute mother who can meet his needs and whom he can tolerate without ambivalence. There is much here that many will want to dispute. But there is also much brought to the surface that many of us have probably been realizing subliminally. In any event, it is an article worth reading.

In "Huck Finn's Search for Identity" (*MTJ*, XIII, iii, 11–14) Marvin I. LaHood argues that like other classic American frontier heroes Huck Finn gains knowledge of himself only through repudiation, not acceptance. And Abigail A. Hamblen in "The Best-Known Teenager: Huck Finn" (*MTJ*, XIII, iii, 15–18) believes that the book is an account of the growth of a personality. She finds Huck realistic, shrewd, naive, tender, poetic, and so on—almost a paragon.

Concerned only with the first chapter, James R. Bennett in "The Adventures of Huck Finn in Chapter One" (*IEY*, XII, 68–72) suggests that by the time Huck drops out of the window at the Widow Douglas's, all of the major motifs of the novel have been introduced: freedom, slavery, religion, money, illusion, the family, superstition, loneliness, death, and moral growth. Roger B. Bailey discovers high symbolism in the last paragraph of Chapter One and the first paragraph of Chapter Two, "Twain's *The Adventures of Huckleberry Finn*, Chapters 1 and 2" (*Expl*, XXVI, Item 2). Tom steps on a twig and makes it snap. The incident, suggests Mr. Bailey, calls to mind Cooper's Indians and therefore becomes a sly satire on romantic fiction. Huck, however, trips over a root. The detail is more realistic and in keeping with Huck's character. Jumping to a later chapter, "Twain's *The Adventures of Huckleberry Finn*, Chapter 37" (*Expl*, XXVI, Item 20) by Allison Ensor offers the possibility that there is undetected irony in Uncle Silas' selection of Acts XVII as a text since there is a verse in it that can be read as a condemnation of slave holders (e.g., Uncle Silas).

"*Huckleberry Finn*: Why Read the Phelps Farm Episode?" (*RS*, XXXV, 189–197) by Gerald W. Haslam makes a case for the last ten chapters as a logical extension of the moral texture of the novel. The reader's discomfort in reading these chapters is not due to Twain's flawed execution but to the cruel treatment Jim is made to endure. Yet this treatment is essential to the novel, Mr. Haslam believes, because through it Twain is able to give the final emphasis of the book to the impossible moral position of a slave society. John S. Hill sees the return of Tom Sawyer in the final section as made necessary by the pattern of the book, "Huck Finn's Reaffirmation of Rejection," (*MTJ*, XIII, iv, 16–17). Chapters 1–6 show Huck under the rule of the South. Chapters 7–32 show Huck the rebel. If Twain is then to convince us of Huck's moral growth, he must place him again under the rule of the South, hence Chapters 33–42. An especially impassioned case for the ending appears in Spencer Brown's "*Huckleberry Finn* for Our Time: A Re-Reading of the Concluding Chapters" (*MQR*, VI, 41–46). Assuming that the book is primarily an attack upon slavery, Mr. Brown asserts that the last chapters are integral

to this attack and indeed its most envenomed point. Furthermore, he
declares, the writing here is deliberate and sophisticated, and it exhibits the ultimate degradation of all of the main characters, even
Huck and Jim. Mr. Brown's introduction of such terms as "gradu-
alist" and "civil-rights romantic" gives his argument a contemporary ring.

In the last study to be noted here on the concluding chapters
M. J. Sidnell in "Huck Finn and Jim: Their Abortive Freedom Ride"
(*CQ*, II, 203–211) attacks Eliot and Trilling on the one hand for
evading the moral issue of the novel and Leo Marx on the other for
attributing to Mark Twain a lapse of moral vision. His contention is
that Mark Twain refuses to be *sivilized* to the extent of offering us
a happy ending. Instead Mr. Sidnell shows the book riddled with
ironies, none more savage than those in the last chapters where
Twain presents Huck and Jim presumably successfully escaping
from bondage but really being more thoroughly enchained than ever.
For their enslavement now is to Tom's debased imagination, to the
genteel tradition, and to the stereotype of the Southern black. Huck
and Jim succumb to Tom's authority because they respect his social
superiority. Thus it is a tough-minded ironic Mark Twain who writes
the ending, not an uncertain writer seeking refuge in farce.

That Huck's final resolve to "light out" for the territory is nothing
more than a device to pave the way for further adventures is Eugene
McNamara's conclusion in "Huck Lights Out for the Territory: Mark
Twain's Unpublished Sequel" (*UWR*, II [1966], i, 68–74), an essay
he wrote after reading the manuscript of *Huck Finn and Tom Sawyer Among the Indians*. Having paved the way for the new book,
however, Mr. McNamara believes that Mark Twain was not able to
do much with it because he had no theme in mind.

Two critics compare *Huckleberry Finn* and *Finnegans Wake*.
Anthony Burgess in "Mark Twain and James Joyce" (*MTJ*, XIII, iii,
1–2) discusses Joyce's use of the name of Mark Twain and the names
of some of his major characters. Huck and Tom, for example, cor-
respond to the "twain" sons of the aging Earwicker. In a much more
detailed article, "To Give Down the Banks and Hark From the
Tomb!" (*JJQ*, IV, 75–83), James S. Atherton says that entries from
Huckleberry Finn were among the last to be inserted into *Finnegan's
Wake* and hence are relatively easy to trace. On the whole, Joyce
used the *Huckleberry Finn* material for his own purposes and with no

great regard for the original meanings. Nevertheless Tom fits nicely into the Shaun role, and Huck into the role of Shem the Penman. In an appendix Mr. Atherton reproduces the "H.F." pages from Joyce's holograph notebook. A comparison of *Huckleberry Finn* and the writings of Ernest Hemingway appears in Bryant N. Wyatt, "*Huckleberry Finn* and the Art of Ernest Hemingway" (*MTJ*, XIII, iv, 1–8). Mr. Wyatt finds stylistic parallels (the raising of colloquial speech to a literary language and the use of objective narration) and affinities in subject matter (the polarity between reality and illusion, the significance of folk beliefs and superstitions, the symbolic significance of rivers, and the search for self-realization). One of the more interesting parts of the essay is a comparison between passages in *Huckleberry Finn* and "My Old Man."

In "The Failure of Tom Sawyer and Huckleberry Finn on Film" (*MTJ*, XIII, iv, 9–10), Robert Irwin compares four films based on the lives of the two boys. Before a 1900 production of "Tom Sawyer" Mark Twain wrote the adapter Paul Kester that he could "turn the book upside-down and inside-out . . . add people, incidents, morals, immorals, or anything else." Mr. Irwin's point is that every producer has done precisely that.

In "Teaching *Huckleberry Finn* to Foreign Students" (*MTJ*, XIII, iii, 5–7) Robert H. Woodward tells of his happy experience teaching the Duke and the Dauphin excerpts to a group of students from the Republic of Mali.

vi. Later Works

A thorough study of the *Yankee* occurs in James D. Williams' "The Genesis, Composition, Publication and Reception of Mark Twain's *A Connecticut Yankee*" (*DA*, XXVII [1966], 1798A–1799A). Mr. Williams pretty well scotches the idea that Mark Twain's irritation with England was a controlling force behind the material and structure of the novel. Twain's notes and notebook entries of the 1880's show that he wrote it impulsively, that he relied increasingly on satire, that he cut many passages just before publication that were potentially offensive. Despite vigorous promotion the book did not sell well, and the critical reception was, on the whole, unenthusiastic.

"*The American Claimant*: Reclamation of a Farce" (*AQ*, XIX, 86–103) by Clyde L. Grimm is a valiant attempt to elevate the novel.

Mr. Grimm talks over-generously of the "meaningful satire" in the book and of the "clearer and more mature statement" of the cultural issues that Mark Twain had been writing about for years. He is more persuasive when he discusses the broad scope of the criticism in the *Claimant* and the varied facets of its attack on American democracy. Mark Twain's personal identification with Sellers seems worth stressing too, witness the notebook entry that Mr. Grimm quotes and that I repeat here only in part: "I have never been properly and humbly satisfied with my condition. I am a democrat only on principle, not by instinct—nobody is *that*."

In "Pudd'nhead Wilson's Calendar" (*MTJ*, XIII, iii, 8–10) Jim Wayne Miller attempts to relate the aphorisms in the Calendar to what is taking place in the book proper. His conclusion is that the aphorisms are a legitimate part of the novel, providing not only characterization but commentary upon the action.

After carefully going over the manuscripts of *Following the Equator*, Sydney J. Krause concludes in "Olivia Clemens's 'Editing' Reviewed" (*AL*, XXXIX, 325–351) that Twain was much less under Livy's influence than many have supposed. Livy's notes on this book provide the most complete record that we have of her "editing." Mark Twain accepted 64 of her suggestions, rejected 15. But it should be noted that Livy's suggestions are haphazard, and that Twain made more changes on his own to avoid minor improprieties than were suggested by Livy. Furthermore, many of Livy's suggestions were in the interest of precision. What is especially interesting, however, is that Twain *added* improprieties and that serious social criticism got by Livy's so-called censorship. Mr. Krause's contention is that though Twain gave in to Livy on minor, almost petty, considerations, he operated on the theory that there were more things in heaven and earth than were dreamed of in her philosophy—and inserted gross irreverences and serious criticisms with the confidence that they would stay put. Mr. Krause adds nine additional comments by Livy which have not yet been reported in print. The argument is documented substantially enough to persuade the reader that *Following the Equator* would not have been substantially different had Livy never seen the manuscript.

University of Iowa

6. Henry James

William T. Stafford

No startlingly new directions were apparent in the criticism devoted to James during 1967. The quantity of material may well have been reduced somewhat, for it was a year—surely the first one in a decade or so—which saw only a single new book in English on the subject, J. A. Ward's *The Search for Form*. Briefer studies were perhaps also fewer, with only one new explication of *The Turn of the Screw*. But critical quality was not necessarily reduced. Some of the short studies are very good indeed. And at least four of them seem to me worthy of special commendation: John Goode's essay on James's "The Art of Fiction," John Felstiner's study of James and Max Beerbohm, Robert J. Reilly's exploration of the Jamsian morality, and Caroline G. Mercer's article on Adam Verver.

i. Manuscripts, Bibliography, Biography

James Kraft records a modest find in "An Unpublished Review by Henry James" (*SB*, XX, 267–273), a hitherto unknown manuscript which reviews *Two Men*, a little known novel by Elizabeth Stoddard, wife of Richard Henry Stoddard. Written late in 1865 (and obviously for Norton and the *North American Review*), it was probably not published, speculates Kraft, because of the "harshness of James's judgments of the wife of a contemporary literary figure." Perhaps of more importance today for what it reveals about James's reading than for what it says—there are allusions in it to *Hard Times*, to Trollope, and to Mrs. Stoddard's first novel, *The Morgesons* (1862) —it is a useful little document to have in print.

Robert A. Hall, Jr.'s "Some Recent Books on Henry James" (*AION-SG*, IX [1966], 49–64) purports to be a survey of books written on James during the 1960's. In fact, most of his pages are given over to Geismar's book, whose exaggerations and distortions Hall sees well enough, but many of whose reservations about James Hall shares. And although he mentions, in addition, works by Stallman, Edel, Dupee, Cargill, McElderry, Gale, Poirier, Marks, Holland, Wiesenfarth, Krook, Clair, and Blackall (among others)—it is apparently D. W. Jefferson's little book that most closely wins his approbation.

In "Henry James: The Americano-European Legend" (*UTQ*, XXXVI, 321–334) Leon Edel, in his usually informed and elegant way, recapitulates James's prophetic insight into modern cosmopolitanism, in his life and in his writing, in his travel essays and in his fiction. Many of James's achievements are widely recognized. But "still . . . to be fully learned," concludes Edel, is "the lesson and the vision of his cosmopolitanism—of 'differences and hindrances surmounted' among the nations, *urbi et orbi*."

ii. Criticism and Drama; Sources, Influences, Parallels

Of great importance in John Goode's "The Art of Fiction: Walter Besant and Henry James" (*Tradition and Tolerance*, pp. 243–281) is the rich, rich context in which Goode's analysis is made: the context of Besant's fiction and of James's, the context of the influences on them from France and elsewhere, and the context of the literary life in the England of the 1880's. James's great essay, moreover, is seen precisely for what it is: the turning point from Victorianism to modernism in English. James's essay is minutely analyzed—with sensitivity, wit, and erudition—and then imaginatively applied to the literary achievement of *The Bostonians* and *The Princess Casamassima*. This may well be the final word on the importance of James's famous essay.

Also enlightening, if brief, is Roger B. Stein's account of James's views of Ruskin in *John Ruskin and Aesthetic Thought in America, 1840–1900* (Cambridge, Harvard Univ. Press, pp. 210–217). Stein records James's objections to the painter's "theological spirit" and to the "narrow dogmatism of his point of view." He also pays some attention to James's uses of European art in his early international tales as a means of defining theme. And he sees in the short chapter given over to Newman and Babcock in *The American* "a piece of imaginative cultural history" that is unsurpassed in capturing "the dilemma of the American approach to art."

Patricia Kane adds very little that was not already known in her survey of public and private estimates James and Howells made of one another's books during their life-long friendship, in her "Mutual Perspective: James and Howells as Critics of Each Other's Fiction" (*MinnR*, VII, 331–341). Rather well-known ground is also covered in David L. Swartz, Jr.'s "Bernard Shaw and Henry James" (*ShawR*, X, 50–59). And conventional enough is Kimball King's "Theory and Practice in the Plays of Henry James" (*MD*, X, 24–33) in its view of why James's early plays were failures and in its conviction that the last ones were improved. He follows Bruce McElderry, Jr., in seeing *The Other House* as James's best, the one play by James that might well be successful today.

New ground, however, is broken in John Felstiner's "Max Beerbohm and the Wings of Henry James" (*KR*, XXIX, 449–471), a lengthy and original study of the multitude of things James meant to Beerbohm over a long period of years. In fact, says Felstiner, "Beerbohm's maturest values start in the comic dispute made up by his caricatures and parodies of Henry James." There are more of both than one might have suspected (15 caricatures and several parodies), and James appears to have been delighted with many of them even as he comes close to parodying Beerbohm's parodies of himself in some of the letters here used. But the ultimate intention here is a serious one, for Felstiner can conclude that in one sense (for Beerbohm) "James stood for the whole of fiction, and parody for its possible criticism." Moreover, the general questions a parodist asks may well be "the radical questions of literature."

Two studies examine French influences on James's *The American*. Maurita Willett, in "Henry James's Indebtedness to Balzac" (*RLC*, XLI, 204–227), presents an extended view of the public pose he took toward Balzac in his essays and reviews (although curiously excluding his Prefaces) as prefatory to a long comparison of *Le Père Goriot* with the James novel, seeing both negative and positive influences at work, but seeing most importantly James's gaining from Balzac some sense of the sacredness of the artistic imagination. C. E. Maguire, in his "James and Dumas, fils" (*MD*, X, 34–42), does not add a great deal on the influence of *L'Etrangère* on *The American* that had not previously been suggested by Professor Cargill's study in his *The Novels of Henry James*.

Robert O. Stephens and James Ellis, in "Hemingway, Fitzgerald, and the Riddle of 'Henry's Bicycle'" (*ELN*, V, 46–49), quote from a letter from Fitzgerald to Maxwell Perkins to confirm a previous contention that the allusion in *The Sun Also Rises* to "Henry's Bicycle" was to James and his "obscure hurt."

iii. Criticism: General

J. A. Ward's *The Search for Form: Studies in the Structure of James's Fiction* (Chapel Hill, Univ. of N. C. Press) is in at least one sense a companion volume to his earlier book-length study of James (*The Imagination of Disaster: Evil in the Fiction of Henry James*, 1961), for a conclusion in each book is that James's ultimate position, about morality *and* technique, is a pragmatic one. The two opening chapters of *The Search for Form* trace, through James's critical comments and general practice, his developing esthetic: the giving way, in the first instance, of preconceived ideas of what the form of a work should be to some organic development of the germ; the growing concern, in the second instance, "for logical and spatial conceptions of relationships rather than chronological ones." Chapters then follow on *Watch and Ward*, "Madame de Mauves," *The Europeans*, *The Princess Casamassima*, *What Maisie Knew*, and *The Wings of the Dove*. The concluding chapter on *The Golden Bowl* is a summing-up—an analysis of a novel wherein "characteristic methods and principles of earlier works achieve their highest development." The final point there made (and it works beautifully in *The Golden Bowl*) is in fact *the* point toward which the thesis of this entire study moves: for, says Ward, when we see that Maggie Verver "discovers that a form is preserved only as it is strained," we also see that, for James, "the perfection of form consist[s] in the violation of form."

Some of Ward's chapters are more convincing than others, although I think one would not argue with the selections he makes in terms of the need for chronological spread and variety of types. *Watch and Ward* and *The Europeans* may well be too thin for the amount of critical attention they receive, but to see so clearly the extracted "formal" problems of *The Princess Casamassima* or to read Maisie's dilemma (and the novel's) as a conflict between an "idea of form" and the "life" it is attempting to contain—is all refreshing enough. The book is thus clearly structured and coherent. Although some might well object to the narrow context in which the study is set—its relative lack of attention to the sources of James's technique or its indifference to the developing comparable techniques of James's great contemporaries—Ward makes perfectly clear *his* awareness of the many, many things he is here not doing. What he does do, in short, is well worth doing, narrow and special in a sense though it is.

Robert J. Reilly's "Henry James and the Morality of Fiction" (*AL*, XXXIX, 1–30) is another good study, so good, in fact, that it was awarded the Norman Foerster Prize of $250 for the best article to be published in *AL* during 1967. It is not difficult to see why, for Reilly goes right to the heart of the problem of determing how one determines morality in fiction. He of course concludes that one can not, that one does not. "Fiction," he says, "is no more moral than life, but no less either. The substantial connection between life and imitative art is that neither is the cause of either goodness or wickedness but that both present to man the essential condition of morality." Enough said, but a great deal more is done here, including a learned and enlightening discussion of just how the many, many Jamesian critics (from Joseph Warren Beach, in 1918, through Dorothea Krook, in 1962) who have attempted to determine the specific nature of the Jamesian morality have never more than partly seen this elementary truth. Reilly also demonstrates how William's conception of what is "moral" informs Henry's: "Both brothers show [a] . . . profound respect for singularity." Both "have the psychologist's love of endless particularity." His final point is another illuminating tie, for the "typical Jamesian protagonist," Reilly concludes, "is an Emersonian individual." He will be led to "unique moral action." "Henry's protagonists . . . are moral originals."

Charles Child Walcutt's "The Illusion of Action in Henry James," in his *Man's Changing Mask* (pp. 175–211), may serve its function within his book well enough; the chapter does not, however, add much to our knowledge of James's fiction. For Walcutt, it is James who initiated the "aesthetic notion of objectivity." He means by this the Jamesian ideal of allowing "scene and dialogue" to "speak for themselves, without auctorial commentary or explanation." In practice, however, James "loaded his stories with personal discussion." And the damage was done when readers "accepted humbly as if it were only objectivity" what "was offered as objectivity" but was "in fact ambiguity." Joyce was the great extender of this method, says

Walcutt, "performing an extraordinary reduplication . . . of the
Jamesian doctrine." The thesis is thus provocative enough, but in the
analyses that follow—of "The Real Thing," "The Beast in the Jungle,"
The Bostonians, The Portrait of a Lady, The Golden Bowl, and (very
briefly) *The Ambassadors*—what most often results is simply repeated contentions that James's obtrusive and continued analyses of
his characters prohibit their achieving any kind of intrinsic dramatic
reality in the readers' minds as things in themselves. The "organic
unity of action, character, and theme" are defined to perfection by
James; but "the ideas and the characters are not contained in the
action and expressed through it" in his practice. *The Portrait* is the
great exception.

Special in a different sense is Viola H. Winner's "Pictorialism in
Henry James's Theory of the Novel" (*Criticism,* IX, 1–21), a lengthy
exposition of the extent to which James's knowledge of art affected
his conception of fiction in theory and in practice. Mrs. Winner even
provides a "Glossary of Art Metaphors"—definitions of the special
literary uses to which James put such words as *chiaroscuro, color, per-*
spective, photograph, picture, portrait, sketch, study, tone, and *value.*

The more important of two general studies examining the Gothic
elements in James is Martha Banta's "The House of Seven Ushers
and How They Grew" (*YR,* LVII, 56–65). After discussing the
earlier Gothicism of Poe, Hawthorne, and the standard English ex-
emplars, Miss Banta identifies a New Gothicism, which was tied "to
psychological developments of the period." James, of course, was a
superb practitioner of the latter; and she presents a fine comparative analysis of *The Portrait of a Lady* and *The Wings of the Dove.*
She demonstrates that "what had been implied crudely in earlier
Gothic tales was implied with finesse" in *The Portrait,* and "what was
implied with finesse [in *The Portrait*] was made the strong center
of the psychological Gothicism" of *The Wings.* Raymond Thorberg's
brief study of the "terror" in the late ghostly tales, in his "Terror
Made Relevant: James's Ghost Stories" (*DR,* XLVII, 185–191),
reaches roughly similar conclusions. For Miss Banta, "the terrors of
a new Gothicism . . . revealed the self as victim of its own self-
villainy." For Mr. Thorberg, the terror of the late ghost stories is not
in external trappings, but in "that consciousness which may be called
the soul."

Two other general studies look at the uses of marriage in James's fiction. "Marriage longed for or schemed for, marriage postponed, marriage thwarted, marriage triumphant"—such, says Munro Beattie, in "The Many Marriages of Henry James" (*Patterns of Commitment*, pp. 93–112) is precisely that which "defines and directs the action" in tale after tale, novel after novel, in the fiction of Henry James. Although the stories of writers and artists are those one might expect to find most relevant to this particular approach and are indeed the fiction to which Beattie gives most attention, the critical results of the analyses do not carry much conviction. For Stephen E. Teichgraeber, in "The Treatment of Marriage in the Early Novels of Henry James" (*DA*, XXVIII, 1830A), characters "can be definitely placed . . . regarding their relative merits and degrees of awareness and sensitivity through a study of their ideas about the manner in which they attempt marriage."

Five additional dissertations were also concerned with general studies of James. Thomas J. Bontly, in "The Aesthetics of Discretion: Sexuality in the Fiction of Henry James" (*DA*, XXVII, 3446A–3447A), finds James's indirection and discretion to have allowed him to treat with freedom and with intellectual integrity problems which were central to his age. Courtney Johnson, Jr., in "The Problems of Sex in the Writings of Henry James" (*DA*, XXVIII, 679A–680A), sees in James "the solution to a character's sexual problems" as "inseparable from the solution to his moral, aesthetic, and spiritual" problems. Barry M. Menikoff, in "Style and Point of View in The Tales of Henry James" (*DA*, XXVIII, 686A–687A), restricts his study to tales narrated by a third person and the concomitant problems of how the author introduced himself into the fiction and also how he maintained his characters' internal narratives. Kirby L. Duncan, in "The Structure of the Novels of Henry James" (*DA*, XXVIII, 2242A–2243A), sees a single "structure" in thirteen James novels: "one or more central characters, and the two opposing poles which he or they must chose between, attempt to synthesize, or reject." And Alfred C. Habegger, in "Secrecy in the Fiction of Henry James" (*DA*, XXVIII, 1077A–1078A), examines the intrigue plot in the canon. James is also the subject of the central chapter in Peter K. Garrett's "Scene and Symbol: Changing Mode in the English Novel from George Eliot to Joyce" (*DA*, XXVII, 4251A).

iv. Criticism: Individual Tales

"The Aspern Papers" was the subject of two studies during the year. Mildred Hartsock's "Unweeded Garden: A View of *The Aspern Papers*" (*SSF*, V, 60–68) is a provocative and inclusive reading that plays down the diabolical in Juliana to point to the ways "the aged woman directs all her wily perceptions to the . . . salvaging of life for Tina." In this view, the narrator is seen more sympathetically than in most other views, and the "thesis" of the tale thus becomes the recognition that although "the past has a continuity and a beauty to which the imaginative man must be sensitive," he "cannot light all his candles for the dead. . . . He must turn at last to seeing and living and loving." For Robert C. McLean, in " 'Poetic Justice' in James's *Aspern Papers*" (*PLL*, III, 260–266), the tale is "neither an Eliotic study of the spiritually dead narrator nor a tragic 'parody of the creative process' "; it is instead "a comic study of poetic justice in which rewards and punishments are appropriately distributed."

Two studies of "The Real Thing" also appeared. David Toor, in "Narrative Irony in Henry James' 'The Real Thing' " (*UR*, XXXIV, 95–99), sees the irony in the story turned toward the narrator, not the Monarchs, and thus sees the theory of art the narrator there promulgates as faulty. Harold Kehler's "James's 'The Real Thing' " (*Expl*, XXV, Item 79) is a brief explication of the "charming" word play with the name of Miss Churm in the tale.

In "Another Twist to *The Turn of the Screw*" (*MFS*, XIII, 167–178), a professor of psychiatry, C. Knight Aldrich, M.D., turns his professional clinical gaze upon Mrs. Grose. His conclusion: the tale "is a tragedy about an evil older woman who drove an unstable younger woman completely out of her mind, and whose jealousy was the indirect cause of a little boy's death."

E. Duncan Aswell, in "James's *In the Cage*: The Telegraphist as Artist" (*TSLL*, VIII [1966], 375–384), would refute those readings of the story which see it celebrating a young girl's acceptance of her dreary lot after a life of fantasy and heartbreak. James's intention instead, says Aswell, is to use "her voice to comment ironically on high and low society, but the last laugh is always at the expense of the girl herself as she unwittingly reveals traits and feelings identical with those she most condemns in others."

Finally, we have two studies of "The Jolly Corner." Courtney Johnson, Jr.'s "Henry James' 'The Jolly Corner': a Study in Integration" (*AI*, XXIV, 344–359) is an elaborately psychoanalytic analysis of this already often psychoanalyzed tale—but in this instance focusing on the *two* missing fingers, the *dual* nature of Brydon's fear (masculine *and* feminine, father *and* mother, America *and* Europe). In his view, the tale of course both projects the duality and resolves it, in a final "rebirth of both sides with a new capacity of giving and receiving love, realized in the [now] conscious self" of Brydon. J. Delbaere-Garant, in "The Redeeming Form: Henry James's *The Jolly Corner*" (*RLV*, XXXIII, 588–596), also sees Brydon redeemed, by virtue, however, of his having "created" (in a parable of art) a vision of his limited self which frees him from his former self, his terror, and his death-in-life.

v. Criticism: Individual Novels

Charles Fish's "Form and Revision: The Example of *Watch and Ward*" (*NCF*, XXII, 173–190) is a study that supplements but does not supplant B. R. McElderry, Jr.'s pioneering analysis of its revisions (in *MLN*, LXVII [1952], 457–461). Fish's is the more elaborate analysis, seeing James's revision in 1878 (from the serial version of 1871) as achieving several improvements—by removing a number of obtrusive auctorial intrusions, by occasionally strengthening point of view and center of interest, by deleting some unnecessary description, and by sharpening characterization, especially that of George Fenton.

The Portrait of a Lady provoked two books and several articles during 1967. This writer edited *Perspectives on James's* The Portrait of a Lady: A Collection of Critical Essays (New York, N.Y.U. Press), and David Galloway wrote a 61-page monograph, *Henry James: The Portrait of a Lady* (London, Edward Arnold).[1] *Perspectives* reprints some twenty analyses of the novel, including James's own comments both before and after he wrote it; contemporary reviews from England and America; and representative essays that explore such problems as the novel's techniques, sources, revisions; its place in British

---

1. The latter, for some unaccountable reason, was unavailable to me, from its English publisher *and* its American one (Barron's Educational Series), even after I offered to purchase it!

and American literary history; and its special methods and over-all achievement. It contains in addition an Introduction and a 100-item bibliography by the editor.

Of three new articles on the novel, clearly the most important is Charles R. Anderson's "Person, Place, and Thing in *The Portrait of a Lady*," *Essays on American Literature* (pp. 164–182). He not only presents a fine reading of the novel in terms of its elaborate imagery and narrative structure, but he also clearly sees its place within the James canon, marking as it did his "first real break with the traditional novel and his pioneering of new techniques," its place within the history of fiction, enabling it to "break away from the conventional realism of Howells and Trollope, even Flaubert," and its paving the way "for the bolder new departures" for his own later work and, ultimately, that of Joyce and Faulkner. J. M. Newton's "Isabel Archer's Disease, and Henry James's" (*CQ*, II, 3–22) is an unconvincing attempt to explain Isabel's marriage to Osmond in terms of James's own attraction to the "ideal" Osmond represents. And Sister Lucy Schneider, C.S.J., in "Osculation and Integration: Isabel Archer in the One-Kiss Novel" (*CLAJ*, X [1966], 149–161) examines each and every kiss in the novel (there are some twenty of them!) in order to conclude that Isabel's "return to Rome is to her previous experiences in her European adventures what Caspar's kiss is to the kisses that have preceded it."

David B. Green's "Witch and Bewitchment in *The Bostonians*" (*PLL*, III, 267–269) is a brief note purporting to find "white witch" imagery in the novel, especially as it relates to Verena, and thus to see a comic and pathetic irony in the various beguilments at work in the tale.

For John L. Kimmey, in "*The Princess Casamassima* and the Quality of Bewilderment" (*NCF*, XX, 47–62), contradictory opposites control the conception and the structure of the novel. Consequently, Hyacinth, "the plot that enmeshes him, the world he inhabits, his friends, and the very diction and imagery that reveal him" are all seen as manifesting this guiding principle.

Philip L. Greene's "Point of View in *The Spoils of Poynton*" (*NCF*, XXI, 359–368), is an elaborate and on the whole convincing defense of Fleda Vetch as "a reliable reflector" of the novel's affirmed values. "She is the renouncing sensibility who is capable of love." Alan W. Bellringer's "*The Spoils of Poynton*: James's Intentions"

(*EIC*, XVII, 238–243) is a retort to an objection raised by John Lucus to a previous study by Bellringer on this novel. (See *ALS*, 1966, p. 74).

More ambitious and rewarding than any of these are three substantial studies of *The Awkward Age*. James W. Gargano, for example, in "The Theme of 'Salvation' in *The Awkward Age*" (*TSLL*, IX, 274–287) provides a good analysis of the way James's "social" comedy seriously dramatizes the collision between competing saviors, "one representing innocence [Mr. Longdon] and the other intrigue and experience [Mrs. Brook]." Especially provocative here is the view of Longdon who, says Gargano, "plays a disruptive, almost sinister role" yet nonetheless "succeeds in planting truth where illusion flourished, in fixing boundaries to possibility." Mildred Hartsock's analysis, in "The Exposed Mind: A View of *The Awkward Age*" (*CritQ*, IX, 49–59), focuses on Nanda, whose developing consciousness, her concern for "knowing," is seen as the very center of the novel's purpose. And Elizabeth Owen, in " 'The Awkward Age' and the Contemporary English Scene" (*VS*, XI, 63–82), sees both the form and content of the novel "to be very much a product of its decade." Its dialogue form, she says, may in fact be more the result of James's attempt to outrival some contemporary best sellers in similar form than a result of the dramtic years. Its major worth may well be as history rather than as art, in its "brilliant analysis" of a certain section of near-Edwardian society, "its freedom and gaiety" but also "its precariousness and frivolity, its irresponsibility and cruelty." Miss Owen's is an important essay.

The Ambassadors, like *The Portrait of a Lady*, continues to be among the most popular of James's novels, and the amount of criticism devoted to it reflects that popularity. It was the subject of two dissertations, one in German, and four ambitious articles. Frieder Busch's *Erzähler-, Figuren und Leserperspektive in Henry James Roman* The Ambassadors (München, Max Hueber), is concerned with the techniques of the novel, while Charlotte A. Alexander's "The Emancipation of Lambert Strether: A Study of the Relationship Between the Ideas of William and Henry James" (*DA*, XXVIII, 661A–662A) focuses on the development of Strether as enlightened by a knowledge of William's thinking.

Robert C. McLean's "The Completed Vision: A Study of *Madame de Mauves* and *The Ambassadors*" (*MLQ*, XXVIII, 446–461) reveals

parallels between the tale and novel in characterization, scenic structure, and theme. More importantly, contends McLean, it "clarifies"
our understanding of Strether's relationship to Mme de Vionnet by
seeing that she in fact rejects him, not he her. And the Strether who
emerges is one capable of defying "determinism on a 'philosophical
level' by coming to terms with himself, by gaining inner knowledge."
The point by point contrast with the tale is interesting enough; the
analysis of Strether reaches conclusions others have reached before.
Alwyn Berland's "Americans and Ambassadors: On Henry James"
(*WascanaR* I, [1966], ii, 53–82) also places Strether in a large context: as he appears in the 100-page scenario James wrote for the
novel, and as foils to him appear in other American businessmen
James portrayed (Newman, Adam Verver, Abner Gaw, Caspar
Goodwood, etc.). Strether of course rises above them all, emerging,
concludes Berland, "as with a sense of glory, as James's great tribute
to the idea of civilization." Somewhat similar conclusions about the
novel are reached by both L. Moffitt Cecil and Daniel J. Schneider
in, respectively, " 'Virtuous Attachment' in James' *The Ambassadors*"
(*AQ*, XIX, 719–724) and "The Ironic Imagery and Symbolism of
James's *The Ambassadors*" (*Criticism*, IX, 174–196). For Cecil,
Strether is one who has outgrown "both the Woollett and Paris codes
and has gained a moral insight that is superior to either." For
Schneider, in a much more elaborate study of the imagery in the
novel, Strether also sees both cities as "but moulds into which 'the
jelly of consciousness' may be poured to harden and, hardening, to
die." Although fifty-five years old, Strether at the end "toddles off
to live his own life, the freest and youngest person in the book."

John Hagan's "A Note on a Symbolic Pattern in *The Wings of the
Dove*" (*CLAJ*, X, 256–262), although the brief single article exclusively on this complex novel in 1967, is a neat explication of how the
symbolic imagery in the early cliff scene, which criticism has often
noted, prefigures a larger pattern which recapitulates Milly Theale's
three-part development from "initial acceptance of London society,
through disillusionment, to the renunciation she first disdains."

Finally, in Caroline G. Mercer's "Adam Verver, Yankee Businessman" (*NCF*, XX, 251–269) we have a crucial study of *The Golden
Bowl*. It elaborately and convincingly places Verver in the tradition
of American humor, sees him as James's exquisite refinement of the
Yankee trader, and reads sympathetically his subtle "trading" near

the end of the novel as a "gain" even while his "losses" are made perfectly clear. Important enough for its reading of *The Golden Bowl*, this article is equally important for its documented demonstration of James's wide and intimate knowledge of a significantly American literary tradition. It is an excellent essay.

Purdue University

7. Faulkner

Robert A. Wiggins

The quantitative level of Faulkner scholarship remains constant. There have been some shifts of interest as noted in the appropriate places. The decline of dissertations to only one in 1966 proved temporary. There are six listed in *DA* not previously reported. There is a decrease in the imagery studies so popular a couple of years back. There is a considerable increase of interest in Faulkner's sources. Stylistic and characterization studies are at about the same level of quality and quantity. There has been a noteworthy upsurge of attention given to *Absalom, Absalom!* over all other novels for 1967. Two journals—*Mississippi Quarterly* and *Modern Fiction Studies*—devoted entire issues to Faulkner.

i. Bibliography, Texts, and Biography

The single important bibliographical item is the checklist by Maurice Beebe in the special Faulkner issue, "Criticism of William Faulkner: A Selected Checklist" (*MFS*, XIII, 115–161). Though selective, it is a very full bibliography that overlooks no really important item. It makes this issue of *MFS* particularly valuable for students and investigators, since it is the most current list that we have.

The lone text of unusual interest is reprinted in connection with William Spratling's "Chronicle of a Friendship: William Faulkner in New Orleans" (*TQ*, IX [1966], i, 34–40). The reprint is a facsimile reproduction of *Sherwood Anderson and Other Famous Creoles*, which was the Spratling caricatures arranged by Faulkner with an introductory parody of Anderson's style. The essay by Spratling is an account of his friendship with Faulkner in New Orleans and on a trip to Europe.

There are two other biographical items. Wilmuth S. Rutledge in "How Colonel Falkner Built His Railroad" (*MQ*, XX, 166–170) reprints a newly discovered letter by Col. William C. Falkner written in 1874 in which he throws some general light on the building of his own railway. Murry C. Falkner, the only surviving brother of William, has published *The Falkners of Mississippi: A Memoir* (Baton Rouge, La. State Univ. Press). This is a book of reminiscences of childhood and later with some new family photographs. In a foreward Lewis P. Simpson perceptively contrasts this with John Faulkner's *My Brother Bill*, which is a more consciously literary work that relates to the Yoknapatawpha myth. Murry's memoir is an old-fashioned, genteel work, probably factually more accurate in that it is not colored by references to Faulkner's novels, and dwells upon family lore and personal memories. It should prove to be useful background material for Faulkner biographers, though it gives us nothing essentially new. "The Falkners of Oxford: The Enchanted Years." (*SoR*, III, 357–386) is a chapter from the book.

ii. Criticism: General

The principal dissertations can appropriately be reviewed here, since they deal with general topics. John M. Ditsky in "Land-Nostalgia in the novels of Faulkner, Cather, and Steinbeck." (*DA*, XXVIII, 1072A) defines land-nostalgia as "a feeling for or about the land that is both intellectual and emotional, involving the presence of Nature as a character in American fiction by virtue of the special relationship between man and the land." The tangled rhetoric of this definition, when applied to Faulkner, produces the complicated conclusion that for Faulkner the land is used as a complex, multiple symbol for 1) "good" influence on human personality, 2) a link between the pagan past and the dark forces of fertility, 3) a covenant with man, 4) a basis for a dynastic social structure, and 5) a basis for technical experimentation with time.

Ben M. Vorpahl, "Such Stuff as Dreams are Made on: History, Myth and the Comic Vision of Mark Twain and William Faulkner." (*DA*, XXVIII, 698A) finds certain similarities between the two writers studied. Assuming the frontier origins of their humor, he goes on to view their comic attitudes toward history as the failure of Edenic hope, incongruous beside the truth of reality. In "Primitivism in the Fiction of William Faulkner" (*DA*, XXVIII, 695A–696A) George W. Sutton finds Faulkner to be partial toward primitive characters (children, idiots, Indians, hunters, poor whites, and Negroes) as embodiments of virtues which modern man can at best imitate.

Egbert W. Oldenberg uses the unpublished fragment of *Elmer* and Faulkner's poetry to demonstrate an Impressionist influence on Faulkner's early experiments in technique: "William Faulkner's Early Experiments with Narrative Techniques" (*DA*, XXVII, 2158A). In "Faulkner and the Negro" (*DA*, XXVII [1966], 1385A) Aaron Steinberg argues that Faulkner began his writing with a latent hostility toward the Negro and could never come to treat the Negro as a fully developed character. He neatly dodges the complication that Joe Christmas presents by asserting that Faulkner does not treat him as a Negro; he becomes a Negro only at the end of the novel. The conclusion is that the best Faulkner could achieve in Negro characterization was to use the Negro as a "touchstone-catalyst" figure relating to white behavior.

In *The Thirties* (pp. 55–62) Warren French has a fine essay, "William Faulkner and the Art of the Detective Story." He discusses Faulkner's ventures in the genre of the detective story and his extensive use of the form in his other work. The thesis has special relevance to *Absalom, Absalom!, Intruder in the Dust, Knight's Gambit, The Sound and the Fury,* and *The Bear.* There is also an essay by John T. Flanagan (*Folklore Studies*, pp. 135–145) titled "The Mythic Background of Faulkner's Horse Imagery." Flanagan claims that "Faulkner wrote of the horse because of his own personal liking for the animal and because it represented a significant phase of the Southern economy. But the horseman as an image provides another dimension to his fiction and has connotative values far beyond the literal." What he actually demonstrates is that the Confederate cavalryman is a common figure in Faulkner's work.

M. E. Bradford in "On the Importance of Discovering God: Faulkner and Hemingway's *The Old Man and the Sea*" (*MissQ*, XX, 158–162) examines Faulkner's review of Hemingway's novel and finds that he singles out for admiration those qualities he lists in his Nobel Prize address. There are no surprises in Wallace G. Kay's "Faulkner's Mississippi: The Myth and the Microcosm" (*SoQ*, VI, 13–24). As the title suggests, he examines Faulkner's fictional world compared with the actual South and concludes that Faulkner starts with the actual South of his experience, imaginatively fills in details to create myth that raises the work beyond reality to cosmic significance.

Elmo Howell has made the point before in other essays that Faulkner made no pretension to accuracy in discriminating between

Chickasaws and Choctaws. In "William Faulkner and the Mississippi Indians" (*GaR*, XXI, 386–396) he goes on to a conclusion based on examination of the four principal short stories about Indians. Unlike Cooper and some later Eastern writers, Faulkner, Twain, and others have dealt realistically with the Indian, but only Faulkner has achieved a combination of realism and mirth with moral implications in the use of Indian characters.

In *Patterns of Commitment* (pp. 181–192) Michael Millgate has an interesting essay titled "William Faulkner: The Problem of Point of View." He convincingly argues that through Faulkner's experiments with point-of-view we come to gain some understanding of his remarkable technical accomplishments and indeed their unobtrusive insistence upon what Cleanth Brooks calls his "Sense of Community." Another look at technique is Eric Larsen's "The Barrier of Language: The Irony of Language in Faulkner" (*MFS*, XIII, 19–31). Here he details Faulkner's view of the inadequacy of words to convey truth, but ironically while language is indeed a barrier to truth, it is also the primary medium by which an artist like Faulkner can create non-verbal, experimental truth. In a slight book, *Faulkner's Twice-Told Tales: His Re-Use of His Material* (The Hague, Mouton [1966]), Edward M. Holmes points out that Faulkner's rhetoric is transformed from comparatively simple patterns toward "formality and increased intensification and complexity." This development parallels his method of expanding short-story material to novel form with the addition of details. This study pretty much documents a point made by other critics that characteristically Faulkner composed in discrete units which he later combined into novels. Robert Strozier, in "Some Versions of Faulkner's Pastoral" (*ForumH*, V, i, 35–40), analyzes characterization chiefly in what he calls the "pastoral" novels to show Faulkner's mastery of a variety of styles which are dictated by the manner of characterization chosen.

As mentioned earlier, there has been a decline in imagery counting. But one essay deserving mention is William J. Palmer's "The Mechanistic World of *Snopes*" (*MissQ*, XX, 185–194). It finds the main symbolic pattern unifying the Snopes trilogy to be based on imagery of the machine. Another is "Empty Steeples: Theme, Symbol, and Irony in Faulkner's novels" (*ArQ*, XXIII, 197–206) by Jessie Coffee. She finds that church bells, spires, and steeples constitute one group of symbols frequently used to produce irony by recalling the church community at a given moment to produce contrast with the actual community.

Elmo Howell, in "William Faulkner's Southern Baptists" (*ArQ*, XXIII, 220–226), argues that "Faulkner's reaction to religious cant, and particularly Baptist cant, is so strong that he fails to present fairly and fully one aspect of Southern experience." Continuing the religious theme, H. L. Weatherby in "Sutpen's Garden" (*GaR*, XXI, 354–369) finds Faulkner to be rich in Christian images but generally ignorant of Christian theology. Sutpen's garden evokes Edenic suggestions in Faulkner of a "sense of what a Christian society should long for." This distinguishes Faulkner from his more thoroughly secular contemporaries.

Glenn Sandstrom cleverly invokes Eric Erikson's theory of identity found in "The Problem of Ego Identity." In "Identity Diffusion: Joe Christmas and Quentin Compson" (*AQ*, XIX, 207–223) he makes a revealing psychological analysis of two characters to confirm Faulkner's profound insight into human nature. In *Essays on American Literature* (pp. 108–125) Richard Beale Davis has an essay titled "Mrs. Stowe's Characters-in-Situations and a Southern Literary Tradition." He defines a tradition in the Southern slavery novel initiated by Mrs. Stowe which broadens out to include Mark Twain, G. W. Cable, and Faulkner. Mr. Davis is careful to point out that these writers are heirs, not imitators, of this tradition of the "characters-in-situation" created by Mrs. Stowe. It is an ingenious argument, but I had the nagging suspicion in reading it that Mrs. Stowe was getting more credit than she deserved.

Elmo Howell in "Inversion and the 'Female' Principle: William Faulkner's 'A Courtship'" (*SSF*, IV, 308–314) examines one short story to provide insight into how Faulkner characteristically handled romantic love from a basically comic viewpoint which emphasizes female practicality as superior to male imagination, or "the inevitable triumph of matter over mind." David M. Miller in "Faulkner's Women" (*MFS*, XIII, 3–17) classifies white female characters into earth-mothers and ghosts. But Naomi Jackson finds the terms demon-nun and angel-witch more meaningful in "Faulkner's Women: 'Demon-Nun and Angel-Witch'" (*BSUF*, VIII, i, 12–20). On the other hand, Louise Blackwell maintains that Faulkner's female characters resist easy categorization because they are primarily individuals. Faulkner "has created a gallery of very lifelike women figures": "Faulkner and the Womenfolk" (*KM*, pp. 73–77).

There was a considerable increase in 1967 of notes and discussions on sources and influences. Eric Solomon, for example, in "Joseph Conrad, William Faulkner, and the Nobel Prize Speech" (*N&Q*, XIV, 247–248) finds verbal echoes in the Nobel Prize address and the "Thursday Night" section of *A Fable* from Joseph Conrad's 1905 essay "Henry James: In Appreciation." Joel A. Hunt, "Thomas Mann and Faulkner: Portrait of a Magician" (*WSCL*, VIII, 431–436) finds thematic similarities between "Mario and the Magician" and Faulkner's story "An Error in Chemistry." In "*Soldier's Pay* and the Art of Aubrey Beardsley" (*AQ*, XIX, [3]–23) Addison C. Bross professes to see a pervasive influence of Beardsley's drawings in *Soldier's Pay* manifested in black and white contrast, the costuming of characters, the gesturing hand, dressing table scenes, and formal garden scenes. This influence in turn may have been an early contribution to the rich pictorial quality of Faulkner's prose. Except for a mildly mauve mood in this one novel, the argument is not very convincing. The industrious Elmo Howell discusses the use of "Christmas Gift" as a greeting in the old South in "William Faulkner's 'Christmas Gift'" (*KFR*, XIII, 37–40). Michael A. Fredrickson, using internal evidence alone, makes a weak case in "A Note on 'The Idiot Boy' as a Probable Source for *The Sound and the Fury*" (*MinnR*, VI [1966], 368–370). Matthew Bruccoli in "A Source for Sartoris?" (*MissQ*, XX, 163) contributes a short note on *Two Little Girls in Blue* (1922–23), Dolly and Polly Sartoris, as possibly providing at least the name Sartoris for Faulkner's twin characters in *Sartoris*. Ida Fasel contributes "A 'Conversation' Between Faulkner and Eliot" (*MissQ*, XX, 195–206) in which she makes a comparison of the language between *The Wasteland* and *The Sound and the Fury* to conclude: "the effect of Eliot on Faulkner was an efflorescence, as when the Elizabethans expanded by hundreds of lines Ovid's slenderly told stories"—to which I can only react by feeling perhaps, but I'd like to see more evidence. Bruce Harkness remarks on a brief description in *The Hamlet* that parallels a scene in Scott's *The Talisman* in "Faulkner and Scott" (*MissQ*, XX, 164). And finally James M. Mallard in "The Biblical Rhythm of *Go Down, Moses*" (*MissQ*, XX, 135–147) finds *Go Down, Moses* to be structured in thematic cyclical rhythms that closely parallel Biblical thematic rhythms. I would not want to deny such source hunting as an esoteric indoor sport, but it does seem rarely to contribute much to serious scholarship or understanding of the creative process. Invariably the authors of such pieces must conclude that such slender bits of possible reading represent no more than a minor fraction of the total experience upon which Faulkner drew.

Other general studies deserving some brief mention are Michel Gresset's "Faulkner essayiste" (*NRF*, XV, 309–313), a brief note of general interest, but containing nothing novel for American readers; Patrick G. Hogan's "Faulkner's New Orleans Idiom: A Style in Embryo" (*LaS*, V [1966], 171–181); Irena Kaluza, *The Functioning of Sentence Structure in the Stream-of-Consciousness Technique of William Faulkner's* The Sound and the Fury: *A Study in Linguistic Stylistics* (Krakow, U.J.) and Kenneth E. Richardson's *Force and Faith in the Novels of William Faulkner* (The Hague, Mouton).

iii. Criticism: Individual Works

John T. Frederick in "Anticipation and Achievement in Faulkner's *Soldier's Pay*" (*ArQ*, XXIII, 243–249) claims that *Soldier's Pay* has been wrongly neglected; it is important for anticipating Faulkner's later evocation of place and foreshadowing certain motifs. Ralph Page in "John Sartoris: Friend or Foe" (*ArQ*, XXIII, 27–33) maintains that the character of Bayard Sartoris can best be understood in terms of "that shadowy, nebulous figure, his twin brother, John." He finds Faulkner essentially retelling the story of Cain and Abel.

Henry J. Underwood, Jr. in "Sartre on *The Sound and the Fury*: Some Errors" (*MFS*, XII [1966], 477–479) has a note on Sartre's "Time in Faulkner: *The Sound and the Fury*." He finds that Sartre errs in four quotations on time from Faulkner, which, of course, weaken Sartre's case that Faulkner's metaphysic is time. In "'The Beautiful One': Caddy Compson as Heroine of *The Sound and the Fury*" (*MFS*, XIII, 33–44) Catherine B. Baum feels that Faulkner must be taken literally when he said that the novel was a "tragedy of two women: Caddy and her daughter." Caddy is more centrally the concern of the novel than other critics have admitted. In "Nihilism in Faulkner's *The Sound and the Fury*" (*MFS*, XIII, 45–55) John V. Hagopian concentrates upon the concluding section of the novel. Using the Gestalt concept of "closure," he provides a scheme

of structural analysis that demonstrates the novel to be antagonistic
to Christian values and confirmation of Cleanth Brooks's nihilistic
view that it has to do with the discovery that life has no meaning.
Other studies relating to *The Sound and the Fury* are Emily K.
Izsak, "The Manuscript of *The Sound and the Fury*: The Revisions
in the First Section" (*SB*, XX, 189–202), and Jesse C. Gatlin, Jr.'s
"Of Time and Character in *The Sound and the Fury*" (*HAB*, XVII
[1966], ii, 27–35).

R. W. Franklin in "Narrative Management in *As I Lay Dying*"
(*MFS*, XIII, 57–65) critically examines the novel and finds the use
of present-tense narration to be inconsistent; it is faulty at points,
resulting in anachronisms, probably the result of "the great haste in
which it was written." Robert L. Mason in "A Defense of Faulkner's
Sanctuary" (*GaR*, XXI, 430–438) insists that *Sanctuary* is a better
book than most critics have held. Temple is adequately motivated by
a preference for evil, the events are adequately prepared, and the
book is artistically organized. Mr. Franklin's discussion revolves
around Temple and insistence upon her proclivity toward evil. Frank
Baldanza in an especially perceptive and illuminating essay on "The
Structure of *Light in August*" (*MFS*, XIII, 67–78), contends that a
Faulkner novel is customarily organized around "theme clusters."
He convincingly analyzes *Light in August* in detail to show how the
"theme cluster" theory of structure accounts more fully than other
theories for the "short story anthology" organization of the major
novels. In "Faulkner's Lena Grove" (*GaR*, XXI, 57–64) Robert W.
Kirk thinks Lena Grove has been taken too seriously by critics. She
is essentially a comic character, and her characterization is an end in
itself as part of the countrybred atmosphere.

David Levin has a chapter on Faulkner in his *In Defense of Historical Literature*. Chapter six is titled "*Absalom, Absalom!* The
Problem of Re-Creating History." Levin contends "the search for
historical knowledge dominates the central action and justifies—if it
does not determine—the narrative method." "[It] is a fine historical
novel about the nature and meaning of history, not merely the influence of the past in the present but also the reconstruction of the past
by present observers, the value of historical witnesses, the relationship between interpretation and fact, the importance of understanding the past." In *The Limits of Metaphor: A Critical Study of Melville, Conrad, and Faulkner* (Ithaca, Cornell Univ. Press) James

Guetti studies three novelists concerned with the inadequacy of language. Their narrator characters seek a rhetoric adequate to relate the experiences in which they are involved. He finds *Absalom, Absalom!* to be a hunt for the right words that ultimately fails. The three viewpoints in the novel suggest "that human experience cannot be understood, that order cannot be created." The novel is testimony to the failure of language; metaphor breaks down, and the result is no novel at all, its potential never realized. I find the essays by Levin and French much more instructive about this novel.

Floyd C. Watkins, in "What Happens in *Absalom, Absalom!*" (*MFS*, XIII, 79–87), comments upon the great number of inconsistencies and discrepancies in the novel. The lapses of the author's memory, however, blend unobtrusively into the design of the work, for they can be laid to the fact that the narrators could not realistically be expected to agree on all points of fact. James W. Mathews, "The Civil War of 1936: *Gone with the Wind* and *Absalom, Absalom!*" (*GaR*, XXI, 462–469) writes an interesting minor chapter in the history of literary taste. He summarizes the reviews that appeared shortly after the publication of the two Civil War novels that appeared in the same year. In "Geschichte als Geschehen und Erfahrung: Eine analyse von William Faulkners *Absalom, Absalom!*" (*Archiv*, CCIV, 26–50) Ursula Brumm produces a methodical and detailed analysis, chapter by chapter, of the novel, showing that it is far more than the historical novel that it first appears to be. It is an important psychological and philosophical link in the creation of Faulkner's world.

Thomas M. Lorch, in "Thomas Sutpen and the Female Principle" (*MissQ*, XX, 38–42), finds that "*Absalom, Absalom!* presents male aspiration and will and the passive, enduring, absorbent Female in more closely balanced conflict than we find in Faulkner's other novels." In "Is King David a Racist?" (*UR*, XXXIV, 121–126) William G. Clark follows a curious psychological line of reasoning to argue that Sutpen's antagonism toward the introduction of Negro blood into the Sutpen dynastic line is more than the conventional Southern racist attitude of blood purity. It is deeply involved in the trauma of Sutpen's youth when the Negro butler turned him from the front door. A drop of Negro blood (evoking the butler) would destroy Sutpen's ambitious design that was motivated by proving his right to enter the front door. The purity of the design is necessary to prove his worthiness to a Negro. Also on the same novel is Marvin K. Singleton's "Personae at Law and Equity: The Unity of Faulkner's *Absalom, Absalom!*" (*PLL*, III, 354–370).

Other individual novels receive less attention. Carolyn N. Reaves in "*The Wild Palms*: Faulkner's Chaotic Cosmos" (*MissQ*, XX, 148–157) feels that the imagery of the novel—especially the air, earth, water, fire imagery—creates a timeless, chaotic world. Richard K. Cross in "The Humor of *The Hamlet*" (*TCL*, XII, 203–215) provides an analysis of the strains of frontier humor and surrealistic humor in this novel. Richard A. Lawson in "Patterns of Initiation in William Faulkner's *Go Down, Moses*" (*DA*, XXVII [1966], 1372A) says the novel shows ambivalence operating in each individual's search for identity through initiation. Each individual is marked by his ability or inability to come to terms with life. The dream of an Eden (that Ike McCaslin has) is impossible for the South. The dream of a Promised Land was never for an Eden. There is a factual account of Faulkner's most notable venture in the theater in Nancy D. Taylor's "The Dramatic Productions of *Requiem for a Nun*" (*MissQ*, XX, 123–134).

Thomas P. Carpenter in "A Gun for Faulkner's Old Ben (*AN&Q*, V, 133–134) finds Faulkner's men of the "deep South as provincial, excessively conservative, and cruel." They therefore hunt Ben with woefully inadequate weapons—shotguns and popgun carbines—weapons totally inadequate for bringing down a 700 pound black bear. A better understanding of the story is provided in Melvin E. Bradford's "The Gum Tree Scene: Observations on the Structure of 'The Bear'" (*SHR*, I, 141–150). John Feaster, in "Faulkner's *Old Man*: A Psychoanalytic Approach" (*MFS*, XIII, 89–93), argues that the convict voluntarily returns to the prison as a womb-substitute. Elmo Howell, in "Sam Fathers: A Note on Faulkner's 'A Justice'" (*TSL*, XII, 149–153), finds the ambiguity of Sam Father's parentage a source of irony in the story. And finally Elizabeth M. Kerr, "*The Reivers*: The Golden Book of Yoknapatawpha County" (*MFS*, XIII, 95–114), examines *The Reivers* as a conclusion to the Yoknapatawpha saga, and as such it takes on a greater importance for its recapitulation of themes and motifs in earlier novels.

University of California at Davis

8. Hemingway and Fitzgerald

William White

Before surveying the 1967–1968 year's work in Ernest Hemingway-F. Scott Fitzgerald scholarship, we may profitably take a brief glance at what we have in the total picture up to now, and also an equally short look at the future. Both the past and what's-to-come are better, I think, especially for Hemingway in the latter, than the present year. On balance, Carlos Baker's *Hemingway: The Writer as Artist* (Princeton, N.J., Princeton Univ. Press, 1952, 1956, 1963) remains the best critical study of the author of *A Farewell to Arms*, certainly in its revised and enlarged third edition; a fourth edition was issued as a $2.95 Princeton Paperback in November 1967. Less ambitious and second to the Baker book I should place Earl Rovit's *Ernest Hemingway* (TUSAS, 1963), in which the Freudian and Jungian explications do not get out of hand as Philip Young's *Ernest Hemingway* (New York, Rinehart, 1963) was apt to do in its psychological approaches; this account, now revised as *Ernest Hemingway: A Reconsideration* (Univ. Park, Pa. State Univ. Press, 1966; revised in paperback, New York, Harcourt, Brace & World [1967]) is exciting and was found indispensable to many readers. Shorter yet, at 150 pages, Sheridan Baker's *Ernest Hemingway: An Introduction and Interpretation* (New York, Holt, Rinehart, and Winston) is penetrating, well-written, and balanced, even saying kind words about *Across the River and into the Trees*, though I cannot agree with Baker that *Green Hills of Africa* is Hemingway's "most mature book" and that *To Have and Have Not* "comes near to equalling Hemingway's best."

In the case of the author of *The Great Gatsby*, I do not feel that Henry Dan Piper's *F. Scott Fitzgerald: A Critical Biography* (New York, Holt, Rinehart, and Winston, 1965) has wholly supplanted Arthur Mizener's *The Far Side of Paradise: A Biography of F. Scott Fitzgerald* (Boston, Houghton, Mifflin, 1951). We could not possibly ask for more in a specialized study than we have in Matthew

J. Bruccoli's *The Composition of* Tender Is the Night (Pittsburgh, Univ. of Pittsburgh Press, 1963); and for a full and satisfying treatment we must turn to Robert Sklar's *F. Scott Fitzgerald: The Last Laocoön* (New York, Oxford Univ. Press). In every way that Sheridan Baker's *Ernest Hemingway* is successful, Milton Hindus' *F. Scott Fitzgerald: An Introduction and Interpretation* (New York, Holt, Rinehart and Winston, 1968), in the same American Authors and Critics Series, is not; where Mr. Baker's account is a good place to begin a study of Hemingway, Mr. Hindus' does not fill one with confidence. If Andrew Turnbull's edition and selection of *The Letters of F. Scott Fitzgerald* (New York, Scribner's, 1963) did not please all the critics on its appearance, we have no edition of Hemingway's letters at all, and by the dictates of his will are not likely to have, although Audre Hanneman's *Ernest Hemingway: A Comprehensive Bibliography* (Princeton, N.J., Princeton Univ. Press) pp. 256–266, lists no less than 110 published letters.

Carlos Baker has finished *Ernest Hemingway: A Life Story* (its probable title), and its publication by Charles Scribner's Sons is promised for 1969; it will run to approximately 700 pages, most of it from manuscript sources, chiefly letters, and personal interviews. It begins with Hemingway's first visit to Bear (later Walloon) Lake at the age of six weeks and ends with the shotgun explosion on July 2, 1961.

After forty numbers the valuable and outspoken *Fitzgerald Newsletter*, produced by Matthew J. Bruccoli, ceased publication in Winter, 1968, to be replaced by *The Fitzgerald-Hemingway Journal*, to appear annually.

i. Bibliographies and Texts

Miss Hanneman's Hemingway bibliography and Jackson R. Bryer's *The Critical Reputation of F. Scott Fitzgerald: A Bibliographical Study* (New York, Archon Books), both reviewed by the late Fredrick Hoffman in last year's *ALS*, will be all that scholars need for some time to come. Eventually, book collectors and those interested in the various Fitzgerald editions and impressions will welcome a full-dress bibliography, with descriptions and collations, perhaps by Mr. Bruccoli, whose new *Journal* will include yearly checklists of Hemingway and Fitzgerald.

My own *By-Line: Ernest Hemingway* (New York, Scribner's),
sympathetically reviewed in these pages by Mr. Hoffman last year,
was surprisingly (to me) on the national best-seller list for several
weeks; an English edition was published by Collins, London, in late
February, 1968, and was as favorably received by reviewers as the
American edition; and a paperback edition (New York, Bantam,
1968) was issued in July. I am now preparing a collection of all the
identifiable Hemingway journalism—about 300 pieces, of which 77
appeared in *By-Line*—which Charles Scribner's Sons will publish,
perhaps in 1970.

After fifty years, which included searches by the late Charles A.
Fenton and others, unsigned pieces which Hemingway wrote as a
cub reporter for The Kansas City *Star* have been identified. In an
article by Mel Floor, "Remembering Hemingway's Kansas City
Days," in *The Star*, July 21, 1968, four news features are reprinted,
with evidence of Hemingway's authorship and other background
material: "Throng at Smallpox Case," February 18, 1918; "At the
End of the Ambulance Run," January 20, 1918; "Kerensky, the Fighting Flea," December 16, 1917; and "Mix War, Art and Dancing,"
April 21, 1918. (The Kerensky story had been reprinted earlier in
The Kansas City *Star*, in January, 1968.)

ii. Memoirs and Biography

The most important biographical publication of the year, dealing
with either Hemingway or Fitzgerald, is Nicholas Joost's *Ernest Hemingway and the Little Magazines: The Paris Years* (Barre, Mass.,
Barre Publishers, 1968). It deals in some detail with the other side of
Hemingway's 1921–1926 "career" from the one my *By-Line* deals
with: his relationship with small or no-pay publications in competi-
tion for his time as European representative of The Toronto *Daily
Star* and *The Star Weekly*—or, in other words, journalism *vs.* literature. Much of Charles Fenton's *The Apprenticeship of Ernest Hemingway* (New York, 1954) treated the same period and material, and
his work is still useful; but Mr. Joost not only has turned up a considerable amount of new source matter but has told his story from the
viewpoint of the various little magazines themselves: *The Dial, The
Double-Dealer, Poetry, the transatlantic review, The Little Review,
Der Querschnitt, This Quarter,* and (very briefly) *transition* and

Ezra's Pound's *Exile*. A certain amount of Hemingway's *A Moveable Feast* naturally comes in for explication, and Mr. Joost is both sympathetic toward Hemingway and scrupulous about setting the record straight: he tells the full story "like it was." (In dealing with Hemingway, *The Dial*, and Ernest Walsh, William Wasserstrom has a piece by that name (*SAQ*, LXV [1966], 171–177) with which Mr. Joost disagrees, saying it is based on a misreading of the text; I am inclined to agree with the Joost view.) It is easy to get lost in the petty squabbles and the mass of information, and it is sometimes difficult to know whom to side with in the *transatlantic* dispute between Hemingway and Ford Madox Ford: Hemingway and others make such a fool of Ford, but Ford is there almost to be made a fool of. In this respect, one should consult Bernard J. Poli's *Ford Madox Ford and* the transatlantic review (Syracuse, N.Y., Syracuse Univ. Press), which Mr. Joost says "is essential but (as regards Hemingway) very biased"; it is generally considered that Hemingway could be brutal and was not always kind to those who helped him, yet there is something in Ford's personality that invites parody, scorn, and worse.

One of the books and its author mentioned several times in Mr. Joost's account of the Twenties is William McAlmon, whose marvelously titled *Being Geniuses Together, 1920–1930* has been revised with supplementary chapters by Kay Boyle (Garden City, N.Y., Doubleday, 1968). Under the Paris imprint of the Contact Publishing Co., McAlmon published Hemingway's first book, *Three Stories & Ten Poems* in 1923, and others by Ezra Pound, William Carlos Williams, H. D., Robert M. Coates, and Gertrude Stein, as well as seven books of poetry and fiction by Robert McAlmon, whom he considered more than their equal. He met everyone who was anyone in the 1920 Paris literary world, including Scott and Zelda, Gertrude and Alice B., James Joyce (a favorite drinking companion), T. S. Eliot, and Sylvia Beach, generously helping many of them with money from his father-in-law, the shipping magnate Sir John Ekkerman, through his (McAlmon's) wife, the poet Bryher. Although McAlmon was a failure as a writer—because, says Malcolm Cowley, "he never in his life wrote so much as a memorable sentence"—*Being Geniuses Together* does capture the era, helped considerably by Kay Boyle's new chapters, though McAlmon's harsh judgments of writers who have since achieved fame, and accounts of their dis-

graceful behavior, make him both small and blind. Hemingway is
far more than the Fitzgeralds in the McAlmon story, with both his
first and second wife, referred to about a hundred times; but Mc-
Almon's opinion of Fitzgerald shows his critical level: "Unlike Gertrude Stein," McAlmon writes (p. 347), "I agree with Scott himself
in thinking that most of his books will not be interesting to later
generations, except to intellectuals who will perhaps 'revive' him in
order to show their own extreme sensibilities."

A literary curiosity, now republished, Zelda Fitzgerald's *Save
Me the Waltz*, with a preface by Harry T. Moore and a note on the
text by Matthew J. Bruccoli (Carbondale, Southern Ill. Univ. Press),
may well be read as a complement to her husband's *Tender Is the
Night*, written at about the same time, and based on several of the
same Riviera scenes, and as Mr. Moore says, "it is of absorbing interest to note the differences between the husband's and wife's
version of what was happening."

In Sara Mayfield's *The Constant Circle: H. L. Mencken and His
Friends* (New York, Delacorte Press, 1968), Zelda and Scott were,
on a number of brief occasions, in the circle; Zelda, indeed, being
known to both the author and Sara Haardt (who later married
Mencken) in Zelda's Montgomery days. Miss Mayfield thinks *Tender
Is the Night* "did as gross an injustice to Zelda and the Sayres as any
author ever had done to his wife and her family" (p. 207). Scott's
pathetic note in Mencken's copy of the book begs him to read it and
support him against the herding critics, but it is not known if H.L.M.
ever read the novel—its pages were uncut when his biographer William Manchester saw Mencken's copy (the pages are now cut). The
Sage of Baltimore had little patience with the disordered lives of
both Hemingway and Fitzgerald, Miss Mayfield reports, and was
inclined to write Fitzgerald off as hopeless. Hemingway is mentioned
only three times in the book: Mencken, who was satirized in *The
Torrents of Spring*, nevertheless praised *A Farewell to Arms* for "its
brilliant evocation of the horrible squalor and confusion of war,"
said *Death in the Afternoon* "invariably falls into banality and
worse," and he felt that Hemingway "failed to make his way into
the first rank of American authors" (p. 201).[1]

A somewhat offbeat interview with Hemingway's sister Sunny,

1. *H.L. Mencken's* Smart Set *Criticism*, edited by William H. Nolte (Ithaca,
N.Y., Cornell Univ. Press, 1968), includes what he said of encouragement to
Fitzgerald; the book appeared too late to be fully reviewed here.

now owner of the old family home on Walloon Lake, is the subject of "Indian Camp Camp," by Donald St. John (*CM*, IX [Winter 1968], 95–109). She showed Mr. St. John the locales of a number of the Nick Adams stories—though she said "it is no fun being a curator in your own house and having strangers knock on your door at all hours"— but denied that many of the tales were based on actual people or events: "Of course not; those were just stories." Leicester Hemingway's *My Brother, Ernest Hemingway* (1961), Sunny said, depended too much on letters ("he was too young to know what really went on"); but of Marcelline's *At the Hemingways: A Family Portrait* (1962), the younger sister was far less kind: "Crap," she said. "C-R-A-P-P, crap."

Malcolm Cowley, editor of the Viking Portable *Hemingway* (1944) and author of *Exile's Return* (1951, rev. 1956) and of numerous articles and reviews of Hemingway from their Paris days on, has more to say in "Papa and the Parricides" (*Esquire*, LXVII [June], 100–101, 103, 160, 162).[2]

iii. Criticism

On the whole, critics of twentieth-century American fiction continued to take the writings of Hemingway and Fitzgerald with great seriousness, and far more was done in books and periodical articles on what they wrote than on their lives and personalities: "Papa" Hemingway, fisherman and big-game hunter, and Scott and Zelda, symbols of the jazz age, are now becoming literary craftsmen of some stature. There will always be trivial publications and many more shorter articles and notes than full-length studies in the realm of ideas, for the obvious reason that not all who write in the scholarly journals are made of the stuff of Aristotle, Plato, Dr. Johnson, or—to be more recent—Vernon L. Parrington or F. O. Matthiessen. Dull or unreadable as some of the pieces were, there need be no apologies for the year's output on E.H. and F.S.F.

2. Worth citing under "Biography" is Harold Loeb's "Hemingway's Bitterness," (*ConnR*, I, 7–24), for Mr. Loeb, the author of *The Way It Was* (New York, 1959), who again reminisces, was the model for Robert Cohn in *The Sun Also Rises*. A far slighter note is Barry Sanders' "An Unresolved Hemingway Enigma" (*ABC*, XVIII, i, 8–9), on where the title, *A Moveable Feast*, comes from: a conversation with A. E. Hotchner, a letter (as Mary Hemingway says), a comment by Zelda Fitzgerald, Camus' *The Stranger*, or Howells' *A Modern Instance*.

It is difficult to know what goes on abroad, for the writings of European and Far Eastern scholars do not get fully reported in this country or even listed in bibliographies. Both writers are read abroad, Hemingway more so than Fitzgerald; as a matter of fact, uniform editions of Hemingway (in translation) are available in several countries: Norway (in nine volumes), Denmark (ten volumes), Japan (nine volumes), including a critical study by Rikuo Taniguchi—(see my "Collected Hemingway: A Japanese Translation," *Serif*, IV, i, 30–32), and Korea (five volumes, 1967, even including the poems and the bull-fighting account, *The Dangerous Summer*, which appears in book form only in a Korean translation). This publishing record is better than in our own country, where no uniform edition exists of either Hemingway or Fitzgerald that approaches anywhere near completeness, though Scribner does have ten volumes of Hemingway in uniform dust-jackets. In "Books About Hemingway Abroad" (*ABC*, XVIII [April, 1968], 23) I deplored the situation in Europe, where the "average" reader in France, Spain, Portugal, Holland, and Belgium was restricted largely to inferior biographies (in translation) by A. E. Hotchner, Kurt Singer, and Leo Lania; but I might ask: how many bookstores in America carry Robert Sklar's study of Fitzgerald or Carlos Baker's *Hemingway: The Writer as Artist* (which is available, or was in Spring, 1967, in Arabic in a Cairo bookstore)?

Five contributions from abroad are Péter Egri's *Hemingway* (Budapest, Gondolat), in Hungarian; I. Finkel'stejn's "Sovetskaja kritika o Xeminguèe" [Soviet criticism on Hemingway] (*VLit*, XI, viii, 174–190) in Russian, a further example of Russia's long and continuing interest, which has been highlighted by Ivan Kashkeen's many books and articles; Jacques Robichon's "Hemingway face à la mort," (*NL*, XXIX [déc., 1966], 1, 11, in French; William V. Nestrick's "F. Scott Fitzgerald's Types and Narrators" (*RLV* [Brussels], XXXIII, 164–184) written on *The Great Gatsby* and *Tender Is the Night* in an academic English and full of such opaque scholarly jargon as to be readable only with great difficulty (if this is so of an American reader, what will a French or Belgian understand?); and Beongcheon Yu's "The Still Center of Hemingway's World," *Phoenix* (XII [Spring, 1968], 15–44), which discusses Hemingway's development as a personal artist whose talent is an outgrowth of his vision of life and death—if we accept Hemingway's wish that he be judged from the inside on his own terms, we are, says Mr. Yu, "grateful for the best he can offer us, his vision that enables us to see anew our existence in its nakedness."

Edwin M. Moseley's *F. Scott Fitzgerald: A Critical Essay* (Grand Rapids, Mich., William B. Eerdmans) is another in the series entitled "Contemporary Writers in Christian Perspective" (Nathan A. Scott, Jr.'s pamphlet on Hemingway in the series was published in 1966). Confining his discussion to Fitzgerald's five novels and restricted to forty-four pages, Mr. Moseley unfortunately can't do full justice to a study of the religious elements in the fiction. Almost nothing is said of the novelist's own Catholic background; and while some suggestive and worthwhile points are developed, especially in *The Great Gatsby* chapter, much needs to be added to the Moseley essay and the passing reference to the subject by other critics and scholars.

The one major work of criticism, dealing with either Hemingway or Fitzgerald, is Robert O. Stephens' 391-page study of *Hemingway's Nonfiction: The Public Voice* (Chapel Hill, Univ. of N.C. Press, 1968). That Hemingway wrote so much journalism is no mystery: my own selection in *By-Line* and Fenton's examination of the early material in *The Apprenticeship of Ernest Hemingway* show what it contributed to the novelist and short story writer. By calling the writing "essays," Mr. Stephens is the first one to make a truly full-scale estimate of the entire body in newspapers, magazines, introductions to others' works, and ephemera, plus *Death in the Afternoon, Green Hills of Africa,* and *A Moveable Feast.* Not only does all this throw light on Hemingway's fiction, but it is worthwhile material on its own. Mr. Stephens divides his book into five parts, beginning with a forty-page survey of Hemingway's career as an essayist, from 1917 through his posthumous work, relating how he changed from the impersonal recorder of society at home and abroad, with an occasional bit of fun, then involved his own personality in his writings, and finally went one step further to make his world a function of his own response to it. Part two goes into Hemingway's essays as a vehicle for his personality, as connoisseur, travel expert, war analyst, literary commentator, and man of letters; part three deals with his "think pieces" on culture, politics, and aesthetics; and part four shows how the nonfiction, instead of draining his energies from his fiction, actually served as sources, analogues, and echoes.

It is these middle parts that make up the bulk of Mr. Stephens' book, the shorter final and fifth part being his conclusions, "Hemingway's Art of the Essay," and evaluations. Of Hemingway's three voices, the personal must be left to inference, the fictional behind the imaginative mask must be put into the roughest equivalent of expository language for critical study, but the nonfictional between these two voices is self-explaining and public, and thus immediately usable for total comprehension. We now have Hemingway's nonfiction studied by Mr. Stephens, in as much depth as we shall presumably need, in this important, ground-breaking, and critically sound volume. "Hemingway's nonfiction should reveal," Mr. Stephens summarizes, "that, in spite of his frequent self-depiction as a lonely man at work outside the mainstream of literary and political fashions, he was very much a public writer for his times."

Of five books containing significant mention of Hemingway or Fitzgerald or both, two deal with war: *World War I and the American Novel*, by Stanley Cooperman (Baltimore, Johns Hopkins Press); and *Writers in Arms: The Literary Impact of the Spanish Civil War*, by Frederick R. Benson (New York, New York Univ. Press). The first has a chapter entitled "Death and Cojones: Frederic Henry (Ernest Hemingway)" in the section on "Antiheroes," in which Mr. Cooperman concludes that Hemingway depends upon ritualized action to escape from his *nada*, and when this fails, the individual is doomed along with his manhood: "Initiative must be regained at all costs, and the demand for initiative is the clue not only to the central drama of *A Farewell to Arms*, but to life—and the death—of Hemingway himself." Mr. Benson's study of European and American Spanish Civil War literature, less compartmentalized and more penetrating than Mr. Cooperman's, concentrates on the works of Malraux, Regler, Hemingway, Orwell, Koestler, and Bernanos, and he examines their treatment of the issues and the impact of the conflict on the intellectual conscience. The war was Hemingway's first step in his personal fight against fascism, Mr. Benson says; but the novelist's concern is with the action of individuals rather than the political or collective elements in the war effort, and he quotes Hemingway on *For Whom the Bell Tolls*: "It wasn't just the civil war I put into it . . . it was everything I had learned about Spain for eighteen years." And Hemingway realized, the critic points out, that the fight to destroy his liberal ideals had only just begun in Spain;

his hatred of fascism and sympathy for the Loyalist Republic, his romantic love of old Spain, and his enthusiasm and anxiety for the future of the world were also to be determined in this crusade.

Arthur Mizener's volume, *Twelve Great American Novels*, is a modest attempt for the reader who wants help in reading novels for himself but doesn't feel at home with them: among the twelve works are *Tender Is the Night* and *The Sun Also Rises*, to which Mr. Mizener devotes fifteen and twenty-two pages, respectively. The approach is straightforward, and if there is little new or startling in interpretation, these are essays full of sympathy, understanding, and appreciation. How helpful these pages will be to students may be seen in this summing-up: "*The Sun Also Rises* is the supreme realistic image of the romantic attitude toward private experience as it existed in the twenties, perhaps the last period of American society in which the private life was still lived in the public world."

The fourth volume (*Explorations of Literature*) contains William E. Doherty's "*Tender Is the Night* and the 'Ode to the Nightingale'" (pp. 100–114), the first attempt to show the relationship between Fitzgerald's novel and Keats's poem which gave it both title and epigraph. As Mr. Doherty puts it, the correspondences between the ode and the novel indicate "a calculated pattern of allusion beneath the literal surface of the novel which deepens the psychoanalytic rationale and adds context to the cultural analysis the book offers." The ode also provides "a sort of thematic overlay which clarifies unsuspected symbolic structures, essential to the understanding of the book." (I might add that Mr. Doherty's language is more readable, relaxed, and restrained when he takes up the similarities between Fitzgerald and Keats.)

A great improvement in every way over a 1966 anthology, *The Twenties*, Warren French has now edited *The Thirties*, to which Sheldon Norman Grebstein contributes "Hemingway's Dark and Bloody Capital" (pp. 21–30) and Jonas Spatz, "Fitzgerald, Hollywood and the Myth of Success" (pp. 31–37). Mr. Grebstein makes a critical analysis of "The Capital of the World," a very good story on "the initiation of an innocent into the bitterness of life through suffering," in which the Spanish boy Paco replaces Nick Adams as victim. Paco's story dramatizes what Hemingway says in a different way in *Death in the Afternoon*, its theme being that the brave, good, and innocent are unfit for life. In technique "The Capital of the

World" differs from many other Hemingway stories in the obtrusive presence of its narrator, who comments upon the characters and action, and in a coda which summarizes the themes and points the story's ironic moral. Mr. Spatz's essay deals largely with *The Great Gatsby*, "The Diamond as Big as the Ritz," and especially *The Last Tycoon*. This last work, he concludes, is Fitzgerald's "final version of the capitalist myth," and while the novelist "regrets the passing of individualism and the degradation of frontier democracy," he sees in Hollywood, for all its vulgarity, the vitality of the lavish, romantic past.[3]

Of the doctoral dissertations, two were written on Fitzgerald and four on Hemingway: Barry E. Gross, "The Novels of F. Scott Fitzgerald: 'The Dominant Idea' " (*DA*, XXVII, 304A); Virginia A. Hallam, "The Critical and Popular Reception of F. Scott Fitzgerald" (*DA*, XXVII, 3456A); Jackson J. Benson, "Ernest Hemingway and the Doctrine of True Emotion" (*DA*, XXVII, 3862A); Forrest D. Robinson, "The Tragic Awareness of Hemingway's First-Person Narrators: A Study of *The Sun Also Rises*" (*DA*, XXVII, 2543A); Bickford Sylvester, "Hemingway's Extended Vision: *The Old Man and the Sea*" (*DA*, XXVII [1966], 1841A); and Samuel E. Vandiver, "The Architecture of Hemingway's Prose" (*DA*, XXVII, 2268A).

The long list of periodical pieces includes only three of a largely psychological nature, all appearing in the same journal. Jackson R. Bryer's "A Psychiatrist Reviews 'Tender Is the Night' " (*L&P*, XVI [1966], 198–199), cites an anonymous reviewer in the *Journal of Nervous and Mental Disease* (LXXXII [1935], 115–117) who concludes that the novel is "an achievement which no student of the psychological sources of human behavior, and of its particular social correlates today, can afford not to read." David Gordon's "The Son and the Father: Patterns of Response to Conflict in Hemingway's Fiction" (*L&P*, XVI [1966], 122–136) is a thoroughgoing analysis of many of the short stories and all of the novels on the hypothesis that the novelist (or his hero), "prevented by guilt from direct gratification of sexual and aggressive impulses, achieved gratification by recasting his motives into forms that demonstrate moral superiority";

---

3. One other book is worth a footnote: James A. Michener's *Iberia: Spanish Travels and Reflections* (New York, Random House, 1968). See "Colloquium on Hemingway," pp. 490–502, which summarizes Michener's ambivalent feeling about Hemingway: "No gracia. No understanding. A good writer. Not the greatest man. But a good writer."

furthermore, Mr. Gordon winds up, "the martyr-hero of Hemingway's fiction is a product of cultural as well as individual psychology." Stanley Wertheim, "The Conclusion of Hemingway's *The Sun Also Rises*" (*L&P*, XVII, 55–56) sees the raised baton of the traffic policeman (as Brett pressed against Jake) as a phallic symbol, "an ironic counterpoint which serves to remind Jake of the felicity he has lost" in the war.

Robert W. Lewis, Jr., and Max Westbrook jointly contribute an essay in "The Texas Manuscript of 'The Snows of Kilimanjaro'" (*TQ*, IX [1966], iv, 66–101), on what the MS tells us of Hemingway and of the story. A deleted epigram from Vivienne de Watteville's *Speak to the Earth* (1935) reveals that her book was an important source to Hemingway and thus helps to illuminate our reading of the story. The MS also reveals significant steps in the creative process of Hemingway's imagination and suggests a new interpretation of the imaginary flight by Harry, who is seen as an amalgam of Hemingway, Scott Fitzgerald, and a fictive Harry. Two short articles, not on so high a level of achievement as the Lewis-Westbrook study deal with the same story: Reid Maynard's "The Decay Motif in 'The Snows of Kilimanjaro'" (*Discourse*, X, 436–439) and Gloria R. Dussinger's "'The Snows of Kilimanjaro': Harry's Second Chance" (*SSF*, V, 54–59). In view of Hemingway's creed, "To be true to the senses is the writer's ultimate duty," Gloria Dussinger says that by recording the sensory impressions of Harry's final flight—colors, textures, temperature—Hemingway thus announces Harry's victory.

Two short pieces are concerned with Hemingway's "The Killers": Edward Stone's (*SSF*, V, 12–17), and Lawrence A. Walz's (*Expl*, XXV, Item 38). Mr. Stone asks about Summit, the small town, where Henry's restaurant is, the two killers, Nick, and calling the police; and he answers by quoting Leicester Hemingway that the restaurant was in Chicago, by quoting A. E. Hotchner that the Chicago mob that sent the killers was still "very much in business" (when the story was written), and that Hemingway left out much ("the whole city of Chicago"); he concludes that "The Killers" is "utterly free and need abide no questions at all." Mr. Walz comments ingeniously on the confused sexuality in the story (the shotgun made a bulge under the gangster's tight overcoat: pregnancy?), saying that "men ought to be men . . . women ought to be women . . . and one should be pregnant with life, not with death." A more sensible item in *The*

Explicator (XXVI, Item 8) is John D. Magee's on Hemingway's "Cat in the Rain": Hemingway's use of natural as opposed to artificial light, as the wife looks out of the window and says she wants a cat (which she sees) when in reality she wants a baby, symbolically represents the wife's empty and sterile existence.

John Reardon, in "Hemingway's Esthetic and Ethical Sportsmen" (*UR*, XXXIV, 13–23), finds that the novelist's fourth dimension—which he mentioned in *Green Hills of Africa*—is esthetic and the fifth ethical; Mr. Reardon makes a good case that Hemingway's sportsman is "the physical manifestation of the writer, who is the esthetic manifestation of the hero, who is the ethical manifestation of the code." The same periodical has an equally well thought out two-part study by Richard Hovey, "*A Farewell to Arms*: Hemingway's Liebestod" (*UR*, XXXIII, 93–100, 163–168), in which he shows that if Frederic Henry's view of love is black, there are but two things to fall back on: faith in God or in death. As the novel ends without a hint of faith in God, "the drift is toward death"; thus *Death in the Afternoon* argues for a mystique of death and Hemingway's next book, *Winner Take Nothing*, "offers his prayer to Our Nada who art in Nada."[4]

Robert B. Holland, in "Macomber and the Critics" (*SSF*, V [1968], 171–178), makes the strong statement that "Macomber" illustrates "how far astray we may go in our judgments of literature, and how greatly and disastrously we may distort and misrepresent the intent, even the plain statement of the author"; for when Hemingway wrote that Mrs. Macomber "had shot at the buffalo," he meant exactly and literally that. Mr. Holland says all the critics are wrong: Mrs. Macomber did not murder her husband. If he's right, then one of the finest of Hemingway's short stories make no sense whatever.

J. F. Kohler is perfectly accurate in saying in his "Confused Chronology in *The Sun Also Rises*" (*MFS*, XIII, 517–520) that days and dates are totally mixed up and that dates of two actual events, the Ledoux-Kid Francis fight and William Jennings Bryan's death, are wrong, and that Hemingway's editor (Maxwell Perkins?) should

---

4. As space makes impossible the discussion of all articles on Hemingway, at least two more may at least be cited: Daniel J. Schneider's "The Symbolism of 'The Sun also Rises'" (*Discourse*, X, 334–342); and Alexander Tamke's "Jacob Barnes' 'Biblical Name': Central Irony in *The Sun Also Rises*" (*ER*, XVIII [Dec.], 2–7), which pleads that Jake's name is an ironic echo of the Biblical Jacob who has fertile loins and God's promise, but I doubt that this is central to the novel.

have held a calendar up to those dates. But *The Sun Also Rises* is neither an almanac nor a statistical table; it is a novel. How relevant are these dates to the story? One whispers, hardly at all. More relevant, but unconvincing is Bickford Sylvester in the same periodical, " 'They Went Through This Fiction Every Day': Informed Illusion in *The Old Man and the Sea*" (*MSF*, XIII [1966], 474–477), who feels that the ritualistic dialogue between the old man and the boy, ritualistic play, and formal devices prepare for Santiago's imminent death. Another *MSF* piece by Ray L. White, "Hemingway's Private Explanation of *The Torrents of Spring*" (XIII, 261–263), paraphrases five unpublished E.H. letters to Sherwood Anderson, in which the younger writer said he meant *Torrents* as a joke, though not a mean one; he hoped Anderson would not be offended, and nothing that is good could be hurt by satire.

By his title, "Hemingway's Staying Power" (*MR*, VIII, 431–439), Edward L. Galligan means Hemingway's influence on Norman Mailer, Nelson Algren, and Vance Bourjaily, all of whom regard Hemingway as "unquestionably one of America's greatest writers [whose] greatness lies in what he discovered about how to live in awareness of the reality of death."

The periodical criticism of Fitzgerald is about on the same level as the Hemingway material; it's only that there isn't as much of it, if we exclude the 13 pieces in the *Fitzgerald Newsletter* (all of them worthwhile contributions, plus notes, reviews, and Matthew J. Bruccoli's quarterly checklist: its demise can only be regretted by F.S.F. enthusiasts). Of these 13 *FitzN* articles, the most informative, and of a specialist's concern, is the five-part "F and the Princeton Triangle Club," by Donald Marsden, the last three parts in 1967–68 (No. 38, pp. 1–3; No. 39, pp. 8–11; No. 40, pp. 11–14). R. E. Long has three items in *FitzN*: "Dreiser and Frederic: The Upstate New York Exile of Dick Diver" (No. 37, pp. 1–2), on how *An American Tragedy* and *The Damnation of Theron Ware* influenced *Tender Is the Night*; "*Vanity Fair* and the Guest List in *GG*" (No. 38, p. 4), noting that both Thackeray's and Fitzgerald's novels include "a satirical sketching of a motley social group"; and "*B&D*: Nathan and Mencken as Maury Noble" (No. 40 [1968], pp. 3–4), pointing out the composite nature of Noble. Mario L. D'Avanzo's "Gatsby and Holden Caulfield" (No. 38, pp. 4–6) has both protagonists as idealists, kind, charitable, trusting, and believing they can recapture the past.

The Great Gatsby takes up almost all the space in No. 39 of *FitzN*:
Sister Margaret Patrice Slattery discussing the function of time (pp.
1–4); Paul Sawyer, Jay Gatsby's boyhood schedule (pp. 4–7); James
F. Slevin, the water images (pp. 12–13); and Richard A. Burleson,
the color imagery (pp. 13–14). David J. F. Kelley's account of "The
Polishing of 'Diamond' " (No. 40, pp. 1–2) testifies as to Fitzgerald's
craftsmanship; Alexander R. Tamke, in "Michaelis in GG; St. Michael
in the Valley of Ashes" (No. 40, pp. 4–5) calls attention to the appearance of the archangel in modern guise at a crucial point in the
novel; and John S. Hill's "Henry James: F's Literary Ancestor" (No.
40, pp. 6–10) shows an overlooked relationship between *The Ambassadors* and *Gatsby* "as sharers of disillusionment about the American dream."

Jackson R. Bryer's "F. Scott Fitzgerald as Book Reviewer" (*PBSA*,
LX [1966], 369–370), on Fitzgerald's casual review of Sherwood
Anderson's *Many Marriages*, feels it shows "his quite acute literary
perceptions and ability to write perceptive literary criticism," a
somewhat strong statement for the small evidence. Victor A. Doyno,
"Patterns in *The Great Gatsby*" (*MFS*, XII [1966], 415–426, makes a
close study of Fitzgerald's craftsmanship, centered around four inserted picture titles—the pencil MSS, galley proofs, and revisions
show that the novelist wrote "something new—something extraordinary and beautiful and simple and intricately patterned." Robert
Forrey finds in "Negroes in the Fiction of F. Scott Fitzgerald"
(*Phylon*, XXVIII, 293–298) that blacks are generally relegated to
clownish or inferior roles and rich ones are ludicrous, while in real
life the appearance of a Negro was usually the signal for Fitzgerald
to promote a prank; but in *The Last Tycoon*, however, Fitzgerald
(Monroe Stahr) introduces a Negro at an important point without
any of the accoutrements of racism.

Richard Foster, "Fitzgerald's Imagination: A Parable for Criticism" (*MinnR*, VII, 144–156), a bit defensively and uncritically,
refutes the accusation that Fitzgerald's prose was impersonal, following the lead of Joyce and Yeats; and he also answers yes to the question, "Was Fitzgerald an artist as well as a writer?" Using F. S. F.'s
letters, as well as comparing early books and stories and nonfiction
in his full researched study, Mr. Foster shows that the gaining of
self-knowledge was synonymous with his development of knowledge
about his art. "The simplicity and purity of Fitzgerald's loyalty to

the life of his imagination," this essay concludes, "makes him rare and moving in the role of artist in the twentieth century."

John H. Randall, III, suggests, in "Jay Gatsby's Hidden Source of Wealth" (*MFS*, XIII, 247–257) that Gatsby and Wolfsheim were involved in the 1919 Teapot Dome scandal; but *FitzN* (No. 39, p. 17) replies that it is at least as likely that their illegal activity was something like the theft of $5,000,000 of Liberty Bonds for which Nicky Arnstein went to jail in 1922. A more diffused, subjective, and less tangible general approach to the same novel occurs in Robert and Chris Richards' "Feeling in *The Great Gatsby*" (*WHR*, XXI, 257–265), in which the two authors see that this "color, this feeling of perspectives and distances . . . sustain this novel . . . and make it immediate and vital"; and what gives *Gatsby's* greatest pleasure is its color, "an opalescent quality which is the source of pleasure." Two better essays, with some similarity of approach to each other, are Benjamin T. Spencer's "Fitzgerald and the American Ambivalence" (*SAQ*, LXVI, 367–381) and David F. Trask's "A Note on Fitzgerald's *The Great Gatsby*" (*UR*, XXXIII, 197–202). In responding to the dichotomy of the North and South and the East and West, Fitzgerald was typically ambivalent, says Mr. Spencer, who sees "all human experience, at least in the American-European world, [as] an endless counterpoint of westward thrust and eastward recoil," and the Gatsby and Diver tragedies show him "neither the collapse nor the punitive culmination of the American dream, but rather its betrayal by the non-dreamers." And here is Mr. Trask on *Gatsby*: "inescapably a general critique of the 'American dream' and also of the 'agrarian myth'—a powerful demonstration of their invalidity for Americans of Fitzgerald's generation and after." He says Hemingway's emphasis "is on method—on how to live in the revolutionalized context," while Fitzgerald dealt with "the bankruptcy of the old way . . . and could discern no beauty in the city to compare with the beauty, however meretricious, inherent in Gatsby's Platonic conception of himself."

iv. Conclusion

In all this wordage, which shows no sign of abating, we can only say what has been said before: Fitzgerald and Hemingway continue to be taken as serious artists, and their place in American literary history is so secure that editors, bibliographers, critics, and scholars treat what they have written with the greatest respect. Even the trivia, despite its appearance of overwhelming us, make a minor contribution; and among the lengthier and more fully developed interpretations and evaluations, those that succeed do so, not because of what Fitzgerald and Hemingway wrote or how badly or well they wrote it, but because of sensitivity, intelligence, and the ability of the interpreters and evaluators to say what they have to say.

Wayne State University

Part II

9. Literature to 1800

Richard Beale Davis

That twenty-five per cent more books and essays on early American literature appeared during 1967 than during the preceding year is one evidence of the lively and growing interest in the area. Some two dozen items were edited texts, more than a dozen collected or single works of one author in book form, and five others anthologies. These help to supply our greatest need. There were several biographical studies, none a full-length survey of a major figure, but two good comprehensive sketches of significant minor writers appeared. The preponderance of the writing dealt with criticism and literary and cultural history and included dozens of good essays and at least two books of major importance.

i. Bibliography, Libraries, and Publishing History

Practically useful for the scholar and entertaining for the bibliophile is Roger J. Trienens, "The Library's Earliest Colonial Imprints" (*QJLC*, XXIV, 186–200), a listing and discussion of these books in the Library of Congress. From the Massachusetts *Bay Psalm Book* of 1640 (acquired in 1966) through a Georgia *Almanack* of 1763, it is principally a collection of Acts of Assembly and Laws; but several volumes of sermons and almanacs represent literary endeavor. *Bookbinding in Colonial Virginia* (Williamsburg, Colonial Williamsburg), by C. C. Samford and John M. Hemphill, is one of our few studies of this art so closely allied to book-composition. Incidentally it locates in colonial bindings copies of such rare works as Samuel Davies' *Miscellaneous Poems* (1751–1752) and the printed and manuscript material ordered bound by author-owners such as Thomas Jefferson, William Stith, Henry Timberlake, William Byrd, and Richard Bland. Though its title is promising, Joseph M. Carrière's "French Books in Colonial Virginia" (*PICLA*, II, 1184–1188) is brief and inconclusive.

"The First English Editions of John Lawson's 'Voyage to Carolina': A Bibliographical Study" (*PBSA*, LXI, 258–265), by E. Bruce
Kirkham, demonstrates that this was a popular book with five "editions" in the first ten years, but that all of the five were mere re-issues
of the original Stevens' 1709 publication. Edward G. Howard in "An
Unrecorded Baltimore Imprint from Philadelphia" (*PBSA*, LXI,
121–123) shows how a recently acquired copy of Charlotte Turner
Smith's *The Romance of Real Life* (1799), with a Baltimore imprint,
is the same publisher's Philadelphia printing with a new title page.
Thus another detail of late eighteenth-century publishing practices
is revealed. R. Reed Sanderlin, "A Variant version of 'The Child of
Snow'" (*EALN*, II, ii, 22–26), compares a second recently discovered version of an early American short story with the first (see *ALS*,
1966, p. 111). A similar article is J. Philip Goldberg's "Some Con-
jectures upon John Shippen's 'Observations on Novel Reading'"
(*EALN*, II, i, 6–11), which refutes William Free's attribution (see
ALS, *1966*, p. 111) to Shippen of an anonymously published text.

Edgar C. Reinke's "A Classical Debate of the Charleston, South
Carolina, Library Society" (*PBSA*, LXI, 83–99) is concerned with
the old subject of the colonial attitude toward the study or reading
of the classics. Reinke finds that a full decade before the Revolution
a majority of members of this library society rebelled against spend-
ing money on the Greek and Latin authors, though Christopher
Gadsden (see p. 120) was among the minority who championed the
ancients. "David Hall and the Stamp Act" (*PBSA*, LXI, 13–37), by
Robert D. Harlan, uses Franklin's former partner as an example of
how the Stamp Act affected a printer in economic and psychological
ways so as to cause him to turn radical. G. Thomas Tanselle's "Author
and Publisher in 1800: Letters of Royall Tyler and Joseph Nancrede"
(*HLB*, XV, 129–139) gives information about publishing arrangements at the end of the eighteenth century. In their matching of wits,
the flattering but self-declared impecunious publisher never did
bring out the proposed volume of stories and sketches by the author
of *The Contrast*.

ii. Texts

The corpus of known early American literature was increased in
1967 by the publication for the first time of two diaries, two satires,

and a number of individual poems. The writings of half a dozen men better known for their achievements in non-belletristic work are also of great significance. Gatherings and translations of obscure works by early Americans, new editions of three or four now rare standard works, and a number of anthologies, several quite distinguished, round out the text-publication for the year.

"The Diary of Jeremiah Dummer" (*WMQ*, XXIV, 397–422), edited by Sheldon S. Cohen, traces the life of a born Puritan to the period of his breakdown into worldliness. Interesting for both personal and political reasons, the journal retains the introspective and blame-of-self qualities of the early Puritans and reveals finally a very human and curious creature who ended life as a Tory exile, but not as the infidel his enemies claimed he was. From the South comes "The Diary of Frances Baylor Hill of 'Hillsborough,' King and Queen County, Virginia (1797)" (*EALN*, II, iii, 3–53), edited by William K. Bottorff and Roy C. Flannagan, an excellent picture of social and intellectual life in the Tidewater at the end of the century. The diarist was a young woman of the upper classes who sewed, cooked, prescribed medicine, attended equally balls and church services, composed and sang her own songs, and read fairly widely. Slightly more introspective than Byrd's diary, this resembles his in its relative objectivity more than it does that of her sombre fellow-Virginian Landon Carter. Also may be added to the body of Virginia literature two satires, one poetic and the other prose, edited by Richard Beale Davis as *The Colonial Virginia Satirist* (Philadelphia, Amer. Philos. Soc.). The verse, "Dinwiddianæ," is really a collection of political satires (probably by James Mercer) and some quasi-dialectal letters. This attack on a colonial governor is clearly representative of many such literary-political exercises composed in the Chesapeake Bay region during the whole century preceding the Revolution. The prose satire, "The Religion of the Bible and the Religion of K[ing] W[illiam] County Compared," by James Reid, is an attack upon the worldliness and lack of religion of upper-class Virginians in 1769. Erudite, discerning, descriptive of weaknesses, it is as relentless in its moralism as a tract by any Puritan of New England might be.

Isolated poems of intrinsic and/or historical value appeared: "Two Unpublished Colonial Verses" (*BNYPL*, LXXI, 61–63), edited by Kenneth Silverman, are by Philadelphian Joseph Breitnall about 1740, and by South Carolinian "Captain Martin" about 1769, two poems contrasting in their displayed affection for country or city life; "Benjamin Colman's 'Hymn of Praise': Text and Comments" (*EALN*, II, ii, 27–31), edited by Leo M. Kaiser, prints Coleman's poem from manuscript along with someone else's later Latin translation; "An Unpublished Latin Poem of James Logan" (*SCN*, XXV, 43), also edited by Kaiser, is actually a translation of a Greek poem by Heinsius; "An Unpublished Latin Poem of Benjamin Church" (*SCN*, XXV, 42), edited again by Kaiser, is a Latin acrostic on John Hancock's name. Thomas E. Johnston in "A Translation of Cotton Mather's Spanish Works: *La Fe del Christiano* and *La Religion Pura*" (*EALN*, II, ii, 7–21) gives English renderings of a catechism and a commentary on the language of church services and a declaration of the entire sufficiency of the Bible for Christian guidance, the one a statement of Puritan belief, the other a condemnation of Roman Catholicism. Three unrecorded printings of occasional verse are brought to light by Lewis Leary in "Unrecorded Early Verse of William Dunlap" (*AL*, XXXIX, 87–88); each represents a different facet of American literary interest of the 1790's. Philip L. Barbour prints with commentary "Two 'Unknown' Poems by Captain John Smith" (*VMHB*, LXXV, 157–158), significant among other things in proving the author a poet of some ability.

Gradually the titles known primarily from literary histories are appearing in good modern editions. First-generation Virginian Ralph Percy's *Observations Gathered out of 'A Discourse of the Plantation of the Southern Colony in Virginia by the English,' 1606* (Charlottesville, Univ. Press of Va.), edited by David B. Quinn, gives in convenient form these comments on the New World scene. Royall Tyler's novel, *The Algerine Captive* (SF&R), has been edited with a good introduction by Jack B. Moore from the London edition of 1802. *The Anarchiad: a New England Poem (1786–1787)* (SF&R) "written in concert" by Barlow, Humphreys, Trumbull, and Hopkins, has been re-edited from the 1861 edition by William K. Bottorff. For the second straight year (see *ALS, 1966*, p. 100) an edition of Cotton Mather's *Bonifacius: An Essay upon the Good* (SF&R), edited this time by Josephine K. Piercy, has appeared. Every library should have this facsimile as well as the new letterpress edition of last year. George W. Pilcher has used both of the original manuscripts in republishing in *The Reverend Samuel Davies Abroad: The Diary of a Journey to England and Scotland 1753–1755* (Urbana, Univ. of

Ill. Press), a valuable journal buried before this in abbreviated form in W. H. Foote's *Sketches of Virginia, 1st Ser.* The growing realization of Davies' significance as a literary figure is enhanced in this presentation of one of the great subjective diaries of colonial America.

Homer D. Babbidge, Jr.'s edition of *Noah Webster: On Being American, Selected Writings, 1783–1828* (New York, Frederick A. Praeger) is fairly representative, despite the limitations implied in its title, of the mind of the great lexicographer. Curiously it shows him as a nationalist in theory who is preeminently parochial, a man who proclaims his breadth but remains in many respects narrow indeed. A most valuable new edition of the complete works by one writer is Jeannine Hensley's *The Works of Anne Bradstreet* (Cambridge, Mass., Harvard Univ. Press), a careful reproduction in letterpress (with certain corrections) of the second edition of 1678. It includes a good critical and textual introduction and history of previous editions—though it does not entirely supersede the Ellis edition. Harvey Wish's edition of *The Diary of Samuel Sewall* (New York, Putnam) is a fairly good abridgement, with too few notes. It may be useful to the undergraduate. Much better is *William Byrd's Histories of the Dividing Line betwixt Virginia and North Carolina* (New York, Dover), with the notes and introduction of an earlier edition by William K. Boyd, and with an additional introduction and a revised text (by adding from recently discovered manuscripts inserted leaves at the proper places) by Percy G. Adams. This will be from now on the basic parallel-text edition, and one may add that it goes beyond Louis B. Wright's fine non-parallel edition of a year or two ago in its emendations of the previously printed versions of both histories.

At least two of the great editions of our colonial and Revolutionary political writers continued their series of volumes this year. *The Papers of Benjamin Franklin,* Volume XI, January 1 to December 31, 1764 (New Haven, Yale Univ. Press), edited by Leonard W. Labaree and others, contains as do the earlier volumes a rich gathering of letters on science, pamphlets on politics, and essays on humane and humanistic subjects. *The Papers of James Madison,* Volume V, 1 August–31 December 1782 (Chicago, Univ. of Chicago Press), edited by William T. Hutchinson and W. M. E. Rachal, is not so rich in humanistic terms, but does show Madison's interest in science and above all his growing skill as political negotiator. Richard Walsh has edited complete in one volume *The Writings of Christopher Gadsden: 1746–1805* (Columbia, S.C., Univ. of S.C. Press), the works of a major Revolutionary figure who was one of the first movers for independence and whose letters to the press are among the more significant pamphlets in the progress towards independence. Complete in two volumes are *The Works of James Wilson* (Cambridge, Mass., Harvard Univ. Press, Belknap), edited by Robert G. McCloskey, an enlightening collection of letters, lectures on law, pamphlets, and other materials, which enable us to understand both the ability and relative obscurity of this Founding Father of the Republic who was too ambitious in too many things. All four editions are capably edited, with excellent head and foot or tail notes.

Among the editorial work of the year five anthologies loom large, three of them works of real distinction. Rex Burbank and Jack B. Moore's *The Literature of Early America* (Columbus, Charles E. Merrill) is organized according to literary genres. Hopelessly parochial and unbalanced in its selections, it is valuable primarily for some of the short fiction it brings into print again. Robert E. Spiller as editor of *The American Literary Revolution 1783–1837* (New York, New York Univ. Press) attempts "to document from contemporary sources some of the ways in which the burst of revolutionary enthusiasm was carried over . . . from the issue of political to that of literary independence" and to trace that progress up to the writers of the American Renaissance. This is a most useful anthology of what amounts to American nationalism in literature and to development of definitions of the nature, function, and quality of American literature. Included are some genuinely significant but previously not readily available materials, the kind of thing that always enhances the value of an anthology.

An anthology for Italian readers, Biancamaria Tedeschini Lalli's *I Puritani* (Bari, Adriatica, 1966), is impressive in its selections (given in English) and critical introductions and notes. It is highly regrettable that the English-language texts are marred by careless punctuation and capitalization, omission of lines, erratic spacing, and other corruptions, and that the bibliography and Table of Contents also contain several inaccuracies. The two most useful and well-edited anthologies of the year are made up largely of tracts and/or sermons. Merrill Jensen's *Tracts of the American Revolution 1763–1776* (Indianapolis, Bobbs-Merrill) gives a much better balanced sampling from much the same sources than does Bernard Bailyn (*ALS, 1965*, p. 116) in his comparable collection. Though limitations of space prevented Jensen from including as lengthy and as elaborate an introduction and other comments as Bailyn, Jensen's collection is much more representative geographically and equally as good in quality. In other words, other sections than New England wrote as well or better on liberty than the inhabitants of the northeast. Both Bailyn's and Jensen's books suggest our need for a more comprehensive collection of political tracts, colony-by-colony, from any and all sources (both these men limited themselves as to sources in one way or another) if we are to visualize the body of Revolutionary political literature. *The Great Awakening: Documents Illustrating the Crisis and Its Consequences* (Indianapolis, Bobbs-Merrill), edited by Alan Heimert with the assistance of long notes from Perry Miller's writings, is a much better balanced book in its selections than Heimert's *Religion and the Amercian Mind* (*ALS, 1966*, pp. 112–113) is in its discussions. Heimert includes selections from writers here whom he has barely mentioned in his earlier study. He still rides his thesis of Calvinist as liberal and Liberal as conservative, but this is a highly useful and revealing anthology of the religious literature of the colonies just before the Revolution.

iii. Biography: Narrative and Critical

A number of small new bits of information or corrections or annotations for earlier published biographies appeared this year. Robert E. Hemenway in "Charles Brockden Brown's Law Study: Some New Documents" (*AL*, XXXIX, 199–204) discusses two recently discovered papers of some significance. Alyce Sands, "Establishing John Saffin's Birthdate" (*EALN*, II, i, 12–17) discovers and then draws conclusions from a combination of British and American documents, altogether giving us a nice bit of investigation. Leo M. Kaiser in "On Mussi's *In virgam Franklinianam*" (*WMQ*, XXIV, 288–291) traces the text and shows variants of a poem written in 1784 and included in William Temple Franklin's *Memoirs of the Life and Writings of Benjamin Franklin* (1818). A. O. Aldridge's "The First Published Memoir of Franklin" (*WMQ*, XXIV, 624–628) shows that an episode included in the later *Autobiography* appeared in a London newspaper as early as 1778. Aldridge comments upon the possible significance of the differences between the two texts. James A. Bear, Jr., has edited together two useful recollections, one by a slave and one by an overseer, in *Jefferson at Monticello: Memoirs of a Monticello Slave* ... [and] *The Private Life of Thomas Jefferson* ... (Charlottesville, Univ. Press of Va.). A few lines are added to the biography of the great theologian in Leonard T. Grant's "A Preface to Jonathan Edwards' Financial Difficulties" (*JPH*, XLV, 27–32) and Edwin Sponseller's *Northampton and Jonathan Edwards* (Shippensburg, Pa., Shippensburg State Coll.).

Two books in a new series offer a multiple-sided presentation of the lives and characters of two major political writers. Merrill D. Peterson in *Thomas Jefferson: A Profile* (New York, Hill and Wang) has brought together eleven selections from specialists and a brief biography of his own. Ideas, interests, achievements, character, are among the subjects of individual sections. The same thing has been done by Jacob E. Cooke in *Alexander Hamilton: A Profile* (New York, Hill and Wang), with thirteen essays focused on character and various activities and events. More narrative biography is the excellent concise sketch of Jefferson's and Hamilton's Tory contemporary, "The Reverend Jonathan Boucher, Turbulent Tory (1738–1804)" (*HMPEC*, XXXVI, 323–356), by Ralph E. Fall. Parts of John Woolman's life and character are appraised in two essays: Phillips Moulton, "John Woolman's Approach to Social Action—as Exemplified in Relation to Slavery" (*CH*, XXXV [1966], 399–410) suggests individual qualities of the Quaker which help to account for his effectiveness; Henry J. Cadbury, "Sailing to England with John Woolman" (*QH*, LV [1966], 88–103), uses twenty-one recently uncovered letters from Woolman's traveling companion. Several significant details as to Woolman as social creature and as strong individualist are revealed.

Philip M. Marsh, one of the most indefatigable of Freneau scholars, added to his several books and many essays and edited documents a biography, *Philip Freneau, Poet and Journalist* (Minneapolis, Dillon Press). Feeling a double need, a biography less scholarly in style than Leary's and at the same time one which emphasizes the prose to a greater extent, Marsh has drawn an enormous knowledge of his subject's prose writings and given in one volume a great deal of material Leary did not include. Unfortunately, in the effort to write in a "popular" form, the author has given only rather vague bibliographical documentation for his ascriptions of much of the prose, presumably expecting the scholarly reader to look up the scattered essays and editions which offer his real proof of argument. The style is breezy, the sections within chapters somewhat choppy because of their brevity. But the book is readable, and the intellectually curious who are not academics may find it worthwhile reading. Its greatest value for the scholar may lie in the large section on the Santa Cruz years, for Marsh visited the site and used local documents. And the extensive and extended review of Freneau as journalist is impressive and enlightening despite the scholar-reader's uneasy feeling in many places that he would like the reasons for ascription to the Poet of the Revolution.

Two segment-biographies of major figures, both with grave shortcomings, add little to our knowledge of their subjects. The first of these, on the same author as Marsh's study, is not so reliable. Jacob Axelrad's *Philip Freneau, Champion of Democracy* (Austin, Univ. of Tex. Press) has a promising subject, but despite a wealth of available materials it adds almost nothing to our knowledge of its subject even from the one point of view announced in the title, and it contains some careless errors in fact (pp. 392, 411). Roger Burlingame's *Benjamin Franklin, Envoy Extraordinary, The Secret Missions and Open Pleasures of Benjamin Franklin in London and Paris* (New York, Coward-McCann) is a popular biographical sketch of some interest to the general reader but marred by factual error and highly doubtful and exaggerated conclusions.

The best critical "biographies" of the year were of minor figures, both dramatists. Rodney M. Baine in *Robert Munford, America's First Comic Dramatist* (Athens, Univ. of Ga. Press) gives a well-researched study of Colonel Munford's life in Virginia and a good analysis of his plays. One feels the need of more context, of some suggestion of the potential significance of the writing of these plays, and of their rural production and performance, in the Virginia of the Revolutionary decade. G. Thomas Tanselle, who has already written several essays regarding his subject, gives us what he calls "a starting point for further research" in *Royall Tyler* (Cambridge, Mass., Harvard Univ. Press). This is really a critical study with biographical introductions and "settings" for studies of Tyler's plays, poetry, novel, and essays. Despite the author's modest assertions that this is only introduction, the comments on most of the longer and better-known writings seem adequate for the general student.

Though this book could have been placed in the next section of this
essay with as much reason as in this one, it *is* our first real investigation of this man and his work, from beginning to end.

iv. Criticism and Literary and Cultural History

Of all the seventy-six or more books and essays of criticism and
literary and cultural history only a part can be discussed in the space
available. The explications of Taylor's verse, the new analytical
studies of Charles Brockden Brown, and the usual additions to all
phases of Franklin's work are the three largest groups of material.
But Edwards, Cotton Mather, Roger Williams, Jefferson, John Smith,
Hooker, and Brackenridge received attention more than once.
Eighteenth-century writers were discussed more often but the seventeenth century was by no means neglected.

"The Puritan Poetry of Anne Bradstreet" (*TSLL*, IX, 317–331),
by Robert D. Richardson, Jr., shows her "Contemplations" to be an
expression of the conflict between "love of this world and reliance
on the next," which is New England Puritanism. Her other poetry is
also given a good, sound, though by no means original, analysis.
Everett H. Emerson's "Thomas Hooker, The Puritan as Theologian"
(*ATR*, XLIX, 3–16) is the best examination to date of Hooker's
theological views, what they do and do not include. Elémire Zolla,
"Lo stile di Thomas Hooker" (*SA*, XI [1965], 43–52), asserts that the
plain style of this theologian, as expressed in his sermons, is actually
not so plain, and is to be understood only in the author's own
rhetorical, classical, and general cultural background. Sacvan Berco-
vitch writes of "Cotton Mather Against Rhyme: Milton and the
Psalterium Americanum" (*AL*, XXXIX, 191–193), arguing that the
American's defense of unrhymed (not blank) verse owes more to
Milton's practice and theory in *Paradise Lost* than it does to Mather's
British neo-classical contemporaries. Ross L. Morton's "Hawthorne's
Bosom Serpent and Mather's *Magnalia*" (*ESQ*, No. 47, p. 13) sug-
gests an episode copied into the *Magnalia* as a possible source, in-
stead of Spenser, for Hawthorne's story.

Everett H. Emerson considered two important aspects of our
earliest major prose writer in "Captain John Smith, Autobiographer"
(*EALN*, II, i, 18–23) and "Captain John Smith as Editor: *The
Generall Historie*" (*VMHB*, LXXV, 143–156). Of the eight essays

and one monograph on Edward Taylor's verse attention should be called to the thoughtful study of his imagery, Peter Nicolaisen's *Die Bildlichkeit in der Dichtung Edward Taylors* (KBAA, IV, Neumünster, Karl Wacholtz, 1966), which lays stress on the Bible, not his New England experience, as the principal origin of his figures. More than imagery is included: Taylor's problem of method, his use of the abstract, his relation to his British contemporaries and predecessors, are considered. Ursula Brumm replies to Cecelia Halbert's study (*ALS, 1966*, p. 106) of Tree-of-Life imagery in "Der 'Baum des Lebens' in den Meditationen Edward Taylors" (*JA*, XII, 109–123), in which Brumm quarrels with Halbert on the ground that the biblical-theological source of the image is *the* significant thing. Brumm seems to miss Halbert's point, which does not really conflict with her own. Allen Penner, "Edward Taylor's Meditation One" (*AL*, XXXIX, 193–199) argues that this poem functions as a prologue for *Preparatory Meditations* and analyzes the poem to prove his point. A general re-examination is Evan Prosser's "Edward Taylor's Poetry" (*NEQ*, XL, 375–398), which points out significant relationships between *Preparatory Meditations* and *God's Determinations*. Other essays (see *MLA* International Bibliography, 1967) discuss self-depreciation, the use of text of sermons in the verse, the occasion and the audience, the momentum of metaphor, the diction, and individually, "Meditation Forty-Two." Metaphor and doctrine receive most attention.

Two books on Williams' religious or governmental theories are of some importance. Irwin H. Polishook, *Roger Williams, John Cotton, and Religious Freedom* (Englewood Cliffs, N.J., Prentice-Hall), in an extensive introduction considers Williams' interpretation of the role of government as contrasted with Cotton's, and then presents a useful series of documents from the two, preceded by or interspersed with other pertinent materials, such as the "civil-magistrates" selection from Winthrop's *Journal*. The selections are perhaps too brief to satisfy the general scholar but should be useful to the student who seeks some understanding of the controversy. Edmund Morgan's *Roger Williams: The Church and the State* (New York, Harcourt, Brace, and World) is a fine concise exposition by a major historian of a major phase of Williams' thought. It is the structure of that thought, the intricate and beautiful symmetry of ideas broken occasionally when "he succumbed to the temptation to argue from a

position that he himself had rejected but knew his opponents accepted," that Morgan wishes to analyze and to demonstrate. He declares that Williams cannot be examined in nineteenth- or twentieth-
century terms, but in the intellectual milieu of his own century, in
which "he dared to think." The notes may not be detailed enough
for the scholarly reader who wishes to know *exactly* all the sources
and all the detailed ramifications of Williams' thought. But Morgan
has given us a masterly context of "thought-climate" and Williams'
reaction to it. This is a book to be read by every student of the New
England mind. Here are the bases for fresh analyses of that which
is significant.

Besides the two biographical studies of Edwards, there were
three critical essays of some value. Gerhard T. Alexis, "Jonathan Edwards and the Theocratic Ideal" (*CH*, XXXV, 328–343), gives a
survey of Edwards' consideration of an earthly kingdom or theocracy
by relating his works to what was going on around him. Clifford
Davidson in "Jonathan Edwards and Mysticism" (*CLAJ*, XI, 149–
156) sees the Puritan preacher as standing above both rationalism
and mysticism, a man who united pietism and orthodoxy. And Clyde
A. Holbrook, "Edwards and the Ethical Question" (*HTR*, LX, 163–
175), analyzes Edwards' views of true virtue in relation to those of
Francis Hutcheson but spends most space indicating ways in which
Edwards' view may or may not be applicable today.

Mary Maples Dunn in *William Penn: Politics and Conscience*
(Princeton, Princeton Univ. Press) has surveyed the Founder's life
from the point of view he displays in his actions and writings on the
relation between politics and conscience. The key to his politics, she
tells us, was liberty of conscience. She points out the paradoxes of
his character and his career, concluding that "For all his mistakes,
and in large part from religious motives, he helped to create a secular
world and a new empire enjoying a new freedom."

Charlotte Kretzoi's "The Concept of Poetry in Colonial America"
(*HSE*, III, 5–21) shows some superficial reading of New England
poets represented in anthologies, too frequently outdated ones, but
comes nowhere near developing its announced subject. Eighteenth-
century poets, who frequently did have a theory or concept, are almost totally ignored. Satiric verse, at least next to the elegiac in
popularity, goes unnoted, as does natural description. It is an un-

fortunately poor presentation of colonial verse and theory to Hungarian readers.

Franca Rossi's "Le prime relazioni inglesi sulla Virginia" (*SA*, XI [1965], 7–41) surveys the earliest exploration literature from the Roanoke Voyages to John Smith and sees in it a contradiction of good and bad, of the strange and the familiar, which contributed to a development toward reality and realism during the half century in which it appeared. Ola Elizabeth Winslow's "Seventeenth Century Prologue" (*Essays on American Literature*, pp. 21–29) is a well-written, sympathetic brief survey which catches the spirit of the early writing of such transplanted Englishmen as Josselyn, Norwood, Hariot, and Whitaker. In the same collection Theodore Hornberger's "Thomas Prince: Minister" (pp. 30–46) considers the colonial historian and bookman as he was, first of all, a preacher. In Prince's sermons Hornberger considers style, theme, erudition, scientific attitude, and religious conviction. The analysis of Prince's funeral sermon will be useful as a criterion for the study of other works in this genre.

As the notices of texts and biography above have attested, Franklin received as usual much attention. A. O. Aldridge in "Form and Substance in Franklin's Autobiography" (*Essays on American Literature*, pp. 47–62) adds further interpretation to the many studies of the *Autobiography* noticed in previous issues of *ALS*. Aldridge feels that recent critics have made too much of conscious art and perfected method, and therefore attempts to get straight at its essential qualities by analyzing parts. He concludes finally that the delight from reading this book is primarily psychological rather than artistic. Nancy T. Clasby's "Franklin's Style: Irony and the Comic" (*DA*, XXVIII, 622A) sees Franklin's style as "the product and essence of a lifetime of expressive action." J. Y. Brinton, "Franklin and the Conspiracy of Cataline" (*LC*, XXXIII, 3–7) indicates in a particular example how Franklin used the classics intelligently even though he was by no means a classical scholar. James A. Sappenfield, "The Growth of the Franklin Image: The Philadelphia Years" (*DA*, XXVII, 3469A) suggests that the symbolic Franklin's qualities later established in the public mind were already present by 1758. Marie Fletcher in "Benjamin Franklin's *General Magazine*: An Image of the Colonial Mind" (*McNR*, XVII [1966] 3–12) shows that the three

principal concerns of the time were the war with Spain, the problem of currency, and the Great Awakening (especially concerning
Whitefield).

One of the most important books in several years on the Philadelphian is Alfred Owen Aldridge's *Benjamin Franklin and Nature's
God* (Durham, N.C., Duke Univ. Press), easily the best study of the
subject. Aldridge has uncovered some unknown Franklin writings
illustrating religious attitudes and some new sources for all that
Franklin has to say on the matter of organized and personal religion.
The two other perspectives of the book are an examination of Franklin's *credo* and a tracing of his relationship to churches and sects.
Perhaps a bit more indicative title might have been "Franklin's relation to the various religions and religious bodies of his time." This
is a superb book, necessary equally to the student of Franklin and
the student of eighteenth-century deism.

Three chapters of David Levin's *In Defense of Historical Writing*
(New York, Hill and Wang) are concerned with literature to 1800.
Beginning with the premise that "in formal history the highest literary
art is that combination of clear understanding and exposition which
brings us closest to a just evaluation of the past now present to us,"
Levin examines the uses made of the unpublished "Paterna" by later
historians who establish a character for Mather which does not embody all the available facts. This is his chapter on "The Hazing of
Cotton Mather," already noticed in its separate periodical publication (*ALS*, 1963, p. 100). Even more incisive in its analysis and suggestion of method and aim is "The Autobiography of Benjamin
Franklin: The Puritan Experimenter in Life and Art" (*ALS, 1964,*
p. 100), a study in Franklin's literary skill and of modern interpretation of what he said. In "Historical Fact in Fiction and Drama: The
Salem Witchcraft Trials," the author studies Hawthorne's "Young
Goodman Brown," Miller's *The Crucible*, and other recent works in
their success or lack of it in pointing up in graceful and vivid form
qualities of Puritanism which documents have brought to us. These
are incisive criticisms of the difficulties of understanding biographical
characters portrayed by eighteenth-century and twentieth-century
writers, and of the value of fact to the contemporary writer on older
themes, times, and persons. A book to be pondered by scholar and
creative writer.

Of the four essays on Jefferson, two deal with his religion, which

was close akin to Franklin's. M. J. Mehta, "The Religion of Thomas
Jefferson" (*IAC*, XVI, 95–103), gives a clear but hardly original
statement of the Virginian's position. Elliot K. Wicks in "Thomas
Jefferson—A Religious Man with a Passion for Religious Freedom"
(*HMPEC*, XXXVI, 271–284) summarizes his subject's religious philosophy and then shows how it led to his struggle for religious
liberty. "Thomas Jefferson: Educational Philosopher" (*PAPS*, CXI,
1–4), by Samuel A. Pleasants, describes a recently discovered letter
to Charles Sigourney in which Jefferson again states his educational
views. John Krnacik's "Thomas Jefferson's Interest in Italian Life,
Language, and Art" (*KFLQ*, XIII [1966], 130–137) brings together
about all the known materials on the subject but proves little. Jefferson's great lifelong friend-and-enemy is the subject of Earl N. Har-
bert's "John Adams' Private Voice: The *Diary* and *Autobiography*"
(*TSE*, XV, 89–105). This is a significant study in its appraisal of
Adams as stylist and in its pointing up of his model-forming method
for the history of literature and the writing of his own family in
future generations. Henry Adams is anticipated in a dozen ways in
these writings of his ancestor.

Daniel B. Shea, Jr.'s "Spiritual Autobiography in Early America"
(*DA*, XXVII, 2135A) is an avowed attempt to penetrate the conventions of Quaker journal and Puritan spiritual narrative in order to
discover where the autobiographer confronted his experience and
shaped it to a purpose. The author finds change and development
toward didacticism in the Mathers and a final abandonment of the
exploratory function for a guidance one in Franklin. Kenneth J.
Spencley, "The Rhetoric of Decay in New England Writing, 1665–
1730" (*DA*, XXVII, 3851A), shows the sources and nature of the
metaphorical language used by the Puritans from the first generation to the death of the Mathers. E. S. Morgan's "Puritan Hostility
to the Theatre" (*PAPS*, CX, 340–347) enables us to understand more
clearly the reasons for the New England opposition to players and
acting commented upon in every history of the early theater. He
shows that Puritans gave valid moral reasons for their hostility, but
that there was also the strong and immediate additional one that the
sermon could not compete with the play.

Perhaps the most intriguing thing about "Arthur Blackamore:
The Virginia Colony and the Early English Novel" (*VMHB*, LXXV,
22–34), by Richard Beale Davis, is the suggestion that possibly at

least one of Blackamore's two novels of 1720 and 1723 was written before he left America and might therefore be our first novel. Dedications are to Virginians, and at least one character in each is modelled on a person Blackamore knew in Williamsburg. Peter Thorpe's "Sarah Kemble Knight and the Picaresque Tradition" (*CLAJ*, X [1966], 114–121) demonstrates ways in which the New England schoolmistress followed and strayed from the conventions of the picaresque tradition in her *Journal*. Helen Loschky, "The 'Columbiad' Tradition: Joel Barlow and Others" (*BBr*, XXI, 192–206) offers interesting evidence of Barlow's use of imitations of his own *Vision* in the reworkings which turned the earlier poem into the *Columbiad*, "a strange example of an artist emulating himself through his reflection in the work of other artists."

William K. Bottorff, "Humphreys' 'Ode to Laura': A Lost Satire" (*EALN*, II, ii, 36–38) reads this poem from Elihu H. Smith's *American Poems (1793)* (*ALS, 1966*, p. 102) as a mock-serious rather than serious love poem. This classification from today's point of view is more flattering to the author, but the arguments are not really convincing. Humphreys' French-American contemporary is studied in Elayne A. Rapping's "Theory and Experience in Crèvecoeur's America" (*AQ*, XIX, 707–718), where the "Farmer" is seen as demonstrating, in eighteenth-century context, how dream and reality in American life differ, how in practice theory breaks down, as shown by Crèvecoeur's experiences as he moves in space and time. "*Democracy* and *Republic* as Understood in Late Eighteenth-Century America" (*AS*, XLI, 83–95), by Robert W. Shoemaker, quotes or refers to Madison, Paine, James Wilson, and other political writers in drawing significant but hardly new distinctions between the meanings of the two words.

The writings of two figures concerned primarily with fiction were examined from several points of view. William L. Nance in "Satiric Elements in Brackenridge's *Modern Chivalry*" (*TSLL*, IX, 381–389) concludes that the author derived his satiric technique almost entirely from the great masters of the art who preceded him and that the satiric emphasis brought a unity of tone to a work which was structurally disunified. This is a pioneer analysis of a phase of Brackenridge which should be investigated further. William B. Craddock's "A Structural Examination of Hugh Henry Brackenridge's *Modern Chivalry*" (*DA*, XXVII, 3040A) presents a highly interesting summary of his findings, showing the great differences between Parts One and Two, and how the 1819 revised text gives numerous clues to what Brackenridge intended but never accomplished. Daniel Marder's longer study, *Hugh Henry Brackenridge* (TUSAS, No. 114), views Brackenridge as a son of the Scottish Enlightenment trying to plant its literary values in the life of the frontier. Marder also sees his subject's Revolutionary writings as preeminently oratory, whether poems, plays, or essays. He concludes that in sum Brackenridge's work anticipates by a full generation the literature of romantic attitudes attentive to the West, for he portrays a new country free from English dominance, the America which Emerson was later to say began west of the Alleghenies.

For the second straight year Charles Brockden Brown was a favorite subject. That the interest in him is not confined to the United States may be noted by the appearance of a competent study by an Italian scholar, Marisa Bulgheroni, in *La Tentazione della chimera: Charles Brockden Brown e le origini del romanzo americano* (Rome, Edizione di Storia e Letteratura, 1965). Dated 1965 but not available until 1967, Mrs. Bulgheroni's study has expanded the essay on Brown she published in *Studi americani* in 1964. She views the work of Brown as "documento singolare delle origini della narrativa americana preludio alle scoperte di Poe e di Hawthorne, constituisce, al di là del suo apparente provincialismo, un capitolo della storia del romanzo moderno, ricco di anticipazioni e di alchimi e tematiche." Further Italian interest in Brown is shown in a review-article by Claudio Gorlier, "Due classici dissepolti: *Wieland* e *Clarel*" (*Approdo*, XII [1966], 3–8), which discusses Brown's novel recently translated into Italian. It is a fair critical evaluation, showing an understanding of Brown's mechanics and emphasizing the "black" qualities of the work.

Other work on Brown is both general and specific. Kenneth Bernard, "*Edgar Huntly*: Charles Brockden Brown's Unsolved Murder" (*LC*, XXXIII, 30–53), "proves" through imagery, parallelism, psychoanalysis, identifications in symbols, and ingenious reasoning that Edgar Huntly himself committed the murder on which the plot turns. Thus he proposes a solution which he believes explains Clithero and other garbled character and action in the novel. E. Bruce Kirkham in "A Note on *Wieland*" (*AN&Q*, V, 86–87) explains the elder Wieland's actions as the result of his reading the seventeenth- and eighteenth-century Camisards, who wrote mystical works in which singing voices, persons with the gift of prophecy, and dependence on the Bible for guidance in earthly action are normal ingredients. Among the more general works, Morton Shapiro looks at "Sentimentalism in the Novels of Charles Brockden Brown" (*DA*, XXVII [1966], 1384A), pointing out that though Brown is usually treated as a Gothic or philosophic-reform novelist, many elements of sentimentalism in technique, characterization, and theme are present in all of them. This is a suggestive summary of a study which perhaps should be published in full. Arthur G. Kimball in "Rational Fictions: A Study of Charles Brockden Brown" (*DA*, XXVIII, 232A) summarizes the findings of his dissertation, placing Brown squarely in the literary philosophical tradition of his own time, with emphasis on its—and Brown's—Lockean background. In "Savages and Savagism: Brockden Brown's Dramatic Irony" (*SIR*, VI, 214–225) Kimball sees most previous studies as misinterpretations of the role of the Indian in *Edgar Huntly*, for he believes Brown was using the term "savage" ironically as a commentary on the white man rather than the red. Through Huntly's discovery of his own savage potential Brown is protesting Enlightenment optimism and commenting ironically on man's rational and irrational behavior. Robert E. Hemenway's "The Novels of Charles Brockden Brown: A Critical Study" (*DA*, XVIII, 676A) sees both the Gothic and sentimental traditions in Brown but shows how, by a "unique blend of metaphor and myth, rhythm and stasis," peculiarly American fictional qualities, Brown transcends both the older traditions. Though none of these studies of our first major novelist is startlingly original, several of them do represent fresh critical insight as to the mind and method of the artist.

In his *Belief and Disbelief in American Literature* (Chicago, Univ. of Chicago Press), Howard Mumford Jones begins with a discussion of a figure from our period. He chooses Thomas Paine as the representative American writer of the Revolutionary and post-Revolutionary period not because he was our greatest thinker but because he is the principal ancestor of "the radical fringe in American religion" which yet continues. Much of the secularization in once church-related institutions in later America, as well as our progressing study in comparative religions, is reflected in Paine's utterances.

Richard M. Gummere, who has written extensively of the classics and classical influences in colonial America, has added to his earlier studies *Seven Wise Men of Colonial America* (Cambridge, Mass., Harvard Univ. Press), a series of sketches of Hugh Jones, Robert Calef, Michael Wigglesworth, Samuel Davies, Henry M. Muhlenberg, Benjamin Rush, and Thomas Paine. Really a sequel to his *The American Colonial Mind and the Classical Tradition* (1963), which was devoted mainly to major intellectual figures and reactions, the present book shows how seven able and highly individualistic men used the classics themselves but denied that the classics should be a part of the training of the ordinary citizen. Each case-figure is a fascinating story in itself. Except for Wigglesworth, Rush, and Paine, these men have been too generally neglected. Even this approach from one angle suggests their more general significance. The use of Jones, Davies, and Muhlenberg indicates our growing interest in non-Puritan religious literature. And the attitude of all or most of them toward popular classical education is one of our earliest historical explanations of its gradual demise. Deceptively light and easy in tone, this is a suggestive little book.

This latest gathering of the late Perry Miller's essays, *Nature's Nation* (Cambridge, Mass., Harvard Univ. Press, Belknap), with an introduction by Kenneth B. Murdock, represents the great scholar at his best, and of course that is saying a great deal. One agrees with Murdock that this book is "an indispensable guide to full understanding of Perry Miller's achievement, in effect a summary of the basic elements of his thought." Fifteen essays, several previously unpublished, begin with Puritan covenant theology and, as they go on, shift the emphasis from religion "to the philosophy of nature to the development of an original literature." Frequently Miller is analyzing at the same time all three sorts of quests for self-identity. The collection is at once one of the major examples of a great author's work, a fuller explication of his particular use of terms and events he touches upon in previous books (as *jeremiad* and *benevolence*), and an example of the narrowness of his colonial concept—that is, New England is America. One essay, " 'Preparation for Salvation' in Seventeenth-Century New England" is on a subject recently better and more elaborately handled by Norman Pettit. One or two essays (as Number Five) are dull and insecure in the foundations of their reasoning. But most of them are brilliant imaginative triumphs.

The University of Tennessee

10. Nineteenth-Century Fiction[1]

Joseph V. Ridgely

Though still far outshone by the five luminaries not surveyed here, Crane, Howells, and Cooper managed to sustain their lesser-magnitude brightness in 1967. Other rankings remained relatively unchanged, though our busy explorers in the field inflated the MLA International Bibliography with more than 160 contributions. Only the comparatively more significant of these will be commented on.

i. General Topics

Several doctoral dissertations explore general subjects or themes, sometimes helping to create a context for greater works. John H. McElroy's "Images of the Seventeenth-Century Puritan in American Novels, 1823–1860" (DA, XXVII, 3845A) reports that twenty-eight novels treated the Puritan either as the self-sacrificing father of democracy, as the stern figure who tried to force the individual into orthodoxy, or as the imperialist expanding into Indian territory. Arthur L. Madson, in "The Scapegoat Story in the American Novel" (DA, XXVII [1966], 1828A), cites three works of this period—Cooper's *The Bravo*, Howells' *A Hazard of New Fortunes*, and Frederic's *The Copperhead*—in identifying a ritual pattern in which a young hero or middle-aged chieftain is sacrificed to revitalize the community. Conceding that in a "classical sense" the term grotesque cannot be defined, Malcolm A. Griffith, in "The Grotesque in American Fiction" (DA, XXVII, 3047A), nevertheless finds in the work of Crane and Norris that the grotesque character is intended to be a reproduction of a real human being who deviates widely from the norm. Ruth A. Coplan's "A Study of Predominant Themes in Selected Best-Selling American Fiction, 1850–1915" (DA, XXVIII, 191A–

1. This essay excludes five major figures: Hawthorne, James, Melville, Poe, and Twain.

192A) examines seventy-one best-sellers, concluding that seventy
per cent deal with one or more of four major themes: the movement
west and migration from farm to city, reform movements, religion,
and the rise to the top. Both in his dissertation (*DA*, XXVIII, 2224A)
and an article (*MASJ*, VIII, i, 90–97) Robert J. Ward focuses on
"Europe in American Historical Romances 1890–1910" to learn that
118 romances used the matter of European history in a generally
favorable way, reflecting America's growing awareness of an Old
World it had once spurned.

Three articles also attempt wide-ranging analyses. John O. Wal-
ler traces the changing attitudes toward the novel from outrage to
acceptance to pride by studying "*The Methodist Quarterly Review*
and Fiction, 1818–1900" (*BNYPL*, LXXI, 573–590). Elmer F. Suder-
man cites works by Margaret Deland, James Lane Allen, Henry
Adams, Harold Frederic, and Mark Twain in assessing "Skepticism
and Doubt in Late Nineteenth Century American Novels" (*BSUF*,
VIII, i, 63–72). He finds that novelists began by showing that new
scientific knowledge, while lending weight to skepticism, also gave
man a firmer faith; they ended, however, by anticipating more
recent fiction in declaring that man is incapable of discovering God's
existence. Henry Nash Smith's title is promising: "The Morals of
Power: Business Enterprise as a Theme in Mid-Nineteenth-Century
American Fiction" (*Essays on American Literature*, pp. 90–125).
The article, though, is largely concerned with Judge Pyncheon of
The House of the Seven Gables and Colonel Sellers of *The Gilded
Age*, as Smith explores "the first gropings toward literary treatment
of the forces released by the industrial revolution."

ii. Irving, Cooper, and Their Contemporaries

The year's most notable general study of this period is James T.
Callow's *Kindred Spirits: Knickerbocker Writers and American Artists, 1807–1855* (Chapel Hill, Univ. of N.C. Press). Cooper and
Irving figure largely in this studious examination of the mutually
beneficial relationships between writers and artists.

A comparatively neglected artist and author, Washington Allston,
also achieved separate revaluation. Nathalia Wright's informative
introduction to a facsimile edition of his *Lectures on Art and Poems*

(1850) and Monaldi (1841) (SF&R) argues that his achievement in
both fields is without parallel in America. John R. Walsh's "Washington Allston, Cosmopolite and Early Romantic" (*GaR*, XXI, 491–
502) is primarily biographical, but it offers the challenging judgment
that he was a "greater factor in the American romantic movement
than his obscured reputation now indicates."

While we await the new edition of Washington Irving, scholars
continue to garner fragments about his life and writings. Ben H. Mc-
Clary produces the texts of nine new letters in three separate articles
(*PQ*, XLVI, 277–283; *N&Q*, XIV, 304; *SSL*, IV [1966], 101–104);
five of these deal with his aid to brother authors and three with his
relationships with the John G. Lockharts. Daniel R. Barnes's "Washington Irving: An Unrecorded Periodical Publication" (*SB*, XX,
260–261) reprints an 1852 item, "Our Changing Sky and Climate."
Dahlia J. Terrell's "A Textual Study of Washington Irving's *A Tour
on the Prairies*" (*DA*, XXVIII, 245A) declares that no edition has
printed the full text accurately; the study contributes some significant emendations. Two articles are primarily critical appraisals.
Donald A. Ringe's "New York and New England: Irving's Criticism
of American Society" (*AL*, XXXVIII, 455–467) analyzes those works
in which the regional conflict—grounded on the New Yorker's objections to what was seen as the New Englander's materialism, lack of
tradition, and social fluidity—is made to serve a satiric end. Henry A.
Pochmann's "Washington Irving: Amateur or Professional?" (*Essays
on American Literature*, pp. 63–76) reaches the balanced conclusion
that Irving carefully calculated his own potentials as an artist, a fact
that makes him less an amateur "toying with esoteric aspirations beyond his reach than the canny professional gauging his grasp by
his reach."

Much headier claims are still being advanced for the artistry of
James Fenimore Cooper; the year saw—in addition to the usual rash
of minor notes and rehashed critiques—one uneven but still useful
book and several solid critical essays. In *James Fenimore Cooper:
The American Scott* (New York, Barnes & Noble), George Dekker,
an American scholar teaching in England, has produced the first full-
length survey of Cooper's fiction to come from a British University.
Though he occasionally relies heavily on his predecessors, Dekker
is essentially an intuitive critic, seeking some means of substantiating
his sense that Cooper is a more distinctive artist than is generally

conceded. Such a dichotomy is evident, for instance, in his comment that *The Deerslayer* has on him "the impact of major fiction" but he finds it difficult to explain why this is so. Justification for such impressions is finally sought in discussions of Cooper's social and political views and in his "assimilation and development of the historical novel as first perfected by Sir Walter Scott." As a whole the book is engagingly written, though individual judgments are often quirky.

Dekker's high estimate is generally echoed in David Howard's "James Fenimore Cooper's *Leatherstocking Tales*: 'without a cross'" (*Tradition and Tolerance*, pp. 9–54). Howard reasserts the established judgment that Cooper is "no longer the mere adventure writer" but a serious critic who must be dealt with seriously. Not only the "inventor and master of literary genres," he is also—and more importantly for Howard—one of the first to concern himself with the fundamental theme of all American writers, "the confrontation of American and European experience." Another European critic, Klaus Lanzinger, offers in "James Fenimore Coopers progressive Haltung zur Westexpansion" (*NS*, XV [1966], 456–470) the rather flat conclusion that between *The Pioneers* and *The Oak Openings* Cooper's attitude toward the march of civilization became increasingly affirmative. A more specific treatment of the civilization-wilderness conflict is found in E. Arthur Robinson's "Conservation in Cooper's *The Pioneers*" (*PMLA*, LXXXII, 564–578). Robinson acutely sees the novel as being structured about the three chief ways in which characters regard the heritage of nature: the belief that natural resources exist for personal benefit; Judge Temple's conviction that resources must be conserved with an eye to the future; and Natty Bumppo's doubly opposing vision of "an almost complete preservation of a state of nature."

In the year's only reported dissertation, "Patterns of Action and Imagery in the Leatherstocking Tales" (*DA*, XXVIII, 2254A), Laurence E. MacPhee also seeks to advance claims for Cooper's artistry. Such patterns are described as "dialectical; they counterpoint fixed moral and intellectual qualities whose conflict is predictable in Cooper's world." A useful source study is James H. Pickering's "*Satanstoe*: Cooper's Debt to William Dunlap" (*AL*, XXXVIII, 468–477). A chapter in the history of Italian-American literary relations is documented by James Woodress' "The Fortunes of Cooper in Italy" (*SA*, XI [1965], 53–76). The first American novelist translated into Italian (1828), Cooper has enjoyed continuous popularity among Italians: 148 editions in 138 years.

The "Southern Cooper," William Gilmore Simms, continued to entice authors of dissertations but otherwise drew negligible comment. David A. McDowell undertook the ambitious task of surveying "The Place of William Gilmore Simms's Fiction in American Literature: A History of the Criticism From 1833 Through 1965" (*DA*, XXVII, 3464A). Two conditions have confused the issue of Simms's literary reputation, McDowell thinks: his character and personality promised more of literary art than he ever delivered and he became the subject of "sectional irrelevancies." Though Simms's works collectively have about the place they deserve, "separate episodes, tales, character portrayals, and flashes of creative insight provide a wealth of material for criticism and study." The assessment is unexceptionable, if unexciting. Iris S. Argo remines an old vein in "Simms and the Elizabethans" (*DA*, XXVII, 3004A), developing the thesis that he drew the principles for his fiction largely from his readings in Elizabethan drama. Another not unexpected source is tracked in Mary A. Wimsatt's "Simms and Irving" (*MissQ*, XX, 25–37). The youthful Simms, she says, borrowed both techniques and material; in later life, despite his growing dissatisfaction with Irving, he continued to draw upon him.

Harriet Beecher Stowe was the subject of two solidly informed contributions to *Essays on American Literature*. Richard B. Davis' "Mrs. Stowe's Characters-in-Situations and a Southern Literary Tradition" (pp. 108–125) discerns that in *Uncle Tom's Cabin* and *Dred* she "presented a peculiar variety of characters and their unusual tragic situations with such force as to indicate to later writers the potentialities of the plantation novel as a vehicle of depth and complexity and moral seriousness." James Woodress adds another chapter to the history of the widespread influence of her major book in "*Uncle Tom's Cabin* in Italy" (pp. 126–140). Citing the somewhat surprising fact that no other American book has been so widely distributed and read in Italy, Woodress finds that the chief difference between its nineteenth-century and its present status lies in its "emergence as a child's classic and its gradual decline as a novel for adults." Though it has never been out of print, its three periods of maximum popularity have coincided with the emergence of major political crises.

iii. Humor, Local Color, and Popular Fiction

General theorists and historians of humor and local color are for the moment quiescent, though the business of issuing anthologies and exhuming individual writers goes on as usual. John Q. Anderson's *With the Bark On: Popular Humor of the Old South* (Nashville, Vanderbilt Univ. Press) brings together under thematic headings brief items largely garnered from the New York *Spirit of the Times.* The editor's knowledgeable introduction and headnotes argue that the minor humorists "made an important contribution to the humor of the Old Southwest, which, in turn, contributed to the rise of realism." M. Thomas Inge has compiled some further sketches and tales by George Washington Harris in *High Times and Hard Times* (Nashville, Vanderbilt Univ. Press). The anthology, which includes penetrating critical commentary, collects all of Harris' known work except for the Sut Lovingood yarns printed in the 1867 edition. Inge's estimate may also be sampled in "The Satiric Artistry of George W. Harris" (*SNL*, IV, 63–72); Harris' method is said to be Menippean, the construction of a fable which involved his victims in a particular historical occasion.

The South was the region most frequently mapped by investigators of the local color movement. Merrill A. Skaggs, in "The Plain-Folk Tradition in Southern Local-Color Fiction" (*DA*, XXVII [1966], 1839A), traces the presence in fiction from 1830 onwards of "large numbers of common people who lived humble but honest lives of self-respect"; this interest is contrasted with the "plantation tradition." Lewis Leary concentrates on the earlier Hearn in "Lafcadio Hearn, 'One of Our Southern Writers': A Footnote to Southern Literary History" (*Essays on American Literature*, pp. 202–214), supporting the judgment that during his New Orleans days "there was not another in the South who dedicated himself more assiduously and successfully to literature as an art." Richard Cary, a Jewett specialist, turns to another woman local colorist in *Mary N. Murfree* (TUSAS, No. 121), correcting the unjust impression created by anthologists and historians that she wrote of nothing but Tennessee mountaineers. Each of eight chapters deftly explores a single facet of her canon, but most readers will still find little of her total output recoverable. One of the year's weightier essays is George Arms's "Kate Chopin's *The Awakening* in the Perspective of Her Literary Career" (*Essays on American Literature*, pp. 215–228), which places the short novel in the context of her other tales and provides a disciplined analysis of its major themes.

New England lagged somewhat behind, though it inspired a subtly penetrating article in Paul J. Eakin's "Sara Orne Jewett and the Meaning of Country Life" (*AL*, XXXVIII, 508–531). Containing, inevitably, a fresh reading of *The Country of the Pointed Firs*, it also considers at length the "moral impulse behind her realism, [which was] determined by her conservative view of the village community and of the individual within it." Eakin is particularly good in isolating a basic "visit pattern" in the fiction—a narrative design based on an outsider who makes a visit to a village or country locale. Richard Cary adds a footnote to Jewett biography and the record of her foreign readership in "Miss Jewett and Madame Blanc" (*CLQ*, VII, 466–488); portions of Madame Blanc's 1885 review of Miss Jewett are given in English translation (pp. 488–503). Scholars should also be aware of Cary's enlarged edition of *Sarah Orne Jewett Letters* (Waterville, Me., Colby Col. Press).

A New Englander often linked with Jewett is scrutinized by Perry D. Westbrook in *Mary Wilkins Freeman* (TUSAS, No. 122). The author prefers to call her a "regionalist" since the term includes both local color and "realistic evocation of a place and its people without excluding the idealism and ethical didacticism that was part of the spirit of New England." Though this critique sets Mrs. Freeman's work solidly in its cultural context, it is not likely to inspire the reader to further digging in the canon. Thomas R. Knipp's "The Quest for Form: The Fiction of Mary E. Wilkins Freeman" (*DA*, XXVII, 2501A) includes a searching examination of the New Englander's continued search for a literary vehicle suitable to regional themes. Knipp has praise for Mrs. Freeman's "remarkable powers of observation" in many of her shorter tales, but he faults most of the novels for succumbing to Dickensian melodrama.

Richard O'Connor, who has previously packaged Bret Harte and Jack London for popular consumption, now offers his *Ambrose Bierce* (Boston, Little, Brown). Though O'Connor strives for an up-to-the-minute air—"If [Bierce] is rediscovered in the near future, it will likely be as the first notable exponent of black humor in America"—he makes only small contributions to biography and adds nothing of moment to the critical estimate. The rationale behind such "popular" biographies—besides, one suspects, the publishers' conviction that they are more "readable" than scholarly works—remains hard to fathom.

Except for some of the dissertations and articles surveyed above under "General Topics," popular literature remained an unpopular subject this year.

iv. Howells, Realism, and Post-Civil War Fiction

Welcome news for period specialists was the founding of a new journal, *American Literary Realism 1870–1910*, edited by Clayton L. Eichelberger. Designed primarily as a research tool with a bibliographical focus, *ALR* proposes in future issues to provide thorough, annotated bibliographies of secondary comment on individual authors, to stimulate interest in lesser figures, and to act as a newsletter. The first issue (Fall, 1967) offers reviews by specialists of the present state of scholarship on seventeen figures, Bellamy, Bierce, Cable, Churchill, De Forest, Eggleston, Frederic, Garland, Hearn, Herrick, Jewett, Kirkland, London, Murfree, Norris, Page, and O. Henry. Like most present-day scholars, the editor confesses to uneasiness about the definition of "realism"; but the practical scope of the journal is indicated by the statement that it will be "concerned with all American writers of the designated period who struggled, no matter how falteringly, to incorporate 'the objective representation of contemporary social reality' in their work."

An ambitious general survey which extends somewhat beyond this period is undertaken by Jay Martin in *Harvests of Change: American Literature 1865–1914* (Englewood Cliffs, N. J., Prentice-Hall). With varying degrees of insight (and accuracy), Martin devotes a large portion of his book to discussions of a number of minor novelists under several catchall headings. "The Great American Novel" examines De Forest, Howells, Crane, and Norris; some specific comment will be noted below. "Paradise Lost" looks at a group of local colorists and regionalists of the South, West, and East, finding a tendency among them either to reconstruct myth romantically or to destroy it realistically. "Paradises (To Be) Regained" and "The Visible and Invisible Cities" contrast the worlds of the utopians, the muckrakers, the naturalists, and others. As a comprehensive review which attempts to abstract some unity from a period of radical change, the book will prove of considerable usefulness to students at large, but it is likely that the specialist on any one figure will have quibbles about the ways in which he is here categorized.

With the announcement of *A Selected Edition of W. D. Howells* the Howells revival has attained a summit of sorts.[2] Under the general editorship of Edwin H. Cady, the Indiana University Press will publish nearly forty volumes of fiction, criticism, travel writings, memoirs, letters, and a complete bibliography; a collected edition is a feat which the "Dean" himself was never able to manage. Meanwhile, Howells continues to run second only to Stephen Crane in general appeal. Unfortunately, the year's only book is a brief and somewhat timid one. In *Literary Realism of William Dean Howells* (Carbondale, Southern Ill. Univ. Press), William McMurray offers a reading of twelve major novels to support his thesis that Howells' literary realism closely resembles William James's pragmatism. Too often, however, the author relies heavily on plot summations and quotations from earlier commentators. McMurray's conclusion seems sound enough: "both Howells and James conceived man as living in an open world, a world which is yet unfinished in its meaning and in which man himself is the maker of that meaning." But, on the whole, the discussion is too sketchy to shed much illumination on his view that Howells was a more self-aware and skilful novelist than his critics have granted.

Though a pamphlet, William M. Gibson's *William D. Howells* (UMPAW, No. 63) successfully says a good deal in brief compass and is particularly good in its summation of Howells' theory of fiction. Gibson suggests further directions in his comment that interpretation of the novels is further advanced than is elucidation of his critical principles or the full range of his practical criticism. George E. Fortenberry devotes his dissertation to "The Comic Elements in the Fiction of William Dean Howells" (*DA*, XXVIII, 228A–229A), asserting that Howells' interest in Spanish literature led him to believe that there was an affinity between Spanish and American humor, particularly in their loose structure and geniality. Douglas R. Picht emphasizes the author's intention rather than method in tackling the vexed problem of realism in "William Dean Howells:

---

2. The first volume to be issued (*Their Wedding Journey*) actually appeared at the end of 1967 but carries a copyright date of 1968 and will be noticed in the next volume of *ALS*.

Realistic-Realist" (*RS*, XXXV, 92–94). Two articles discuss Howells' social attitudes. Arthur Boardman is critical in "Social Point of View in the Novels of William Dean Howells" (*AL*, XXXIX, 42–59), urging that the "world that matters" is "the world of the highest level of society presented"; in other words, "the attitudes shown have the effect of contradicting the egalitarian theme" Howells expressed in the novels protesting social injustice. Frank Turaj's "The Social Gospel in Howells' Novels" (*SAQ*, LXVI, 449–464) reviews his attraction to Christian Socialism, and comes to the not unexpected conclusion that, in the seven novels discussed, his basic position is that religion should be concerned with welfare.

Several critics addressed themselves to Howells' work outside the novel. Studying nine of "The Short Novels of William Dean Howells" (*DA*, XXVII, 2529A), Argle S. Garrow, Jr., deduces that for Howells the form was primarily a genre for character or theme revelation. Anthony Dubé's "William Dean Howells's Theory and Practice of Drama" (*DA*, XXVIII, 1816A) comes to an equally commonplace conclusion: Because his theory of drama was based largely on his concept of realism, it was irreconcilable with the traditional artistic intentions of the stage; his plays are failures as "good theater." George Arms, in "Howells' English Travel Books: Problems in Technique" (*PMLA*, LXXXII, 104–116) detects in these usually neglected works a creative solution to the problems which the genre presented. They remain of importance not only for their social and literary criticism but also for their style, use of dramatic encounters, image clusters, and a complexly conceived narrator. Patricia Kane considered relationships with another author in "Mutual Perspective: James and Howells as Critics of Each Other's Fiction" (*MinnR*, VII, 331–341). Work covering some fifty years is examined in determining that Howells often functioned as a justifier for James and laid down the main lines of Jamesian criticism. James reviewed Howells less frequently but showed that he understood his aims and achievements. The article contains good summary statements of the specific views of each. Martin's creditable summation in *Harvests of Change* is a reflection of renewed critical respect: Howells was the "first to understand the whole history of the American imagination. He carried the history of American culture in his consciousness."

Henry Adams' two novels continue to attract probing comment.

Charles Vandersee, in "The Pursuit of Culture in Adams' *Democracy*" (*AQ*, XIX, 239–248), points to a larger world of reference than the political sphere; Adams is also satirizing the ostentatious American pursuit of culture in the uncritical worship of Europe and the fanatical but superficial lust for education. Pairing the two books in "*Democracy* and *Esther*: Henry Adams' Flirtation with Pragmatism" (*AQ*, XIX, 53–70), Michael Colacurcio argues that the flirtations of his sensitive and instinctively moral heroines with bold and direct men stand as the metaphor of Adams' own attractions to pragmatic doctrine, even though it is finally "absolutism-as-usual" in both works. In his brief but relevant analysis in *Harvests of Change*, Martin treats the novels as products of Adams' "double": a self "determined to find meaning where the historian can find none."

The minor work of John W. De Forest stirred up some interest this year. James B. Durham's "The Complete Short Stories of John William De Forest" (*DA*, XXVIII, 193A–194A) is an annotated edition of forty-five tales which appeared in periodicals between 1856 and 1884. An introduction assesses De Forest's contributions to the short story as slight but finds him of significance as an early realist, a reporter of the national scene, and the creator of a wide range of American characters. Alfred Appel, Jr., edits and introduces the first book publication of *Witching Times* (New Haven, Col. and Univ. Press). It will be welcome for classroom use, but some scholars will object to the fact that the text is "modernized." Martin gives some space to De Forest in *Harvests of Change*, asserting that by making a "National Novel" he "helped to make a Nation." Yet eventually he fell victim to the drive to produce the Great American Novel.

The utopianists received some valuable new critiques. John L. Thomas' 88-page introduction to Edward Bellamy's *Looking Backward 2000–1887* (Cambridge, Harvard Univ. Press, Belknap) is a first-rate essay which, drawing on the unpublished Bellamy papers, illuminates both his other work and that of the whole movement. The novel is deftly characterized as providing for many readers a "moral restorative" not so different from the "patent-medicine panaceas of the day." Alexander Saxton probes deeply into Ignatius Donnelly in "*Caesar's Column*: The Dialogue of Utopia and Catastrophe" (*AQ*, XIX, 224–238). The paired images of utopia and catastrophe suggest, he acutely observes, "that the utopian novels

of the nineties sink roots into a deeper American past than the reaction to industrial growth and urbanization alone can quite account
for." Part Five of *Harvests of Change* includes a wide-ranging survey
of the utopian and dystopian novel.

Harold Frederic has been undergoing a modest boom in the
1960's, which his admirers would label a revival. The subject of
American Literary Realism's first annotated bibliography, he has
also won for himself a newsletter, the *Frederic Herald*, edited by
Thomas F. O'Donnell. The first two issues contain brief biographical
and bibliographical items. Stanton Garner's "Some Notes on Harold
Frederic in Ireland" (*AL*, XXXIX, 60–74) discusses the Irish tales
and uncovers a Frederic far different from the New York State
regionalist. J. R. K. Kantor adds a few more items in "Autobiography
and Journalism: Sources for Harold Frederic's Fiction" (*Serif*,
IV, iv, 19–27).

Finally, Constance Fenimore Woolson was briefly resurrected.
Rayburn S. Moore edits and introduces her For the Major *and
Selected Short Stories* (New Haven, Col. and Univ. Press)—a short
novel and eight stories. Robert L. White has a look at "Cultural
Ambivalence in Constance Fenimore Woolson's Italian Tales" (*TSL*,
XII, 121–129), showing how her work was symptomatic of the
ambivalent responses of nineteenth-century Americans to Italy—
the land which they found both the most attractive and the most
repulsive.

v. Stephen Crane

The Crane revival has passed into the ultimate stage of the Crane
industry. Though a scholarly edition is now under way at the University of Virginia, the texts continue to multiply. Thomas A. Gullason has added as a companion volume to his *Complete Short Stories
and Sketches* (1963) *The Complete Novels* (Garden City, N. Y.,
Doubleday). It is the year's bargain book, containing not only the
first-edition texts of the six novels but also the most important variant
readings from the 1893 *Maggie* plus the newspaper version of *The
Red Badge of Courage*. A 93-page introduction provides one of the
most balanced essays on Crane in recent years. Joseph Katz's dissertation "The Poems of Stephen Crane: A Critical Edition" (*DA*,

XXVIII, 2250A) has now appeared as a book under the same title
(New York, Cooper Square). While reviewers have quibbled over
some textual points, there is agreement that this is the most nearly
definitive edition of the "lines." Katz has also introduced "The Red
Badge of Courage" (SF&R), a facsimile of the New York *Press* text
of December 9, 1894. (Gullason prints the text from the serialization
in the Philadelphia *Press*.) R. W. Stallman continues his publication
of minor, scattered writings with "Stephen Crane: Some New
Sketches" (*BNYPL*, LXXI, 554–562), pieces about Mexico City, and
with "Stephen Crane and Cooper's Uncas" (*AL*, XXXIX, 392–396).
(The piecemeal, often competitive, reprinting of Crane's lesser items
continues to be a topic for scholarly acrimony; see the exchange between Stallman and E. H. Cady in *AL*, XL [1968], 83–85.)

Oddly, *The Red Badge of Courage* received little significant
comment during the year. John Fraser's "Crime and Forgiveness:
'The Red Badge' in Time of War" (*Criticism*, IX, 243–256) attacks
today's "rampant formalism" in criticism as he presents the book as
it might be taught to students themselves facing war. Fraser's challenging reading insists that a transformed Henry Fleming at the end
of the story is in a better position to face the "moral claims of events";
critics who feel he has been brutalized are influenced by a "certain
naive liberalism." And he concludes flatly that "Crane has helped to
show up the fashionable nihilisms of today as the effete and schizo-
phrenic things that they are." The critical battle will no doubt continue. C. B. Ives, in " 'The Little Regiment' of Stephen Crane at the
Battle of Fredericksburg" (*MQ*, VIII, 247–260) sees Crane mocking
at popular idolatry of military courage in *The Red Badge* in order
to test his own courage. But his source materials also led him to
express admiration in the story "The Little Regiment," which, Ives
explains, was actually New York's "Fighting Sixty-Ninth."

Among the few articles dealing with the shorter fiction, George
Monteiro's "Whilomville as Judah: Crane's 'A Little Pilgrimage' "
(*Renascence*, XIX, 184–189) is a thorough explication of the Biblical
themes behind Jimmie Trescott's disturbing experience with Sunday School.

Selected criticism of Crane, mostly reprinted, is represented in
Maurice Bassan's volume in the Twentieth Century Views series
(Englewood Cliffs, N. J., Prentice-Hall). The *Stephen Crane News-*

letter published four issues in 1967. The items are predominantly biographical and bibliographical rather than critical; a few new letters and texts of varying importance are printed.

vi. Naturalism and Beyond

American Literary Realism promises to include debate over the meaning of naturalism in forthcoming issues. Meanwhile, little was published this year which could help a student form his own conclusions. Martin's *Harvests of Change* glances at "The Continuity of Naturalism" (Henry B. Fuller and Norris) without attention to definitions.

Frank Norris continues to attract and to puzzle critics. Three authors viewed the vexed question as to the sources and extent of his naturalism with typically varying degrees of emphasis. Robert B. Olafson's "Frank Norris' Seven Novels: A Study of the Mosaic of Tensions Between Critical Realism and Naturalism in the Works" (*DA*, XXVII [1966], 1831A–1832A) acknowledges the influence of Zola but finds the vein of critical realism richer than the one of naturalism. Don D. Walker's "The Western Naturalism of Frank Norris" (*WAL*, II, 14–29) notes what most readers note: that his fiction betrays a basic confusion of values. Yet Walker concludes that Norris was more naturalistic than romantic, closer to Zola than to Wordsworth. Philip Walker agrees in *"The Octopus* and Zola: A New Look" (*Symposium*, XXI, 155–165), though with significant qualification. Walker concedes the obvious similarities noted by earlier critics, but he argues that—unlike the richness, depth, and coherence of Zola's vision—Norris' views had not coalesced in *The Octopus.*

On balance, the year offered no surprises. As usual, critics were drawn principally to fashionable figures like Crane or to the genuinely (and often quite deservedly) neglected. A continuing difficulty is the critic's uneasiness as to how one should best explicate a minor work. For what it contains of "art"? For its "ideas" if it has little or no redeeming "aesthetic value"? For whatever it may contribute to literary history? The problem is raised again by Robert E. Spiller in his review of *Essays on American Literature*, in which he approvingly notes that several emphasize the importance of the minor writer to literary history—"a much needed emphasis in these days of concentration ad nauseam on a selected few masterpieces" (*AL*, XL [1968], 86–88). But no one surveying the year's scholarship in this field could find any more agreement about methods than does Spiller in analyzing a typical symposium.

Columbia University

11. Poe and Nineteenth-Century Poetry[1]

J. Albert Robbins

This seems to have been a year for basic tools, what with the first two volumes of Andrew Hilen's significant edition of Longfellow's letters, an updating of Ostrom's edition of Poe's letters, Dameron's checklist of Poe criticism, the Dameron-Stagg index to Poe's critical vocabulary, and Regan's collection of recent Poe criticism. Though he writes on a minor poet, O. W. Frost's book on Joaquin Miller is a model of scholarship, critical assessment, and good writing. Among the scholarly articles and essays, Arnold, Connor, and Smith on Poe and Ehrlich on Lowell impress me by their substance and clarity.

i. Edgar Allan Poe

a. **Letters, reference works, and general articles.** In the eighteen years since John Ward Ostrom's *Letters of Edgar Allan Poe* appeared, new letters have come to light and their text has been published in a number of periodicals. These are now collected in a supplement to the original *Letters* in a new edition (2 vols., New York, Gordian Press, 1966). The original Harvard University Press edition of 1948 has been photographically reproduced and a 56-page supplement added, in which Ostrom includes six new letters or portions of letters (92a, 106a, 228a, 296a, 302a, 307a), two dozen letters previously published by Ostrom or others, and an improved text for eleven letters (now published from ms. or photostats of mss.). The six new letters are minor ones, but of more interest is Letter 79—a lengthy letter to George W. Poe on the Poe family and Edgar Poe's life, now expanded from the mere four-sentence excerpt in the 1948 edition, and a genealogical chart of "The Descendants of John Poe" added. Os-

---

1. Beginning this year, scholarship on Emily Dickinson is reviewed in Chapter 4.

trom also corrects and adds to his original notes and checklist and gives other new data. There is an index to the supplement and a new list of known manuscript collections.

Mr. Ostrom discussed the problems of editing Poe's letters in a recent address to the Poe Society of Baltimore and the text of his talk is available in the *Baltimore Bulletin of Education* (XLIII, i, 1–8) under the title, "The Letters of Poe: Quest and Answer." He discusses the buying, selling, forging, and collecting of letters; problems of editing; and the importance of the letters to Poe scholarship.

In three or four year's time we shall have a detailed checklist of critical books and articles on Poe from 1827 to 1960. Irby B. Cauthen, Jr., will revise his thesis and contribute items from 1827 to 1941. Meanwhile J. Lasley Dameron provisionally offers his segment of the two-man enterprise under the title, *Edgar Allan Poe: A Checklist of Criticism, 1942–1960* (Charlottesville, Bibliographical Society of the Univ. of Va., 1966). Mr. Dameron cites 595 titles in English and 328 in foreign languages, listed alphabetically by author. Many entries carry brief descriptions, and there is an index. I have found only one error of substance: item T.23 is duplicated and attributed to the wrong author under B.31.

Mr. Dameron has supplemented his checklist with an essay surveying "Poe at Mid-Century: Anglo-American Criticism, 1928–1960" (*BSUF*, VIII, i, 36–44). He sees, between 1928 and 1941 "a growing reaction against the application of psychoanalytical theories of his works" (p. 37), and after 1942 an affirmation of Poe as a major figure, with praise for psychological verisimilitude in the fiction and a relevance to contemporary literature.

Dameron and Louis Charles Stagg have compiled a useful *Index to Poe's Critical Vocabulary* (Hartford, Conn., Transcendental Books, 1966; *ESQ*, No. 46, pp. 1–50). Here, under scores of terms and concepts (such as Beauty, Character, Imagination, Genius, Style) the authors give the phrase in which the terms occur and cite volume and page in the *Letters* (1948 edition of Ostrom) and the *Complete Works* (1902 edition of Harrison).

A collection of criticism on Poe was published by Eric W. Carlson last year (see *ALS, 1966*, pp. 129–130) and another, edited by Robert Regan, has appeared this year (*Poe: A Collection of Critical Essays*, Englewood Cliffs, N. J., Prentice-Hall). Within the larger span of 316 pages, Carlson includes pieces from 1829 to 1963; whereas, confined to this century and 183 pages, Regan has room for only a dozen essays (as against nineteen for the twentieth century in Carlson). There is little duplication (three essays), so that both collections will be useful. Let me mention (but not deplore) that, both in Mr. Regan's introduction and in his choice of essays, the emphasis is heavily upon Poe's fiction.

The last college anthology of Poe was Edward Davidson's in 1956. A new one edited by Eric W. Carlson (*Introduction to Poe: A Thematic Reader*, Glenview, Ill., Scott, Foresman) gives a broad selection of poems, tales, and criticism, running to 601 pages. There are features which are admirable: he specifies copy text, includes variants of some poems, and adds tales and critical pieces not normally anthologized ("The Duc De L'Omelette," "Mellonta Tauta," and "The Light-House," for example). But several things bother me. The thematic arrangement, despite the editor's insistence that it is suggestive rather than prescriptive, is worrisome and, in some cases, wrong-headed. I question the wisdom of citing as text the correct periodical, yet using as "basic text" Harrison (even though "errors in that edition have been corrected"). In a brief check, I find one error in "Mellonta Tauta" and three in "A Descent into the Maelström." The notes are no better than those in most anthologies, with some errors and silence on difficult passages. The note on Martin Van Buren Mavis (p. 586) is wrong, for example: it is a pun upon Andrew Jackson Davis; and other problems in "Mellonta Tauta" are wrongly construed or ignored. Mr. Carlson commits the usual error on the Nubian Geographer, who confronts us both in "Eleonora" and "Mellonta Tauta": it is Idrisi, not Claudius Ptolemy; and, regarding the important allusion to the well of Democritus in "Maelström" and "Ligeia," he explains only the source in Glanvill. (There is a meaningful version of this old saying in Rees's *Cyclopaedia*, which Poe used: "This mode of acquiring certain knowledge he confessed to be very difficult, and, therefore, he used to say that truth lay in a deep well, from which it is the office of reason to draw it up.")

In his important book on the *Frontier: American Literature and the American West* (Princeton, N. J.: Princeton Univ. Press, 1965) Edwin Fussell devotes a chapter to Poe (pp. 132–174) and cites many forms of reference to the West, with, of course, special attention to *Pym* and *Julius Rodman*. He has interesting things to say, as well, about such shorter pieces as "The Island of the Fay," "Morning on the Wissahiccon," and "The Masque of the Red Death" (Prospero representing the United States and the Red Death, "the shape of the American conscience").

On the subject of "Edgar Poe and the University of Virginia" (*VQR*, XLIII, 297–317), Floyd Stovall comments upon Poe's classes; the books he withdrew from the library; Poe's habits, literary efforts, "vices," and membership in the Jefferson Society. There was no local notice of his death, but a parody of "The Raven" appeared in the campus magazine in 1850. "Serious student interest" in Poe, he says, "was greater between 1885 and 1900 than between 1867 and 1885, but less than during the four or five years immediately preceding the Civil War" (p. 316).

Sidney P. Moss turns his attention to "Poe, Hiram Fuller, and the Duyckinck Circle" (*ABC*, XVIII, ii, 8–18) and in considerable documented detail gives week-to-week battle reports on the War of the Literati, with particular attention to Fuller's dislike of Poe from 1845 to 1847. Catching Poe without a journal to serve as a base for retaliation, "Fuller and his allies were able to defame him to the limits of their ability in one *ad hominem* attack upon another."

In the last year of his life Poe visited the Richmonds in Lowell, Massachusetts, and met a young lady whom he referred to in one of his letters as "Miss B." By searching local documents Fred B. Freeman, Jr., has found "The identity of Poe's 'Miss B'" (*AL*, XXXIX, 389–391): Eliza J. Butterfield.

In a paper much too long and garrulous, Burton R. Pollin ("Poe as 'Miserrimus': From British Epitaph to American Epithet," *RLV*, XXXIII, 347–361) recounts how the one-word epitaph on a gravestone in Worcester Cathedral led Wordsworth and two lesser poets to write sonnets on it and Frederick Mansell Reynolds a novel. Poe knew the novel and mentioned it often in his criticism. Furthermore, Mr. Pollin proposes, Poe may have absorbed and used themes and stylistic echoes from the Reynolds novel. If Poe did cry out for Reynolds on his deathbed, it could have referred to the Englishman, F. M. Reynolds, not the American, J. N. Reynolds.

Another address to the Poe Society of Baltimore has been printed. Taking the general topic, "Edgar Allan Poe: A Study in Heroism" in the *Curious Death of the Novel* (Baton Rouge, La. State Univ. Press, pp. 47–66), Louis D. Rubin, Jr., touches upon the poetry with critical skepticism ("A little 'sinfully scintillant planet' goes a long way"; Poe's verse about bells is the kind that appeals to persons who seldom read poetry, and "is the kind of poetry my father-in-law recites"), then goes on to view "Edgar Allan Poe as a hero, both in his career, in what he stands for in American literary history, and in the courage of his vision." Mr. Rubin defines his heroism as the capacity to see through all the optimism and progress around him to the depravity and horror in men that we of the next century have found to be all too true.

b. **Fiction.** The greater part of an essay by Sidney P. Moss on "*Arthur Gordon Pym*, or The Fallacy of Thematic Interpretation" (*UR*, XXXIII, 299–306) argues the point, already noted by others, that *Pym* consists of two distinct narratives, that the two are imperfectly joined, and that there are flaws in narration and characterization. The final two and a half pages treat the fallacy mentioned in the subtitle. Convinced that the novel lacks unity, Mr. Moss believes that those who affirm an overall thematic unity, despite narrative disunity, are guilty of critical fallacy. Mr. Moss's discussion would benefit a good deal by an awareness of the important article by Ridgely-Haverstick published a year earlier (see *ALS, 1966*, p. 132), but I dare say that Moss's manuscript was finished and on the desk of the *UR* editor before that article appeared.

John H. Stroupe ("Poe's Imaginary Voyage: Pym as Hero," *SSF*, IV, 315–321) proposes that Pym is a true narrative hero because he elects to go to sea to face life at its most intense and to complete himself; because he is a subjective narrator, interpreting action; and because his superiority increases throughout the story. What has sent him to sea is the mystery and fear of death. In facing death he can "discover its true nature and relationship to life."

Raymond Tarbox has published an essay in *AI* (XXIV, 312–343) on what he labels "Blank Hallucinations in the Fiction of Poe and Hemingway." What I am inclined to call a psychoanalytic reading is, the editor of *AI* tells me, wrong. Rather, he says, the author treats "the dynamics of psychoanalytic forces in the narratives." At any rate, Tarbox deals with "MS. Found in a Bottle" and more extensively with *Pym*, whose hero seeks narcissistic identification with Augustus Bernard and Dirk Peters, and illustrates "the close relationship between depersonalization, stupor, and the dream screen" (p. 334). In "MS. Found" the basic pattern "is an appeal to a paternal figure for help, failure of the appeal . . . , followed by feelings of desolation or depersonalization." In "The Snows of Kilimanjaro" Mr. Tarbox finds that the oppressive weight of the "devalued hyena" is familiar in case histories, as are the hallucinated details of the airplane journey ("regressive signals which usually appear in our stories before the emergence of the elaborated dream screen").

Looking at seven tales—the three Dupin stories and those about disturbed young men ("Berenice," "Morella," "Ligeia," and "The Fall of the House of Usher")—Marvin and Frances Mengeling (in "From Fancy to Failure: A Study of the Narrators in the Tales of Edgar Allan Poe," *UR*, XXX, 293–298; XXXI, 31–37) argue that Dupin succeeds because he uses " 'true' imagination" and that the others fail because they depend upon fancy. Since so much depends upon the words *fancy* and *imagination*, the authors summarize Poe's uses of the terms in criticism but the distinction is in peril because Poe's usage of the terms shifts. I find it difficult to explain the seven tales on so simple and exclusive a premise as the one proposed: "Poe meant success or failure to depend chiefly on the *method* of solution used" (p. 293). There are statements which I question, such as the assertion that Dupin "admirably attained through a combination of imagination and reasoned analysis solutions to all problems that confronted him" (p. 294). The truth is that Poe does not see Dupin as having solved all problems, as paragraphs 5–8 of "The Murders in the Rue Morgue" will indicate. There are a few instances of manipulated evidence and one of error in the article: "Morella" was not written to "modify" "Ligeia" (p. 33). It was the other way around.

Under the topic, " 'The Cask of Amontillado': A Masquerade of Motive and Identity" (*SSF*, IV, 119–126), James G. Gargano considers as central to the story the idea that "human division is more 'real' than union," that man is unable to live with his kind in harmony. As to the once honored and now aggrieved Montresor, Mr. Gargano believes that a part of the irony and a key to the meaning is that he "resembles Fortunato in being the dupe of his own crazed obsessions" and that he "is broken on the wheel of a world in which violence is simultaneously an internal and an external action" (p. 125). Clearly, this is opposed to the reading by John H. Randall III (see *ALS*, *1964*, p. 124), who considers Montresor the true gentleman punishing the imposter and suffering no sense of guilt.

There are three articles on "Ligeia," none of them remarkable. In a curiously disjointed essay, Joy Rea considers "Classicism and Romanticism in Poe's 'Ligeia' " (*BSUF*, VIII, i, 25–29). Part of it goes like this: Ligeia's song or poem, "The Conqueror Worm," tells us the meaning of the story. A key is "bloodred thing" (a synonym for romanticism) and the condor (a synonym for science). "Out comes the bloodred worm, or romanticism, and devours" the people. "For Poe, science and romanticism work together against the poetic truths found in classicism" (p. 28). The rest of the essay is not much more cogent. In "Poe's 'Ligeia': An Analysis" (*SSF*, IV, 234–244) Claudia C. Morrison believes that Poe was largely unconscious of the theme of the story, believes that the story "is rooted in the child's fantasy that the dead mother can return to him through the strength of her love and the force of her will" (p. 242) and that its impact upon readers derives from an underlying vampire theme. Looking at "The Conclusion of Poe's 'Ligeia' " (*ESQ*, No. 47, pp. 69–70), D. Ramakrishna has little to say other than that, at the end, the reader is left confused and uncertain.

The footnote in "Usher" about Watson's *Chemical Essays* is thoroughly explored in Herbert F. Smith's "Usher's Madness and Poe's Organicism: A Source" (*AL*, XXXIX, 379–389). Believing that "Poe's debt to Watson does not end with this footnote," Mr. Smith examines Watson's book and suggests that there Poe found a scientific basis for the relationship between organic plants, capable of feeling, and the non-organic materials around them. Out of a knowledge of Watson Poe has fashioned an environment in which "the algae of the house of Usher have organized themselves—the stones of the house, the air around them, and even the mind of Usher himself—into what can only be described as a single, unified organism" (p. 387). Moreover, Smith says, Poe went on to a broader use of organicism in *Eureka*—"perhaps the most extended development of the organic metaphor ever written" (p. 386).

Three minor tales have received attention. "Another source for Poe's 'The Duc De L'Omelette' " (*AL*, XXXVIII, 532–536), David H. Hirsch finds, is (beyond Benjamin Disraeli's novel, *The Young Duke*, proposed thirty years ago by Ruth Hudson) the review of the novel published in the *Westminster Review*, for some details in the story have parallels only in the review. In an interesting article, "Poe's 'Lionizing': The Wound and the Bawdry" (*L&P*, XVII, 52–54), John Arnold finds the narrator in the long tradition of the

"wounded alienate." He claims that Poe "is probably the first . . .
American author who clearly enunciates in fiction . . . the wounded
man—the alienate—the impotent—the anti-hero as hero," plus bawdry,
which becomes "a tonal correlative necessary to particularize the
wound and define the first American Lion whose Lionship derives
from his sexual impotence" (p. 54). In "Poe's 'Von Kempelen and
His Discovery': Sources and Significance" (*EA*, XX, 12–23), Burton
R. Pollin gives a great deal of detailed attention to the sources—
biographical and literary. As to significance he considers the tale
"the culmination of Poe's efforts in the field of the literary hoax"
(p. 12) and, more questionably, says that it reflects Poe's poverty
and self-delusion that all was going well.

After citing statements by psychologists about the primary fears
of infants and children, Robert J. Blanch itemizes some of these
fears (fear of falling, fear of being hurt by animals, fear of snakes,
for example) and cites examples, allusions, and verbal echoes in
Poe's writings. Some of these citations are absurd: Ligeia's eyes
"blazed" is classified under Fear of Being Hurt by Fire; the verb
"writhe" is included under Fear of Snakes. The article ("Poe's Imagery: An Undercurrent of Childhood Fears," *FurmS*, XIV, iv, 19–25)
is falsely conceived, poorly argued, and unimpressive in thesis and
conclusions. A final article: in "Poe's 'The Man That Was Used Up' "
(*Expl*, XXV, Item 70) Thomas O. Mabbott suggests that the sur-
name of Theodore Sinivate is Cockney for *insinuate*.

Two dissertations pertain to Poe's fiction. In "Narrative Point of
View in Edgar Allan Poe's Criticism and Fiction" (*DA*, XXVII,
3880A–3881A) Calvin L. Skaggs claims that Poe is truly an innovator. With daring and variety, Poe experimented and made the psychological states of his unreliable narrators reveal themselves
deceptively and dramatically, making this, rather than violent physical experiences, the focus of his tales. In examining "The Grotesque
in American Literature: Poe, Hawthorne, and Melville" (*DA*, XXVII,
3840A–3841A) David G. Halliburton subscribes to Wolfgang Kay-
ser's thesis "that the grotesque is a process of estrangement arising
from man's inability to find a home in the physical universe" and believes that it depends heavily on the sense of play and "may also aid
in consciousness in knowing, and in being as well." Viewing the
three authors, he says that "Melville's breadth of perspective brings

him closer to the ironic, sympathetic Hawthorne than to the detached and even indifferent Poe."

c. Poetry. I am of two minds about the first of two general essays on Poe as poet. E. San Juan, Jr., attacks a basic problem in "The Form of Experience in the Poems of Edgar Allan Poe" (*GaR*, XXI, 65–80), but the result, for me at least, is marred by an unfortunate, glutinous style. Mr. San Juan believes that there is a "quest for being and permanence," for "the absolute—for identity, being, as opposed to death or nothingness symbolized by the Raven" (pp. 66, 68); he says that, in trying to transcend the limitations of time and space, Poe creates a topography of the unconscious (p. 71); and asserts that the poet sought "to essentialize experience and reduce sensory impressions and material data into forms of beauty" (p. 80). This is a piece whose merits the reader should determine for himself. In the other general essay, on "Stanza Patterns in the Poetry of Poe" (*TSL*, XII, 111–120), James L. Allen, Jr., disagrees with those who have contended that stanzaic irregularities are lapses and that some poems are so free that they almost defy analysis. Out of the fifty some odd poems, five are stanzaically regular, nine or so are in verse paragraphs, and the remainder are in units "that clearly manifest elements of consciously wrought internal structure or pattern." He examines the variations of rhyme and meter in "Annabel Lee" to show that they are consciously handled and are functional.

The most intensive study of a single poem is "Poe's 'The City in the Sea' Revisited" (*Essays on American Literature*, pp. 77–89). William O. Clough views the poem as cosmological, akin to Poe's prose pieces which posit a negation of humanity. Here, then, are "the dissolving atoms, embodied in the last symbols of human pomp and circumstance when the human life has departed from them; and the slow sinking into the waiting void . . . . There Death itself, in its proud tower, sinks with the rest, for there is no more death where nothing lives" (pp. 87–88).

While the image of the worm can be traced to Byron and others and the phrase, "conqueror worm," to Spencer Wallis Cone, Poe's handling of materials is entirely his own, Klaus Lubbers says in "Poe's 'The Conqueror Worm'" (*AL*, XXXIX, 375–379). The Elizabethan metaphor of the world or universe as a stage is retained but

the order of things (God, angels, man) Poe changes to a new triad:
the Conqueror Worm, "vast formless things," and mimes. The "music
of the spheres" now is fitful and discordant music. There are un-
answered questions remaining, but, placed in the context of "Ligeia,"
the Conqueror Worm must be Death, not Satan, dramatizing "the
seemingly unexceptionable lot of man which is, at least for a short
while, overcome by Ligeia's will" (p. 379).

In two notes, J. Lasley Dameron ("Schiller's 'Das Lied von der
Glocke' as a Source of Poe's 'The Bells'," *N&Q*, XIV, 368–369) cites
two magazines where Poe could have read translations of the Schiller
poem; and Thomas O. Mabbott ("A Poem Wrongly Ascribed to
Poe," *N&Q*, XIV, 367–368) says an eight-line poem which Amelia
Poe sent to Ingram is a concoction of lines from "The Raven" and
"Dream-Land."

d. Eureka and criticism. While many are familiar with "Dr. Nichols"
from the reference to him in "The Murders in the Rue Morgue,"
few know of Poe's awareness of this Glasgow astronomer, John
Pringle Nichol, and of the role his nebular cosmogony played down
to the publication of *Eureka*, where there are several unobserved
parallels. Frederick W. Conner, in "Poe & John Nichol: Notes on a
Source of *Eureka*" (*All These to Teach*, pp. 190–208), explores these,
along with Poe's condescending attitude to Nichol. In "Poe's *Eureka*
and Hindu Philosophy" (*ESQ*, No. 47, pp. 28–32) D. Ramakrishna
says that again and again statements by Poe conform to ideas in the
Upanishads and the Bhagavad Gita.

Because Poe defined the short story in his review of Hawthorne's
tales and because Brander Matthews in an article in 1885 echoed
many of these precepts, Richard Danner uses the term, "The Poe-
Matthews Theory of the American Short Story" (*BSUF*, VIII, i, 45–
50), in reviewing the emergence of critical ideas about modern
short fiction. In a gracefully written essay, Richard Cary considers
"Poe and the Literary Ladies" (*TSLL*, IX, 91–101) and believes that,
because Poe idealized womanhood, he could not treat women with
critical objectivity. "Moments of uncontaminated analysis are few"
for "he converted every woman into a blend of Venus and the Virgin
Mary" (p. 101).

Richard P. Benton views "The Works of N. P. Willis as a Catalyst
of Poe's Criticism" (*AL*, XXXIX, 315–324) and, in a detailed review

of Poe's criticism of Willis' writings, he contends that, in the process, Poe developed two basic critical concepts—totality of effect and the four faculties of the creative process (imagination, fancy, fantasy, and humor). Willis seems to be more a subject or target than a catalyst and Mr. Benson admits that both concepts were postulated earlier in regard to other writers.

ii. Longfellow, Whittier, Lowell, Bryant, Tuckerman, Stowe

Since 1954 Andrew Hilen has been at work editing Longfellow's letters. Now the first two volumes are in print, *The Letters of Henry Wadsworth Longfellow* (Cambridge, Harvard Univ. Press, Belknap, 1966), a major work of editorial scholarship. The two volumes provide some 800 letters from 1814 (age six) to the end of 1843 (age thirty-six) when he was an established author and newly married to Frances Appleton. Mr. Hilen has provided a clear reading text, with data and notes conveniently following each letter. He not only annotates persons, places, and events but identifies an impressive array of quotations without textual clue (for example, "expressive silence," from James Thomson's *A Hymn on the Seasons*). The editorial apparatus—including chronology, genealogical tables, section headnotes, illustrations and translations of foreign language passages—seems to me perfectly executed. There will surely be a general index when the final volume appears.

How far we have come from the documents and the view of Longfellow that Samuel Longfellow created in the 1886 *Life*! The poet's love for Frances Appleton, so apparent in the unabridged letters, became antiseptically impersonal in the *Life*: "In July he was married to Miss Frances Elizabeth Appleton, the daughter of Mr. Nathan Appleton, an eminent and highly esteemed merchant of Boston." We can readily sample the silent "editing out" of phrases and sentences which Samuel Longfellow deemed necessary by considering a long and revealing letter to George W. Greene of October 22, 1838 (*Life*, I, 300–303; Hilen, II, 106–110). Gone, in the *Life*, are references to "Madonna Francesca" and "the '*Dark Ladie*' who holds my reason captive" and the revealing part of another sentence (italicized): "*Meanwhile* I labor and work right on with what heart and courage I may, *and despise all sympathy; and am quite reasonably cool for a mad-man.*" Gone such a telling sentence as "But for all these things I care not a straw; being wholly taken up with myself and my *sorrows-of-Werter* kind of Life." On the novelist, Joseph Holt Ingraham, Longfellow wrote: "He is a tremendous ass!! really *tremendous!*" and his brother records it as "He is tremendous—really tremendous." Gone is the reference to Prescott's being "fond of good wine" and gone the damning middle section of "Now I shall take a glass of Whiskey-punch and go to bed."

The letters show more of Longfellow than there is space here to detail. From early youth he was a serious lad and sure he could force the world to grant the eminence due him. He danced and he drank, but he had remarkable self-discipline. He stood up strongly for what was due him, but took adversity manfully. Frances stirred him more than his first wife, Mary. Longfellow is here, complete and alive.

Michael Zimmerman gives a close reading to a seldom anthologized, seldom discussed poem in "War and Peace: Longfellow's 'The Occultation of Orion'" (*AL*, XXXVIII, 540–546) and finds that in it the poet is "ambiguous, paradoxical, emotionally perplexed," inasmuch as its theme is "the uncertainty of peace triumphing over war and violence" (p. 541). The poem shows Longfellow deeply concerned with political issues and facing the uncertainties of the Forties with intellectual candor. In eight new letters written to the youthful Miss Cornelia Fitch in 1864–65 (Sargent Bush, Jr., "Longfellow's Letters to Cornelia Fitch," *BI*, No. 6, pp. 13–19, 23) we see the poet, after the death of his second wife, finding a charming female acquaintance and a source of pleasure for his five motherless children, until Miss Fitch's engagement ended the relationship.

Edward Wagenknecht's volumes of character studies of nineteenth century figures has reached five with *John Greenleaf Whittier, A Portrait in Paradox* (New York: Oxford Univ. Press). Aside from the need for a separate chapter on pacifism and attitudes toward war, the book follows the pattern of the others with chapters on personal matters, on the world about him, on matters intellectual and esthetic, and on religion. As usual, there is a minimum of critical judgment, but Wagenknecht does consider *Leaves from Margaret Smith's Journal* "his one prose work of the first rank" and "one of the inexplicably neglected classics of American literature" (p. 7). On the question of Whittier's political sense, Mr. Wagenknecht admits that he could be "shrewd and cunning," but apparently does not agree with Perry Miller that Whittier had "a fair amount of guile, which he employed most systematically in building up the legend of his guileless simplicity" (see *ALS*, *1964*, p. 129). The author's final assessment is that Whittier "was not a great poet" and "was not even the best among American poets" but was the only one before Robert Frost "able to capture both the face and the soul of New England in verse" (pp. 193, 194).

Wagenknecht says that "the authoritative account now" on "John Greenleaf Whittier and Mary Emerson Smith" (*AL*, XXXVIII, 478–497) is the article by John B. Pickard. In six early letters to his distant cousin, Whittier showed deep interest in his career and only a brotherly interest in Miss Smith. Indeed, in the second letter (Whittier was twenty-one), he shuddered at the thought of being "perched upon the 'high seats' with a Quaker intended." "Horrible!" he exclaims. "Is it not a terrible picture? but such *must* be my lot, unless, indeed, I come to the conclusion to lead a life of 'Single Blessedness' " (p. 486). It would seem that he had already so concluded.

In a search for patterns of conflict in Whittier's poetry ("John Greenleaf Whittier: Focus on Yesterday," *DA*, XXXVIII, 1791A–1792A) Richard Dale Olson examines conflicts relating to art, nature, the past, industrialization, and disengagement from conventional life. "His life, in work and love," he believes, "describes a series of feints toward involvement succeeded by withdrawal."

Five years ago in a brief headnote on Lowell in Perry Miller's anthology, *Major Writers of America*, William Charvat raised some relevant issues by saying that Lowell had no understanding or tolerance for "that literature which celebrates the ego of the individual," that he was "uneasy among the multiplying confusions of the nineteenth century," and that only rarely could he approach the level of great poetry. In all 108 pages of her book on *James Russell Lowell* (TUSAS, No. 120) Claire McGlinchee is silent upon all such matters. She has only pleasant and innocuous things to say about her subject, fails to compare him with his contemporaries or place him properly in American literature, and refuses to make critical commitments— except in the last five sentences of the book. The serious student of Lowell will find very little of interest in this volume.

In his article Heyward Ehrlich has important things to say about "Charles Frederick Briggs and Lowell's *Fable for Critics*" (*MLQ*, XXVIII, 329–341), some of it coming from previously unpublished letters of Briggs. The friendship was such a close one that "Briggs was able to turn Lowell slowly from his early interest in social reform" toward satire and invective. They shared a dislike of Cornelius Mathews and Margaret Fuller ("the female ass of the Tribune," Briggs wrote; an "unparalleled sternutator," Lowell replied). "Undoubtedly," says Ehrlich, "Lowell never would have undertaken *A Fable for Critics* without Briggs's guidance and assistance" (p. 340).

Robert A. Rees explores the correspondence between Lowell and his successor to the ambassadorship in Spain, General Lucius Fairchild in "James Russell Lowell in Spain and England: New Letters" (*ESQ*, No. 47, pp. 7–13). The nine letters are of biographical, not literary, interest.

Two unpublished juvenile poems of Bryant written at age 12, are transcribed from the manuscripts in the Barrett Collection at the University of Virginia (Richard E. Peck, "Two Lost Bryant Poems: Evidence of Thomson's Influence," *AL*, XXXIX, 88–94) and a reliance upon James Thomson noted. The verses show a fresh view of nature which antedates Bryant's acquaintance with Wordsworth. A total of thirty-seven new Bryant letters are given in four articles in *ESQ*, Number 48. The more interesting are found in David R. Rebmann's "Unpublished Letters of William Cullen Bryant (pp. 131–135), especially one on a word change in "The Death of the Flowers" and on his favorite poems ("The Past" and "The Dream"), and another on the coming Civil War. The arrangement between "Bryant and the *United States Literary Gazette*" for contributions is the subject of eleven letters between 1823 and 1825 in Joseph G. Ornato's article (pp. 135–139). Three letters presented by Paul Crapo (pp. 139–140) show us "Bryant on Slavery, Copyright, and Capital Punishment"; and fifteen rather ordinary ones, edited by Edward J. Lazzerini, are called "Bryant as a Writer of Friendly Letters" (pp. 125–131). In a study of "William Cullen Bryant's *New York Evening Post* and the South, 1847–1856" (*DA*, XXVIII, 698A–699A) Thomas G. Voss finds that Bryant and the paper agreed with Southern attitudes in the early years, but after the annexation of Texas, the Compromise of 1850, and the Kansas-Nebraska Act, he found it necessary to oppose extension of slavery. In 1854 the paper saw a sectional struggle as inevitable.

Edwin H. Cady sees "Frederick Goddard Tuckerman" (*Essays on American Literature*, pp. 141–151) as a minor but true poet and specifies four sources of poetic power in the sonnets: "the implied drama of the *persona*, the speaking voice, the figure observed or observing, sometimes the 'I' of the sonnets; the diction; the beautifully controlled tonalities; the often superb imagery" (p. 143). He gives a convincing reading of the sestet of Sonnet X, First Series, a passage which puzzled Yvor Winters. Considering Tuckerman's much-praised "The Cricket," N. Scott Momaday ("The Heretical Cricket," *SoR*, III, 43–50) summarizes facts about the poem, discusses themes and organization, compares it with Bryant's "Thanatopsis," and says that it is unique in several ways—in a hard response to nature, in dramatic structuring, in its precise symbolic object, and in its moral and intellectual integrity.

Anyone finding occasion to use "Collected Poems of Harriet Beecher Stowe" (*ESQ*, No. 49, pp. 1–100) should beware the editing of John M. Moran, Jr. The hymn, "Nearer My God to Thee" is by the English poetess, Sarah Flower Adams, not Stowe. The editor found a holograph poem with Stowe's autograph, appropriated the opening words, "Oh Love Divine," as a title, and includes it as hers. (Its title is "Hymn of Trust" and it can be found in Holmes's *Professor at the Breakfast Table*.) He takes a piece titled "The Church and the Slave Trade," observes the line lengths and prints it as a poem—though obviously it is prose. The final four stanzas of a poem on page 49, by some accident, are not included. Several "Poems on Slavery" from a volume titled *Pictures and Stories from Uncle Tom's Cabin* are included as hers, though there is every reason to suspect her authorship. There probably are other errors, but these should suffice to indicate the poor quality of the enterprise.

iii. Miller, Lanier, Dunbar, Taylor, Timrod, Tabb

The studies of poets outside New England are miscellaneous, with O. W. Frost's book clearly the most substantial. His *Joaquin Miller* (TUSAS, No. 119), the first since M. Marion Marberry's *Splendid Poseur* (1953), is critically honest, beautifully proportioned, and well-written. And impressive in its scholarship, with generous use of documents, manuscripts, and frontier newspapers. That this former renegade, Miller, could teach himself enough of the art of poetry to construct an international reputation, and with such materials as Stalwart Western Hero, Fair Woman, scenery, sentimentality, optimism, and stale rhetoric, is, though true, a tall tale. Among many frank things Mr. Frost says in his fine chapter on Miller's craft are these: "A versifier of noble, elemental feelings, he is a moralist who usually lacks precision, subtlety, and originality. Most importantly, he is no thinker, no philosopher; and he is, therefore, in the most elevated conception of the word—no poet" (p. 97).

In a useful general view of "Lanier as Poet," Edd Winfield Parks (*Essays on American Literature*, pp. 183–201) surveys the span of Lanier's poems, touches upon his impulse toward freer verse forms, examines individual poems of worth, and places Lanier as an American poet. He was not the great poet that he aspired to be and, though his defects are many and severe, Lanier deserves a better reputation than he now has. "The Marshes of Glynn" is his best long poem and there is a handful of fine lyrics. He is, Mr. Parks believes, "one of our most vital and most interesting minor poets" (p. 201).

In his general essay on "Paul Laurence Dunbar: The Rejected Symbol" (*JNH*, LII, 1–13) Darwin T. Turner tries to correct some errors of fact (the "legend of his enforced silence," 1898–1903, for example) and answer current critics who damn him as a too-acquiescent black writer. Looking more at the prose than at the poetry, Mr. Turner cannot disprove the critics, but only can suggest that "perhaps readers have demanded too much of Dunbar as a symbol"— more than any Negro writer of that day could achieve.

Though not a Quaker, Bayard Taylor became a perceptive observer of the distinguishing qualities of Delaware Valley Quakers in his day. With fidelity Taylor recorded such qualities as "adamant sobriety," discipline, patience, sense of order, and masked emotions. His works, William Hannan says ("Bayard Taylor's Portrait of Pennsylvania Quakerism," *PF*, XVI, i [1966], 8–14), are a rich source for social information.

In his dissertation, "A Critical Study of the Poetry of John Banister Tabb," John J. Williams treats two 1910 collections and attempts to place Tabb as a Southern and as an American poet (*DA*, XXVII, 3474A).

iv. General

The amateur verses of Army men on frontier duty are discussed by an historian, James T. King, in "The Sword and the Pen: The Poetry of the Military Frontier" (*NH*, XLVII [1966], 229–245). The topics are what one would expect—some romanticizing ("Oh the life of a soldier is wild and romantic") but more lamenting the decrees of officers, the cruelty of Apaches, and the monotony of hard-tack and beans.

In "The Poetry of Mind and Nature: A Study of the Idea of Nature in American Transcendental Poetry" (*DA*, XXVII, 2496A) Carl E. Dennis says that, unlike the English romantics, American poets place the mind, not nature, at the center; and notes that their emphasis on correspondence established a tradition followed since by Stevens, Williams, and Frost. The title of "The Prophetic Vision in American Poetry, 1835–1900" (*DA*, XXVII, 3461A) sounds promising until Aaron Kramer explains that "prophetic" to him means representing the conscience of his age and that he takes "five areas of specific iniquity" (two wars, Fugitive Slave Law, mob violence, mistreatment of Indians) for admeasuring prophetic vision.

Indiana University

12. Fiction: 1900 to the 1930's

Warren French

Several developments during 1967 are disturbing: the redundancy of book-length studies of much-discussed authors; the continued lack of scholarly editions of established works (perhaps partly as a result of continuing uncertainty over the provisions of a new copyright act); the lack of more broad studies like Stanley Cooperman's *World War I and the American Novel* (Baltimore, Johns Hopkins Press) that enable us to contemplate both major and minor fiction against a background of the times that produced it.

i. General Studies

Comprehensive critiques of the fiction of this period were rare in 1967. The most noteworthy contribution to the study of this material—although not limited in its utility to this period—is *The Twentieth-Century Novel in English: A Checklist*, compiled by E. C. Bufkin (Athens, Univ. of Ga. Press). The only book to treat critically of the whole period is Nicholas J. Karolides' pedestrian survey, *The Pioneer in the American Novel 1900–1950* (Norman, Univ. of Okla. Press), which discusses only slightly more than a hundred novels, of which not more than twelve have enduring artistic value. Karolides has exhaustively classified plots, themes, settings, and attitudes reflected in the novels, and his chapter on "The Moral Fiber" is especially valuable for its portrayal of the change from the Victorian prudery of novels written just after the turn of the century to the freedom and explicitness in the treatment of sex in the novels of the Thirties and Forties. This change, however, probably reflects a general shift in public taste rather than a specific evolution in literary attitudes toward pioneers, so that Karolides' findings will be of most value when incorporated with similar studies into general cultural histories of the first half of this century.

A number of novelists of this period are also analyzed in Charles

Child Walcutt's *Man's Changing Mask*, which argues that there have been significant changes since 1900 not only in the mode of American life, but also in fictional modes of characterization and in the relationship of characters to action in novels. Walcutt documents his thesis with discussions of many British and American writers, including James Gould Cozzens, Sinclair Lewis, John O'Hara, Katherine Anne Porter, and John Steinbeck. No synthesis emerges, however, because Walcutt introduces writers in random order and confines his comments to a single novel by each, so that he conveys no sense of any progression in modes of characterization. What does emerge unmistakably is Walcutt's almost unqualified distaste for the treatment of character by American writers since 1920, revealed by his statement that the hero of the modern novel "is usually involved in a psychological conflict: fears, neuroses, complexes, inhibitions are almost the air he breathes; but they are *not part of the self*. They have been so thoroughly explored and defined and catalogued by the psychoanalysts that they cannot be seen any more as individual eccentricities." The loss of critical objectivity turns a study of a subject of great importance into what its author acknowledges is a "tirade." A book that touches even more lightly upon some of the authors considered in this chapter (London, Dell, Hecht, Bodenheim, Stein) is Emily Hahn's charming but superficial *Romantic Rebels: An Informal History of Bohemianism in America* (Boston, Houghton, Mifflin).

The most valuable contribution during 1967 to study of fiction of the first decade of this century was the founding at the University of Texas at Arlington of the semi-annual journal *American Literary Realism 1870–1910*. The first number (Fall, 1967) is devoted to bibliographical studies of seventeen novelists, including Winston Churchill, Robert Herrick, Jack London, and O. Henry. Churchill and Herrick are also represented, along with Hamlin Garland, W. A. White, Booth Tarkington, Lincoln Steffens, Alfred Henry Lewis, Elliott Flower, David Graham Phillips, Upton Sinclair, Brand Whitlock, and Frank Norris, by samples of their fiction in *Political Literature of the Progressive Era*, edited and with an introduction by George L. Groman (E. Lansing, Mich. State Univ. Press).

Several important novelists of the period before World War I are isolated for treatment in Jay Martin's *Harvests of Change: American Literature 1865–1914* (Englewood Cliffs, N. J., Prentice-Hall), which advances the unassailable argument that "the changes that took place in America between the Civil War and the First World War were remarkable for their completeness and for their rapidity." Martin produces no noteworthy generalizations about the novels of the period, nor does he make a full-scale study of any novelists discussed in this chapter (as he does of Henry James). He produces, however, a useful survey of recent scholarship about significant patterns of imagery in the novels of Wharton, Dreiser, and London.

One of the best books written in this or any other year about a sub-genre of American fiction is Cooperman's *World War I and the American Novel*, which aims "not merely to 'criticize' a literary period, but rather to re-experience it, to get at something of the essence which made of the twenties so vital a decade in American letters." This ambitious aim is accomplished in two long chapters, "The Bold Journey" and "The Broken World," that sum up the enormous impact that World War I had on both American life and literature. Using generous excerpts from novels to convey the at first idealistic and later bitterly disillusioned responses of Americans to this first technological war, Cooperman brings to life this nation's loss of innocence as the senseless horror of war forced upon our people the recognition of the differences between propaganda images and actual experience.

The next three chapters explore the principal American novels about the War in terms of the heroism or anti-heroism of the principal characters. The opening and closing analyses of Willa Cather's *One of Ours* and Ernest Hemingway's *A Farewell to Arms* are particularly brilliant treatments of works that represent the extreme ends of the idealism/despair spectrum. In a final chapter, Cooperman surveys chronologically the criticism of the war novels, calling attention to the differences between fiction dealing with the two World Wars and exposing the irrelevance of "humanist" criticism of war literature because of the anachronistic expectations of the critics. The book is not only a definitive study of a sub-genre, but a model for the exploration of similar subjects, which will be especially welcomed in American Studies courses for its wise blending of historical and literary scholarship.

The second part of the title of Thomas Reed West's *Flesh of Steel: Literature and the Machine in American Culture* (Nashville, Vanderbilt Univ. Press) suggests the ambitious subject of a book that deals with the fiction of the Twenties less successfully than Cooperman's. The opening chapter is a useful survey of nineteenth-century attitudes toward the emerging machine culture; but the essays on Sherwood Anderson, Waldo Frank, John Dos Passos, Sinclair Lewis, Thorstein Veblen and others fail to add up to a meaningful whole. The author, who admits that the book is "not to be taken as a literary study," is much more successful in summarizing the views of essayists than in clarifying the novelists' metaphorically projected attitudes toward machine culture.

We may well recall 1967 as the year in which the critical exploitation of the 1930's reached major proportions. *The Thirties: Fiction, Poetry, Drama*, edited by Warren French, is a collection of twenty-three original essays with prefatory remarks by the editor and a bibliographical checklist by Jackson R. Bryer. The section on fiction opens with the statement that "this was a great age of the novel"; the supporting essays on Dos Passos, Wolfe, Steinbeck, Cain, Miller, West, Henry Roth, and the proletarians will be discussed at the appropriate points in this essay. A useful (although unintentional) companion volume is *Years of Protest: A Collection of American Writings of the 1930's*, edited by Jack Salzman and Barry Wallenstein (New York, Pegasus), which contains specimens from the works of most of the writers mentioned above and many others. Indispensable also to an understanding of the fiction of the Depression years are *Crisis of the American Dream: A History of American Social Thought 1920–1940*, a collection of essays edited by John Tipple (New York, Pegasus), and *Between the Wars: America, 1919–1941*, by David A. Shannon (Boston; Houghton, Mifflin), which contains an essay on "Literature and Art of the Depression," characterizing Dos Passos, Farrell, and Steinbeck as "the major novelists most in tune with the mode of militant democratic egalitarianism."

Literature about the Spanish Civil War attracts increasing attention. John F. Muste's *Say That We Saw Spain Die* (Seattle, Univ. of Wash. Press, 1966) contains detailed analyses of Hemingway's and Dos Passos' fiction. Frederick F. Benson's *Writers in Arms: The Literary Impact of the Spanish Civil War* (New York, New York Univ. Press), deals only in passing with American writers other than Hemingway.

To order the survey of writings about individual novelists active principally between 1900 and 1939, I divide them again into the six groups set up last year as most helpful in illuminating patterns in the development of our fiction. With the addition to the writers previously considered of Henry Miller, B. Traven, Nathanael West, and Thornton Wilder, the groups take on clearer definition.

ii. The Inheritors of the Genteel Tradition

The three ladies whom Howard Mumford Jones regarded as those who best "bridge the gap" between the novelists of the "golden age" late in the nineteenth century and the raucous moderns continue to attract admiring attention.

K. A. Heinemann explains in "Ellen Glasgow: The Death of the Chivalrous Tradition" (*ForumH*, IV, xi, 37–41) that through her insistence on the rights of women and the dignity of the common man, she broke the spell that the chivalrous tradition had cast over writers of Southern fiction. Julius R. Raper, Jr.'s dissertation, "Ellen Glasgow and Darwinism, 1893–1906" (*DA*, XXVII, 2541–2542A), advances a provocative argument about the influence of *On the Origin of Species* on the novelist's early fiction.

Arthur Mizener selects Edith Wharton's *The Age of Innocence* as one of *Twelve Great American Novels* and analyzes it principally in relation to the events of the author's life that she was reticent to discuss. He concludes that the "epilogue" to the novel is the most explicit expression of "her beautifully balanced sense, implicit everywhere in the book, that the only endurable life is the one that preserves the values" that "can be preserved only at the cost of gradually starving the individual emotions that give them life and significance." Jay Martin similarly argues in *Harvests of Change* that Mrs. Wharton "used literature as a means of preserving, establishing, and even of creating her ideals for culture and civilization."

Richard H. Lawson in "Hermann Sudermann and Edith Wharton" (*RLC*, XLI, 125–131) points out that Mrs. Wharton was commissioned by Mrs. Patrick Campbell to translate the German's play *Es lebe das Leben* (mistitled in English *The Joy of Living*) and that Lily Bart, the heroine of *The House of Mirth*—the first novel Mrs. Wharton wrote after completing the translation of the play—bears a remarkable resemblance to Sudermann's heroine as "a victim of a fixed and remorseless society." In "Circularity: Theme and

Structure in *Ethan Frome*" (*S&C*, I [1966], 78–81), Charles Bruce maintains that "the circular image involved in the technique of the flashback contributed to the book's effectiveness by emphasizing the inescapable pattern of events controlling Ethan's life." In a snippy note, "Edith Wharton's Foreknowledge in *The Age of Innocence*" (*TSLL*, VIII [1966], 385–389), Lillie B. Lamar asserts that a close examination of the first edition of the novel reveals that Mrs. Wharton did not have her characters' family trees as firmly in mind as she claimed in *A Backward Glance*.

Two of the finest books for review this year are tributes to Willa Cather. Tasteful editing makes James Schroeter's *Willa Cather and Her Critics* (Ithaca, Cornell Univ. Press), which reprints 34 critical assessments of her life and work, a model for the increasingly frequent collections of this kind. The essays, which range from H. L. Mencken's first excited review in *The Smart Set* in 1916 to Schroeter's own essay on *The Professor's House* published in 1965, are divided into six groups that reflect shifts in interest in the novelist from her enthusiastic early reception as a challenge to the genteel tradition that she came at last to represent to recent assessments of her place in American literature and of the mythic qualities in her work.

Most other Cather scholarship stresses—in this or in any other year—regional aspects of her work. The triumph, however, is Bernice Slote's *The Kingdom of Art: Willa Cather's First Principles and Critical Statements, 1893–1896* (Lincoln, Univ. of Nebr. Press), which brings together excerpts from the often anonymous criticisms that Miss Cather contributed to Lincoln newspapers. The double aim of the book is to show that—contrary to past speculation—Willa Cather was continually active during the years that saw the Midwestern college girl transformed into the editor of a national magazine and that most of the critical principles upon which the author operated all her life had been clear in her mind before she left Nebraska. These theses are advanced in two elegant prefatory essays by Miss Slote: "Writer in Nebraska," which meticulously corrects and amplifies earlier accounts of Miss Cather's activities during the years under consideration, and "The Kingdom of Art," a long analysis of the principles reflected in the three-hundred pages of reprinted criticism of plays and other works.

Nebraska's pride in Willa Cather is emphasized also by two articles about her in the mammoth Nebraska Centennial issue of *Prairie*

Schooner (Summer, 1967). In "The Nebraska Encounter: Willa Cather and Wright Morris" (XLI, 165–167), James E. Miller, Jr., forcefully argues that "Nebraska has inadvertently provided in her two major fiction writers, an account of the twentieth-century experience . . . a foreshortened history of the American imagination, its growth and expansion with the American West, its decline and withdrawal with the disappearance of the frontier, its alienation and collapse in confrontation with modern urban and suburban America." Morris' world, Miller maintains, is Cather's inverted. George Seibel in "Willa Cather and the Village Atheist" (XLI, 168–171) adds a colorful sketch about Willa Cather's attending a Tom Paine birthday celebration held by the local Secular Society during her residence in Pittsburgh.

Another regional journal, Kansas City's *University Review*, carries analyses by Lavon M. Jobes of two Cather novels: "Willa Cather's Last Novel" (XXXIV, 77–80) argues that, although critics have called the portrait of Sapphira in *Sapphira and the Slave Girl* unsympathetic, she is portrayed "with a great deal of sympathy and understanding"; "Willa Cather's *The Professor's House*" (XXIV, 154–160) reads the interpolated story of Tom Outland as "an implied condemnation of the shocking concern with trivialities exhibited in the modern world" described in the opening and closing sections of the novel.

Sister Lucy Schneider, C. S. J., also emphasizes a regional problem in "Willa Cather's Early Stories in the Light of Her 'Land-Philosophy,'" (*MQ*, IX, 75–94), arguing that these early stories show an ambivalent attitude toward the land, which, on the one hand, suggests "ugliness, bitterness and impoverishment," but, on the other, "implies satisfying reality, generosity, and hope of fulfillment." Sister Peter Damian Charles, O. P., examines in "My Ántonia: A Dark Dimension" (*WAL*, II, 91–108) the role of the narrator, Jim Burden, and argues that his character merges with that of Ántonia's father to produce a death figure, "a single dark shadow which emphasizes the brilliance of Ántonia's life-force."

The interest kindled in 1966 in other Trans-Mississippi writers by the founding of *Western American Literature* has flared up with the launching in 1967 of a "Southwest Writers Series" of pamphlets —the first similar to the Minnesota pamphlets on American authors to deal only with writers of a particular region. Of greatest concern to this chapter is Edwin W. Gaston, Jr.'s *Eugene Manlove Rhodes: Cowboy Chronicler* (SWS, No. 11, Austin, Steck-Vaughn), an analysis of an often praised writer who has never managed to win a secure place in the history of American letters. Gaston summarizes Rhodes's achievement with an economy of expression other writers might well cultivate, but he underrates his subject when he asserts that what Rhodes did was to "describe Western landscapes and to explicate the Western occupations of mining and ranching." Rhodes created a body of Western fiction that is still unique because his characters triumph by using intelligence rather than brute strength.

Another significant regional contributor to the genteel tradition was Kentucky's Elizabeth Madox Roberts. In "The Mind and Creative Habits of Elizabeth Madox Roberts," a contribution to *All These to Teach* (pp. 237–248), Herman Spivey examines her second novel *My Heart and My Flesh* and opines that it has not been popular because there is "too much humble acceptance and too little rebellion, ranting, and disillusionment for the American public of the 1920's."

Getting back to the mainstream of the genteel tradition, one of the most welcome books of 1967 is *The Genteel Tradition: Nine Essays by George Santayana*, edited by Douglas L. Wilson (Cambridge, Harvard Univ. Press), which brings together the writings that provided an indispensable term and traced the history of its application. In "George Santayana and the Uses of Literature" (*YCGL*, XV [1966], 5–18), Newton P. Stallknecht argues that *The Last Puritan* embodies the philosophy expounded in the essay "The Genteel Tradition at Bay" that "mind was not created for the sake of discovering absolute truth," but for "creating all those private perspectives, and those emotions of wonder, curiosity, and laughter, which omniscience would exclude."

Of the small group of novelists born in the twentieth century who attempt to write in what Santayana would consider the original rationalistic framework of the genteel tradition only James Gould Cozzens continues to excite interest. R. W. Lewis' "The Conflicts of Reality: Cozzen's *The Last Adam*" in *Seven Contemporary Authors* (pp. 3–22) points out that in this early novel the author succeeds in fully and fairly drawing two opposing types of modern hero: Herbert Banning, who is "wealthy and powerful, well-educated and well-born, but . . . caught in dilemmas and indecisions

and conflicts and tensions that will not be resolved except by death,"
but also Dr. Bull, "an Adam, a man who has hope, who demonstrates
hope without thinking about it." Richard A. Long's "The Image of
Man in James Gould Cozzens" (*CLAJ*, X, 299–307) calls Cozzens
"the novelist of the conservative and correct class," who, because
he spares himself both hope and pity, is "at best an accomplished reporter in self-imposed exile from the house of art." Although not so
identified, the approbatory essay on *Guard of Honor* in Arthur Mizener's *Twelve Great American Novels* is a reprinting of "The Undis-
torting Mirror" (*KR*, XXVIII [1966], 595–611), discussed last year
(*ALS, 1966*, p. 155).

A wistful footnote to the decline of the genteel tradition is provided by Abigail Ann Hamblen's effort in "Judge Grant and the
Forgotten Chippendales" (*UR*, XXXIII, 175–179) to revive the reputation of *The Chippendales*, a novel portraying nineteenth-century
Boston society, by Robert Grant, a Boston jurist who was once president of the National Institute of Arts and Letters, but who is recalled
today principally as one of the three members of the special com-
mittee that reported on the fairness of the Sacco-Vanzetti trial. Miss
Hamblen's sympathetic analysis suggests that the novel is of little
artistic interest, but of great sociological value as evidence in support
of Santayana's diagnosis of the reasons for the decline of the genteel
tradition.

iii. The Ungenteel Voices of Protest

Interest in those whom Philip Rahv branded "redskins" in contrast
to the "palefaces" of the genteel tradition continues to rise, with
Jack London especially being touted by a small but determined band
of supporters who have brought their energies into focus by launching the *Jack London Newsletter.* Most of the first issue is devoted to
Earle Labor's "Jack London's *Mondo Cane: The Call of the Wild*
and *White Fang*" (I, 2–13), which argues that the former novel is
"an unforgettable classic," because it "points to something awesome
and marvelous within man's own heart of darkness," whereas the
latter is "merely a very memorable 'story about a dog.'" The issue
also contains many bibliographical notes.

Labor collaborates with King Hendricks on "Jack London's
Twice-Told Tale" (*SSF*, IV, 334–347), which reprints the original
juvenile version of "To Build a Fire" from *Youth's Companion* (1902)

and compares it with the later story for adults. Hendricks also provides a powerful tribute to the novelist in *Jack London: Master Craftsman of the Short Story* (Logan, Utah State Univ. Faculty Assoc.) which discusses four stories that illustrate London's "tremendous ability to create character," his ability to create an atmosphere," and "his masterful use of irony." London receives more balanced consideration in Franklin Walker's "Ideas and Action in Jack London's Fiction" (*Essays on American Literature*, pp. 259–272), which ventures the opinions that the Klondike novels are valued for plot, character, and setting, not intellectual concepts and that "London is never less successful than when he is putting theories obtained from his reading into fiction." Jay Martin, on the other hand, argues in *Harvests of Change* that London "wrote in a philosophical tradition rather than a literary one" and was "perhaps the last of the writers whose work was vitalized by the remarkable efflorescence of utopian ideas in the nineteenth century." James Ellis' "A New Reading of *The Sea Wolf*" (*WAL*, II, 127–134) supports Martin's view by maintaining that Wolf Larsen is meaningful not as "a naturalistic superman," but "as man in conflict torn between allegiance to his animal reason or acquiescence to his human heart." London's concern with ideology is also stressed in Richard VanderBeets' "Nietzsche of the North: Heredity and Race in Jack London's *The Son of the Wolf*" (*WAL*, II, 229–233), which argues that London's "racism" is apparent from his earliest work, which attacks not Orientals—as did much of his later work—but Alaskan Indians.

Writings about Theodore Dreiser concentrate on individual works, although Jay Martin observes generally in *Harvests of Change* that because Dreiser "treated the city not as a moral, but an aesthetic aspect of experience," he was "the first man to accept and reveal, in all its massive incomprehensibility, the modern city." Jack Salzman attacks in "The Publication of *Sister Carrie*: Fact and Fiction" (*LC*, XXXIII, 119–133) the legends surrounding the event and argues that Frank Norris' role has been exaggerated, because Arthur Henry appears the champion to whom Dreiser was most indebted. Yoshinobu Hakutani in "*Sister Carrie* and the Problem of Literary Naturalism" (*TCL*, XIII, 3–17) attacks another stereotype about the novel by arguing that it is not truly naturalistic because Dreiser's subjective treatment of characters departs substantially from Zola's "systematic theory of behavior deduced from scientific observations."

Turning to a less frequently discussed novel, Walter Blackstock maintains in "The Fall and Rise of Eugene Witla: Dramatic Vision of Artistic Integrity in *The Genius*" (*LangQ*, V, i–ii, 15–18) that Witla's achievement of responsible selfhood as an artist is more important than Dreiser's dramatization of the theory of "varietism." The subjective romantic element in Dreiser's work is also stressed in Francesco Binni's "Dreiser oltre il naturalismo" (*SA*, XI [1965], 251–269), which discusses *The Bulwark* as a romance curiously detached from the literary development to which Dreiser had contributed so much. The most impressive study of a Dreiser novel to appear in 1967 is Strother B. Purdy's *"An American Tragedy* and *L'Etranger*" (*CL*, XIX, 252–268), in which it is argued that the two novels present the same conclusions: (1) man is alone in an indifferent universe, (2) there is nothing beyond this life, (3) society is organized to pretend this isn't true, (4) crime is a social invention.

The only volume in the ever proliferating Twayne series to fall this year within my purview is Paul J. Carter's *Waldo Frank* (TUSAS, No. 125), which displays an encyclopedic knowledge of Frank's life and works, but which gives an uncomfortable sense of having been drastically cut from a much longer manuscript. Calling Frank "a naturalistic mystic," Carter concludes that "if a mechanistic and mechanical society continues to search for some meaning to justify its existence, it may yet rediscover Waldo Frank," but his book offers little hope that it will, because the detailed analyses of Frank's works continually remind one of Carter's own objection to Frank's second novel, "The difficulty in *The Unwelcome Man* is one that plagues the subsequent novels: the protagonist is an abstraction; his struggles are shadowy projections of psychological twists of mind."

Other "redskins" find defenders. John E. Hart's "Heroism through Social Awareness: Ernest Poole's *The Harbor*" (*Crit*, IX, iii, 84–94) maintains that the hero of the novel illustrates that "the achieved wisdom of self-understanding and insight comes not from internal vision and private contemplation, but from actual experience with social and economic conditions." Frank Norris' influence on the novels of his neglected younger brother are explored in Arnold Goldsmith's "Charles and Frank Norris" (*WAL*, II, 30–49), a study of Charles's admiration of his brother and his use of Frank as a prototype for certain characters. In "O. Henry as a Regional Artist" (*Essays on American Literature*, pp. 229–240), E. Hudson Long illustrates that O. Henry's "keen interest in setting" made it possible for him to do for New York and Texas what local colorists like Harte and Cable had done for California and New Orleans.

Two provocative essays relate "redskins" to important intellectual trends of the period. John M. Harrison argues in "Finley Peter Dunne and the Progressive Movement" (*JQ*, XLIV, 475–481) that Dunne belongs to a group who were, "in varying degrees, philosophical anarchists" and objected to Woodrow Wilson, for example, because they abhorred intellectual reformers in both domestic and international affairs." David Singer points out in "David Levinsky's Fall: A Note on the Liebman Thesis" (*AQ*, XIX, 696–706) the way in which Abraham Cahan's novel may provide valuable support for the revolutionary theory of Professor Charles Liebman that "most of the nominally Orthodox [Jewish] immigrants who came to the United States were bound by commitments that were ethnic rather than religious."

The mysterious B. Traven, who may well be called "the last of the redskins," has been enjoying a good press lately. In "The Mystery of B. Traven" and related pieces (*Ramparts*, VI, ii, 31–49, iii, 55–75), Judy Stone theorizes that Traven is an illegitimate son of Kaiser Wilhelm II of Germany and that under the name of Ret Marut, Traven published an anti-war newspaper in Munich during World War I. Charles R. Humphrey's dissertation, "B. Traven: An Examination of the Controversy over His Identity with an Analysis of His Major Work and His Place in Literature" (*DA*, XXVII, 3049–3050A) rejects this story and claims that the author's importance rests upon his influence on Mexican President Mateos' land reform program. Charles H. Miller in "Our Great Neglected Wobbly" (*MQR*, VI, 57–61), refuses comment on the Marut legend and attacks other writers for promoting myths about the man instead of the books of "a unique story-teller, whose passion for lowly individuals, whose love of liberty and human dignity, and whose wholeness of life, all mark him apart from the preoccupied partyliners of proletarian literature."

iv. The Iconoclasts

Interest in the Twenties continues. Writings about the group who began immediately after World War I to create and promote a disillusionment with some of our most sacred national stereotypes make up a substantial part of this year's critical assessment of the fiction of the first four decades of this century.

It was an especially big year for Sherwood Anderson. After a lapse the American Authors and Critics series has resumed activity under a new imprint with David D. Anderson's sound and reliable *Sherwood Anderson: An Introduction and Interpretation* (New York; Holt, Rinehart and Winston), in which it is argued that Anderson's works, "in all their variety of forms, from short story to essay to novel to autobiographical memoirs, must be approached as a unit," because "the works as a whole provide the record of one man's attempt to understand the relation between the individual and the time in which he lived and to determine the ultimate meaning of that relation."

The source of Anderson's achievement during his final years is explained by editor Ray Lewis White in his introduction to the tastefully designed and illustrated *Return to Winesburg: Selections from Four Years of Writing for a Country Newspaper* (Chapel Hill, Univ. of N. C. Press). White suggests that perhaps because Anderson had no formal training in editing papers, he created in the two weeklies he took over in Marion, Virginia, "distinct products of his own mind," news items that combine "the characteristics of the short story with those of the familiar essay."

Two dissertations deal also with this last phase of Anderson's life: Welford D. Taylor's "Sherwood Anderson's 'Buck Fever': A Critical Edition" (*DA*, XXVII, 3883A) brings together all the columns in the tradition of Southwestern humorous journalism that Anderson wrote under this pseudonym (many are included in White's book); G. Bert Carlson, Jr.'s "Sherwood Anderson's Political Mind: The Activist Years" (*DA*, XXVII, 3864–3865A) traces the way in which Anderson became increasingly radical after 1929, but avoided commiting himself to Communism and supported Franklin D. Roosevelt.

The road that led Anderson to Marion began in Elyria, Ohio, from which he mysteriously disappeared in 1912. William A. Sutton collects in *Exit to Elsinore* (Muncie, Ind., Ball State Monograph No. 7) all the documents pertinent to this legendary incident to demonstrate that Anderson suffered an amnesiac attack.

Study of *Winesburg, Ohio*, Anderson's most admired work, is likely to be accelerated by John H. Ferres' impeccable new edition of the text (New York, Viking Press, 1966), along with statements from Anderson's letters and memoirs, six early reviews and twenty reprinted critical essays that center primarily on the nature of the short-story cycle. Meanwhile two new essays have been added to the growing body of studies of *Winesburg*. In "The Theme of Sublimation in Anderson's *Winesburg, Ohio*" (*MFS*, XIII, 237–246), George D. Murphy classifies the "grotesques" in the book into "four distinct types on the basis of their responses to sexual emotion." The most "thematically signifiant category," Murphy maintains, contains those who "are presented as being in the grip of a strong physical passion, which, for one reason or another, they do not consummate." Rosemary M. Laughlin focuses on a single tale in " 'Godliness' and the American Dream in *Winesburg, Ohio*" (*TCL*, XIII, 97–103) and points out that when we consider "Godliness" apart from the cycle, it "is not simply an allegory," but reflects "in part the ethic and experience of the Protestant settlers in America," by showing a character turned into a "grotesque" by "the belief in material prosperity as the sign of divine favor."

Turning to a later story, Sister Mary Joselyn, O.S.B., points out in "Some Artistic Dimensions of Sherwood Anderson's 'Death in the Woods' " (*SSF*, IV, 252–259) that through the depiction of four interlocking transformations the story shows how the young boy who witnessed the original events became the artist who portrayed them.

Two further books are at hand about writers who jolted American complacency at the end of World War I. D. J. Dooley's *The Art of Sinclair Lewis* (Lincoln, Univ. of Nebr. Press) appears to have been transcribed directly from note cards. It is scrupulously documented, but its recent predecessors by Schorer and Grebstein make it redundant. Although in conclusion Dooley states that Lewis "went far beyond most of his more illustrious contemporaries in raising questions of enduring importance to national life," his criticisms are mostly fault-finding, and he pays—despite his title—little attention to the aesthetic features of Lewis' work.

Desmond Tarrant's more impressive *James Branch Cabell: The Dream and the Reality* (Norman, Univ. of Okla. Press) also contains much plot summary, but the author's aggressive defense of his subject lends his book a vitality often missing in scholarly labors.

"Cabell," he argues, "is almost alone in twentieth-century literature in presenting man as, if not master of his fate, at least equal to it." As we come to comprehend Cabell's imagination, Tarrant continues, "he may well emerge as the literary giant of the era." One is inclined to think, however, that Edd W. Parks may be right when he maintains in "James Branch Cabell" (*MissQ*, XX, 97–102), one of a series of reassessments of the reputations of Southern writers, that, though Cabell is "the best writer of philosophical romances we have had in this century," he has lost popularity because of the excessive demands he makes upon readers.

Perusing Virginia S. Reinhart's "John Dos Passos, 1950–1966, Bibliography" (*TCL*, XIII, 167–178), one is surprised to find how much the author has written since the appearance of Jack Potter's bibliography in 1950 (19 books, for example!) and how much has been written about him despite a decline in his popularity. Several of the early novels on which Dos Passos' reputation still rests are examined in detail in Stanley Cooperman's *World War I and the American Novel* as exemplary treatments of hero and anti-hero. The earliest of the war novels is also examined in Kenneth Holditch's "*One Man's Initiation*: The Origins of Technique in the Novels of John Dos Passos" (*Explorations of Literature*, pp. 115–123), which argues that although this novel differs from later ones in the author's resorting to "repeated polemics . . . rather awkwardly introduced," it is important as an illustration of Dos Passos' use of "the continuing symbol," foundation for the structure of *Three Soldiers* and *Manhattan Transfer*.

Arthur Mizener's chapter on *The Big Money* in *Twelve Great American Novels* (pp. 86–103), is a conventional analysis of the structural novelties employed in *U.S.A.*, which concludes with the assertion that, though Dos Passos' novels are out of fashion, he is "the only major American novelist of the Twentieth Century who has the desire and power to surround the lives of his characters with what Lionel Trilling once called 'the buzz of history.'" Eleanor Widmer agrees with this assertion in "The Lost Girls of *U.S.A.*: Dos Passos' 30's Movie" (*The Thirties*, pp. 11–19), but, limiting herself to the fresh and provocative subject of the novelist's portrayal of women, she argues that, although he purportedly deals with the newly emancipated female, he nevertheless "handles women with a gentility closely akin to Edwardianism and defeats them by stock situations, lugubrious determinism, and his particular brand of social consciousness *cum* caricature."

The too much neglected writers of an important movement during the Twenties are sympathetically studied by Waters E. Turpin in "Four Short Fiction Writers of the Harlem Renaissance: Their Legacy of Achievement" (*CLAJ*, XI, 59–72), which maintains that, although Jean Toomer, Rudolph Fisher, Langston Hughes, and Claude McKay have been accused of "evoking and perpetuating a vogue of exoticism which tended to foster stereotyping in the treatment of Negro materials," each has a "stylistic sophistication," and "verisimilitude in language, situation and internal logic fused with a sense of irony that gets across any protest unobtrusively," so that they provide "the young Negro writer of today with a lodestar to follow."

v. The Expatriates

Interest in the cosmopolitans who fled these shores for Europe during the era of "normalcy" has shifted from Gertrude Stein's circle to that Peck's bad boy of American letters, Henry Miller. Miss Stein, however, manages to hold her own. Allegra Stewart's *Gertrude Stein and the Present* (Cambridge, Harvard Univ. Press) can only be described as adulatory. Observing that Miss Stein's goal in writing "appears to be something almost quintessential—the mystery perhaps of a power like that attributed to seekers after the philosopher's stone," Miss Stewart makes a detailed analysis of *Tender Buttons* "as a verbal mandala—a work formed . . . by repeated acts of genuine concentration in the attempt to discover fresh language and to effect a breakthrough to deeper creativity." Kemp Malone is less impressed. In "Observations on *Paris, France*" (*PLL*, III, 159–178)—an urbane running commentary on one of Miss Stein's later works—the distinguished scholar makes the point that while her "idiosyncratic style," "commonly though inexactly described as colloquial," is "superficially informal . . . the unstudied effect is contrived and far from thoroughgoing." The cast of mind that accounts for the frequency in Miss Stein's work of words like *never, naturally* and *inevitably*, Malone calls "totalism."

The much more extensive recent contemplation of Henry Miller falls between adulation and contempt. At one end of the spectrum are two dissertations: George P. Cockcroft in "The Two Henry Millers" (*DA*, XXVIII, 669A) attributes the spiritualization of Miller's thinking and writing after 1938 to his discovery of Balzac's mystical novels *Serophita* and *Louis Lambert*; Paul R. Jackson argues in "Henry Miller: The Autobiographical Romances" (*DA*, XXVIII, 678A) that as Miller's career progressed "eclectic religious attitudes replaced the comic and vindictive heroism of the early books."

William A. Gordon's *The Mind and Art of Henry Miller* (Baton Rouge, La. State Univ. Press) develops the thesis that Miller's "voyage of discovery is toward a full acceptance of the possibilities and limitations of the human individual," in the course of which the writer "has reached out beyond the immediately physical in experience to the transcendent, the absolute." His treatment of sex, Gordon explains, should lead theoretically "not to promiscuity, though it seems to justify promiscuity, but to a rethinking, or, better, a re-experiencing of basic sexual attitudes and a revision of them in the direction of a less-restrictive personal ethic," so that "love and excrement must be felt on the same plane of existence, equally acceptable." Gordon's humorless book, unfortunately, loses sight of Miller's ironic playfulness and thoroughly bourgeois sentimentality and sounds like the account of the visits of an earnest, liberal-minded Victorian clergyman to skid rows in order to develop a sense of compassion for his fallen fellow creatures.

A better balanced view of Miller is found in the first half of Ihab Hassan's *The Literature of Silence* (New York, Knopf). Hassan never succeeds in linking Miller's writings to the introductory thesis that "literature, turning against itself, aspires to silence," but he produces incidentally one of the most concise and useful accounts of Miller's life and effusions to appear so far. He admits that Miller's "sacramental vision is backed by an ancient, honorable, and sometimes comic, mystic tradition," but he feels that since the emphasis in *Tropic of Capricorn* is on "desolation," "the mystic recollection must therefore appear to us like some *deus ex machina*, hurriedly summoned to save a darkling day," so that "we cannot finally accept Miller in the way we accept Blake or Whitman, Boehme or Milarepa."

Limiting himself to Miller's famous early works, Alan Friedman in "The Pitching of Love's Mansions in *The Tropics* of Henry Miller"

(*Seven Contemporary Authors*, pp. 23–48) is less impressed. He finds that Miller's focal theme is "disgust and revulsion at the stupidity and ugliness he sees all around him"; but of his flights of fancy Friedman observes, "all this quasi-mystical self-aggrandizing is as much pompous posturing for effect as it is a serious attempt to find proper expression for an ever recurring sense of hopelessness." The late Frederick J. Hoffman strikes the happiest balance between recent attitudes toward Miller in a short meditation, "Henry Miller, Defender of the Marginal Life" (*The Thirties*, pp. 73–80), in which he observes that Miller "is often not at all profound when he thinks he is or he wishes he were; he is often quite strikingly witty when he is least pretentious," so that "the effect of the writing is at once half-profound and half-comical . . . it enlists our sentimentality and our wit at the same time."

vi. The Cosmogonists

Six writers—Faulkner, Porter, Steinbeck, West, Wilder, Wolfe—in perspective appear more and more to have been, because of their perception of universal meaning in the experience of a particular region, the seminal writers of the Thirties. Faulkner is treated elsewhere in this book.

One of the least satisfactory pamphlets in the new "Southwest Writers Series" is—through no fault of its author—Winfred S. Emmons' *Katherine Anne Porter: The Regional Stories* (SWS, No. 6, Austin, Steck-Vaughn). As Emmons acknowledges, Miss Porter is not primarily a regionalist, so that isolating from her work the eleven pieces with recognizably Texan settings leaves the critic little to do but retell the stories. Malcolm Marsden penetrates much more deeply into Miss Porter's work when he argues in "Love as Threat in Katherine Anne Porter's Fiction" (*TCL*, XIII, 29–38) that there are three basic ways in which the stories imply that love must include hate. In some stories, lovers who quarrel "move in a normal pattern through purgation and renewal," in others "a defective link makes renewal impossible," in a third type, "a character's fear of extinction is so excessive that he isolates himself emotionally from all human contact." All three types of story are woven together in *Ship of Fools*. Concentrating on a single story, Peter Wolfe in "The Problems of

Granny Weatherall" (*CLAJ*, XI, 142–148) reads the tale of her "jilting" as "a celebration of man's spiritual and practical energies rather than a record of despair."

One of the most useful reference tools to appear during 1967 is Tetsumaro Hayashi's *John Steinbeck: A Concise Bibliography (1930–1965)* (Metuchen, N. J.; Scarecrow Press). Though not free of typographical errors, this lengthy compilation of writings in English by and about the novelist will provide the long-needed foundation stone for other investigations of his work. Also important is William R. Osborne's "The Texts of Steinbeck's 'The Chrysanthemums' " (*MFS*, XII [1966], 479–484), which points out that it has not been noticed that there are two different texts of the story in circulation, one based on the version that appeared in *Harper's Magazine* in 1937 and the other on the text found in *The Long Valley* (1938).

A familiar aspect of Steinbeck's work is explored in Harland S. Nelson's "Steinbeck's Politics Then and Now" (*AR*, XXVII, 118–133), which argues that the novelist is not a politician but a visionary and that his politics "are a set of attitudes (more felt than thought) about the state of man in his society and in the world." The attitudes, Nelson feels, have not changed from *The Grapes of Wrath* to *The Winter of Our Discontent*, but the difference between the works is accounted for by the author's loss of confidence, possibly because vision cannot survive without an ideology. An entirely fresh look at Steinbeck's work is taken in Pascal Covici, Jr.'s "John Steinbeck and the Language of Awareness" (*The Thirties*, pp. 47–54), which maintains that "the achievement of John Steinbeck in the 30s was to present not only the land, with the people and the social forces that made life upon it so engrossing and sometimes so terrifying, but also the struggle of people toward the awareness that is 'locked in wordlessness,' " which the writer seeks the symbols to unlock.

Randall C. Reid's dissertation has already—much too quickly—been converted into *The Fiction of Nathanael West: No Redeemer, No Promised Land* (Chicago, Univ. of Chicago Press), an unhappy example of those rushed productions that are not nearly so good as they could have been. I learned a great deal from thinking about this perceptive study, but I had to piece the illuminating fragments together into a sustained argument. Although the thesis that West is a parodist is announced in an introductory chapter and developed in the discussion of *The Dream Life of Balso Snell*, it is lost amidst a welter of other material in the overlong chapter on *Miss Lonely-hearts*, in which the author is reluctant to put his finger on the intellectual pretenders parodied. Finally the term "parody" almost disappears from the epilogue, so that a potentially valuable book becomes almost a fit candidate for parody itself.

In the ten pages of "The Sweet Savage Prophecies of Nathanael West" (*The Thirties*, pp. 97–106), Kingsley Widmer provides a far more coherent interpretation of West's distinctive genius than Reid. Observing that West's "imaginative grotesques" although seemingly demanded by his age are missing in the work of most of his contemporaries, Widmer theorizes that "especially concerned with the fatuous and machined dreams counterfeiting that reality [of the Depression], West foresaw the apocalyptic violence of warped and cheated humanity." "That West can treat the apocalypses of the mass-technological civilization and its counterfeited dreams as comedies," Widmer concludes, "provides a kind of parody of the ancient metaphysical proof of deity from design."

Commentators continue to throng around *Miss Lonelyhearts*. Roger D. Abrahams' "Adrogynes Bound: Nathanael West's *Miss Lonelyhearts*" (*Seven Contemporary Authors*, pp. 49–72) argues that "the pathos of Miss Lonelyhearts' condition is that he knows that he is sick, but finds that he can do nothing about it," because "he cannot abstract himself from his feelings and thus go about acting on them." Thomas M. Lorch's "Religion and Art in *Miss Lonelyhearts*" (*Renascence*, XX, 11–17) maintains, on the contrary, that Miss Lonelyhearts undergoes "a positive religious development . . . toward Christ-like love and sacrifice, and from doubt to faith," as West explores "the ability of Christianity to help the individual achieve self-realization." C. W. Bush's "This Stupendous Fabric: The Metaphysics of Order in Melville's *Pierre* and Nathanael West's *Miss Lonelyhearts*" (*JAmS*, I, 269–274) argues, from yet another point of view, that in both novels "inherited visions of ideal Christian order fail and both heroes are forced to make their own 'stupendous fabric' out of the remnants of the old . . . Both books have a nightmare quality because the heroes achieve their dreams of order only in death."

Bibliographical material on West accumulates. W. Keith Kraus in "Nathanael West: A Further Bibliographical Note" (*Serif*, IV, i, 32) notes a motion picture version of *Miss Lonelyhearts* and its reviews and also in "An Uncited Nathanael West Story" (*AN&Q*, V, 163–164) adds "A Barefaced Lie" (*Overland Monthly*, July, 1929), to the West canon. William White in "'Uncited West Story': A Dissent" (*AN&Q*, VI, 72–73, 1968) challenges the accuracy of the attribution.

One of the great literary events of 1967 was the publication of Thornton Wilder's *The Eighth Day*, which is causing this author who has generally been regarded for three decades as a playwright once more to be considered primarily as a novelist. Criticism continues to stress the plays, but Alexander Cowie's "The Bridge of Thornton Wilder" (*Essays on American Literature*, pp. 307–328) reviews the early novels and argues that Wilder is the most difficult American writer to evaluate because of the exasperating coolness and lack of involvement in his work. Cowie wisely concludes, however, that Wilder "insists not only upon the dignity of man, but also upon his capacity for the enjoyment of life."

Andrew Turnbull, who has apparently become Scribner's "house biographer," has turned his attention from Fitzgerald to Wolfe. His *Thomas Wolfe* (New York, Scribner's) might better be titled "Maxwell Perkins and Thomas Wolfe," for it concentrates on the relationship between the men and ends abruptly with Wolfe's death, much of his work still unpublished. A gossipy, illustrated work, it will appeal much more to general readers than to literary critics. Much more provocative is Richard Walser's "The Transformation of Thomas Wolfe" (*The Thirties*, pp. 39–45), which attributes the break between Perkins and Wolfe to the novelist's increasing intellectual development and political awareness as signaled in stories like "Death—the Proud Brother" (1933) and "I Have a Thing to Tell You" (1935).

Several critical articles on Wolfe have appeared recently in German and Polish journals, but I have been able to locate only Heinz Ludwig's "Ein Beitrag zum Verständnis von Thomas Wolfes 'Death the Proud Brother'" (*NS*, XV [1966], 173–182), which calls this story as important as Walser does because in it Wolfe finds in "the gate of death" "the unfound door" that he was seeking at the end of *Look Homeward, Angel*. Clayton L. Eichelberger also argues for the importance of a neglected work in "'No Door' and the Brink of Discovery" (*GaR*, XXI, 319–327), claiming that this four-part story is perhaps the author's "most effectively controlled presentation of the dominant theme of loneliness and aloneness which stands central in his life and work."

vii. The Tough Guys and Others

General critical neglect of the tough and proletarian authors continued through 1967 (though their turn is coming in 1968). A general survey of the shortcomings of the abundant proletarian fiction of the Thirties, "Reading the Proletarians: Thirty Years Later" (*The Thirties*, pp. 89–95) is the result of David G. Pugh's browsing through Granville Hicks's anthology *Proletarian Literature in the United States* (1935). Pugh observes that "even if a reader under thirty is willing to grant, 'OK, that's how life must have been in those days,' he may be put off by the flatness of the vocabulary and syntax, the obviousness of the style." Propaganda literature, Pugh concludes, suffers more from the passage of time than reportage or reminiscences. Even the reliability of such documents is brought into question, however, by Daniel Aaron (author of *Writers on the Left*) in "The Treachery of Recollection: The Inner and Outer History," his contribution to *Essays on History and Literature* (pp. 3–27), in which he explains the internal and external problems confronting the historian seeking information on the writers of the Thirties, especially concerning their political activities. The "generation gap" that Pugh notes is exemplified by "A Literary Note" from James T. Farrell (*ABC*, XVII, ix, 6–8), which accompanies the first publication of a 1935 preface intended for a Chilean edition of *Studs Lonigan*. Farrell takes a jaundiced look at more recently risen writers of fiction and says that he is "as little in sympathy" with many of his juniors as they are with him.

Edward Dahlberg suffers from no such misunderstanding, for Paul Carroll's introduction to *The Edward Dahlberg Reader* (New York, New Directions), which brings together passages from memoirs, letters, and criticism, asserts that this "Job of American letters" is "our one mythological poet." "Myth is as natural to Dahlberg's sensibility," we are informed, "as air, earth, water, and fire. He never uses myth simply as a literary device; instead he lives myth, expressing his deepest feelings and life in terms of myths."

In "Henry Roth and the Redemptive Imagination" (*The Thirties*, pp. 107–114), William Freedman finds a new depth in much discussed *Call It Sleep*, which he explains as a mixture of "myth, symbol, and profound realism." The frequent comparisons to Joyce's *A Portrait of the Artist as a Young Man*, Freedman believes, are "more apt than is realized" by many who make them, because "in a very real sense, these moments of mystical transformation, of blinding radiance" that are frequent in the novel "are moments of imaginative transcendence, experiences through which David momentarily transcends the chaos of his physical universe" and develops the ability to order and deal with his world.

David Madden's essay "James M. Cain and the Tough Guy Novelists of the 30s" in the same collection (*The Thirties*, pp. 63–71) concentrates almost entirely on Cain's first novel, *The Postman Always Rings Twice*, which Madden feels remains Cain's best. "In its special way," Madden theorizes, "the tough guy vision scrutinizes one of the central themes in American literature: the fate of American land, character, and dream. . . . Leaving out the subtle phases between, the tough novelists show the failure of the dream by a camera-cold recording of the nightmare." Madden also points out a resemblance not only between Frank Chambers of Cain's novel and Meursault of Camus' *The Stranger*, but also "an astonishing structural similarity" between the books. Walter Blair examines another author that Madden mentions in "Dashiell Hammet: Themes and Techniques" (*Essays on American Literature*, pp. 295–306) and finds the detective-story writer's work of "more than ephemeral value" because he is a technician of unusual skill in handling point of view.

With a single striking exception, little criticism appeared during 1967 of the more conventional romancers of the Thirties, although MacKinlay Kantor found occasion in *The Historical Novelist's Obligation to History* (Macon, Ga., Wesleyan College) to attack Stephen Crane's *Red Badge of Courage* and to maintain that the historical novelist "must be an antiquarian of the first water." A regional journal also saluted two historical novelists: Ronald W. Taber's "Vardis Fisher: New Directions for the Historical Novel" (*WAL*, I, 285–296) maintains that Fisher writes about the past "to aid contemporary man in his quest for knowledge"; Orlan Sawey's "Bernard DeVoto's Western Novels" (*WAL*, II, 171–182) finds that the basic theme of the books is "the redemption found in separation from the degrading forces of the East."

The hero of the year was, however, Jesse Stuart. As if in answer to Frank H. Leavell's plea a year earlier for more consideration of the Kentucky writer, Stuart was the subject of two books. Everetta Love Blair's *Jesse Stuart: His Life and Work* (Columbia, Univ. of S. C. Press) is a biography with a chatty introduction by Stuart himself. Lee Pennington's *The Dark Hills of Jesse Stuart* (Cincinnati, Harvest Press) is a much more intensive analysis of the development of a single theme dominant in Stuart's first book of poems through eight of his novels. Both books plead strenuously that Stuart is not merely a regional writer, but an artist of universal significance. Pennington argues with impressive force that Stuart "selected the subject of a particular region simply because a dying culture offered the best example to portray his vision. Just as Stuart's cycle in *Harvest of Youth* begins with death and works forward to a rebirth in youth, his novels start with a dead culture and work toward a rebirth through the youth of that culture."

Perhaps William Saroyan's fiction is rarely discussed because it eludes categorization. In "Komik und Humor in William Saroyans Erzählung "The Pomegranate Trees,'" (*NS*, XV [1966], 372–377), Rudolph Fabritius finds that Uncle Melek's effort to make a garden bloom in a waste land recalls Don Quixote's tilting with windmills, so that in this story—like Cervantes in his great novel—Saroyan creates "the tragi-comedy of mankind."

University of Missouri/Kansas City

13. Fiction: The 1930's to the Present

Richard D. Lehan

In 1965, *Book Week* polled some two hundred novelists, critics, and editors. The consensus was that Bellow was the most distinguished novelist in the 1945–1965 period, followed by Nabokov, Malamud, Salinger, Ellison, Mailer, Flannery O'Connor, Robert Penn Warren, John Updike, and William Styron. While *Invisible Man* was the favorite single novel, four of Bellow's six novels were voted among the twenty best: *Herzog* (4th), *Seize the Day* (5th), *Augie March* (6th), and *Henderson the Rain King* (15th). Except for Nabokov, who placed *Lolita* and *Pale Fire*, no other author had more than one title on the list.

Although Salinger has slipped badly in the last few years while Heller's *Catch-22* has attracted considerable attention, this poll faithfully reflects the critical interest of 1967. And interest there was. In writing this review, I read, in whole or in part, twenty books or monographs and almost 200 articles. While the recent novel has attracted some good critics, much of this writing is pedestrian, concerned with themes and images in one or two novels or even stories, with fitting the novels into arbitrary literary categories or conventions, and with value judgments based on highly debatable criteria. Too many academic journals publish too much marginal and even irrelevant criticism. Very few of the critics tell us why a novel is relevant as literature or pertinent to the modern reader. And even fewer of these critics seem concerned with the relevance of their own writing. After reading this much criticism, I feel a bit like Hamlet who, when Polonius asks him what he is reading, answers "words, words, words."

i. General Studies

To begin this way, however, does an injustice to three excellent full-length studies of recent fiction. The late Frederick J. Hoffman's *The*

Art of Southern Fiction (Carbondale, Southern Ill. Univ. Press) treats Eudora Welty, Carson McCullers, James Agee, Flannery O'Connor, Robert Penn Warren, Katherine Anne Porter, Truman Capote, William Styron, Walker Percy, Reynolds Price, William Humphrey, Shirley Ann Grau, and a number of other Southern writers. While Hoffman is fond of literary categories, and of abstract theories of "space and time," this is not a pretentious book. Hoffman brings twenty-five years of study and reflection to his subject, and he has remarkable insight into the thematic continuity of Southern fiction as well as the complexity and relevance of each author's work. While he relies heavily on other critics, he does so judiciously, and his evaluation of the existing criticism is part of the importance of this significant book.

Another important book is Howard M. Harper, Jr.'s *Desperate Faith* (Chapel Hill, Univ. of N. C. Press). Harper attempts to read Saul Bellow, J. D. Salinger, Norman Mailer, James Baldwin, and John Updike as existentialist novelists. This attempt is somewhat frustrated by a loose definition of existentialism ("Like Camus, our contemporary writers are pessimistic as to man, but optimistic as to men. Their fiction is the testament of that desperate faith.") This lack of precise definition, however, turns out to be a virtue because it gives Harper the room to read each novel on its own terms and not with pre-established ideas or categories in mind. As a series of critical readings, *Desperate Faith* is superb. As a study of literary existentialism, it misses the mark, especially with Salinger and Baldwin, although the chapters on Mailer and Updike are extremely good, particularly the discussion of the religious elements in Updike's fiction.

Still another important book is Robert Scholes's *The Fabulators* (New York, Oxford Univ. Press). Scholes treats a number of novelists who have been overlooked—writers like Vonnegut, Terry Southern, John Hawkes, and John Barth—overlooked perhaps because critics have had difficulty in coming to terms with them. Scholes is an expert reader, and he is up to the complexity of the novels he discusses. Because he has pointed to a whole sub-genre of fiction that must be more fully investigated, *The Fabulators* is a pioneering work. The book, however, is not entirely satisfying. Scholes is never sure for whom he is writing. When discussing Vonnegut (the weakest part of his book) and John Hawkes, he assumes the

reader has not read *Mother Night* and *Charivari*; but when discussing Iris Murdoch and John Barth, he assumes the reader has a
detailed understanding of *The Unicorn* and *Giles Goat-Boy*. Scholes
may be right in what he takes for granted, but he also gives the
reader the impression of discussing the novels he wants to discuss
and ignoring those he wants to ignore—and doing this in a random
way. The final point of reference in this book is Scholes's interest
and taste, and many readers may feel that both are arbitrary.

Furthermore, Scholes is too much concerned with the conventions of fiction. His main thesis—that "as the realistic novel was
rooted in the conflict between the individual and society, fabula-
tion springs from the collision between the philosophical and mythic
perspectives of the meaning and value of existence"—may be true,
although it does ignore the obvious social elements in writers like
Vonnegut and Barth. But his attempt to place the new fiction in a
tradition of medieval fable is a gimmick, as he himself admits.
Scholes seems less pretentious when he tells us that "it is surely
better to think of Voltaire and Swift when reading Vonnegut and
Barth than to think of Hemingway and Fitzgerald." Maybe so, but
why must we think of either team, or at least think of them so inclu-
sively as to eclipse other concerns? If the new novel has affinities
with the medieval fable or with eighteenth-century satire, it does
not have its origin there. Its beginnings are not in 1484, "in the eighth
fable of Alfonce, as these fables were Englished by Caxton," but in
the modern world; and Scholes's study suffers from his insistence
upon conventions which subsume the novel and which fail to account for its personal and cultural motives—and for its twentieth-
century relevance.

A book which makes passing reference to recent fiction is Charles
Child Walcutt's *Man's Changing Mask*. Since Walcutt's ideal novel is
Pride and Prejudice, where character exists to act and where personal and social motives are one, he is not very sympathetic to
recent fiction which, he insists, lacks these literary imperatives. Each
novelist is analyzed in terms of his prime fault. Styron's *The Long
March* and Wouk's *Caine Mutiny* stunt the hero's moral growth and
make him subservient to theme and idea. Calder Willingham allows
situation to determine character. Joseph Heller violates credulity.
John Updike's Peter Caldwell and Salinger's Holden Caulfield are
contained by action which overwhelms them, action as force or "a

closed circuit of energy in which the characters can only react in repetitive pattern." Given Walcutt's starting point, most of the conclusions follow. Despite what amounts to a plea for a new humanism, for the marriage of "reason and beauty, form and passion, lucidity and humanity," not all of us will grant him this starting point. For in his insistence upon the inseparability of character and action, of self and society, he seems intent upon returning to a lost world, one that recent novelists can never again know or portray.

The other general discussions of recent fiction are a bit of a potpourri. Lewis A. Lawson in "The Grotesque in Recent Southern Fiction," *Patterns of Commitment*, (pp. 165–179) believes that the newer Southern writers like William Styron and Flannery O'Connor depict the disintegration of the individual more than the disintegration of tradition and are thus closer in literary spirit to Poe than to Faulkner. Marvin Mudrick, "Who Killed Herzog? Or, Three American Novelists" (*UDQ*, I, i, 61–97), seems unduely worried—as well as imprecise and arbitrary—about what is going to happen to Roth, Bellow, and Malamud now that "the American Jew has disappeared into their novels," that is, been absorbed by concerns more encompassing than how it feels to be a Jew. And Joseph Taylor Skerrett, Jr., in "Dostoyevsky, Nathanael West, and Some Contemporary American Fiction" (*UDR*, IV, i, 23–35), argues that the Black Humor of such novelists as Heller, Purdy, and Bruce Jay Friedman originates in Sterne, Fielding, Dostoyevsky, and the pessimism of Mark Twain and Nathanael West.

ii. James Baldwin

Charles Newman's "The Lesson of the Master: Henry James and James Baldwin" (*YR*, LVI, 45–59) studies two forms of American exile. Newman argues that both James and Baldwin expose the American success legend. Both create "powerless, feeling young men," who seek some kind of "transfiguration." James's characters, however, never give up; they seek new experiences because of their faith in their own possibilities, and they remain open-minded enough to avoid despair in themselves and life. Baldwin's characters, especially in *Another Country*, accept easy conclusions, believe that resistance is an end in itself, have no reality beyond that resistance, and end up "lacking the energy to achieve the *engagement* to which [they pay] coffee-house lip-service." It is an interesting essay, but Newman would be safer if he did not endow James's characters with a kind of freedom they do not have, for they often retreat into consciousness that involves the same kind of solipsism that he condemns in Baldwin.

While C. W. E. Bigsby in "The Committed Writer: James Baldwin as Dramatist" (*TCL*, XIII, 39–48) concentrates on *Blues for Mr. Charlie*, he also discusses Baldwin as a novelist. Bigsby feels that Baldwin sentimentalizes the Negro in the same way that the writers of the Thirties sentimentalized the worker and that Baldwin's work suffers from a distorted commitment to the Negro.

Addison Gayle, Jr., would disagree completely with Bigsby. In "A Defense of James Baldwin" (*CLAJ*, X, 201–208), Gayle defends Baldwin as the only Negro who fully sees the source of the Negro's plight in America. He rejects Robert Bone's belief that Baldwin suffers from an adolescent's sense of frustration and hate, and he has no sympathy for Eldridge Cleaver, who dislikes Baldwin's homosexuality. Gayle feels that Baldwin has rightfully condemned Richard Wright's "naturalistic-protest" novel, which depicts man as controlled by environmental forces. Gayle believes that the American people —not something as abstract as environment—are the source of the Negro's lack of power and that Baldwin puts the blame where it belongs, even if he is as much a defeatist in his own way as Richard Wright.

iii. Saul Bellow

This was the year of Bellow criticism with one book, two monographs, one collection of essays, eight lengthy articles, and one chapter in a book devoted to his work. Keith Opdahl in *The Novels of Saul Bellow* (Univ. Park, Penn. State Univ. Press) depicts Bellow concerned with an over-intellectual society, one afraid of life and death, dedicated to the abstract, and fearsome of flesh and blood realities. Bellow's characters are in need of the community from which they feel cut off. His characters are religious men who must lose their fear of the world, "achieve a sense of self which cannot be absorbed by it," and eventually define themselves through "communal action"—that is, acts of love. Opdahl relates this urge to the principles of Hasidism, "the Jewish movement which feels the presence of the divine within the factual world." He then analyzes each novel, discussing patterns of "resistance, embrace, and release." Although he is fond of tedious plot-telling and sometimes the obvious meaning, Opdahl nevertheless supplies a meaningful and illuminating context for the study of Bellow's fiction.

Equally stimulating is Earl Rovit's succinct and well-written *Saul Bellow* (UMPAW, No. 65). While Rovit and Opdahl share some opinions, Rovit believes that Bellow's view is a less heroic one than does Opdahl, that the pattern of his characters is less clear-cut, and that their salvation is more problematical. He sees Bellow's characters as lonely, suffering men, often separated from their families, yet unable to resign themselves to their loneliness or their suffering. Like Opdahl, Rovit believes that they have too much integrity, too much respect for their own moods, to accept a meaningless system. Unlike Opdahl, he sees them as consciously quixotic blunderers who never expect to escape their despair even though they never willingly accept it. They find salvation in laughter, refuse to take themselves seriously, ridicule their own defeat, and thus prepare for the next assault.

Half-way between Opdahl and Rovit is Howard Harper in his chapter on Bellow (*Desperate Faith*, pp. 7–64). Harper sees Bellow's characters caught between a desire for order and meaning and a society that offers chaos and meaninglessness. Like Rovit, he believes that they must earn their faith in life through a "profound despair." Like Opdahl, he believes that the final "range of human possibilities" that Bellow gives them is "great indeed." Both Harper and Opdahl would be more convincing if they were more specific about what these possibilities entail. Perhaps Bellow's own vagueness on this point has trapped his critics.

The least convincing study of Bellow in 1967 was Robert Detweiler's 48-page *Saul Bellow: A Critical Essay* (Grand Rapids, William B. Eerdmans) in a series entitled "Contemporary Writers in Christian Perspective." While Detweiler is aware that it is difficult to bestow a Christian perspective upon a Jewish writer, he does not let this discourage him in this vague and wooly-headed study. After discussing the novels in general terms, he analyzes the various points of view and use of imagery. He is interested in language because he believes—it is not quite clear how—that in Bellow's words we can find the Word, Christ emerging out of literary technique. "Bellow's fiction shows us," says Detweiler, "how [Christ] may be present, how the word is incarnate in words." Detweiler compares Bellow's "vision" to the Gospel of John, and sees Bellow as a modern Saint Paul writing for later-day Gentiles. If this were not enough, Detweiler concludes that Bellow's "characters illustrate the types that Northrop Frye defines in his influential *Anatomy of Criticism.*"

The problems that the critics have had with Bellow can be seen in Irving Malin's useful collection of essays, *Saul Bellow and the Critics* (New York, New York Univ. Press). Malin's brief introduction is helpful in isolating these problems, and the thirteen essays (all previously published) reveal the wide range of critical contexts that have been used to discuss Bellow.

The same kind of divergence can be found in the eight critical essays devoted to Bellow in 1967. Irvin Stock's "The Novels of Saul Bellow" (*SoR*, III, 13–42) depicts Bellow as a neo-romantic who believes that harmony and joy of life come when we cease from striving and live with "feelings open," accepting the present, seizing the day. He believes that Bellow depicts a kind of Christ-like character who takes on the suffering of others and becomes a kind of deliverer. Stock is a serious critic, with a penetrating eye, which perhaps becomes blurred when he compares English Romanticism to Jewish parents who "learned that feelings matter, that we should love and be good to each other, that the child is dear and precious—*a zisse neshumeleh.*"

Stock's belief in the romantic nature of Bellow's work is shared by Clinton W. Trowbridge in "Water Imagery in *Seize the Day*" (*Crit*, IX, iii, 37–61) and also in another sense by Franklin R. Baruch who in "Bellow and Milton: Professor Herzog in His Garden" (*Crit*, IX, iii, 74–83) maintains that a character like Herzog finds redemption and returns to the garden by "becoming part of nature."

Albert J. Guerard, "Saul Bellow and the Activists: On *The Adventures of Augie March*" (*SoR*, III, 582–596), believes that Bellow found a new kind of language for the fiction that he was writing. Along with Philip Roth, Herbert Gold, Walker Percy, Bernard Malamud, James Baldwin, Jack Kerouac, Ken Kesey, and Wright Morris, Bellow brought a "conscious reaction to themes of defeat, apathy, and acquiescence. All repudiate the close analysis of the guilt-ridden solitary and his psychological 'case.'" Bellow also moved us away from the more refined fiction of Elizabeth Bowen, Jean Stafford, Mary McCarthy, and Truman Capote.

Sheridan Baker in "Saul Bellow's Bout with Chivalry" (*Criticism*, IX, 109–122) believes that Bellow moved from the dead-ended existentialism of *Dangling Man* to a new humanism in *Augie March* and *Herzog*. In the later novels, Bellow reconciles "a feeling heart curbed and empowered by a sympathetic higher will."

Patrick Morrow in "Threat and Accommodation: The Novels of Saul Bellow" (*MQ*, VIII, 389–411) maintains that for Bellow "man's living within society is preferable to self-imposed alienation," and he discusses the ways the Bellow hero fails or succeeds in "accommodating" life as he finds it. Like so many other critics, Morrow discusses Bellow's "romantic suffering" and his ability to reconcile a "tragic role within a comic perspective."

Abraham Chapman in "The Image of Man as Portrayed by Saul Bellow," (*CLAJ*, X, 285–298) depicts Bellow's characters caught between a desire for success and a fear of failure and between materialistic and idealistic imperatives. As a Jewish-American, Bellow sees that suffering, scorn, and rejection can be transcended by the "tempered soul." His characters, aware of their own limitations, try to make sense out of life without illusions, evasions, and *a priori* systems.

Robert Detweiler's "Patterns of Rebirth in *Henderson the Rain King*" (*MFS*, XII, 405–414) traces animal and rebirth motifs connected with Henderson, whom Detweiler sees as a mythic hero. He suggests that Henderson is a product of his own imagination and thus needs an ideal if he is to transform himself. He brings up the question of when illusions are justified and when they are destructive. Detweiler here stops short of making Bellow's quixotic characters into modern Christs and the act of writing into a kind of religious experience, and this essay is far more effective than his monograph (see p. 195) on Bellow.

This brief and inadequate summary of these essays and books proves one thing: most of the critics see Bellow's characters as lonely men trying to find themselves within the community of man. How these characters are to become whole, however, is the problem that separates the critics. Some believe that Bellow offers salvation through a comic or ironic perspective, others through a kind of religious existentialism, still others in a neo-romanticism, or a neo-stoicism, or even neo-Christianity. While the confusion on this point remains, not one of the critics has suggested that the vagueness here might reflect a confusion in Bellow himself, that the inadequacy of the criticism reveals the amorphous meaning—especially with the endings—of so many of the novels themselves.

iv. Joseph Heller

Joseph Heller's *Catch-22* continues to keep him in the critical spotlight. Richard Lehan and Jerry Patch in "*Catch-22*: The Making of a Novel" (*MinnR*, VII, 238–244) examine the novel in terms of interviews with close friends of Heller who have pointed out the similarities between Heller's boyhood experiences in Brooklyn and the events in *Catch-22*. The character of Milo, for example, is modelled on a boyhood friend; and George Mandel, another friend, influenced the actual writing. Lehan and Patch show the similarities and differences between Madel's war novel, *The Wax Boom*, and Heller's *Catch-22*. They also show the influence of Celine and compare and contrast Heller with Camus, Sartre, and Kafka in an attempt to place him within the traditions of a literature of the "absurd."

Vance Ramsey's excellent article, "From Here to Absurdity: Heller's *Catch-22*" (*Seven Contemporary Authors*, pp. 99–118) also places Heller in the tradition of absurd literature as well as that of more recent "black humor." Ramsey discusses both the merits and limitations of the novel, especially the weaknesses with the ending. He describes Heller's characters as threatened by a "nothingness" that negates their very sense of self. In this world, the ideal and the real are "radically incompatible," social commitment is an invitation to death, and cowardly flight becomes the only alternative to madness or death.

Caroline Gordon and Jeanne Richardson in "Flies in Their Eyes? A Note on Joseph Heller's *Catch-22*" (*SoR*, III, 96–105) compare *Catch-22* to Lewis Carroll's *Alice in Wonderland*.

Jan Solomon in "The Structure of *Catch-22*" (*Crit*, IX, ii, 46–57) believes that Heller created an absurdist novel by juxtaposing Yossarian's psychological sense of time against Milo Minderbinder's chronological sense of time. Yossarian and Milo give different times for key events, and their contradictions lead to "chronological impossibility." "The irreconcilability of the two chronologies serves the effect of absurdity." Solomon has very nicely pin-pointed narrative confusion in *Catch-22*. Whether such confusion was inadvertent or intended remains, however, problematical.

Minna Doskow in "The Night Journey in *Catch-22*" (*TCL*, XII, 186–193) discusses the novel as a "symbolic journey to the underworld" represented by Yossarian's night trip to Rome. She believes that here Yossarian finally recognizes evil, sees the need to resist it, and heads for Sweden spiritually renewed. The trouble is that Yossarian had been aware of evil long before the trip to Rome, has really no means available to resist it, and heads for Sweden more in flight than spiritually renewed. Also, as Lehan and Patch show in their article (cited above), Heller wrote the ending of *Catch-22* in haste to meet the contractual demands of his publisher, and he seems to have abandoned his original plans.

v. Norman Mailer

After Saul Bellow and Vladimir Nabokov, Norman Mailer received the most critical attention in 1967. One of Howard Harper's best chapters (*Desperate Faith*, pp. 96–136) is on Mailer. Harper points out that from Hearn (of *The Naked and the Dead*), to Lovett (of *Barbary Shore*), and to Sergius (of *The Deer Park*), Mailer's characters progressed "from external to internal choices and justifications." Harper sees Mailer as an American existentialist, committed to an action that breaks Philistine restraint and affirms the self, often through violence. Rojack (of *An American Dream*) is Mailer's white Negro, his Hipster, the psychopath, who lives on the "edge of violence, always ready to defeat fear by action." For him, reality is not objective, to be perceived; but subjective, to be created. Paul B. Newman in "The Jew As Existentialist" (*NAR*, II [1965], iii, 45–55) pursues these ideas. Newman also believes that for Mailer "the act of self-awareness is always poised against the act of violence."

Robert Solotaroff in "Down Mailer's Way" (*ChiR*, XIX, iii, 11–25) helps bring the ideas of Harper and Newman into focus. Solotaroff believes that Mailer had secret respect for General Cummings and Sergeant Croft in *The Naked and the Dead* because both men consent to a "power mortality." While Sergius of *The Deer Park* rejects such a point of view, Solotaroff believes that Mailer could not firmly believe in Sergius because from his first novel on, Mailer had been heading toward an egoism which wants power so as to resist the emasculating will of society. In *The Deer Park*, Marion Faye, the sadistic pimp, emerges as the central character and anticipates the psychopathic hero like Stephen Rojack, whose acts of violence are in defiance of society. James Toback discusses this kind of psychopathic character in his excellent "Norman Mailer Today" (*Commentary*, LXIV, iv, 68–76).

While Solotaroff and Toback are not explicit on this point, they come the closest to seeing that Mailer's prototypical hero is both a John F. Kennedy and a Lee Harvey Oswald. Kennedy tapped the open circuit of American political power, while Oswald short-circuited it. Mailer unconsciously gives consent to both kinds of men, a fact that his critics never fully realize. Mailer has moved beyond the estranged character to the power maniac. Unlike Camus, he has not set limits beyond which human action cannot go, a fact which separates him from at least one form of existentialism, and which bedrocks his whole literary world upon destructive principles.

vi. Vladimir Nabokov

The best critical writing on Nabokov can be found in the superb collection of eleven essays and in interviews published in *Wisconsin Studies in Contemporary Literature* (VIII, 111–364), ed. by L. S. Dembo. Alfred Appel's interview is particularly valuable. Appel was Nabokov's student at Cornell University in 1954, knows Nabokov personally, and has read his novels—and the novels which interest Nabokov—with deep understanding and appreciation. For once we have an interviewer who is intellectually equipped to interview, one who knows the critical questions to ask. The essays treat individual novels, Nabokov as playwright and translator, and the influence of Jorge Luis Borges. Claire Rosenfield's discussion of *Despair* (despite Nabokov's own disclaimer about doubles in fiction) and Appel's essay on *Lolita* are particularly informative. Also of great value is Jackson R. Bryer and Thomas J. Bergin's checklist of Nabokov criticism.

There were several other essays on Nabokov in 1967. Although Nabokov has spoken harshly of Freud, L. R. Hiatt in "Nabokov's

Lolita: A Freudian Cryptic Crossword" (*AI*, XXIV, 360–370) has convincingly pin-pointed the Freudian elements in *Lolita*. In "Nabokov's *Kunstlerroman*: Portrait of the Artist as A Dying Man" (*TCL*, XIII, 104–110), Robert W. Uphaus sees in *Lolita* a "contest between artist and society" and "the Dionysian and Apollonian" vision, aspects of Humbert's own character. And in "*Pale Fire*: The Labyrinth of a Great Novel" (*TriQ*, VIII, Winter, 13–36), Andrew Field discusses *Pale Fire* in terms of, among other matters, the fact that it emerged from the incomplete novel *Solus Rex*.

vii. Walker Percy

The publication in 1966 of his second novel, *The Last Gentleman*, probably accounts for the new surge of critical interest in Walker Percy. Unlike so many other writers, Percy is not reluctant to talk about the meaning of his fiction, and we have two very interesting interviews with him. In Ashley Brown's "An Interview with Walker Percy" (*Shenandoah*, XVIII, iii, 3–10) Percy tells us that he has been most influenced by existentialism, particularly Dostoyevsky, Kierkegaard, Heidegger, Gabriel Marcel, Sartre, and Camus. More specifically, he tells us that he modelled Will Barrett of *The Last Gentleman* on Dostoyevsky's Prince Myshkin—and that Sartre's *La Nausée* "is a revolution in its technique for rendering a concrete situation, and it has certainly influenced me." Percy again discusses some of these matters in another interview with Carlton Cremeens "Walker Percy, The Man and the Novelist: An Interview" (*SoR*, IV [1968], 271–290). Percy also discusses here the nature and responsibility of the novelist in the modern world. He believes that the Jewish and Southern writers have a great deal in common, agrees with Ralph Ellison that the writer has to avoid thinking of life in terms of sociology and abstractions, and believes that alienation is a very "ancient, orthodox Christian doctrine. Man is alienated by the nature of his being here. He is here as a stranger and as a pilgrim."

Besides the two interviews, several articles were devoted to Percy's work. Richard Lehan in "The Way Back: Redemption in the Novels of Walker Percy" (*SoR*, IV [1968], 306–319) compares Percy's and Faulkner's haunted and prolapsed narrative worlds. In each, an order has been destroyed in the backrush of time, and

characters struggle to find meaning in the broken design, a narrator
hanging suspended from his own consciousness. Lehan reads *The
Moviegoer* and *The Last Gentleman* in terms of Percy's essays on
existential philosophy, especially the idea of an "existential com-
munion"—an overlapping of consciousness which breaks down the
barriers between individuals. This process involves (to use Percy's
own terminology) "alienation" (the starting point), "rotation" (the
aimless journey), and "return" (which brings one to terms with the
haunted past by changing the perspective from which it is seen and
shared—for the return is always for two). Lehan believes that in
his fiction Percy is least effective in describing the "return."

Robert Maxwell in "Walker's Percy's Fancy" (*MinnR*, VII, 231–
237) also reads the novels, particularly *The Last Gentleman*, with
Percy's existential terminology in mind; but because only two pages
are given to the novels themselves, he does not take us very far.
Michael T. Bloudin in "The Novels of Walker Percy: An Attempt at
Synthesis" (*XUS*, VI, 29–42) makes some interesting observations
on Percy's concept of the family, his use of Dostoyevsky's Myshkin
in *The Last Gentleman*, and the meaning of the novel's resolution.

viii. William Styron

As *The Last Gentleman* sparked new interest in Walker Percy, so
The Confessions of Nat Turner generated interest in William Styron.
Of prime importance is "An Interview with William Styron" by
Robert Canzoneri and Page Stegner (*Per/Se*, I [1966], ii, 37–44), an
interview which took place while Styron was at work on *Nat Turner*.
Here Styron discusses at length what Nat Turner means to him and
what he is trying to do in the novel. He comments on the novel's
point of view, its structure, and the meaning of characters. He also
discusses Nat and Margaret Whitehead, especially the sexual nature
of their relationship, revealing motives which perhaps tell us more
about Styron than about the factual reasons for Nat's murdering
Margaret. An interview of this importance should be more accessible
than it is in *Per/Se*.

The critical argument over *The Confessions of Nat Turner* will
undoubtedly go on for some time. One of the best critical essays to
appear so far is Louis D. Rubin, Jr.'s "William Styron and Human
Bondage: *The Confessions of Nat Turner*" (*HC*, IV, v, 1–12). Rubin

believes that Styron has written a novel that goes beyond Negroes and slavery. "A Negro seen by William Styron is in no important or essential way different from a white man. Social conditions, not heredity and biology, set him apart." Rubin sees Nat cut off from the whites and blacks alike, torn by decisions and indecisions that reveal general humanity, and caught in a gratuitous situation which calls for commitment. Rubin sees Nat as a kind of modern, tragic hero. He is the lonely rebel who rejects his absurd condition and acts in the face of the system which cancels the very meaning of his action.

If one substitutes the Marine Corp for Southern slavery, Rubin's reading of *Nat Turner* is not very different from August Nigro's reading of *The Long March*: "The Long March: The Expansive Hero in a Closed World" (*Crit*, IX, iii, 103–112). According to Nigro, Mannix rebels against his bondage, asserts his right to freedom, but "the pride and will that move him to rebellion are also the tragic flaws that blind him to his own tyranny."

Both Rubin and Nigro are in essential agreement with Frederick Hoffman (*The Art of Southern Fiction*, pp. 144–161), who believes that Styron has written "witness novels" that testify to the special depth "of human suffering and struggle."

ix. John Updike

Although much of the criticism on John Updike will have to be reassessed in the light of the recent *Couples*, we do have some important commentary written in 1967. Among the very best is Howard Harper's chapter (*Desperate Faith*, pp. 162–190). Harper treats all the novels and stories in terms of character estrangement. In *The Poorhouse Fair*, the belief in God was a necessity stronger than the welfare state. In the later novels, God began to disappear, until in *The Centaur*, He is a reality for George Caldwell but not his son. When man can no longer look up, he looks in and out and becomes dependent upon himself and others. He sees the destructive consequences of selfishness and of a morality imposed from without. At this point, the moment of love is possible, a moment that is often the resolution of an Updike novel.

Three other essays written in 1967 were devoted to Updike's fiction, two of which try to assess its literary value. Richard H. Rupp's "John Updike: Style in Search of a Center" (*SR*, LXXV, 693–709)

is of more value for its insights into Updike's novels than its judgment of them. Rupp feels that Updike's style blocks off an internal
reality, that it gives us "the outside at the expense of the inside."
Updike, however, usually drenches an object with emotion, and
Rupp seems blind to the way this language evokes a state of mind
or mood.

Bryant W. Wyatt seems equally arbitrary in "John Updike: the
Psychological Novel in Search of Structure" (*TCL*, XIII, 89–96).
Wyatt feels that Updike has never reconciled his highly introverted
characters with the structural demands of fiction. For Wyatt to say
that *The Poorhouse Fair* is "unfocused" is one matter; but for him
to say that Rabbit Angstrom's "misfortune fails structurally because
the heavy depiction of the remembered past pulls the chronology
awry" is to set up criteria which would also work against Proust's
The Remembrance of Things Past; and for him to say that *The
Centaur* fails because the modern-day plot does not fit "the forged
mythical pattern" is to set up another literary principle which could
be used against Joyce's *Ulysses* as arbitrarily as Wyatt uses it against
Updike.

What Fred L. Stanley has to say in "*Rabbit, Run*: An Image of
Life" (*MQ*, VIII, 371–386) seems valid enough, although Stanley
has a fondness for terminology that is at best pretentious. The novel
works in terms of characters who are "pathetic or less-than-tragic,"
and thus beyond "redemption in human experience." Rabbit's sense
of past glory means he is not "disoriented . . . [but] congealed in the
past," and his desire for love is a search for an " 'I-Thou' relationship."

x. Others

The criticism considered here is devoted to the less-heralded novelists. While many of them are minor in comparison to Bellow, Nabokov, Styron, and Updike, a good number—for example, Bernard
Malamud and John Knowles—just did not receive the critical attention that their work deserves.

Peter H. Ohlin's *Agee* (New York, Obolensky) was originally
his Ph.D. dissertation. Ohlin is concerned with Agee as poet, movie
reviewer, screen writer, social commentator, and novelist. Perhaps
his discussion of Agee as novelist is the weakest part of this book,

primarily because it is too bogged down with the obvious meaning of the novels and with plot-telling. This section is in part saved by the interesting discussion of how the literary work creates its own reality, "a transfigured reality," so that it has a "mysterious and miraculous life of its own," an idea that Ohlin believes is central to understanding both Agee's poetry and fiction.

Frank D. McConnell in "William Burroughs and the Literature of Addiction" (*MR*, VIII, 665–680) gives sympathetic attention to *Naked Lunch*, placing it in that romantic tradition with Coleridge's "Kubla Khan" and "Resolution and Independence," De Quincey's *Confessions of an English Opium-Eater*, and Malcolm Lowry's *Under the Volcano*. In these works the "negative euchrist or the outlaw and the sensualist becomes an aesthetic possibility."

Truman Capote continues to receive attention, primarily from the slick journals like *Esquire*, which are interested in his personality. Barbara Long's "In Cold Comfort" (*Esquire*, LXV, vi, 124, 126, 171–181) is an interview based on a weekend visit to Capote's house in Bridgehampton, Long Island. Phillip K. Tompkin's "In Cold Fact" (*Esquire*, LXV, vi, 125, 127, 166–171) is a close study of *In Cold Blood* in terms of the actual facts of the case. Tompkin concludes that Capote sometimes deviated from the actual facts of the Clutter case because he "found it difficult, if not impossible, to understand how a man could kill, and do so without feeling." Tompkin also believes that Capote deviated from the facts for fictional effect. William Wiegand in "The 'Non-fiction' Novel" (*NMQ*, XXXVII, 243–250) enlarges upon this point, insists that Capote used novelistic techniques, and that his book went far beyond strict journalism.

Robert C. Corrigan in "The Artist as Censor: J. P. Donleavy and *The Ginger Man*" (*MASJ*, VIII, i, 60–72) compares the expurgated American version of Donleavy's novel (McDowell and Obolensky, 1958) to the first version published in Paris by the Olympic Press and concludes that the American edition "conforms rather carefully to the general tone of acceptable sexual practices in the United States among members of what Alfred Kinsey has described as the grade-school educated group."

One of the most interesting—and most illuminating—documents on Ralph Ellison is the interview he gave James Thompson, Lennox Raphael, and Steve Canyon ("A Very Stern Discipline: An Interview with Ralph Ellison," *Harpers*, CCXXIV, March, 76–95). Ellison insists that the Negro novelist must first see the "American-ness" of his experience, write out of a base broader than his sense of being a Negro, and take all literature for his model. The writer's responsibility to literature is both deeper and more burdensome than his responsibility to politics because literature draws "from literature itself, and upon the human experience which has abided long enough to have become organized and given significance through literature." Ellison believes that Hemingway has told us more what it is like to be a Negro than have Negroes who write directly about the Negro. Hemingway's characters offer a "metaphor" for post-World War I, which "includes the way Negroes were feeling and acting." His characters seem to intuit the truths of the jazz musician who lives by a code of withdrawal, understands technical and artistic excellence, rejects the respectable society, replaces abstract ideals with more physical values, and knows the needs of both skepticism and stoicism. The insights of both Hemingway and Faulkner, Ellison concludes, reveal that "we are bound less by blood than by our cultural and political circumstance."

David Sanders' *John Hersey* (TUSAS, No. 112) is an informed account of a novelist-journalist whose interest in the topical—the atom bomb, the tortured Jews in Poland, child education in America, and the race problem in general—have made him a popular but not critically respected writer. Sanders is particularly good in describing Hersey's career as a novelist, his method of writing (particularly *The Wall*), and the relevance of his fiction. Sanders believes that Hersey's diminished reputation is an injustice to a novelist who belongs with those recent writers of "radical innocence" who came from sheltered origins, were shocked by modern atrocities, and affirmed "the human will to survive." While Hersey's themes may be similar to these more recognized novelists, his novels do not explore the complexity of these themes, and Sanders seems too generous in his final praise of Hersey.

John Knowles is just beginning to get the critical attention that he deserves. James M. Mellard's insightful "Counterpoint and 'Double Vision' in *A Separate Peace*" (SSF, IV, 127–134) shows that when Gene causes Finny's fall, Finny comes to understand the meaning of evil, while Gene comes to understand "his own duality." The story involves the loss of a prelapsarian world. Simply by growing up, both boys become subject to the realities of the outside world, a world significantly at war. If Finny absorbs the worst of Gene, Gene absorbs the best of Finny. While Gene can never be innocent again, he can "measure others, as well as himself, against Phineas." James L. McDonald further develops these themes in "The Novels of John Knowles" (*ArQ*, XXIII, 335–342). He believes that the conflict in a Knowles novel is between a world of innocence and experience. Comparing Knowles's fiction to that of James and Fitzgerald, he shows how characters come to an understanding of cultural and moral realities.

Bernard Malamud deserves more attention than he received last year. Two articles by James M. Mellard—"Malamud's Novels: Four Versions of the Pastoral" (*Crit*, IX, ii, 5–19) and "Malamud's *The Assistant* (*SSF*, V, 1–11)—are far off the mark. While no one can deny that Malamud makes use of nature imagery and symbols, especially in *The Natural*, Mellard distorts the issue when he insists that Malamud's novels are modern pastorals with "proletarian types" taking the place of "conventional shepherds" (surely a contradiction in terms), nature imagery taking the place of nature, and vegetation myths celebrating "the cycles of death and renewal in nature."

Flannery O'Connor continues to receive critical attention but not in the abundance of 1966. Frederick Hoffman's chapter (*The Art of Southern Fiction*, pp. 81–95) is particularly good. Hoffman sees Miss O'Connor's characters fighting their way through religious denial, usually in the face of violence, to an acceptance of Christ. Stuart L. Burns in " 'Torn by the Lord's Eye': Flannery O'Connor's use of the Sun Imagery" (*TCL*, XIII, 154–166) convincingly demonstrates that in Miss O'Connor's fiction the sun functions as a "visible manifestation of some Divine Agency, intervening in or judging the affairs of men." That this kind of symbolism conflicts with Miss O'Connor's Catholic beliefs is not a matter Burns pursues. And William A. Fahey in "Out of the Eater: Flannery O'Connor's Appetite for Truth" (*Renascence*, XX, 22–29) discusses the need for Miss O'Connor's central characters to act, rather than remain passive, even if misled by skeptical rationalists or by the "denying devil."

Someday J. F. Powers may justify a critical book but not at the present. Limited to three published books, only one of which is significant, J. V. Hagopian is never able to demonstrate his critical skill or to give substance, focus, or even interest to his subject in this book, *J. F. Powers* (New York, TUSAS, No. 130), heavy with arbi-

trary critical distinctions and plot-telling. Robert G. Twombly, by
necessity, attempts less than Hagopian. In "Hubris, Health, and
Holiness: The Despair of J. F. Powers" (*Seven Contemporary Authors*, pp. 143–162) Twombly rejects the reviewers who see Father
Urban Roche as a Catholic George Babbitt. While Father Roche's
religious values may be hypocritically consistent with a secular
world, Twombly believes that "Powers is here not condemning a
man's sins, but a man's incapacity for either virtue or sin."

Irving and Harriet Deer in "Philip Roth and the Crisis in American Fiction" (*MinnR*, VI [1966] 353–360) show how Roth's characters reconcile the often contradictory demands of being a Jew and
an American. While they have not, of course, intended it, the Deers
have nicely answered Marvin Mudrick's concerns in "Who Killed
Herzog?" (see p. 193).

The Salinger boom seems safely over, if this year's scanty amount
of criticism is any indication. The most extensive treatment was
Kenneth Hamilton's *J. D. Salinger* (Grand Rapids, William B. Eerdmans). Unlike so many of the essays in this Contemporary Writers
in Christian Perspective series, Hamilton reads the novels and stories
on their own terms and does not force them into a Christian mold.
While he discusses Salinger's use of the Bible, he also emphasizes
Salinger's interest in Advaita Vedanta and Taoism; and his study
is as discreet as his conclusions are unambitious. Howard Harper's
chapter on Salinger (*Desperate Faith*, pp. 65–95) makes all the
mistakes that Hamilton avoids as Harper tries unsuccessfully to make
Salinger into a kind of mystical existentialist. The rest of last year's
Salinger criticism—James Bryan's "A Reading of Salinger's 'For
Esmé—with Love and Squalor'" (*Criticism*, IX, 275–288) and
Laurence Perrine's "Teddy? Booper? or Blooper?" (*SSF*, IV, 217–
224)—is concerned with arguing and rearguing the meaning of two
short stories.

And if critical interest in Salinger has fallen off, so has such
interest in Robert Penn Warren. We have three essays on Warren
in 1967. Arthur Mizener's chapter in *Twelve Great American Novels*
(New York, New American Library) is a rather stock reading (he
concentrates on the conflict between innocence and experience and
the necessity for ideals to be tempered by experience) of *All The
King's Men*. Allen Shepherd in "Character and Theme in R. P. Warren's *Flood*" (*Crit*, IX, iii, 95–102) argues that in comparison to

All the King's Men the characters in *Flood* "are inadequate to their assigned tasks." Richard Allan Davison in "Robert Penn Warren 'Dialectical Configuration' and *The Cave*" (*CLAJ*, X, 349–357) sees the same kind of discrepancy between *All the King's Men* and *The Cave*, although he believes Warren's use of imagery ("the vibrant roar of the crickets," the "rotting rope outside John T's window," etc.) reinforces key themes and saves the novel, an assertion that surely puts a high priority on imagery as a criterion of literary value.

But if Davison's criteria seem suspect, they continue to reveal that critics—particularly critics of recent fiction—use a limited number of principles to assess a literary work. The approach is almost entirely exegetical, with few critics interested in biography—especially the meaning of the work to the writer himself, or in cultural criticism—the work's social significance and relevance. Since the critical questions are limited, the critical response is also diminished. Because this literature is so new, one could not expect a consensus. One wonders, however, if the criticism must lack coherence so completely, if the critics could not have a larger frame of critical reference, and if they could not find more vital contexts within which to discuss literary success.

University of California at Los Angeles

14. Poetry: 1900 to the 1930's

Brom Weber and James Woodress

In overall quantity of scholarship, 1967 was an average year for the investigation of poetry written from the turn of the century to the 1930's. For individual poets, however, the emphasis fluctuates annually, and none of the major poets surveyed in this period (Pound, Frost, Hart Crane, Robinson, and Cummings) dominates year after year. In 1966 Frost led his contemporaries with four books and a dozen and a half articles devoted to him, including the first volume of Lawrance Thompson's biography. This year Pound is by far the most intensively studied poet, being the subject of eight books of various sorts, while Crane, usually a poor third behind Frost and Pound, is the subject of five books, among which are studies in French and Italian and an edition of his complete poems and selected letters. Robinson received more attention than usual, and Frost, while by no means neglected, did not enjoy a vintage year.[1]

i. General

There were no major contributions this year dealing broadly with the themes, trends, or movements of poetry during the first third of this century. One must be content, however, with three good articles on *symbolisme*, imagism, and American poetry and the volume edited by Warren French, *The Thirties*, which contains a section (seven essays by various hands) devoted to the poetry of that decade. But even this latter work contains only two general discussions.

The late Frederick J. Hoffman's "*Symbolisme* and Modern Ameri-

1. Works actually copyrighted in 1966, many of which did not appear until 1967, are included here if they were not listed in the annual MLA International Bibliography for 1966. This essay does not review the 13 dissertations completed in the past year on poets included in this survey. The dissertations distribute themselves as follows: Cummings, 1; Frost, 2; Jeffers, 3; Ransom, 3; Robinson, 2; Williams, 2. Interestingly enough, Jeffers and Ransom, while providing fertile subjects for dissertation writers, did not generate enough other attention in 1967 to be treated in this essay.

can Poetry" (*CLS*, IV, 193–199) is a brief but illuminating discussion of a much-discussed subject. "The American *symboliste* line was a small brook, running beside a huge stream in France, Belgium, and Britain," writes Hoffman, who adds that only two modern American poets, Stevens and Crane, were much influenced by *symbolisme*. Stevens, however, was only sporadically influenced, because he was interested in many things and knew French. Crane, on the other hand, "is probably one of the great poets in modern *symboliste* history." Yet even Crane's greatest poetry comes only incidentally from the *symbolistes*. Modern American poets are not advocates of *symbolisme* for the quite simple reason that our disaffections, our attacks, our hopes, are largely best presented in prose of a certain kind, principally non-symbolic. "Our poets have perhaps been more inclined than most to particularization, to the filling in of the image, to the comment within the imagistic frame."

In the same issue of the same journal Warren Ramsay's "Use of the Visible: American Imagism, French Symbolism" (pp. 177–191) investigates the similarities and differences between late nineteenth-century French *symbolistes* and the Anglo-Saxon imagists. Ramsay acutely brings together theory and practice in French and English, throwing light upon such Americans as Amy Lowell, Ezra Pound, Wallace Stevens, and John Gould Fletcher. This essay appears to be part of a larger study.

The most interesting part of *The Thirties* is not the section devoted to poetry, for as the editor, Warren French, says in his introductory chapter (pp. 115–121): "The 30s [for poetry] were an autumnal decade." One has to admit that the verse of that period was not very fresh, and the new voices of that era have mostly proved not very enduring. Times simply conspired against the poet. The Pulitzer prizes chiefly went to established poets for their collected poems, and "between Richard Eberhart's first book in 1930 and John Ciardi's in 1940 sprawls a trackless dumping ground of ill-starred ventures into verse."

What was true of the United States as a whole was also true of the South, as Guy Owen makes clear in "Southern Poetry during the 30s" (*The Thirties*, pp. 159–167). The ferment of the old Fugitive days and the excitement of the Agrarian controversy were past, and Randall Jarrell was the only significant new poet of the decade. Yet by 1940 Southern poetry was finally in the mainstream of American poetry, and the shades of Timrod and Lanier, which had haunted Southern poets as late as 1930, had been exorcised.

Finally, it should be noted that Leonard Unger has edited *Seven Modern American Poets: An Introduction* (Minneapolis, Univ. of Minn. Press), a reprinting of seven of the University of Minnesota Pamphlets on American Writers. There is nothing new here, but it is useful to have these pamphlets available in another and more permanent form.

ii. Ezra Pound

As noted above, 1967 was a vintage year for Pound scholarship. The eight book-length studies devoted to him range widely from critical examinations of his work as a whole to popular biography and letters. The tone also runs the gamut from praise to attack, and there is no doubt that Old Ez continues to perplex and to stimulate. In quantity the attention Pound continues to receive, as he moves well into his ninth decade, is impressive: one volume of essays alone contains twenty-two contributions from various hands, and the title page is a Who's Who of Pound scholars.

One of the most interesting and unexpected volumes is Noel Stock's *Reading the Cantos: A Study of Meaning in Ezra Pound* (London, Routledge and Kegan Paul; New York, Pantheon, 1966). Stock has used the occasion to pen a strong attack upon the poet and his achievement [It comes strangely from someone who was once very intimate with Pound and only about a year before had edited a collection of essays in honor of Pound's eightieth birthday. But such conclusions to adulation and friendship are not uncommon in the literary world.] Stock analyzes each group of the *Cantos* in the Chronological order of publication, concerned with piercing through the fog of Pound's own comments upon the poems, the comments of others, and the propensity of modern critics to find meaning in fragmentation. Stock is no enemy of modern poetry: according to the jacket, he is engaged in writing "a major biography" of the poet; so he apparently finds him important other than in the *Cantos*. With few exceptions, however, these poems are flawed for Stock. He subjects them to formal and thematic and substantive analysis, and concludes that they "do not constitute a poem, but a disjointed series of short poems, passages, lines and fragments, often of exceptional beauty or interest, but uninformed, poetically or otherwise, by larger purpose." The specific judgments which Stock makes of Pound (his intellectual superficiality, his lack of insight into other human beings, his ignorance of history, etc.) make this one of the most formidable, though mild-mannered, attacks upon a writer's work in modern times, particularly since Stock believes in many of the values Pound has espoused but which, according to Stock, the *Cantos* do not exemplify except in brief fragments.

Influence studies can be pedantic and monotonous, but K. L. Goodwin's *The Influence of Ezra Pound* (New York, Oxford, 1966) is lively and informative. Goodwin has made a detailed analysis of Pound's catalytic influence upon modern literature and modern writers, tracing his influence as a literary enterpreneur (magazine editor, adviser to publishers, etc.), of Pound as friend and literary associate of such figures as Yeats and Eliot, as promulgator of critical theories, and as exemplar of practice in his role as poet. Goodwin is careful not to over-emphasize Pound's role, and there are not many strained efforts to insist that all of modern poetry is to be credited to Pound. In general, Goodwin believes that "Pound has probably had no more influence than Hopkins, Yeats, or Eliot, and little more than Dylan Thomas or William Carlos Williams." In fact, Goodwin anticipates that Pound's influence may decline in time because his "habitual tone and his favorite subject-matter are less useful to other poets" than those of Yeats, for example. If Pound's influence is to continue, it will be sustained by his "handling of colloquial language, whether of speech or comment, and his advocacy of certain forms."

Goodwin does not devote much attention to Pound's influence upon Joyce. For this, one must turn to Forrest Read, ed., *Pound/ Joyce: Letters and Essays* (New York, New Directions). This volume contains Pound's writings on Joyce and appendices with such relevant materials as the deletions which Read believes Pound made in a section of the manuscript of *Ulysses* he forwarded for inclusion in *The Little Review* of June, 1918. Much of the value of the book resides in the fact that only twelve of Pound's letters to Joyce, of which there are more than sixty, were included in D. D. Paige's 1950 edition of the letters. Judging from Goodwin's documentation, he did not have access to all of the letters in the Read book. Linking together all the materials in the book are Read's commentaries. Apparently Pound aided Joyce with the publication of *Ulysses* but lost interest in Joyce when he began to write *Finnegan's Wake*. Neither ignored the other, however, for Pound appears in *Finnegan's Wake*, and Pound eulogized Joyce upon the latter's death.

An additional collection of Pound letters, though of minor importance, also appeared in Carlo Izzo's *Civiltà americana, vol. II: impressioni e note* (Rome, Edizioni di Storia e Letteratura). It consists of twenty-four letters and nine postcards written between 1935 and 1940 when Izzo was translating Pound into Italian. The letters show Pound's careful interest in helping Izzo get the exact shade of meaning in turning his poems into Italian.

Following up his earlier study, *The Poetry of Ezra Pound: The Pre-Imagist Stage* (1960), Christoph De Nagy has brought out a second volume dealing with the years 1911–1921: *Ezra Pound's Poetics and Literary Tradition: The Critical Decade* (Bern, Francke, 1966). This is a dense, sometimes awkwardly written, but nonetheless useful book. To explain the dwindling of Pound's reputation in the late 1920's and thereafter, he concludes that his critical contributions had been so well absorbed into modern literature (American primarily) that any reiteration, especially by Pound, began to seem anti-climactic and redundant. An inevitable desideratum began to be the application of the poetics, and here Pound did not take the dominant lead. Nagy's summation of Pound's poetics makes the problem of initial impact and subsequent redundancy clear:

> Pound's poetics are primarily guidelines helping the poet to find his relationship to the literature of the past and that of his own time; it is a norm of Pound's poetics that such a relationship should be developed in full consciousness and should be based on the assimilated knowledge of the greatest possible number of existing literary forms. Only this knowledge will enable the poet to make an adequate choice regarding the form to be used by him; he may make his choice among pre-established 'normative' forms, but they are not binding for him in any way; there is no norm prescribing the use of one particular form rather than another or, generally, the use of an existing form. The poet may, if he feels it imperative, evolve a new 'organic' form; but the new form will in some manner be blended with existing ones by any poet who is

saturated with the tradition of his art: the new poetry will likely encompass existing forms.

Evidence of Pound's international stature, in addition to De Nagy's publications in Switzerland, comes this year from Germany where two significant books have appeared: Eva Hesse, ed., *Ezra Pound: 22 Versuche über einen Dichter* (Frankfort, Athenäum) and Lore Lenberg, *Rosen aus Feilstaub: Studien zu den Cantos von Ezra Pound* (Wiesbaden, Limes, 1966), the latter being the outgrowth of a Freiburg dissertation in 1958 on the *Pisan Cantos*. Eva Hesse, who is Pound's chief German translator, has assembled and ably commented on twenty-two monograph extracts, symposium contributions, and articles, eight of them previously unpublished. All were translated into German, except the few originally written in it. Major critics and Pound specialists like Albert S. Cook, Guy Davenport, Donald Davie, Richard Ellmann, John Espey, Hugh Kenner, Earl Miner, N. Christopher De Nagy, Noel Stock, and J. P. Sullivan appear as well as less well-known scholars. These studies too throw light on neglected aspects of Pound's work (e.g. Murray Schafer, "Der absolute Rhythmus," or Rudolf Sühnel, "Ezra Pound und die homerische Tradition"). Hemingway's "Homage to Ezra" (1925) is dug up from the Paris periodical *This Quarter*, while Iris Barry's "Ezra Pound in London" is from the London *Bookman* (1931). All of the other publications, however, were originally printed between 1954 and 1965. Thus this anthology, lavishly indexed and with a German version of Gallup's bibliography as well as with Canto CXVI (1962 fragment) appended, presents an instructive, though limited and chronologically not quite coherent, spectrum of American, Australian, British, Canadian, German, Italian, and Swiss Pound criticism. In Miss Lenberg's volume, *The Pisan Cantos* are seen as a system of correlations. With 'persona,' 'image' (as distinct from 'symbol'), 'dynamic image,' 'ideogram,' 'interpretive metaphor,' and 'logopoeia' selected as controlling concepts, Pound's literary theory supporting the Cantos is clearly, though conventionally, defined. The first two Cantos, introducing the basic themes of the descent to Hades and an Ovidian Metamorphosis, are treated as a frame of reference for the interpretation of the whole cycle.

The last two book-length studies of Pound this year are of lesser importance. Michael Reck's *Ezra Pound: A Close-Up* (New York, McGraw-Hill) is mostly biographical and is based on 15 years of

conversations with Pound, first at St. Elizabeth's Hospital in Washington and later in Italy. While most of the biographical data is familiar and adds nothing new, Pound's conversation is worth having
in print, although the author does not let him talk enough. Reck,
eager to present Pound, has some good material, but he unfortunately
tries to write a popular and easy book. There are less than 16 ounces
in this Pound. Edward L. Meyerson's *The Seed is Man: A Collection
of Poetry and an Essay on Ezra Pound* (New York, Frederick-
William) is a well-intentioned survey of Pound's letters, essays, and
poetry in twenty-two pages, but because of its length and scope it
is necessarily superficial and presents no new insights.

An article by Max Halperen, "Ezra Pound: Poet-Priest, Poet-
Propagandist" (*The Thirties*, pp. 123–131), deals with an aspect of
Pound's career most scholars would like to forget: his dismal foray
into economics and politics in the Thirties. Halperen tries to explain
how the man who was so ready to help younger writers and to feed
all the cats in Rapallo and who was so astonishingly broad in his
literary taste and knowledge could have written *Jefferson and/or
Mussolini* (1935). Summarizing Pound's ideas, Halperen writes: "As
a sensitive receiver of impressions, as the antenna of his race, the
poet is, apparently, peculiarly equipped to discern and define those
patterns that make for a decent, orderly society." So Pound was led
down the primrose path.

One final item should be noted briefly in this round-up: Karl
Malkoff's "Allusion as Irony: Pound's Use of Dante in 'Hugh Selwyn
Mauberly'" (*MinnR*, VII, 81–88). Malkoff sees Pound's poem as "a
parody of Dante's *Commedia*," and his use of allusions to it "provides
a consistent ironic framework for the poem."

iii. Hart Crane

The increasing importance of this poet has been buttressed by a
second collected edition of his poetry that replaces the first collection
(1933) edited by Waldo Frank. *The Complete Poems and Selected
Letters and Prose of Hart Crane* (New York, Doubleday Anchor and
Liveright, 1966), edited by Brom Weber, is faithful to Crane's arrangement of the manuscripts in the "Key West" collection left unpublished at the poet's death; adds seventeen poems not in the first
edition and excludes four poems in that edition; corrects textual

errors in the first edition; and presents the uncollected early and late poems in three chronologically ordered sections. Augmenting the poetry is a selection of Crane's reviews, letters, and essays setting forth his ideas on literature and poetics. Another stimulus to renewed study of Crane is Kenneth A. Lohf's *The Literary Manuscripts of Hart Crane* (Columbus, Ohio State Univ. Press), which meticulously lists and describes almost 280 poetry and prose items in various American collections. Because its publication overlapped issuance of the second edition of Crane's poetry, Lohf's essential guide is collated with the first edition alone.

What was awaited as a major work turns out to be less substantial than expected. Despite the critical talent of R. W. B. Lewis, *The Poetry of Hart Crane* (Princeton, Princeton Univ. Press) is an over-simplification of Crane's complexity in order that (1) he be accommodated to Lewis' vision of the poet as an apocalyptic visionary, and (2) Crane's poetry be shown to exemplify this vision. Lewis' readings of the poems are useful despite their thesis-ridden character because he illuminates words, phrases, and lines on many occasions. His guiding pattern is his conception of Crane as a romantic, post-Christian "religious poet," of Crane's theme as "the visionary and loving transfiguration of the actual world," and of his career as a "journey" of the apocalyptic poetic imagination through "the broken world" undertaken in order to "heal . . . transform" and redeem that world "by poetry." A monolithic book such as this is grist for the negative mill of a hostile critic such as Joseph Riddell, whose "Hart Crane's Poetics of Failure" (*ELH*, XXXIII, 473–496) reiterates Barbara Herman's judgment in 1950 that "the nearest that Crane could approach the Word he vainly invoked in poem after poem was simply the word." Riddell stresses that failure was inherent in Crane's attempt to escape human limitations (e.g., language, history, poetry, mortality) so that he inevitably collapsed as poet and man. Riddell is apprehensive lest "the academic . . . 'New Paganism,'" exemplified for him in the collaborative *Start with the Sun* (1960) by James E. Miller, Karl Shapiro, and Bernice Slote, replace the rejected style of Eliot with a new "'official' style, no less contrived for its appearing spontaneous." He posits the alternative of a "post-transcendental, humanistic poetics like that of Wallace Stevens, which, denying resolution, throws the poetic self back upon the resources of an all-too-human imagination that can discover its identity only in the act of relating itself to others . . . the poet . . . creating not the Word but himself." Riddell's closely argued case against Crane is impressive, but it rests on the assumption, which need not be shared with him, that the academic New Pagans are justified in regarding Crane as their "immediate forerunner" and the modern American exemplar of their desired "religious, physical, passionate, incantatory . . . cosmic consciousness."

A French critic—Jean Guiguet—has taken his cue from Crane's stated belief in "the so-called illogical impingements of the connotations of words on the consciousness (and their combinations and interplay in metaphor on this basis)" and boldly proceeded in *L'Univers poétique de Hart Crane* (Paris, Minard, 1965) to trace the connotations of Crane's dominantly recurring words in order to test the merit of Crane's additional belief that his difficult poetry would become lucid for average readers when, "by some experience of their own, the words accumulate the necessary connotations to complete their connection." Guiguet has divided his word studies into three categories and their subdivisions: (1) *physical elements*, including water, fire and light, air, and earth; (2) *civilization*, including cities, ports, trains and roads, vessels, and bridges; (3) *motion*, including circles and gyrations, breaking and scattering, reunion fusion, and rising and falling. The book encourages a fuller response to the connotative resonance of Crane's words and bodies forth an interesting approximation of an abstract poetic world. A reasonable objection to Guiguet's method is that essentially he has created a general universe, whereas Crane's poetic universe is initially at least that of the particular poem, in which alone such words as appear in it can reverberate with meaningful connotations that in context become specific rather than general.

A more important study than Guiguet's is the work of an Italian scholar, Pietro Spinucci, who has written the best work on Crane so far produced in Europe: *Il Ponte di Brooklyn di Hart Crane e la poesia americana degli anni venti* (Milan, Società Editrice Vita e Pensiero, 1966). Although Spinucci concentrates on *The Bridge*, which no longer seems *the* critical fulcrum for lifting meaning from Crane's works, he gives the poem a sensitive and illuminating reading. He explicates *The Bridge* in the currently fashionable terms of religious unity and in addition puts Crane into the context of his age. Spinucci began this study as preparation for translating Crane, which one hopes he soon will do. In the meantime this book will unlock the riches of a difficult poet for many Italian readers.

Milne Holton's " 'A Baudelairesque Thing': The Directions of Hart Crane's 'Black Tambourine" (*Criticism*, IX, 215–228) is a careful examination of one of Crane's earliest successful poems in the context of Crane's literary and personal life. Holton feels that "Black Tambourine" is "one of several poems which, taken together, mark the change from Hart Crane's poetic adolescence to his artistic majority. Henceforth he dealt with "the poet and the poetic imagination in a contemporary environment . . . his major achievement." This is a fine article.

The early poetry not included in *White Buildings* (1926) is considered jointly with some of the poetry in that volume by Maurice Kramer in "Hart Crane's 'Reflexes' " (*TCL*, XIII, 131–138). Kramer misinterprets Crane's reference to "reflexes" in "Recitative" as implying involuntary "motions of mind," i.e., predictable patterns of thinking and structuring akin to involuntary muscular patterns, so that the critic freely can search for these patterns in other poems. This appears to be a desire for critical order driven to excessively radical solutions.

Robert L. Perry's *The Shared Vision of Waldo Frank and Hart Crane* (Lincoln, Univ. of Nebr. Press, 1966) is a monograph containing the first extended study of Crane's intellectual life since Brom Weber's *Hart Crane* (1948). Perry shows plausibly that Frank's "mystical geometry" of curve imagery and metaphor, incorporated in his fiction and other prose writings, antedates Crane's and probably encouraged him in *The Bridge* to emulate Frank's models. Perry also holds that Frank was a disciple of the pseudo-philosopher P. D. Ouspensky and strengthened Crane's dependence upon Ouspenskian thought, although this has been denied by Gorham Munson, an intimate of Frank's and Crane's in the 1920's. The influence of Frank was pervasive in other respects upon Crane. After due allowance is made for Whitman's centrality in Crane's life, for example, there is little reason to disagree with Perry's statement that "when Crane answered the call to write a religious myth, he was answering Frank's call."

Although Perry and others have not hesitated to ascribe Crane's theory and practice to mysticism, Joseph J. Arpad insists in "Hart Crane's Platonic Myth: The Brooklyn Bridge" (*AL*, XXXIX, 75–86)

that the poet's "Platonic idealism" must not be equated with "romantic mysticism" if we are to comprehend his "myth." Arpad
declares that Crane transcended Plato's negative conception of poetry as "mystical" and "dream-visionary" and formulated his "logic
of metaphor" in accordance with Plato's positive conception of the
philosopher's "technique of acquiring knowledge." The Platonic philosopher's "Idea-vision . . . was a product of the 'rational intuition'
(*noesis*), the highest form of cognizance; his was a 'synoptic view'
of experience which allowed him to perceive the universal Form or
Idea in particular objects or events." Armed with this as the rationale
for his poetic technique, Crane achieved coherence in *The Bridge*
despite the absence of a "linear progression of ideas or images"; coherence accrues by dialectical interplay of the progressively unfold-
ing "new insights afforded into the bridge's meaning" in the poem's
sections until the Idea, synthesis of the "material ideal of a nation"
and the "spiritual ideal of the individual," is attained in the concluding section, "Atlantis."

Interest in Crane's life has picked up now that fear of intentional
and genetic fallacies has died down. The most lively piece in this
area is Gorham Munson's "Chaplinesque" (*ForumH*, V, 20–26)
which provides anecdotal information about the response to Crane's
"Chaplinesque" by the poem's subject, Charlie Chaplin, and Munson
himself. John Unterecker's "A Piece of Pure Invention" (*ForumH*,
V, 42–44) focuses on the relatively neglected personal warmth of
Crane as revealed in a "bon-voyage poem" he wrote in 1924 for an
aunt leaving on a European trip. Unterecker properly asserts that the
poem reveals Crane's "facility in light verse"; he might also have
pointed out that it is one of his weakest efforts in that line. Although
Hunce Voelcker's *The Hart Crane Voyages* (New York, Brownstone)
is allegedly criticism and biography, it is essentially fictional autobiography in the Jean Genet mold. The best thing about it is Robert
Duncan's deadpan eulogy on the back cover, in the tradition of the
burlesque sermon, that "deep studies, not only in Crane's work and
letters and in the whole field of literary criticism related, but also in
mythopoeic lore, inform Voelcker's work. . . ." Those who wish to inform themselves on Voelcker's literary ability to transport himself
back in time, metamorphosed into one of Crane's most intimate companions, will find this attractively printed volume relevant.

iv. E. A. Robinson

On the basis of this year's scholarly interest in Edwin Arlington Robinson, one might tentatively predict an upturn in his critical fortunes. There have been two important books, five significant articles, and a scattering of lesser items. The fact that four dissertations also have been written on Robinson in the past two years adds to the evidence of Robinson's returning favor.

The most ambitious study is W. R. Robinson's *Edwin Arlington Robinson: A Poetry of the Act* (Cleveland, Western Reserve Univ. Press). This is a book in the tradition of the 1960's established by such critics as Roy Harvey Pearce (to whom the author acknowledges his debt), in which the value of an author is asserted to lie in his ability to embody in word and deed the quintessential character of his age, Existentialism (the non-institutionalized religious variety) in the case of modern twentieth-century Americans. The format for such criticism is exemplified by this book. It is written in a dense often highly "personal" style, and finds Robinson encompassing all the attitudes (e.g., the "alienated self"; the development of abstraction in language and articulation; the refusal to take solace in pre-modern orthodoxies, religious and secular; the belief in the centrality and pre-eminence of aesthetic experience and expression, as well as the artist; the rejection of the dualism characteristic of pre-modern thought; anti-materialism; etc. etc.) of Western modernism.

Essentially, the pattern of modernism is applied to Robinson and enough reference is made to his work to support the attribution of the pattern. W. R. Robinson admittedly has made the philosophic character of Robinson (not his ideas, which were few and unsystematic) the prime factor in his evaluation. The result is that Robinson is shown to be in the radical empirical tradition of Whitman-William James-Dewey, thoroughly modern; but much less attention has been given to Robinson's poetry in this book than is warranted, even to the later poetry which—contrary to most treatments of Robinson—is here regarded as the most dynamic body of expression produced by the poet.

Ultimately, this book never makes clear that Robinson's poetry is qualitatively valuable in a critical sense—the value resides in the poet's modernity. Essentially, then, this book is primarily concerned with the intellectual climate of the American spirit from 1890 to 1930 and with Robinson primarily as he exemplifies that spirit. The primary achievement of this book is its delineation of that intellectual climate, and here W. R. Robinson is very knowledgeable. Also, it must be said that this book will surely re-open the issue of Robinson for students of modern American poetry and turn him into a "question" arousing increasing attention. The result will be salutary, for the book not only praises the open-endedness of Robinson's poetry but demonstrates the value of such open-endedness in its commitment to a secular existentialism which has permitted the author to scrutinize the intellectual and functional significance of an important and yet fashionably neglected poet.

Complementing W. R. Robinson's book is Wallace L. Anderson's, *Edwin Arlington Robinson: A Critical Introduction* (Boston, Houghton Mifflin). Mr. Anderson modestly asserts an intention to fill the gap that exists in Robinson studies because "there has been no book for the college student and general reader that combines biographical and critical material." Like Edwin H. Miller's book on Whitman in the same series (Riverside Studies in Literature), however, its achievement is greater than its expression of purpose. Robinson has not been neglected by any means, but it has not been possible for recent critics to deal comprehensively with him, because of the revolutionary iconoclasm of the New Criticism which sought to bury the "false" revolutionary character of the pre-1920 American poetry (the American Renaissance of the 1910's) with which Robinson had been associated historically. The result was that Robinson was thrust back into the nineteenth century, sometimes grudgingly considered to be a transitional figure leading into the twentieth century from which he withdrew in the 1920's as his method and values made him feel increasingly anachronistic. Additionally, as has been pointed out, his penchant for the long poem of discursive character was contrary to the emphasis upon the short poem which seemed to dominate the post-1910's.

Mr. Anderson's book is successful far beyond its author's hopes in evoking a fresh interest in Robinson's poetry and an awareness of his great stature in the first half of the twentieth century because the book deals with Robinson's poetry at length and in detail, and with the poetry of his whole career rather than the early works, or the works of the 1910's, or another limited segment. Mr. Anderson is not thesis-ridden, which enables him to function objectively, or at least to give the impression that he has escaped his biases for the time involved in writing the book. He can approach the Arthurian poems of the 1920's with as much freshness of perception and judgment as the shorter vignettes which customarily appear in anthologies. He can appreciate Robinson's humor, as in the long "Captain Craig" where it is extended and serious and also in "Isaac and Archibald" where it is more limited. In short, Anderson opens up Robinson's poetry for the reader, uses the facts of biography without confusing them with the facts of the poetry, and makes sound judgments about the literary value of the poems as separate entities and about Robinson's poetry as a whole.

Mr. Anderson believes that only two of Robinson's contemporaries—Frost and Eliot—are of "equal stature" with him, and Anderson gives persuasive grounds for believing that in a few respects Robinson may have gone beyond them. Admirers of Stevens and Williams will be up in arms at this; they will have to read Robinson's poetry before taking issue with Anderson, and this will be the best testament to the importance of Anderson's book in the late 1960's.

Of a piece with the books by Robinson and Anderson is a felicitously and ably written essay by Floyd Stovall, "Edwin Arlington Robinson in Perspective" (*Essays on American Literature*, pp. 241–258). Stovall, writing in the twilight of his own distinguished career, summarizes and analyzes Robinson's career succinctly, noting the decline in his reputation, which he thinks is not at all deserved. He cites the statistics relating to the declining anthology space that Robinson has received in the past generation and divides the critics into two groups: those who are chiefly literary historians who see Robinson in the long perspective of American letters and those younger critics who are anti-romantics and are inclined to think of Robinson as a belated spokesman for the nineteenth century. He concludes, perhaps prophetically: "This division among critics may not last. Each age, we know, finds newness somewhere in the past." He fears that Robinson's long poems will remain unread because they will not be anthologized, but "even so, he will surely retain a prominent place among the modern poets who were his contemporaries."

The remaining articles of significance include one by Anderson,

which is subsumed in his book, and three others. Paul Zietlow's "The
Meaning of Tilbury Town: Robinson as a Regional Poet" (*NEQ*, XL,
188–211) contrasts Robinson's regionalism with that of Hardy and
Frost and concludes that Robinson's Tilbury Town is isolated from
time and place, lacks particularity, and is essentially "an illusion . . .
malignant and powerful" from which one must escape into transcendental myths, which alone give meaning to life. Gertrude M. White,
in "Robinson's 'Captain Craig'; A Reinterpretation" (*ES*, XLVII
[1966], 432–439), takes issue with earlier interpretations of the
poem by Herman Hagedorn, Yvor Winters, and Ellsworth Barnard,
which she finds limited. She regards the poem as "a somewhat puzzling combination of narrative, didactic poem, and character sketch,"
not necessarily one of Robinson's best poems but an important "dramatization of the fear and conflict within Robinson's own mind as
he struggled to understand himself and accept his destiny."

A final Robinson item, also dealing with Frost, is Barton L. St.
Armand's "The Power of Sympathy in the Poetry of Robinson and
Frost: The 'Inside' vs. the 'Outside' Narrative" (*AQ*, XIX, 564–574).
Armand explores the differences between Robinson and Frost in
terms of their characterizations. Robinson's are done from the inside.
"Captain Craig," for example "is not a character sketch at all but
the most subtle of poetic psychographs." Frost, on the other hand,
"will not let us into the minds of his characters" and we know them
"almost solely through their actions."

v. Robert Frost

Following the large amount of scholarship devoted to Frost last
year, one could have predicted much less attention in 1967. Such has
been the case, but there seems no doubt that Frost's reputation is
permanently fixed on a high level. Frost is the subject this year of
a book-length symposium, a handful of articles, and an addition to
the canon.

In Edward C. Latham and Lawrance Thompson, eds., *Robert
Frost and the Lawrence, Massachusetts 'High School Bulletin': The
Beginning of a Literary Career* (New York, Grolier Club, 1966)
Robert Frost's high-school poetry of the 1890's is presented in a
beautifully printed book, along with facsimiles of the four issues
of the monthly *High School Bulletin*, which Frost edited in late

1891. The editors find that Frost's poetry and prose foreshadow many of his more mature characteristics and attitudes, including his view of the "function and process of the poet," his concern with archeology, and his "devotion to classical learning."

The 142 pages devoted to Robert Frost in the *Southern Review* (II, iv, n.s., Autumn, 1966) have the range and value of a small book. Indeed, the collection of essays and reminiscences has been edited with an eye to formal unity, for the initial essay (by W. W. Robson) is by an Englishman who deals with the relation of Frost to English literary men and the English poetic scene in the mid-1910's, when Frost's first book appeared under an English imprint; the concluding essay is an evaluation of the impact upon Frost's posthumous reputation of the publication of his letters and interviews with him (John A. Meixner).

Robson's essay (pp. 735–761) makes some interesting observations about the state of English letters in the mid-1910's, pointing out that the so-called "Georgian" poets currently held in critical disrepute were actually "modern" poets obsessed "with personal freedom" in their day and that they both strengthened Frost and in turn were positively affected by him. Edward Thomas' review of *North of Boston* in 1914, for example, "put the stress where it should be put . . . on Frost's technical innovation." Robson's subsequent discussion of the elements of the "revolutionary" character Thomas ascribed to Frost's work is extremely illuminating, for it is designed to evoke the impact of Frost's verse in the mid-1910's. Robson is compelled to admit, however, that there is no single great poem to cite and that he finds a "thinness" in the whole corpus. Among the limitations and weaknesses are a lack of profundity, "monotony," "self-indulgence," "no such technical (or personal) development as we find in a Rilke or an Eliot or a Yeats," and "in his quasi-homiletic poetry . . . some vague theological equivalent of a friendliness and cosmic optimism which are antipathetic to his own creative powers." Robson concludes that Frost's "personal poetry" in which "what we are given is the aperçu, the glimpse, the perception crystallized, where the poet seems to be beside the reader, sharing his vision, not gesturing in front," is "highly distinctive, and indeed unique."

Herbert Howarth's essay (pp. 789–799) is designed to correct the recent critical stance which has elevated Frost to great heights and depreciated such contemporaries as Ford Madox Ford, Ezra Pound, and T. S. Eliot. Howarth regards Ford and Pound as catalysts of Frost who "had perceived certain needs and opportunities that they already had perceived; when he met them, he perceived the needs and opportunities more clearly and at once became a more articulate theorist; and he went aside the better to pursue his own solutions, which were only in part, though the more obvious part, different solutions." "Frost's monosyllables" may be discerned in Ford's poetry. Pound, Eliot, and Frost were all affected by Browning's examples. "What Frost's influence has determined is the skill and craftsmanship of this period of American literature. The clean, firm, whittled shapes, the well-restrained rhetoric are his legacy. Only credit must also be given to the work done by Hueffer, Pound, and Eliot; they too imposed the respect for technique, for the virtues of brevity and the intaglio method."

John F. Lynen (pp. 800–816) is concerned that the apotheosis of Frost as "culture hero" whose works "come together as parts of some one great poem which constitutes a life record" may obscure the fact that he actually created a world rather than merely recorded his experience in it and that, therefore, his poems are discrete and can be judged individually in terms of their relative success in discovering an "assumed world." Lynen grants that Frost's poems "*seem*" to be "discoveries of the world he has known all along," but insists that "this is a fiction which the poet himself probably believed and which he has made so credible that the simple truthfulness of his statements or their eloquence often seem the only mysteries of his art."

All of the critical contributions to the *Southern Review* cite and quote specific poems but only one writer—Lloyd N. Dendinger (pp. 822–829)—offers an explication. The poem is "Stopping by Woods on a Snowy Evening." Dendinger believes that the general interpretation of "woods" as "death," of the "lure of the woods" as "death wish" is valid. However, "if we allow the woods to remain 'woods' and call their attractiveness the force of irrational impulse," the poem expands in meaning to become an expression of "the wilderness theme in American literature," itself "a particular historical expression of the larger theme of Western man's attempt to understand the mysterious forces of his world and of his own nature."

Dendinger's reading is persuasive, especially in view of George Nitchie's (pp. 817–821) discussion of Frost's predilection for "irresponsible and self-indulgent" behavior in his early years and his yearning for "reassurance" that his life as a poet had not been wilful, cruel to others and himself.

John A. Meixner's review (pp. 862–877) of the posthumously published letters and interviews and the biographical writings appearing after Frost's death leads him to conclude that Frost's reputation "is likely to sag from the shock of these revelations, but in any long run it can only grow and deepen." For it is now much clearer that "his efforts, and his stance, clearly were in the service of sanity and inner poise. Frost valued most what he needed most." Nevertheless, "this sense of balance . . . is based, in large measure, on personal constriction, with aesthetic and ethical consequences that significantly limited the world that Frost created." He was not, then, "one of the world's great poets" though unquestionably "a great *American* poet."

The reminiscences of Frost's years at Dartmouth, as set down by F. Cudworth Flint, Alexander Laing, and others tend to confirm Meixner's conclusions. Richard Eberhart's lecture (pp. 762–788) on Frost delivered at San Francisco in 1964 also does so. Granting that Frost is representative in many ways of urban, democratic American culture, that "he engages us totally in what is commonly known and felt to be reality and this may be his greatest gift," Eberhart praises Frost for his representative quality and his "masterful poems" and yet emphasizes that Frost's vision was limited: "He has to stand and have his being on reason, on rational grounds, with a nature-penetrating imagination, not a mystery-piercing or a God-piercing one."

Howell D. Chickering, Jr., in "Robert Frost: Romantic Humorist" (*L&P*, XVI [1966], 139–150) seeks to provide "a specific mental structure for this [Frost's] self-image, in order to connect by a single means his humor, terror, lyrical self-projection into nature, and the curious decorum of his pastorals." The key is Frost's "serious" (probably unconscious) use of humor to protect himself from the bruising of his ego as it has been exposed in his poems. The application of this key to Frost's poems by Chickering produces results. For example, it helps to explain a phenomenon of his structure, namely, why Frost's "tone of voice changes at the end of poems" so that "the most committed meanings of the poems" seem to conclude in a "detachment" that masks his increasing commitment to the meanings and protects him from rejection of the meanings. In short, the Romantic excess is controlled by a technique of concealment of the self at its most vulnerable.

In a public address Reuben A. Brower attempts to define the peculiarly American qualities of Frost's poetry ("American and Un-Americanness of Frost" in Martin Shookley, ed., *1967 Proceedings of [the] Conference of College Teachers of English of Texas,* Lubbock, Tex. Tech. College, XXXII, 6–10). His conclusion suggests the difficulty of doing so: "Either there's something universal about Frost—or can it be that there is something universal about Americanness?" Before leaving us with this rhetorical question, Brower does indicate that there is a distinctive "Americanness" in Frost's "*sound*" reposing not in dialect but in rhythms which capture "the arrest and flow of American speech," in the profound response to the " 'wildness' " of nature encouraged by a country in which the landscape was still natural, and "in *the very economy* of Frost's response to the beauty and terror of this world."

Reginald L. Cook in "Frost the Diversionist" (*NEQ*, XL, 323–338) studies Frost as an innovator "in individual variations within the demands of metrical verse," an artist dedicated to "the play of humor and wit," and "a poetic strategist . . . addicted to irony and paradox." Thus he is far more complex than some critics have been willing to comprehend or grant in the face of his "deceptive simplicity."

Finally, Lewis H. Miller, Jr., in "Two Poems of Winter" (*CE*, XXVIII, 314–317) argues that a careful linguistic and literary analysis of Frost's "Desert Places" and the anonymous medieval lyric "Wynter Wakeneth Al My Care" can help students develop a sense of literary history by observing in detail "how a modern poet *makes* meaning out of a neutral universe, while a medieval poet *finds* it." Miller believes that Frost's poem is designed to reveal that Frost achieves meaning by transforming neutral objects into symbols.

vi. Lindsay, Masters, Hilda Doolittle, and Others

It is difficult to interest readers in Vachel Lindsay these days, but two persuasive reappraisals have appeared which try to extract a modest amount of permanent poetry from his uneven and often banal collected poems. Peter Viereck, in "Vachel Lindsay, the Dante of the Fundamentalists: The Suicide of America's Faith in Technology" (Vittorio Gabrieli, ed., *Friendship's Garland: Essays Presented to*

Mario Praz on His Seventieth Birthday, Rome, Edizioni di Storia e Letteratura, 1966, II, 207–232), argues that Lindsay at his best "incarnates for America the importance and dignity of spontaneous song: its ennobling and rehumanizing role in a standardized machine age." This article is based on two tacit postulates: "First, that poetry-readers have no more right to laugh at the homespun Fundamentalist theology of the Old American West than at the subtler but perhaps no more pious-hearted theology of Dante's day. Second, that the American small-town carnival deserved as much respect as Dante's medieval pageants; it was as filling a literary theme; it was no less capable of combining the divine with the humdrum." Viereck concludes that "when Lindsay did voice deeply enough the roots of the human condition, he became a fundamental poet, rather than merely the poet of the Fundamentalists."

The second article, also appearing in a *Festschrift*, is John T. Flanagan's "Vachel Lindsay: An Appraisal" (*Essays on American Literature*, pp. 273–281). Flanagan deplores the shift in popularity which used to give Lindsay adequate coverage in anthologies (twenty-one pages in Matthiessen's *Oxford Book of American Verse*, 1950) and now gives him no representation at all (Allen, Rideout, and Robinson, *American Poetry*, 1965). Without being blind to Lindsay's limitations, Flanagan asserts: "Lindsay's verse has earned him a permanent place in American literature, and future anthologists who deny him that place will reflect only their own myopic vision."

That Edgar Lee Masters seems to interest more Europeans than Americans is attested to by three of the four articles which appeared on him during the past year. Two of them were essays in European *Festschriften*: Harro Kühnelt, "*Maximilian*: Ein Drama von Edgar Lee Masters" (Osmund Menghin and Hermann M. Olberg, eds., *Festschrift: Leonhard C. Franz zum 70. Geburtstag*, Innsbruck, Sprachwissenschaftliche Inst. der Leopold-Franzens-Universität, 1966, pp. 245–260); S. B. Liljegren, "*Père Lachaise* and *Spoon River*: Some Notes on the Dependence or Independence of Literary Motifs in Their Interrelation with Society" (Gerhard Muller-Schwefe and Konrad Tuzinski, eds., *Literatur-Kultur-Gesellschaft in England und Amerika: Aspekte und Forschungsbeiträge. Friedrich Schubel zum 60. Geburtstag*, Frankford, Diesterweg, 1966, pp. 201–208). Kühnelt, besides examining Masters' forgotten play, is interested in other dramatizations of the Maximillian story and appends a bibliography.

Liljegren's article suggests tentatively and unconvincingly that *Spoon River Anthology* owes a debt to De Maupassant. The third article, which is a detailed and significant study, appeared in Italy: Giuseppe Sertoli, "La piccola Commedia di Spoon River" (*SA*, XII [1966], 201–229). Despite the fact that Sertoli takes his title from Pavese's comparison of the *Anthology* with the *Divina Commedia* and Masters' own similar comparison, he sees little Dantean design in the work. The *Anthology* is, however, as is all of Masters' work, held together by Masters' belief in "the myth of the pioneer." Quoting from an interview Masters gave to the New York *Times* in 1942, saying that his roots were in the America of Jefferson and in Greece and that he had an aversion to Lincoln, Sertoli goes on to find these attitudes pervading all of the *Anthology*.

Another Italian scholar, Ruggero Bianchi, in "Saffo in America: Hilda Doolittle" (*SA*, XI [1965], 197–211) sets out to examine H. D. in light of the great reputation she once enjoyed. He finds that her Parnassianism, her Hellenism, her exoticism, and her formalism, which combined to explain not only her reputation but also her relation to imagism, made her a sort of mirror of the complex of aesthetic ideas that flourished in the early years of this century. He concludes, however, that her intellectual limitations are only too evident: a narrowness of inspiration and an inability to breathe life into poetry of large themes; an expertise with the chisel and intaglio which produced minor art, refined but often detached from reality. Hers was a poetry "exquisitely subtile, splendidly elaborated, but in the end too obviously 'feminine.'" On the technical level, her poetry has all the virtues and defects "di una poesia formalistica e neoparnassiana, cioè in fondo 'letteraria.'"

Quite a different sort of thing was the poetry of the Harlem Renaissance that Eugenia W. Collier describes in "I Do Not Marvel, Countee Cullen" (*CLAJ*, XI, 73–87). This article, which is not particularly concerned with Cullen (as the MLA listing suggests), explicates several poems: Cullen's "From the Dark Tower," Sterling Brown's "The Odyssey of Big Boy," and Claude McKay's "The Harlem Dancer." Miss Collier also discusses Black poetry of the Twenties in which the Negro first discovered pride in being black, dropped the false dialect of the Paul Lawrence Dunbar school, and began to "portray realistically the world of the black American."

Another member of the Harlem Renaissance is the subject of

Lynn Adelman's "A Study of James Weldon Johnson" (*JNH*, LII, 128–145), which recounts Johnson's difficulties in realizing himself as a man and writer because of having been born an American Negro and because of having assumed the role of active leadership in Negro journalism and the NAACP.

Finally, this survey of recent scholarship on minor poets of the early twentieth century ends with a handful of short essays in George B. Saul's *Quintet: Essays on Five American Women Poets* (The Hague, Mouton). Totalling only fifty pages, this is an unpretentious little volume that attempts to keep alive interest in Sara Teasdale, Elinor Wylie, Hazel Hall, Abbie Huston Evans, and Winifred Welles. All of these essays have been previously printed.

vii. Aiken, Fletcher, Cummings, MacLeish, Millay, Sandburg, Minna Loy

One of the last survivors of his generation, Conrad Aiken lives in Savannah, Georgia, where Patricia Reynolds Willis interviewed him ("Unabashed Praise of a Poet," *GaR*, XXI, 373–380) and with her tape recorder took down some interesting bits of opinion and reminiscence. His views on martinis, writers' conferences, and literary fashions are here along with his memories of old associations with Pound and Eliot. He reports his recent sharp exchange with James Dickey over a review of *Lord Zero* and recalls his own savage review of Amy Lowell's book on Keats. He also remembers that when he edited Emily Dickinson in 1924 Eliot and Pound were "very much annoyed with me . . . They did their damnedest to stop me . . . I think they thought this was really cutting the ground from under their feet . . . to have a great poet looking over their shoulders suddenly."

Aiken also recalls his endless war with Louis Untermeyer, who nevertheless remains his friend. It was important to fight Untermeyer, he declared, "because his taste was so bad and his influence so enormous; this had to be kicked out. We didn't succeed and he managed to outlast us." Very true, and Untermeyer's voice still comes through loud and clear, only now he is beating the drums for Aiken ("Conrad Aiken: Our Best Known Unread Poet," *SatR*, L, Nov. 25, 28–29, 76–77). Untermeyer suggests that Aiken's prolificity and his unyielding refusal to try to attract a following have led to a dwindling audience. He grants that Aiken has written too much and too easily but praises him for his resistance to fashion and concludes that "the best of his work will stand a long time."

Edna B. Stephens' *John Gould Fletcher* (TUSAS, No. 118) is the first book on Fletcher, a surprising fact in view of his interesting career. The author wrote a dissertation on the Oriental backgrounds of Fletcher's poetry and her presentation of this material in relation to Fletcher's poetry and prose is an important contribution. The book has many of the faults of skimpiness imposed by space limitations in the Twayne Series, yet she does manage to review his vast output in some detail. From these pages it is possible to find out why such an enormously well-known poet and contributor to important magazines in the 1910's and 1920's suddenly dropped from sight, for it appears that his career can be divided into three major phases, with a gradual decline of poetic originality beginning in the second phase.

In his first phase the expatriate Fletcher was an aesthete who produced poetry of great freshness and quality; this was the period when he wrote imagistic verse, his symphonies, and his haikus. His second phase carried him through the Twenties; it saw a heightening of his religious mysticism and the development of an antipathy to the modern world and to such modern writers as Joyce and Eliot, the writing of religious poetry and the conscious search for meaning in American historical materials; the third phase found him returning to the United States, intellectually and socially drawn to the Southern Agrarians but disliking their critical theories and their literary practice, ultimately withdrawing to Arkansas and an agrarian regionalism more intense and lasting than that of any contemporary with the exception of Donald Davidson.

Edna B. Stephens has had to bring together into coherent pattern many diverse and difficult materials; if her book is not entirely a success, she has made clear the need to study Fletcher's first and second phase poetry again and to bring him back into the literary history of modern American literature. The author believes that much of Fletcher's post-1930 poetry was good in its Blakean mysticism and Rimbaudian texture and negation; she observes that he was ignored by some critics (especially the New Critics) and not read by most except for those who were reviewing books in New York papers and magazines; that his long pieces don't lend themselves to anthologizing even if an anthologist dares to be original, and that consequently he cannot be found in more than one or two post-1930 anthologies, especially those used in college classes; further, it is clear that the revival of a post-orthodox Christian religious spirit and Fletcher's dissenting individualism open him up for treatment and an increase of reputation in the manner accorded to such figures as Robinson and Hart Crane in recent years.

The only major consideration of E. E. Cummings in 1967 was an article dealing with *The Enormous Room* and only inferentially with Cummings' poetry: Marilyn Gaull, "Language and Identity: A Study of E. E. Cummings' *The Enormous Room*" (*AQ*, XIX, 645–662). This is a perceptive reading of the novel, which the author concludes is on almost every level—language, form, theme, character—"a metaphor for the Edenic experience of the creating imagination." She believes that in Cummings' assault on the traditional values of words his poetry is little more than "evocative eccentricity," but within the more flexible bounds of prose, "Cummings was able to build up new contexts, to provide the precise associations upon which a creative and functional use of language depends."

This article reminds one that this too-little read novel has a great deal to say that is relevant today in the struggle to maintain individuality. Cummings' assault on the symbols of language is a stylistic device to get at the mindlessness that submits to them. Miss Gaull reminds us that Cummings was imprisoned by the French military police for what appeared to be only a verbal impropriety. When asked, " '*Est-ce-que vous détestez les boches?*' " he replied, " '*Non, j'aime beaucoup les français.*' " The official mind could not tolerate such license, for as Monsieur le Ministre charged, "It is impossible to love Frenchmen and not to hate Germans."

Dan Jaffe's "Archibald MacLeish: Mapping the Tradition" (*The Thirties*, pp. 141–148) stands in sharp contrast with Max Halperen's essay on Pound (see p. 216). Despite the last line of MacLeish's best-known and universally anthologized poem "Ars Poetica" ("A poem should not mean/ But be"), his career during the Thirties and during World War II was anything but a separation of life from art. Those who practice their art in isolation, he called "The Irresponsibles," and during the Thirties he wrote many radio plays dealing with the problems of the times. His poetry also often reflected his social conscience, and his public career reached a climax with his valuable service as Librarian of Congress and during the war as Assistant Secretary of State and one of the founders of UNESCO.

James Gray's *Edna St. Vincent Millay* (UMPAW, No. 64) is a modest attempt to clothe Millay with dignity as a person and with moderate success as a poet; yet Gray cannot make a good case for her literary achievement as a whole. He seems to have been influenced by Millay's self-disparagement during her last years. Gray acknowledges that she wasn't really in tune with the modern spirit despite her acute social consciousness and her assertive femininity. As he points out, and he must, "her impulse toward expression was governed by convention," chiefly convention of the past. Her poetry thus has an opaque quality behind which there is no encouragement for a reader to pass. It is dubious that she will ever be resurrected and taken seriously as a significant poet.

Time is not dealing kindly with Carl Sandburg's reputation, as the meager annual gleanings from the 1967 MLA International Bibliography show: parts of two articles and one bit of reminiscence.[1] In Eleanor G. Vance's "Glimpses of Carl Sandburg" (*NAR*, n.s. IV, ii, 9–10) the poet is seen briefly as he appeared in 1931 in a public recital (reading, singing, and guitar-playing) at Northwestern University. In James B. Anderson's "Frost and Sandburg: A Theological Criticism" (*Renascence*, XIX, 171–183) one reads: ". . . modern American poets, with the exception of Eliot and a few others . . . either oppose Christianity openly or implicity, or weakly hold on to it while they largely ignore it in their poetry." For Sandburg anti-intellectualism apparently leads to "an ignorance of theology"—thus there is "no 'Christian intellect' that governs all his seeing."

Time blurs the past and expediency compels critics and scholars to acquiesce. Kenneth Fields in "The Poetry of Mina Loy" (*SoR*, II, 597–607) sets out to remedy human weakness by providing samples of Mina Loy's poetry together with commentary. Readers of such little magazines and anthologies as *Others*, *The Little Review*, and *The Dial* have come across her poems; her books are scarce, the first apparently printed in Dijon, France, in 1923 and her latest in 1958 by a small private American press. In the history of American poetry (1946) by Horace Gregory and Marya Zaturenska, Mina Loy is con-

---

1. One of the articles is from a Danish *Festschrift* which we have not seen: Poul Sørensen, "To amerikanske prosalyrikere" in Sven M. Kristensen, ed., *Fremmede digtere i det 20. århundrede* (Copenhagen, G.E.C. Gad), I, 25–38.

sidered important enough to be linked with Eliot, Stevens, and Marianne Moore as those whom Alfred Kreymborg discriminatingly published in his *Others* anthologies. Mina Loy's poems were written in free verse; in addition, as Mr. Fields explains, her "versification is unsophisticated and sometimes awkward . . . . Her most serious deficiency is a lack of unity from beginning to end of many of her poems." Balanced against this, Mr. Fields declares that she deals with "ideas" more effectively than Pound, with "subjects" less "trivial" than those of Williams, and that she manifests a "profound" and "bitterly satirical" spirit where Marianne Moore "is clever and superficial . . . amusing." There is enough good poetry presented here and sufficient balanced critical comment to suggest that Mina Loy's poetry has been improperly neglected.

University of California at Davis

15. Poetry: The 1930's to the Present

Oliver Evans

i. General

The most ambitious book-length "overview" of contemporary American poetry to appear in 1967 was M. L. Rosenthal's *The New Poets: American and British Poetry Since World War II* (New York, Oxford Univ. Press), which, notwithstanding its title, tends to focus primarily on the American scene. Underlying the depressive quality of modern poetry on both sides of the Atlantic—what Robert Lowell has termed "our universal *Angst*"—Rosenthal finds certain specific characteristics that he claims are typical of the most recent poetry: a tendency toward what he terms Romantic aestheticism; a tendency to view the individual as the victim of his culture rather than as merely the product of it; and a tendency for the poet to use his private life as a conscious theme, sometimes symbolically identifying a personal predicament with a national or cultural one. He makes the familiar point that "the fragmentation of the long poem is an aspect of alienation," and traces the development of the poem-sequence type from *Song of Myself* to *Paterson* and *Life Studies*, by way of *Spoon River Anthology*, *The Waste Land*, the *Cantos*, and *The Bridge*.

Rosenthal's analysis of *Life Studies* (the book in which he claims Lowell at last "found himself") is probably the most detailed study of this book which has yet appeared. Less satisfactory are his discussions of other "confessional" poets, the most obvious error being one of proportion: thus, twenty-three pages are devoted to Ginsberg, twenty-one to Berryman, and eight to Sexton, while Roethke rates a single paragraph. This is of course the necessary consequence of "thesis criticism," which sacrifices the poet's total achievement to that aspect of him—which in this case is "confessional"—in which the critic happens to be chiefly interested; but the result is unfortunate. Of Roethke he observes: "We have no other modern American poet of comparable reputation who has absorbed so little of the concerns of his age into his nerve-ends." I wonder if this is not a facile judgment, and if the concerns of our age differ so essentially from those of preceding ages that Roethke's poetry may be said to suffer on this account. I suspect the opposite is true, and that the superiority of Roethke over, say, Ginsberg (or LeRoi Jones, who rates four pages in another chapter) lies precisely in the fact that his concern is with themes which are universal rather than temporal.

The chapter entitled "The Projectivist Movement," which takes its title from Olson's influential essay "Projective Verse," wherein a poem was conceived not as an "assembly of ankylosed lines" but rather as a "field," contains discussions of Olson, Creeley, Duncan, Levertov, Blackburn, and LeRoi Jones. Here too one encounters eccentric judgments. Of Duncan, who he says is the most naturally gifted of this group, he writes: "In a number of the poems, too, an acceptance of homosexual love is taken for granted; that is, it is assumed that everyone will share the poet's felt meanings." The assumption that his "felt meanings" will be shared by his readers is surely the assumption of every poet, regardless of his sexual inclinations, so that this observation seems not merely prudish but astonishingly naïve, as will be apparent if one ponders its implications: is the homesexual poet, by virtue of his sexual identity, therefore incapable of writing "good" love poems? A glance at the very considerable number of successful poems (among them, of course, a number of Whitman's) which celebrate unorthodox love is sufficient to refute this suggestion. Must the poet renounce his sexual identity, or assume one other than his own, before he can qualify as a candidate for Mr. Rosenthal's approval?

Those poets who are neither "confessional" nor "projective" are lumped together, rather indiscriminately, in a final chapter which is quite obviously a catch-all and which includes, among others, Nemerov, Weiss, Goodman, Kinnell, Moss, (William) Stafford, Bly, Simpson, Wright, Dickey, Snyder, Shapiro, Snodgrass, Rukeyser, Wilbur, and Jarrell. Their collective guilt derives from the fact that they represent but impurely, if at all, those tendencies which Mr. Rosenthal regards as truly contemporary and which he outlines in his first chapter. While it offers occasional interesting insights on particular poets, the book as a whole suffers from a lamentable want of proportion and commits, on the positive side, a number of serious errors of judgment.

Sister M. Bernetta Quinn, in *The Metamorphic Tradition in Modern Poetry* (New York, Gordian Press), also practices thesis criticism, but because she defines metamorphosis so very generally she does not fall into Rosenthal's error and is not obliged consequently to make similar sacrifices. Indeed, she defines it so generally that there would seem to be almost nothing it is *not*, so that it tends to lose value as the criterion of a "tradition." This, I think, is the central weakness of her book, which is intelligent if a bit academic. Metamorphosis as she uses the term applies equally to the process by which the poet, by means of his senses, transforms one reality to create another one (Stevens); to the process by which a poet achieves unity in his longer works by fusing identities, slipping back and forth among them at will (Eliot and Williams); and to the process by which the poet adapts traditional mythic material to his particular needs (Jarrell). When Sister Bernetta says that "to write a poem is itself a metamorphosis," one is forced to wonder, while conceding the obvious truth of her statement, how, if one conceives of metamorphosis thus broadly, a "metamorphic tradition" would differ from any other. On the other hand, the book makes many specific points with eloquence and erudition; it has a good many adventitious merits (the analysis of *Paterson*, for example, is both shrewd and subtle). There is, however, an unfortunate tendency toward understatement: "Jung and his theories have influenced many modern poets."

Six Poets of the San Francisco Renaissance, edited by David Kherdian, (Fresno, The Giligia Press) contains bibliographies of Ferlinghetti, Snyder, Whalen, Meltzer, McClure, and Brother Antoninus. There is a curious introduction by William Saroyan, who admits to not having read these poets but who says of the editor: "His writing is so good that without knowing the poetry itself of the poets, I am made to feel glad that they are there, and to believe in the unread and to me unknown poetry, which I am sure I shall in time read and know." The checklists are accompanied by biographical sketches of the subjects, and Kherdian also includes material from taped interviews with Snyder and Brother Antoninus.

Seven Modern American Poets, edited by Leonard Unger (Minneapolis, Univ. of Minn. Press), contains essays on Frost, Stevens,

Williams, Pound, Ransom, Eliot, and Tate that were originally published as items in the UMPAW Series. As these have for some time been available in print (for a discussion of the Tate critique, by George Hemphill, see *ALS, 1964*, p. 209), there seems no particular point in considering them here; suffice it to say that the obvious virtue of such a collection lies in its convenience.

Our final book-length item, *Poets in Progress*, (Evanston, Northwestern Univ. Press), has a misleading title, inasmuch as two of the poets which it discusses (Roethke and Jarrell) are no longer alive. The explanation is that this collection is actually a reprint of an earlier edition which appeared in 1962, to which have been added three new essays on Simpson, Sexton, and Levertov. The Levertov article, by Ralph Mills, was first printed in *The Tri-Quarterly* and later included in that critic's *Contemporary American Poetry* (see *ALS, 1966*, p. 206), so that only two of the thirteen essays printed herein have not previously made their appearance in book form— those on Simpson, by Yohma Gray; and on Sexton, by Beverly Fields. Miss Gray begins by noting the disadvantage under which objective criticism of lyric poetry must always labor, then invites us to "consider the difficulty of describing to someone totally ignorant of the experience, how a cello sounds, or how sandpaper feels, or how a puppy's mouth smells." This is perhaps intended to justify her method, which relies too heavily on quotations held together, sometimes rather tenuously, by an occasional sensitive *aperçu*. The Sexton essay suffers from the same defect, and is less gracefully written.

Of items in anthologies, perhaps the two most interesting are "Contemporary American Poetry," by Frederick J. Hoffman, in *Patterns of Commitment*, pp. 193–207, and "Zen Buddhism and Modern American Poetry," by Lucien Stryk (*YCGL*, XV [1966], 186– 191). Hoffman sees four traditions at work in contemporary poetry: the "quietly intellectual metaphysical" mode derived from the Twenties and the Thirties and represented, at its best, by Simpson (Lowell, Roethke, Eberhart, Jarrell and Wilbur are excluded from this category by virtue of their seniority); the poetry of native and local images, represented by Bly and Wright; "projective verse," which, pioneered by Williams and Zukofsky, continues in the work of Olson, Creeley, and Duncan; and the "free-swinging" poetry of the Beat Generation (Ginsberg, Corso, Ferlinghetti). Hoffman clearly favors the first tradition, which he calls the most "substantial,"

but he insists on the right of the others to be recognized. Of the
kind of "place poetry" which Bly writes, he observes that it tends
to settle into "a monotony of almanac observations with a minimum
of drive," and of the Beat poetry he says that it has a vitality "whose
compensating weakness is superficiality."

Stryk notes the similarity to Zen aesthetics of Keats's concept
of Negative Capability, and gives convincing examples of Zen influence on Snyder, Bly, and Wright. He appears insufficiently aware,
however, of the relationships existing among contemporary American poets, as when he writes: "It is the conviction of James Wright
and his friend Robert Bly, and of many fine poets who are learning
from them, including Louis Simpson, Donald Hall and W. S. Merwin,
that American poetry has wasted its life in its pursuit of formal perfection and "outwardness." While Mr. Simpson (for one) might
understandably be gratified at being called a "fine" poet, I suspect
he would be astonished, and not a little indignant, at the news that
he has all this time been going to school of Messrs. Bly and Wright.
The observation is as meaningless as it is insulting, and causes one
to wonder how well Mr. Stryk really knows his subject.

Few periodical items concerned themselves in a general way
with the new poetry. However, the series of essays entitled "The
Wesleyan Poets" by Norman Friedman in *ChiR* (the first two of
which were discussed in *ALS, 1966*, pp. 209–210) continued, with
Parts III and IV, into 1967. Part III (*ChiR*, XIX, ii, 52–73) deals
with the experimental poets published by Wesleyan. As in the first
two essays, he arranges the poets in ascending order of excellence,
placing Ashberry and Combs at the bottom of the ladder (with
Ashberry, whom he declares to be totally incomprehensible, on the
lowest rung); Bly and Ignatow in the middle; and Wright at the
top. The arrangement will probably arouse some objection, especially where the relative merits of Bly and Wright are concerned,
but Friedman defends it vigorously and on the whole intelligently.
(He finds Bly "too taut, too tight, too economical for comfort.")
Among the many interesting observations he makes concerning ex-
perimentalism in poetry, one finds: "The basic fact of the experimen-
talist's position today is its multiplicity, and he can rebel against
Pound in favor of William Carlos Williams, or against Eliot in favor
of Pound, or against both in favor of Williams." But rebellion that is
thus specifically—and thus traditionally—oriented ceases to be experi-

mental in the sense in which he has previously used the term: "Experimental poetry is by nature independent and diverse."

Part IV (*ChiR*, XIX, iii, 64–90) concerns what Friedman refers to as the "in-between" poets, those neither formal nor experimental, whose verse "approximates rather than uses stanzaic patterns, and is at times more daring and open in language than formal poetry." These are Alan Ansen, Robert Francis, Vassar Miller, Hyam Plutzik, and Vern Rutsola. Here again the order is ascending, with Mr. Rutsola making off with the prize partly because, as Friedman puts it, "he seems to me to have one of the keenest senses of contemporary reality that I can remember since Cummings, Auden, the earlier Karl Shapiro, and a few of Simpson's poems." Friedman's insights are generally sound, but his style (of which this last quotation, with its lack of parallelism, is a fair example) is unfortunate, and he seems unnecessarily severe in his judgments.

ii. Individual Poets

a. **Wallace Stevens.** Stevens continues to be the subject of more scholarship than any other individual poet, though this year witnessed an interesting phenomenon: the number of *PMLA* items on Lowell equalled those on Williams, so that both of them tied, so to speak, for second place. In a careful study of Stevens' early poems, Robert Buttel, in *Wallace Stevens: the Making of Harmonium*, traces the formation of this poet's style, which he claims arose out of his "deeply felt need to discover valid ideas of order in an age of cultural change and confusion." Stevens demanded of his poems, in an age which refused to acknowledge that poetry had any connection with reality, that they "contain and elicit the essence of reality itself." The *annus mirabilis* in Stevens' poetic development, he says, was 1915–the year in which "Peter Quince" and "Sunday Morning," among others, made their appearance.

While Buttel regards Stevens' irony as a device for disarming ridicule as he went about his serious task of creating poems whose purpose was to re-order reality, Frank Lentricchia, in "Wallace Stevens: the Ironic Eye" (*YR*, LVI, 336–353), maintains that irony is at the very center of the work. Disagreeing with Miller and Pearce (who take Stevens seriously as a philosophical poet), with Bloom (who views him as playing "a prophetic and apocalyptic" role), and

with Riddel (who sees him as a modern humanist), Lentricchia
argues that although Stevens frequently *begins* with a philosophical
idea, the final effect of his work is usually ironic. At least this is
true, he says, of Stevens' *best* poems: "When the ironic eye blacks
out . . . when the amateur philosopher crowds out the poet, they read
like the monotonous expositions of an aesthetician who had never
had more than one or two ideas." Even in "Sunday Morning," which
is commonly thought of as a complacent pagan poem, endorsing a
kind of genial hedonism, he finds evidence that the poet is "not as
satisfied with chaos as he seems to be." Lentricchia's thesis is certainly interesting, but so radical an interpretation of Stevens' work
requires much further documentation before one abandons in its
favor the more familiar interpretations advanced with such thorough-
ness by other critics.

Another critic with unconventional views on Stevens is J. V. Cunningham, who, in a tightly-organized essay entitled "The Style and
Procedures of Wallace Stevens" (*UDQ,* I, [1966] i, 8–28), claims
that Stevens, like Emily Dickinson, was an amateur rather than a
professional poet, and that, again like her, he had only a few subjects—"a group of rather single-minded ideas and procedures, repetitive ways of getting started with a poem, and getting on with it."
Cunningham classifies these ideas and these procedures in a brisk,
no-nonsense, one-two-three manner, giving examples from the poems.
He finds in Stevens two recurrent underlying concerns: a loss of
religious belief, unaccompanied by a loss of the need for such belief;
and a preoccupation with philosophy. It is the latter in which Cunningham appears to be chiefly interested. Stevens, he maintains,
inherited the ideas that were propagated at Harvard College in the
1890's by Royce, William James, and Santayana and that polarized
subject and object under the "rubrics" of imagination and reality.
Stevens was attracted to the "rubric of imagination," Cunningham
says, and under this heading he discovers in Stevens' work six
"areas" or tendencies: an opposition of the romantic to the realistic
principle (in the usual sense of these terms); a sense of fantasy
associated with a "high-spirited nonsense"; a monistic perception of
resemblances; a process whereby the associations of an object are
abstracted from it "in order to intuit an inherent, a bare reality";
and the discovery that appearance conceals no reality behind it, that
"reality is nothingness." As for Stevens' style, Cunningham argues

he has not one but four: the imagistic, the mannered, the nineteenth-century rhetorical, and the plain. His essay is more readable than this summary might suggest, and his judgments are courageous and emphatic: *Notes Toward a Supreme Fiction* he views as "a failure, on the whole a mess with intermittent successful passages"; "Sunday Morning," on the other hand, is "one of the great poems in the language."

Received too late for inclusion in last year's chapter is an important biographical item, *Letters of Wallace Stevens* (New York, Alfred A. Knopf, 1966), edited by the poet's daughter, Holly Stevens. Nearly nine hundred pages long, this book is indispensable to the serious Stevens scholar, and includes letters to such distinguished contemporaries as Robert Frost, William Carlos Williams, Marianne Moore, John Crowe Ransom, E. E. Cummings, Thornton Wilder, and Allen Tate. As might naturally be expected, they are enormously revealing of their author's habits, both personal and literary, and contain a wealth of informal critical comment. He writes, for instance, to José Rodríguez Feo: "The time to read poetry is before you start to write it; after you start to write it you are afraid to read other people's poetry. Robert Lowell's poetry is a case in point . . . I have never studied any of his work because I don't want to pick up anything. In fact, there is probably no one who reads less poetry than I do." Comparing Winters to Blackmur, he observes that while the latter is an "immeasurably superior" critic, he has "a serious defect . . . and that is that it takes him twenty-five pages what would be much better said if said in one. The result is that, after you have finished twenty-five pages of Blackmur, you haven't the faintest idea what he has been talking about. Either he has too many ideas or too few; it is hard to say which."

b. **William Carlos Williams.** Three periodical items will indicate something of the range of Williams scholarship: "A Bunch of Marigolds," by Linda W. Wagner (*KR*, XXIX, 86–102); "Whitman and the Early Development of William Carlos Williams," by James E. Breslin (*PMLA*, LXXXII, 613–621); and "In the American Grain: William Carlos Williams on the American Past," by Alan Holder (*AQ*, XIX, 499–515). Wagner, examining the late poems, finds evidence that Williams' work continued to improve technically in his later years; there was also, she claims, a change in attitude involving his relationship with the outside world: "The angry younger man of the Thirties . . . had come to realize that private satisfactions are greater than public ones, that his own happiness . . . was more important than the condition of the world surrounding him." As a result of this, she says, the late poems have "an aura of joy, of contentment," and give the impression of a man thoroughly at peace with himself. He also, toward the end, revised and recast much more than in the early work.

Breslin maintains that during Williams' formative years (1902–1914) his most important influence was Whitman. Unable to write in the manner of Pound, whom he also admired, Williams in these years acquired from Whitman the "radical independence, emotional exuberance, bodily energy, and self-admiration" which characterize that poet's work. (As an example of "self-admiration" in Williams, Breslin cites "Danse Russe.") The difference between them, he suggests, is that while Whitman's preoccupation was with the cosmic and the universal, Williams is more down to earth; he attempts to relate this preoccupation to the domestic scene, and becomes (to quote the above-mentioned poem) the "happy genius of his household."

The subject of Holder's essay is Williams' little-known book, first published in 1925, on American history: *In the American Grain*. More often than not, he says, Williams treats the figures he selects for his study (Columbus, Ponce de Leon, De Soto, Raleigh, etc.) as examples of failure rather than success, and concludes that for Williams "one use of the past would appear to be the undermining of characteristic American assumptions about success and failure, the enlarging and complicating of our notions of life's possibilities and values." Holder correctly claims that the book suffers from Williams' obsessive hatred of Puritanism, on which he is inclined to blame almost everything that he dislikes in American life, and from his idealization of the Redskin, who in Williams' eyes could do no wrong.

Other work on Williams in 1967, with one large exception, was mostly explication—five brief discussions of individual poems (four in *The Explicator*) and two studies of *Paterson*: Walter Scott Peterson, *An Approach to Paterson* (New Haven, Yale Univ. Press) and Bernard I. Duffey, "Williams *Paterson* and the Measure of Art," *Essays on American Literature*, pp. 282–294. Peterson's study, which won publication as a prize Senior Honors Essay at Yale, is a felicitously written and well-argued reading of *Paterson I-IV*. Relating *In the American Grain* to Williams' poem, Peterson believes that *Paterson I-IV* celebrates successfully the power of human love and imagination: ". . . man's loving and imaginative 'marriage' to the particulars of his local world can ultimately save him from the death-in-life of 'Puritan' divorce." Because Williams is a poet to whom details are of great importance, the essay sets out to investigate systematically just how the details work in the poem. Central to Peterson's method is Williams' remark: "Place is the only reality, the true core of the universal."

Duffey, on the other hand, sees Williams as more of a poet of ideas than of things. His poetry reflects a varying "imbalance between the world and the poet's own mind." The pervading drama is that of "idea, as theme or form, counterpointed against things." Nowhere is this more plain than in the first four books of Williams' *Paterson*. The subject of *Paterson I-IV* is not things, though these are its occasions: "It is rather the dejection of the idealistic imagination." Duffey concludes his discussion of Books I-IV with a look at Book V (1958), in which Williams' earlier despair gives way to affirmation: a world of art has survived which has "come to heal the nature-mind divorce of Books I-IV." Art, however, does not become a means of special knowledge; it becomes "the area within which mind can exercise itself in the limits and attainments of its own measuring nature."

The large exception to the explications noted above is Hans Galinsky's careful, detailed, and extensive survey of Williams' European reception: "William Carlos Williams: Eine vergleichende Studie zur Aufnahme seines Werkes in Deutschland, England und Italien (1912–1965). Teil II: England und Italien" (*JA*, XII, 167–205). Part I of this excellent study, covering Williams in Germany, appeared earlier (*JA*, XI [1966], 96–175). Galinsky shows that Williams' reputation has grown steadily during the more than half century surveyed and is now secure. He quotes Williams' "The Pink Locust":

> I'm persistent as the pink locust,
> once admitted
> to the garden,
> You will not easily get rid of it.

c. **Robert Lowell.** Having been unable, at this date, to secure a
copy of *The Achievement of Robert Lowell*, edited by William J.
Martz, I shall postpone discussion of it until next year. Of the other
Lowell items, by far the most interesting was a study by a fellow-
poet, Hayden Carruth: "A Meaning of Robert Lowell" (*HudR*, XX,
429–447). Using Lowell's new book, *Near the Ocean* (which he finds
disappointing) as a point of departure, Carruth surveys his entire
career, and though he freely acknowledges him to be our most
important living poet, he is nevertheless dissatisfied with the direction his talent seems to be taking. Lowell's greatest defect, he
maintains, is a "pervasive extraneity" which revealed itself in the
laid-on metaphysical style of *Lord Weary's Castle* and which (after
the relatively relaxed manner of *Life Studies*) again threatens to ruin
his most recent poems, which tend increasingly to revert to formalism. The source of this defect, according to Carruth, is a "discrete
imagination, an imagination which works best in disjunctive
snatches," and his problem as a poet has been to make the best of
this disadvantage while continuing to explore his main theme, which
is guilt. In Lowell, the familiar concept of death as punishment for
sin changes to the concept of death *as* sin: "Our death is our sin, for
which we pay in advance through our guilt." He continues: "Our
death is a crime against every good principle in the universal nature,
God, the human heart. Yet we, the innocent, are the responsible
ones—this is the idea Lowell cannot forego."

d. **Jarrell, Tate, Wilbur, Levertov.** One of the most informative
books of the year, both as biography and as criticism, is the me-
morial volume, *Randall Jarrell, 1914–1965* (New York, Farrar,
Straus), edited by Robert Lowell, Peter Taylor, and Robert Penn
Warren. It consists of twenty-nine appreciations by persons who
knew Jarrell more or less intimately, most of them fellow-poets or
fellow-critics. Among the best of the essays—but almost all of them
are good, in varying degrees and for varying reasons—are those by
Cleanth Brooks, which contains a fine explication of "Eighth Air
Force"; Ransom, who discusses in general terms both the poetry and
the prose; Lowell, whose focus is chiefly on Jarrell's complex personality; Taylor, who fills in the poet's early career as student at
Vanderbilt and teacher at Kenyon; and Robert Fitzgerald, who
knew him during the New York period, when Jarrell was poetry

editor of *The Nation*. As a critic Jarrell was anything but gentle, and it is common knowledge that he made many enemies on this account. "He was immensely cruel," writes John Berryman, "and the extraordinary thing about it is that he didn't know he was cruel." Other contributors agree on this, and on the fear with which he was regarded by potential victims. But if he was feared he was also loved, as is very plain from the evidence of this book. One of the most interesting judgments is that of Allen Tate, who in summarizing Jarrell's career refers to him as "a fine poet and a great prose-stylist."

During 1967 books on three modern poets were issued in the Twayne Series: *Allen Tate*, by Ferman Bishop; *Richard Wilbur*, by Donald Hill; and *Denise Levertov*, by Linda W. Wagner (TUSAS, Nos. 124, 117, 113). Bishop discusses Tate's achievement as poet, as biographer, as critic, and as novelist. The major poems are explicated, and there is a detailed analysis of Tate's single novel, *The Fathers*. Bishop does not ignore his subject's defects, but he passes rather lightly over some of the more serious ones, such as Tate's rationalizations on the subject of slavery. The book is written in a clear, workmanlike style, and is generally competent, though a certain naïveté is occasionally in evidence: "After a brilliant critic like Tate has written on his own poem ['Ode to the Confederate Dead'], what more is one to say?"

Donald Hill's emphasis strikes me as too narrowly explicational (a fault with other items in this series). "I have assumed a reader," he writes in his Preface, "who is ready to provide himself with copies of Wilbur's books, to read them carefully, and to keep them open as he compares his impressions with mine." Few readers will be dedicated to this degree, and Hill shows a decided reluctance to risk certain necessary generalizations. His final chapter, where he is forced into commitment, is so good that one wishes he had shown more enterprise throughout. Of the formalist poets, Wilbur has probably shown the least tendency toward innovation; for this he has been censured by Rosenthal and others, and what Hill has to say in his defense is worth repeating: "There is no value in mere novelty, and from one point of view nothing matters in the end but good poems. If 'making it new' will produce them, it then proves its value thereby; if not, it fails in the essential aim."

Wagner's book is perhaps the best of the three; it is certainly the best written, and her explications have a sufficiently broad context that they do not require the application that Mr. Hill demands of his readers. In accounting for the poems she does not slight the biographical element, and shows particular skill in tracing the influences in Levertov's work, and in defining her relations with her contemporaries of the so-called Black Mountain school.

San Fernando Valley State College

16. Drama

Walter J. Meserve

i. Bibliographies, References, Works, Histories, Dissertations

As scholarly research in American drama becomes generally respected rather than simply tolerated, there is an increased need for bibliographical studies. This year the number of bibliographies and book-length works suggests the growing interest in the history of American drama and in its major figures as well as its current idiosyncracies. The most frequently discussed playwright is still Eugene O'Neill with Arthur Miller and Edward Albee coming close behind. Critical attention to other dramatists and to certain historical periods in the drama, however, distinguishes the scholarship this year.

The interest in American drama bibliography is, indeed, an encouraging aspect of drama scholarship. Clarence Gohdes' *Literature and the Theater of the States and Regions of the U.S.A., An Historical Bibliography* (Durham, N. C., Duke Univ. Press) provides a checklist of monographs, anthologies, pamphlets, book chapters, articles, and a few newspapers. The organization of material according to states and regions is distinctive, and from 1900 through 1964 the work is effective and thorough. Its weaknesses lie in the compiler's decision to omit dissertations and foreign references and to list only a few essays written before 1900. There are a few serious omissions—Laurence Hutton's *Curiosities of the New York Stage*—and some instances where a greater knowledge of drama/theater would have allowed the compiler to list an essay on "Mose," for example, within the area of New York theater. But the fact that this volume exists is a triumph and a valuable reference for drama/ theater students. Another bibliography, Helen H. Palmer and Jane A. Dyson, compilers, *American Dramatic Criticism, Interpretations, 1890–1965, Inclusive of American Drama Since the First Play Produced in America.* (Hamden, Conn., The Shoestring Press, Inc.) does not claim to be exhaustive in listing, alphabetically according to playwrights, books, essays, and monographs from the best-known indexes. Its serious weakness appears in its very limited reference to scholarly journals, and a highly selective list of playwrights which excludes some established playwrights while listing very minor figures in contemporary theater. Along with these two volumes, Phyllis Hartnoll's 3rd edition of *The Oxford Companion to the Theatre* (London, Oxford Univ. Press) should be mentioned. With its English orientation this standard reference does not always do justice to American dramatists. Particularly weak is the section dealing with the drama before 1900. The section on poetic drama does not mention G. H. Boker's *Francesca da Rimini*, and the essay on melodrama omits any reference to an American play. Presumably this edition shows revisions through 1964, but there is no mention of Paul Green's work after 1941, no indication of the later work of George Kelly. A nine-page essay on the "Negro in the American Theatre" is very instructive yet suggestive of imbalance when Japan's drama is treated in three and a half pages, Scandinavia's in seven, Greece in eight, or the United States in fourteen.

A number of brief bibliographical descriptions will be of definite help to scholars in American drama. Vincent L. Angotti's *An Annotated Bibliography and Subject Index to the Microfilm Collection: Source Materials in the Field of Theatre* (Ann Arbor, Mich., University Microfilm Library Series) includes such items as Laurence Hutton's *Manuscript Dramatic Diary, 1870–1885*. Carl Stratman ("American Dramatical Periodicals with Only One Issue, 1798–1959," *AL*, XXXIX, 180–190) lists seventy-six periodicals with all available information. An interest in American theater from 1900 to the present is reported by Barbara Kaiser in "Resources in the Wisconsin Center for Theatre Research" (*AmA*, XXX, 483–492). Robert L. Barlow ("Under My Skin," *YULG*, XLII, 51–76) commented on the American musical theater and the collection for which he was, in part, responsible in the Yale Library. Fredrich J. Hunter's *A Guide to the Theatre and Drama Collection of the University of Texas* (Austin, Univ. of Tex. Press) is a handsome volume; more universities and librarians should be inspired to do this type of work.

The number of books this year dealing with some aspect of the history of American drama is also encouraging. Although in scholarly value they were noticeably uneven, the activity seems healthy. Loften Mitchell's *Black Drama, the Story of the American Negro in the Theatre* (New York, Hawthorne) relates the drama to the social and economic problems of the Negro. Particularly before World War II, the author negates much of his valuable insight by his biased, defensive, and uncritical attitude. One would question, for example, whether Ira Aldridge's obscurity was any more pronounced, or he any more persecuted, than his numerous white contemporaries. Yet Mitchell has a great many facts about plays, playwrights, and theater groups, which blended with anecdotes and emotional wanderings, make a very readable book, most effective on contemporary drama. A more objective book, historically, though with limited material is Langston Hughes's and Milton Metzer's *Black Magic, A Pictorial History of the Negro in American Entertainment* (Englewood Cliffs, N.J., Prentice-Hall). Read with Mitchell's work, it has its value. James Miller's *The Detroit Yiddish Theatre, 1920–1937* (Detroit, Wayne State Univ. Press) adds another chapter to the developing history of the Jewish theater in America. Told with a certain charm, the history briefly suggests the origins of Yiddish theater in America and traces the theater in Detroit with an emphasis on Abraham Littman's Peoples Theatre. In *The American Musical Theatre* (New York, Macmillian) Lehman Engel explores the elements of the successful musical from characters to critics and concludes that the best days of the musical stage are over. For the person who feels the need to know, John L. Tookey provides *A History of the Pulitzer Prize Plays* (New York, The Citadel Press) with very brief plots, some reviews, and a personal summation. Frank Rahill's *The World of Melodrama* (Philadelphia, Univ. of Pa. Press) has an interesting section on the origin and development of melodrama in France with Pixérècourt and in England. The section on America, however, is the weakest in the volume. Although the author touches many of the right bases, his criticism degenerates to sketchy generalization, and he makes numerous errors in dating plays. Joseph Golden in *The Death of Tinkerbell: The American Theatre in the Twentieth Century* (Syracuse, Syracuse Univ. Press) offers a general approach and has very little to say about American plays and playwrights; his concern is the theater. One final book, an anthology which helps fill a most grievous gap was *Best Plays of the Early American Theatre* (New York, Crown) edited by the late John Gassner with Mollie Gassner. Its brief introduction on drama and theater before O'Neill and its comments on the plays and playwrights are satisfactory. The problem comes with the choice of plays (the usual ones before 1900 except for *The Count of Monte Cristo* and *The Mouse-trap*) and an emphasis on the 1900–1911 period (seven of the sixteen plays). There is still room for (1) an anthology which will suggest the development of American drama before World War I and for (2) many more scholarly excursions into the history of American drama.

Persuant to their degrees, Ph.D. candidates added a number of dissertations in American drama. O'Neill, of course, consumed the energies of several: the women in his plays, his religious awareness, his reception in Sweden, his existential themes, his emphasis on Jung. Among the other dissertation topics were Maxwell Anderson's verse plays, dramatic styles in the 1920's, American military heroes and heroines, the criticism of Alan Dale, the businessman in American drama, the American courtroom play, James H. Hackett as actor, the Provincetown players, early dramatic writing in the Virginias and South Carolina, the Theatre Guild from 1928–1939, the major characters in Williams' plays, the reception of Williams' plays in Germany, the plays of Robert M. Bird, and John Gassner as critic and teacher. One that must be noted individually, however, is Neda M. Westlake's "*Caius Marcius*, a Tragedy by Richard Penn Smith Presented by Edwin Forrest in 1831: The Author's Unpublished Manuscript with an Introduction" (*DA*, XXVIII, 1452A).

ii. The Beginning to 1916

Until historical research in American drama becomes sufficiently active to warrant finer lines of division, it is justifiable to use Eugene O'Neill's appearance at the Provincetown as a major landmark. Two very welcome additions to the study of 18th century drama appeared this year. One is Richard M. Baine's *Robert Munford, America's First Comic Dramatist* (Athens, Univ. of Ga. Press), a brief, well-researched book on Munford as student, soldier, planter, politician, and playwright. Prof. Baine is more historian-bibliographer than drama critic and devotes less than half of his book to Munford's plays, but his concern for accurate research and his clear writing make his work valuable. Although he does not evaluate the plays as drama or theater, he effectively relates the plays to a traditional satire and discusses them in terms of Munford's creativity and the times. The second book is G. Thomas Tanselle's study of *Royall Tyler*

(Cambridge, Harvard Univ. Press). Devoting one chapter to *The Contrast* and another to later plays, Tanselle clarifies several issues and presents clear historical studies of the plays. He does not seem comfortable, however, as a critic of the drama, suggesting little about *The Contrast* and attaching a significance to the other plays which is not warranted. His conclusion is that Tyler's writing was the product of "brief idle moments," that he was "not a man of letters." For the student of drama the value of the book is in the author's careful and intelligent research and writing. An essay which adds to the discussion of Tyler's minor plays is Marius B. Péladeau's "Royall Tyler's *Other* Plays" (*NEQ*, XL, 48–60).

Two other texts emphasize theater and drama of the nineteenth century. James K. Dorman, Jr.'s *Theatre in the Ante-Bellum South* (Chapel Hill, Univ. of N. C. Press) is concerned with the development of theater, and with the audience, the plays, and the players. His first part is a clear and well-substantiated discussion which adds to Rankin's work on Colonial Theatre and retraces the activities of Sol Smith, Noah Ludlow, and others which appear sketchily in several works. Dorman supplements the original writings of Smith and Ludlow with evidence to provide a clear picture of Southern theater prior to 1860. The second part of the book is particularly interesting for the comments on the productions of such plays as Payne's *Mazeppa*. Another book emphasizing Southern drama is *Provincial Drama in America, 1870–1916: A Casebook of Primary Materials* (Metuchen, N. J., The Scarecrow Press), edited by Paul T. Nolan. In this text Professor Nolan uses his experience in research and his own essays to interest students in the study of provincial Southern drama. The idea behind this volume is excellent and Nolan has had interesting experiences. As an editor or as an exemplary writer of literary criticism or popular articles, however, he has limitations which give the entire work a disturbing presumption and detract from his stated objectives.

Only a few scholars found material for essays in the pre-O'Neill period—a fact not strange but to be regretted. Although most drama historians accept Boker's *Francesca da Rimini* as the outstanding example of poetic drama written in English in the nineteenth century, few people write about this play. An encouraging exception is Paul C. Sherr who uses *Francesca* to establish Boker "as a sensitive artist, aware of contemporary American literary, social, and political life" ("George Henry Boker's *Francesca da Rimini*, a Justification

for the Literary Historian," *PH*, XXXIV, 361–371). Stanley R. Harrison reprints portions of the letters of a writer of minor dramas in
an attempt to establish him as a critic of late nineteenth-century
life and literature ("Through a Nineteenth Century Looking Glass:
The Letters of Edgar Fawcett," *TSE*, XV, 107–157). Writing about
realism in drama after the turn of the century, Maxwell Bloomfield
errs in his assertion that there was little interest in a "national drama"
before 1898 ("Muckraking and the American Stage: The Emergence
of Realism, 1905–1917," *SAQ*, LXVI, 165–178) and is ungenerous
concerning the work of several playwrights in contending that realism in the drama *emerged* with "Ida Tarbell, the mother of dramatic
realism in the country." He does, however, spend considerable time
with Charles Klein, whose efforts in a social realistic melodrama
bothered such a connoisseur of melodrama as Clayton Hamilton.
Coincident with the fall in popularity of poetic drama and the
gradual rise of realism was the beginning of the Toby character.
Discussing this little known hero and his creators, Jerre C. Mickel
("The Genesis of Toby: A Folk Hero of the American Theatre," *JAF*,
LXXX, 334–340) defined him as "the one outstanding character the
rep shows produced and their one original contribution to the American theatre." In a broad view of American drama before 1916, Bernard Hewitt ("The Americanism of the American Theatre," *The
American Theatre Today*, pp. 3–14) traced Americanism or nationalism in plays from *The Contrast* through *The Great Divide*.

iii. Between Two World Wars

Certainly the most impressive period in American drama, the span
of two decades from 1920 to 1940, still does not attract sufficient
scholarship. Even when the opportunity arises, sometimes little is
done to fill the void. In his book on *Edna St. Vincent Millay* (TUSAS,
No. 116), for example, Norman A. Brittin allowed only seventeen
pages for her drama, which he filled mainly with plots, very little
criticism, and no evaluation of her work in terms of the development
of American drama. Sometimes an essay such as Darwin E. Turner's
work on Jean Toomer ("The Failure of a Playwright," *CLAJ*, X,
308–318) tries to assign present values to past plays. In "Rice's *The
Subway*" (*Expl*, XXV, Item 62) Mardi Valgemae contends that
Rice owes more to Freud (with the subway as a phallic symbol) than

to Marx as previous critics have held. One dramatist of this period whose work deserves much more serious thought is Philip Barry. Although his treatment is not as searching as one would like, James M. Salem ("Philip Barry and the Spirituality of Love," *Renascence*, XIX, 101–109) concludes that Barry came to terms with the problems of his times perhaps more effectively than his contemporaries.

a. **Theater in the Thirties.**　Although the theatre *per se* cannot be the concern of this essay, Jane DeHart Mathews' *The Federal Theatre, 1935–1939, Plays, Relief, and Politics* (Princeton, Princeton Univ. Press) must be noted for its fully researched, pleasingly written presentation of the Federal Theatre's problems and accomplishments. Both the documentation and the discussion are impressive. Gerald Rabkin's "The Federal Theatre Project" (*The Thirties*, pp. 201–210) provides an excellent brief survey. Gerald Weales's "Popular Theatre of the Thirties" (*TDR*, XI, 51–69) comments effectively on representative plays of the decade. Among contemporary critics of our drama, Weales, writing for the now (mid-1968) defunct *Reporter*, becomes more impressive each year and establishes for many that long missing link between the commercial theater and the community of scholars.

In an essay on "The Playwrights of the 1930's" (*The American Theatre Today*, pp. 25–37) Malcolm Goldstein contrasts the Broadway playwrights with the angry playwrights and discusses that "praiseworthy drama which prodded the conscience and stimulated the imagination." Robert J. Griffin's article "On the Love Song of Clifford Odets" (*The Thirties*, pp. 193–200) shows only a limited knowledge of Odets. With an insight that makes his essay the best yet written on Saroyan, James H. Justice ("William Saroyan and the Theatre of Transformation," *The Thirties*, pp. 211–214) discusses Saroyan's notion of transforming love whereby he juxtaposes the real and the unreal in an attempt to find out how to live. Charles Angoff ("William Saroyan: Some Footnotes," *The Tone of the Twenties and Other Essays*, New York, A. S. Barnes, 1966, pp. 203–208) reminisces about Saroyan's philosophy and his undefined style—"a slight touch of phoniness."

b. **Maxwell Anderson.**　One essay that must become basic in American scholarship is Laurence G. Avery's "Maxwell Anderson: A

Changing Attitude Toward Love" (*MD*, X, 241–248). Tracing Anderson's original attachment to love as an ideal in the 1920's to a transitional phase in the 1940's, Avery shows a final antipathy in the little known *Madonna and Child* (1956), which he discusses in some detail. In "Lenormand's *Asie* and Anderson's *The Wingless Victory*" (*CL*, XIX, 226–239), Angela Belli emphasizes the Medea-Jason material which through modern techniques revitalizes the past and reaffirms "the oneness of our culture." Jordan Y. Miller is less enthusiastic in "Maxwell Anderson: Gifted Technician" (*The Thirties*, pp. 183–192), emphasizing a "lack of artistic depth" resulting in an "end product of studied ingenuity."

c. **Eugene O'Neill.** The emphasis this year in O'Neill scholarship was on various influences upon O'Neill, although there also were theme and reception studies. Among the latter, Frederic Fleisher and Horst Frenz ("Eugene O'Neill and the Royal Dramatic Theatre of Stockholm: The Later Phase," *MD*, X, 300–311) survey Stockholm's reaction to O'Neill from the 1953 production of *A Moon for the Misbegotten* to the 1962 version of *More Stately Mansions*, concluding that Sweden provided a major stage for establishing and reviving O'Neill's reputation. In "O'Neill Since World War II: Critical Reception in New York" (*MD*, X, 289–299) William Reardon claims that the revivals of a dozen of O'Neill's plays during this period have solidified his reputation.

The influence studies range widely—through Greek, Italian, German, and English literature. Robert Andreach ("O'Neill's Use of Dante in *The Fountain* and *The Hairy Ape*," *MD*, X, 48–56) contends that O'Neill was indebted to the *Divina Comedia* for a partial framework of each play and supports his argument by demonstrating a man-god relationship in *The Hairy Ape*. In "O'Neill's Use of the Phèdre Legend in *Desire Under the Elms*" (*RLC*, XLI, 120–125), Jay Meyers defends the play as Aristotelian tragedy with a clear moral vision concerning the evil of money and the lust of acquisition. William Brashear's evidence seems somewhat inconclusive ("'To-morrow' and 'Tomorrow': Conrad and O'Neill," *Renascence*, XX, 18–21, 55) as he draws conclusions about the two authors' fascination for the sea, the similarity of jungle symbolism in *The Emperor Jones* and *Heart of Darkness*, and their use of past experiences. Mardi Valgemae ("O'Neill and German Expressionism," *MD*, X, 111–123) makes some very effective observations in his discussion of expressionistic distortion in *The Great God Brown* and his comparison of *The Hairy Ape* to several Kaiser plays as well as to the 1919 German movie, *The Cabinet of Dr. Caligari.* Emphasizing the influences of the past upon the present and future, S. Nagarajan ("A Note on O'Neill's *Long Day's Journey into Night*," *LCrit*, VII [1966], iii, 52–54) compares O'Neill's dialogue with *Macbeth* and praises the poetic language of *Journey*, one of "the few poetic dramas of the American theatre." Robert Lee relates *Long Day's Journey* and *Moon for the Misbegotten* to O'Neill's past with particular reference to his brother in "Eugene O'Neill's Remembrance: The Past Is the Present" (*ArQ*, XXIII, 293–305). With a perceptive scene-by-scene analysis, John Fitzgerald ("Guilt and Redemption in O'Neill's Last Play: A Study of *The Moon for the Misbegotten*," *TQ*, IX [1966], i, 146–158) equates the play to Aristotelian tragedy through the purgation of O'Neill's familial guilt.

There were no book length studies of O'Neill this year. One monograph, Winifred Fraser's *Love as Death in* The Iceman Cometh: *A Modern Treatment of an Ancient Theme* (Gainesville, Univ. of Fla. Press), builds upon the ancient theme relating love to death. Analyzing setting, character, and action, Prof. Fraser explores the vulgar joke and the idea of love as illusion to show the truth that O'Neill felt—"that, to man, love is death." Travis Bogard (*The Later Plays of Eugene O'Neill*, New York, Random House) introduces his collection with a fine essay emphasizing the poet as searcher as well as the technical aspects of the four plays he includes. Doris Alexander ("The Missing Half of *Hughie*," *TDR*, XI, iv, 125–126) comments on the difficulty of staging this play and the injustice done to it in production. An excellent article which also relates East and West is David Y. Chen's "Two Chinese Adaptations of Eugene O'Neill's *The Emperor Jones*" (*MD*, IX, 431–439). Studies without distinction are Gary A. Vena's "The Role of the Prostitute in the Plays of Eugene O'Neill" (*DC*, X, 129–137) the first of two essays, though adding nothing new, and Hugh Dickenson's two-part article measuring O'Neill according to Northrop Frye—"Eugene O'Neill: Anatomy of a Trilogy" (*DC*, X, 44–56) and "Eugene O'Neill: Fate as Form" (*DC*, X, 78–85), which analyze *Mourning Becomes Electra* from ancient myth to modern paradox. Murray Hartman, "The Skeletons in O'Neill's Mansions" (*DramS*, V, 276–279), shows how this play incorporates O'Neill's early use of expressionism as well as such old themes as his war against an acquisitive society and his interest in the Oedipal complex. John J. Fitzgerald ("The Bitter Harvest of O'Neill's Projected Cycle," *NEQ*, XL, 364–374) effectively traces the development of the cycle from the original idea in 1934 to the destruction of the first two plays some years later. In a year which did not contribute a great deal to O'Neill scholarship, this last essay, along with a few previously mentioned, offers some substance.

d. **Thornton Wilder.**   This was something of a big year for Wilder enthusiasts: a book, an issue of *Four Quarters*, and a couple of fine essays by perceptive Wilder critics. Donald Haberman's critical study, *The Plays of Thornton Wilder* (Middletown, Conn., Wesleyan Univ. Press) is particularly valuable for its previously unpublished information and Wilder's personal opinions. He also presents a fine discussion of the effect of the Alcestis legend in Wilder's works. Although Haberman's writing is not always effective and some of his views seemingly weak (such as that on the place of religion in Wilder's art), his chapter entitled "All Times and All Places" is impressive, as he shows with considerable perception the influence of Gertrude Stein and Kierkegaard on Wilder. *Four Quarters* (XVI, iv) includes six essays on Wilder. Richard H. Goldstone, "The Wilder 'Image'" (pp. 1–7), while repeating the views that Wilder has no "image," suggests that he has essentially fused his life with his art; Hans Sahl, "Wilder and the Germans" (pp. 8–9), notes that Wilder, with something of Mozart's serenity, inspired the Germans with a memory of the past and a concern for the future as he became a German *Klassiker*; Joseph Firebaugh, "Farce and the Heavenly Destination" (pp. 10–17), maintains that with a farcical method, combining a sense of surprise with the pleasure of thoughtful implications, Wilder suggests a faith in future generations; Donald Haberman, "The Americanization of Thornton Wilder" (pp. 18–27), comments on the American setting of his major plays and the change in subsequent novels; R. W. Stallman, "To Thornton Wilder: A Note in Gratitude" (pp. 28–29), does not refer to the plays; Isabel Wilder, "Embroidery" (pp. 30–31), provides some sisterly reminiscences. In an essay commenting on Wilder's materials, philosophy, and techniques ("The Bridge of Thornton Wilder," *Essays on American Literature*, pp. 307–328) Alexander Cowie views Wilder as a bridge, a spectacle in the drama of life, one who insists upon the dignity of man and his ability to savor life. Malcolm Goldstein, "Thornton Wilder," (*The American Theatre Today*, pp. 60–72) is particularly effective on Wilder's recent plays and provides a perceptive and intelligent review of his career.

iv. Since World War II

The contemporary period has always stimulated more criticism than earlier periods, but this year, in amount, at least, the balance of criticism is more nearly even. With reference to scholarly value, however, there are more disappointing essays concerned with the contemporary scene, more that should have not been published. *The Modern American Theatre* (Englewood Cliffs, N. J., Prentice-Hall) edited by Alvin B. Kernan offers essays on playwrights and theater since World War II, but emphasizes production problems rather than plays. The introductory essay notes that the volume celebrated a "near-failure" because Americans do not see life "in historic and dramatic terms," and Prof. Kernan's essay on modern drama mentions American drama only vaguely and peripherally. Also disappointing is Eric Bentley's "Comedy and the Comic Spirit in America" (*The American Theatre Today*, pp. 50–59), which wanders considerably from an original thesis and discusses, in the main, *Guys and Dolls* and comic actors with only a brief comment on Miller and Albee. For some pessimistic thoughts on contemporary drama, one can listen to William Inge ("A Conversation with Digby Diehl," *TransR*, No. 26, pp. 51–56) talk about his new play (*Bad Breath*), explain that "you've got to please Walter Kerr or die," and argue that most actors "have no concept of what a play is." Beth Bagby's "El Teatro Campesino: Interviews with Luis Valdes," (*TDR*, XI, 70–80) shows a more optimistic view of that playwright's exciting work with the Farm Workers' Theatre of Delano, California. And then there is a book on *Langston Hughes* (TUSAS, No. 123) by James A. Emmanuel which offers no criticism of his plays.

I have always believed that the interest of poets in the theater and of playwrights in language, even poetic language, is a healthy sign in contemporary American drama. Baruch Hochman ("Robert Lowell's *Old Glory*," *TDR*, XI, 127–138) discusses *The Old Glory* in terms of history rather than language, but observes that "Lowell

the dramatist matches Lowell the poet." Two other essays published
in an Indian journal comment on poetic drama. In "Do Politics and
Poetry Disagree?" (*LHY*, VIII, 74–78) Henry W. Wells astutely
answers his question with reference to *MacBird*, which he calls "a
landmark in the imagination or poetic theatre visible not only to
Americans but to a large portion of mankind." Although H. H. An-
niah Gowda ("*Hogan's Goat* and American Verse Drama," *LHY*,
VIII, 35–41) is weak in placing William Alfred in the tradition of
Anderson, Moody, and Peabody, he offers a clear argument for
Hogan's Goat as "an effective version of a classical play clothed in
modern speech."

a. **Tennessee Williams.**   The most ambitious work on Williams was
Alan Casty's "Tennessee Williams and the Small Hands of the Rain"
(*MRR*, I [1965], iii, 27–43). Casty maintains that E. E. Cummings'
line—"the small hands of the clock"—evoked a "constellation of
images and qualities" which became the "core" of Williams' "vision
of life," so constant a thesis in fact that Casty equates it with the
Jungian mandala, an archetypal dream of a fusion or harmony. In
general, Casty views all of Williams' plays as a part of his struggle
(from the sensual to the spiritual) to achieve this fusion. From
Menagerie to *Milk Train* Casty feels that Williams has progressed
to a new position in which this fusion is at least partially accomplished. An equally admiring critic, Krishna Gorowara ("The Fire
Symbol in Tennessee Williams," *LHY*, VIII, 57–73) traces the fire
imagery in Williams' major plays but draws no conclusions. Paul T.
Nolan's, "Two Memory Plays: *The Glass Menagerie* and *After the
Fall*" (*McNR*, XVII [1966], 27–38) begins with an interesting idea
regarding a new genre "set in the conscious mind of the protagonist"
but fails to develop it logically or substantially and concludes that
the genre is nearer to lyric poetry than objective drama.

   Two essays comment on particular plays. William Peterson,
"Williams, Kazan, and the Two Cats" (*NTM*, VII, iii, 14–20) simply
notes that a play is more than a particular production and that Williams' work should last for itself rather than Kazan's productions.
In "The Tragic Downfall of Blanche DuBois" (*MD*, X, 249–257)
Leonard Berkman claims that her downfall came when she found
herself back in the "whore-image" which she wanted to escape and
that her "tragic power" lies in the acceptance of that future. As
something of a summary comment, Esther Jackson's "Tennessee

Williams" (*The American Theatre Today*, pp. 73–84) treats him as a popular, non-traditional playwright. With the exception of Prof. Casty's interesting, if limited view, none of the essays is outstanding.

b. **Arthur Miller.** Although Miller recently contended that theater people are irresponsible and that very little American theater exists ("Arthur Miller Talks," *MQR*, VI, 153–184), few people evidently felt that he was talking either about them or himself. Tetsumaro Hayashi praised him briefly but enthusiastically and brought a checklist of his writing up to date—"Arthur Miller: The Dimension of His Art and a Checklist of His Published Works" (*Serif*, IV, ii, 26–32). The two book-length studies of Miller present moderate and differing views of his accomplishments, neither writer taking seriously Miller's attempt to write modern tragedy. Leonard Moss (*Arthur Miller*, TUSAS, No. 115), considers Miller a writer of social plays focusing on the struggle of the individual to find his right position in society. Moss's outstanding analysis concerns the technical shortcomings of *After the Fall*. Essentially he offers a chronological study showing little sympathy with or concern for Miller's objectives. Edward Murray (*Arthur Miller, Dramatist*, New York, Fredrich Ungar) notes that his approach is "rigorously inductive." He is concerned neither with theater nor with literature as it reveals insight into life but feels that a close analysis of structure can provide an understanding of Miller's achievement. Not all agree with him. Clearly the most penetrating comment on Miller this year was Gerald Weales's "Arthur Miller" (*The American Theatre Today*, pp. 85–90) in which he concludes from a study of the early and late works of Miller that this playwright's search for identity has become a search for definition, a change from creating characters to making statements.

The Crucible and *After the Fall* received considerable attention from critics, but no essay was outstanding. Those critics who attempted to assess the value of structure were particularly unconvincing. Phillip G. Hill ("*The Crucible*: A Structural View," *MD*, X, 312–317) weakly defends his position that Miller adequately sustains the central action of the play—to find Proctor's soul. Stephen Fender makes the small point that critics and audiences did not always understand Miller's thesis in "Precision and Pseudo-Precision in *The Crucible*" (*JAmS*, I, 87–98). In a more serious essay, Elizabeth Callahan contends that Miller uses the traditional tragic hero and several of the conventions of tragedy in *The Crucible* ("The Tragic Hero in Contemporary Secular and Religious Drama," *LHY*, VIII, 42–49). Much less convincing was Clinton W. Trowbridge's argument ("Arthur Miller: Between Pathos and Tragedy," *MD*, X, 221–232) that Miller's progress in *After the Fall* was away from pathos to the "genuinely tragic." C. W. E. Bigsby ("The Fall and After: Arthur Miller's Confession," *MD*, X, 124–136) effectively praises *After the Fall* as a significant step in which Miller's acceptance of guilt becomes a basis for life but then weakens his thesis by finding the play unsatisfactory in its unbelievable protagonist. John Stinson ("Structure in *After the Fall*, *MD*, X, 233–240) strains considerably in his analysis of what he calls the Marilyn Monroe Act, Act II, to show that both Quentin and Maggie are Christ figures and her death a *felix culpa*. One other structure-style study was "*Death of a Salesman* and Arthur Miller's Search for Style" (*Criticism*, IX, 303–311) in which Arthur K. Oberg observes that as a consequence of Miller's use of the cliché his text is undistinguished and flat. He concludes that one problem for the American dramatist is the "lack of an established and available idiom."

c. **Edward Albee.** It is difficult to take the book-length study of Albee very seriously considering the limited view of the writer, Gilbert Debusscher, who in *Edward Albee, Tradition and Renewal* (Brussels: American Studies Centre) admits that he is concerned with Albee's achievements and not his faults or failures. Debusscher contends that since 1955 neither Miller nor Williams nor Inge has written a good play and that in the Sixties Albee, a defeatist in the tradition of the Absurdists, is singularly important as a representative of the renewal of American drama. With a definite thesis (tradition and renewal) to defend, Debusscher offers little original criticism of Albee's plays. The book, however, has value for its general acceptance of a renaissance in American drama and its interest in Albee's work. Among the year's essays on Albee's plays, two should be singled out for particular attention. Henry Knepler, "Edward Albee: Conflicts of Tradition" (*MD*, X, 274–279) discusses several plays to show Albee's part in the conflict of two traditions—American sense versus the Absurdist view of life—and his use of Absurdist themes in an American manner. Joy Flasch's "Games People Play in *Who's Afraid of Virginia Woolf?*" (*MD*, X, 280–288) is a rather fascinating study of Eric Berne's psychology of human relationships as an approach to understanding a play.

A couple of essays discussed Albee's one-act plays. Mordecai H. Levine, "Albee's Liebestod" (*CLAJ*, X, 252–255) has nothing new to say about the religion-love-hate theme in *The Zoo Story*. Paul Witherington, "Language of Movement in Albee's *The Death of Bessie Smith*" (*TCL*, XIII, 84–88) argues that most critical opinions of the play failed to recognize its complexity and unity because of a misunderstanding of Albee's methods and purpose which are to be discovered in the imagery of movement and inertia. Most of the articles, however, treat some aspect of *Who's Afraid of Virginia Woolf?*. C. W. E. Bigsby, "*Who's Afraid of Virginia Woolf?* Edward Albee's Morality Play" (*JAmS*, I, 257–268) finds the play concerned with the ultimate destruction of illusion, a morality teaching "the primacy of human contact based on an acceptance of reality." Seeing echoes of Shaw in *Virginia Woolf* ("Fun and Games: Two Pictures of *Heartbreak House*," *DramS*, V, 223–236), D. C. Coleman contends that the action in both plays is advanced by fun and sport. "Play-watching with a Third Eye" (*CUF*, X, i, 18–22) by Randolph Goodman is not a very serious or convincing commentary on the influence of Strindberg and Ibsen on Albee's *Virginia Woolf*. Commenting on Albee's games, Louis Paul, "A Game Analysis of Albee's *Who's Afraid of Virginia Woolf?*: The Core of Grief" (*L&P*, XVII, 47–51), argues that the two possible responses to the play (to laugh or to smile and be stirred) suggest that the game or "life project" of George and Martha "represses a core of grief." Arthur Evans, "Love, History and Edward Albee" (*Renascence*, XIX, 115–118, 131) states that Albee's man is "an object of tragedy because [he is] a creature in History and a creator in Love" and that this contradiction is the real subject of *Virginia Woolf*. Anthony C. Hilfer creates an interesting title in "George and Martha: Sad, Sad, Sad" (*Seven Contemporary Authors*, pp. 121–139) but did nothing with it and, in fact, spent a quarter of his essay discussing O'Neill.

v. A Final Comment

It is always interesting, although only occasionally satisfying, to see ourselves through foreign eyes. In his third edition of *New Trends in Twentieth Century Drama* (New York, Oxford Univ. Press, pp.

317–340) Frederich Lumley explains that American drama is now in transition and in that uncertainty "lies its promise." While mentioning most practicing dramatists, he shows reservations about Albee, sympathy for Inge, and some enthusiasm for Jack Richardson and James Baldwin, whom he calls an "outstanding polemical dramatist." As only an Englishman can, he excuses American drama as young and uneven. Another Englishman, C. W. E. Bigsby, came to the conclusion in his Study of Contemporary American Drama, 1959–1966, that Americans could boast an "original contribution to world drama" (*Confrontation and Commitment*, Columbia, Mo., Univ. of Mo. Press). Bigsby sees *confrontation* as underlying contemporary American drama—manifested by a concern for man, the compassion of love, and a sense of rebellion, and found in Gelber, Albee, Miller's *After the Fall*, and Happenings. There is also in American drama a sense of *commitment*—seen in the proletarian theater as a weapon or propaganda and in the work of Negro playwrights. From an American theater reviewer, Martin Gottfried, there comes the comment: "Our drama is schizoid." Forcing himself into a dichotomy which at times defies explanation, Gottfried (*A Theatre Divided: The Post-war American Stage*, Boston, Little, Brown) tries to divide all theater into either Right Wing (Broadway and the Establishment) or Left Wing (Resident Theatres). The difficulty of his thesis appears in such a play as *Hogan's Goat*, a Right Wing play produced on a Left Wing stage. American drama may be at the very least schizoid—a term which Gottfried accepts on a very basic level—but by saying that American playwrights have murdered American drama he poses a thesis which, like his book, must be questioned.

Alan Downer wrote two essays—one concerning the past theater season, the other looking toward the future—which, together, suggest an analogy worth pondering. In his first essay, "The Doctor's Dilemma: Notes on the New York Theatre, 1966–67" (*QJS*, LIII, 213–223), he comments briefly on the season's plays and concludes that the theater is "fat with money, thin in blood, and sickly in the brain." In his other essay, however, he looks optimistically at "The Future of the American Theatre" (*The American Theatre Today*, pp. 193–203), seeing a theater of commitment reflecting a nation. One might make parallel observations concerning our criticism of the drama, both in its objectives and its techniques. Much of it is extremely slight—poorly written, ineffectively substantiated, employing a gimmick, and making confused or commonplace observations. There is also that committed criticism which views playwrights and their plays in meaningful terms and senses both failure and achievement in a developing theater. Fortunately, as several of this year's essays and books with historical and psychological perspective indicate, one can sense the beginning of a meaningful criticism of the drama in America!

Indiana University

17. Folklore

John T. Flanagan

The scholar seeking material on American folklore published in 1967 can avail himself of a number of bibliographical aids. Mary Washington Clarke compiled a list of Kentucky folklore items published in the previous year (*KFR*, XIII, 1–10). William J. Griffin continued his examination of American and Canadian folklore serials by providing discussion of such periodicals as *Autoharp* and *Caravan* (*TFSB*, XXXIII, 121–124). James H. Penrod and Warren I. Titus contributed the section on folklore to "Articles in American Studies" (*AQ*, XIX, 349–354). The first annual bibliography of studies in *Western American Literature*, edited by John S. Bullen and a staff of assistants (*WAL*, I, 323–329), includes some folkloristic items, but the major division is by the authors dealt with. The annual *MLA* International Bibliography (LXXXII, 113–116, 187) has approximately 180 items dealing with ballad, folksong, folk drama, and folk narrative, although they are not exclusively American. *Abstracts of Folklore Studies*, a quarterly journal edited by Donald Winkelman with a corps of assistants and contributors, lists materials from all over the world and provides substantial digests of each item included. A number of esoteric and minor periodicals are reported on here, and the order of listing is alphabetical by journal titles. Although a full index helps to make up for the lack of substantive arrangement, American material is scattered throughout.

As in previous years, however, the single most valuable compilation of folklore material appeared in the *Southern Folklore Quarterly*, the work of Merle E. Simmons (*SFQ*, XXXI, 79–213). The editor utilized ten categories in which to group his material and included both books and articles. Riddle and proverb discussions seem to be in short supply since only eight items relate to the first and only twenty-eight to the latter. On the other hand, the section on prose narrative requires fifteen pages and that on song, dance, and game twenty-eight. An index of the names of contributors is useful and the editorial annotations are invaluable. The coverage in this issue has been expanded to include more items originating in Italy and France and to make at least a bow to Africa and Australia. As in previous *SFQ* bibliographies the American material has not been segregated so that the student must seek for his references within the categories of folklore genres. But despite this limitation the compilation remains as the major bibliographical tool for the folklorist.

i. History and Theory

Two interesting articles on American folklore originally intended for foreign audiences appeared in 1967. Richard M. Dorson's "The Shaping of Folklore Traditions in the United States" (*Folklore*, LXXVIII, 161–183) stressed the point that although the English immigrants brought an enormous amount of lore with them—ballads, songs, superstitions (but not calendar customs and place legends)— Spanish, Indian, and notably Negro influence on American folklore has also been significant. The important Negro folk tradition comprises plantation animal tales, rural stories of hoodoos and superstitions, and urban talk and customs. In addition, the Yankee and the frontiersman have produced a substantial body of folklore, occupational folklore has proved to be rich and varied, and immigrant folklore, especially in the big cities, is still an untapped reservoir. In "The American Concept of Folklore" (*JFI*, III [1966], 226–249), a paper presented at an American-Yugoslav conference, Alan Dundes differentiated the concept of folklore in the United States from that held abroad. He alluded to W. W. Newell's pioneer article in the first issue of the *JAF* (1888) which defined four areas of folklore collecting: relics of English folklore, Negro folklore, Indian folklore, and the lore of the Spanish Southwest. But he observed that Newell's definition was limited and unsatisfactory to contemporary scholars who are constantly enlarging the field and investigating new areas. Dundes presented an interesting list of subjects which challenge attention today, among them nicknames, charms and blessings, formulas for leaving or greeting, mnemonic devices, and graffiti. He admitted that little important folklore theory has originated in the United States and that American scholars have on the whole been imitators rather than innovators. Today the older historical bias seems likely to be modified by psychological and broadly cultural approaches.

Gene Bluestein in "Constance Rourke and the Folk Sources of American Literature" (*WF*, XXVI, 77–87) reevaluated the contribution of Miss Rourke to American folk studies and carefully scrutinized the argument of *American Humor*, the seminal book which appeared first in 1931. Following the German philosopher Herder, Miss Rourke admitted that a sound national literature could not develop without strong folk roots and then proceeded to demonstrate that the United States could indeed display such roots. Indigenous characters like the Yankee and the frontiersman and native movements such as Negro minstrelsy and the popular theater provided exactly the foundation for a healthy and significant literary evolution. It is obvious that subsequent scholars owe Miss Rourke a large debt for her insight into the American creative process.

In "Folklore, Fakelore, and Poplore" (*SatR*, L [1967], Aug. 26, 20–21, 43–44) Marshall Fishwick ventured a definition of folklore (". . . material handed on by tradition—oral or active; by mouth, practise, or custom: folk song, folktale, Easter eggs, dance step, or knocking on wood") and then contended that there is no agreement about what folklore is but a general consensus about what it includes. He cited examples of traditional ballads and noted substantial changes in their American versions (for example, "The Twa Sisters" and "The Three Ravens") and then exemplified fakelore by the synthetic stories about Paul Bunyan, Pecos Bill, and Big Mose. To Fishwick, "fakelore is to folklore what the pseudo-event is to the real event." Poplore represents a new variation and only time can tell if the contributions of Andy Warhol or Bob Dylan have any permanence.

Several writers reported on collecting or classification procedures. In "Some Problems in the Comparative Study of Tall Tales" (*NCF*, XV, 6–8) J. Russell Reaver briefly described his work on a motif-index to American tall tales. He claimed that the tall tale had received inadequate attention in the standard indexes and that the examples cited were often sparse. He also observed that the most common motif was the wonderful hunt (X-1110). Ellen J. Steckert gave an account of the Wayne State University folklore archive (*FFMA*, IX, 61–78), discussing its genesis, describing its classification system, and reproducing sample index cards. Kenneth S. Goldstein in "Experimental Folklore: Laboratory vs. Field" (*Folklore Inter-*

national, pp. 71–82) argued that folklore research can be done experimentally in the field and then described his own experiences in Scotland in 1959–60. He collected devil and ghost stories from two Aberdeenshire sisters at different times and on more than one occasion, and he tried always to glean native folk materials in a context as close as possible to natural conditions. He concluded that it was possible to observe a genuine folk transmission process without dependence on analogy to prove a theory.

The appearance of Ernest W. Baughman's *Type and Motif Index of the Folktales of England and North America* (The Hague, Mouton, 1966), an impressive work which has been many years in preparation, fills an important gap in the indexing of folktales. Using the revised Aarne-Thompson *Types of the Folk-Tale* and the Thompson *Motif-Index* as bases, Baughman expanded the coverage enormously even though he excluded the tales of such foreign-language groups in North America as the French and the Spanish, not to mention the Indian and the Negro. The study includes 13,083 variants of types and motifs and they are preponderantly American. The tall tale (X900–1899) incidentally seems to be overwhelmingly an American form since no less than 3,710 variants are cited. On the other hand, the study shows relatively few märchen and little American interest in fairy stories. Some 371 types of stories are identified here and about a quarter of this corpus is common to the United States and Europe. Included in the *Index* is a valuable bibliography of sources utilized (pp. xxii–lxx).

ii. Folk Heroes

One of the perennial topics for discussion in all countries and in all cultures is the hero, his genesis, his nature, his function. Thus Roger D. Abrahams in "Some Varieties of Heroes in America" (*JFI*, III [1966], 341–362) remarked that although the hero is universally recognized, heroic deeds and traits vary from place to place. Narrators of heroic stories are stimulated by a need to increase their prestige, to repeat the manly deeds of the past, or to provide vicarious achievement for their audience. Typical American Negro heroes are John Henry and Stackolee, while white rural folk regions produce good outlaws like Gregorio Cortez, heroic lumberjacks like Young Monroe, or engineers like Casey Jones. Idealized frontier figures like Daniel Boone and Davy Crockett have strangely enough

produced such offspring as Paul Bunyan, Joe Magarac, the Lone
Ranger, and perhaps even James Bond. Abrahams contended finally
that American heroes despite enormous variation in origin and nature have shared one quality: they have never had a final transforming experience.

Three essays reexamine the cowboy. Joe B. Frantz in "Cowboy
Philosophy: A Cold Spoor" (*The Frontier Reexamined*, pp. 169–
180) gave a capsule history of the cowboy and observed that novelists, scenarists, and even academic specialists have turned their
attention to him. But the cowboy, though given to anecdotes and
hyperbole, was generally quiet and inarticulate; efforts to transform
him into a philosopher have gone sour. Philip Durham in "The
Cowboy and the Myth" (*JPC*, I, 58–62) summarized what recent
writers have said about the cowboy and showed the origin of the
idealized hero. Even though the cowboy's six gun has become a sex
gun and his horse a phallic symbol, his image and his myth seem
permanent. Paul Patterson in "The Cowboy's Code" (*Sunny Slopes*
pp. 39–50) enumerated twelve basic cowboy rules of conduct which
were not only unwritten but unspoken and which no plains rider
dared to violate. Among them were punctuality, respect for fences,
loyalty to the job, and constant control of one's horse.

The idealized outlaw is the theme of John O. West's essay, "Billy
the Kid, Hired Gun or Hero" (*Sunny Slopes*, pp. 70–80). West reviewed the sordid career of this moronic killer and concluded that
even though Billy the Kid was a documented horse thief, gambler,
cattle rustler, and murderer, folk legend is still in the process of transforming him into a glamorous figure.

An equally fraudulent "hero" is the subject of Bruce Jackson's
article, "What Happened to Jody" (*JAF*, LXXX, 387–396). Jody the
Grinder is a Negro folk character found in Negro toasts, army songs,
and even blues. When other men enter military service or are
incarcerated in prisons Jody remains at home, free to pursue his
sexual adventures with the abandon that his nickname implies. Jackson recorded several Jody songs from a Texas penitentiary in 1965
and 1966, one of them called "Jody's Got My Wife and Gone." The
songs, curiously enough, were used as work songs and were lined
out by a leader and responded to by a chorus.

Jody, of course, is a trickster, but older folk heroes were tricksters
and heroes simultaneously. Raney Stanford in "The Return of
Trickster: When a Not-A-Hero Is a Hero" (*JPC*, I, 228–242) reiter-

ated the familiar notion that in folklore and myth the trickster was often at the same time a culture hero. Memorable figures like Loki, Raven, and Hermes combined good and evil attributes: if they lied, stole, copulated freely, they also brought men fire, taught him arts and crafts, made possible his cultural advance. From the ancient trickster via figures like Tyl Eulenspiegel and Reynard the Fox there is a clear descent to the picaro protagonists of early fiction, and from the picaro the line runs to the anti-heroes of contemporary novels. Dostoyevsky's underground man had a significant influence on the characteristic anti-hero of today's fiction, even as represented by the protagonist of Ralph Ellison's *The Invisible Man.* More specific tricksters appear in Bill R. Hampton's article, "On Identification with Negro Tricksters" (*SFQ*, XXXI, 55–65). Concerned chiefly with Negro identification with trickster figures and contending that such figures help individuals and groups to establish both identities and roles, Hampton dealt with Br'er Rabbit, Anansi, and the typical slave John on the antebellum plantation. Today, with social conflict becoming more explicit, such figures have a waning importance, while identification with animal heroes becomes less common with the decline of oral tales. The article makes the interesting suggestion that Langston Hughes's character, Simple, who mingles some of the traits of the trickster and the bad man hero, might well be the prototype for Negroes involved in the civil rights movement.

One aboriginal trickster tale served as a basis for devising a theory of structure. Polly Pope in "Toward a Structural Analysis of North American Trickster Tales" (*SFQ*, XXXI, 274–286) first gave a careful resume of the chief events in the story known as "The Bungling Host." Basic principles were then established: action must be undertaken by a major character in the tale, a major character must also work toward the completion of the event, and there must be interaction between this figure and others. Some seventy bungling stories were utilized by the critic in her effort to arrive at a useful analytical scheme, and charts were supplied to show the distribution of events. This is an article for the specialist; the general reader will be annoyed by the jargon employed.

iii. Ballad and Folksong

Interest in the Child ballads, particularly if they have extensive American variants, remains vigorous. Tristram P. Coffin in "The

Golden Ball and the Hangsman's Tree" (*Folklore International*, pp. 23–28) discussed the basic problem in a widely known ballad which has analogues in tale, drama, cante fable, and play party. Critics have always been puzzled as to why the heroine of "The Maid Freed from the Gallows" was sentenced to death since the narrative is obscure on this point. Coffin read the story as a punishment for the loss of virginity, conventionally symbolized by a golden comb, key, or ball. He cited medical testimony to prove that golden balls were once used as contraceptives. The article uses texts from the Andros Islands, Jamaica, and Missouri. Ed Cray in a discussion of "Barbara Allen" and its frequent cheap reprintings (*Folklore International*, pp. 41–50) printed impressive statistics about this popular ballad: some 600 recoveries of it in the United States alone, some 166 melodies, and at least 56 appearances in periodicals. The ballad varies greatly in length, but it has accumulated few non-narrative stanzas and it is remarkably free from ballad clichés. The attached bibliography includes broadsides, songsters, and such magazines as *Harper's*. William J. Titland compared "The Bitter Withy" with "The Holy Well" (*JAF*, LXXX, 49–70) and considered many variants. Most readers would be more interested in the first ballad with its curious account of Mary disciplining the child Jesus with a bitter withy. Neither song has a substantial American record. On the other hand, Child ballad No. 243, "James Harris," better known in the United States as "The House Carpenter," has had an interesting and well-documented American history. John Burrison in " 'James Harris' in Britain Since Child" (*JAF*, LXXX, 271–284) studied the ballad on both sides of the Atlantic and analyzed variants in texts reported in Great Britain mostly in the present century.

The problem of which Child ballads actually had a history of oral tradition stimulated a carefully reasoned article by J. Barre Toelken, "An Oral Canon for the Child Ballads: Construction and Application" (*JFI*, IV, 75–101). Toelken proposed three criteria to authenticate traditional reliability for the Child ballads: a ballad to be accepted as a genuine oral transmission must have two or more English language variants collected outside England by competent folklorists; it must have at least two traditional tunes connected with it; and it should have variants which again are certified by reputable scholars. By this standard some 135 of the Child ballads are authentically oral and they are enumerated according to their appearance in the five Child volumes. Toelken also identified certain basic themes: the image of a girl sewing, the color green which is associated with misfortune or death, and the pulling of flowers or the picking of a nut as a symbol of seduction to follow. Such images, he contended, were not only familiar to both singer and audience but should be taken as a clue to the folk culture of the society involved. Perhaps the most obvious example is the conventional briar-rose ending of ballads dealing with tragic love: almost invariably the rose grows from the girl's grave, the flower symbolizing the woman in death as it did in life.

Studies of American ballads and folksongs show a wide range. Two articles dealt with verse influenced or stimulated by the Custer massacre of 1876. Brian W. Dippie in "Bards of the Little Big Horn" (*WAL*, I [1966], 175–195) cited poems by Longfellow, Whittier, and Whitman and stressed the tendency of writers to apotheosize Custer. Since no white soldier survived the massacre the imagination of the bards was completely unfettered by evidence, and Custer himself was variously described as having yellow hair, blond hair, or tawny flowing hair. Some of the folk poems were paeans to Comanche, Capt. Keogh's horse also slain on the battlefield. Austin and Alta Fife in "Ballads of the Little Big Horn" (*AW*, IV, 46–49) included the words and music of a number of ballads inspired by Custer's last stand.

Cowboy ballads also attracted attention. John Barsness in "The Dying Cowboy Song" (*WAL*, II, 50–57) contended that most cowboy songs were not authentic but were sentimentalized versions of life on the range written by outsiders or visitors. He was convinced that the average cowboy was too inarticulate or too illiterate to compose ballads. He blamed John Lomax in particular for perpetuating a sentimental image of the cowboy and his singing. An exception to the body of cowboy songs might be "The Old Chisholm Trail," and for many years stanzas of this trail classic have remained unprintable. On the other hand, John I. White in two articles seems to have established the authenticity of one cowboy poet, D. J. O'Malley, who spent several decades in Montana and contributed ballads to the Miles City *Stockgrowers' Journal* in the 1890's. In "A Montana Cowboy Poet" (*JAF*, LXXX, 114–129) White gave a full account of O'Malley's career and emphasized the fact that the famous "When the Work is Done Next Fall" was widely sung by men who had forgotten O'Malley's authorship. Indeed its composition was attributed to another writer. A little less familiar were O'Malley's "Charlie Rutledge" and "D-2 Horse Wrangler," both of which have survived in oral tradition. White repeated some of these facts in "Portraits for a Western Album: I" (AW, IV, 78–79). In a third article White discussed the genesis of "Cowboy Song" originally contributed by Joseph Mills Hanson to a national magazine. In "A Ballad in Search of Its Author" (WAL, II, 58–62) White provided convincing evidence that "Cowboy Song," better known under the title of "Railroad Corral," was Hanson's work and that it appeared in various collections either as anonymous or under some other ascription. Like O'Malley's ballads "Railroad Corral" has become part of American oral tradition.

The two men most intimately associated with the transcription and publication of American cowboy songs are Nathan Howard (Jack) Thorp and John A. Lomax. In his study entitled "Jack Thorp and John Lomax: Oral or Written Transmission?" (WF, XXVI, 113–118) John O. West emphasized the fact that Thorp's little book of 1908 preceded Lomax's first volume by two years and that Lomax incorporated some of Thorp's original contributions without acknowledgement. Lomax, moreover, doctored some of his texts by either alteration or omission. And yet the lover of American folksong and perhaps even the scholar remain indebted to both men. These names also appear in an article by Everett A. Gillis, "Laureates of the Western Range" (Sunny Slopes, pp. 81–88), but a third cowboy composer is mentioned too—Charlie Johnson, author of "The Old Cowboy." The reader of these discussions must conclude that the initial authorship of many cowboy songs which have long been in the public domain may never be established.

Not all familiar songs, furthermore, are genuine folk songs. In "The Penny Dreadful as a Folksong" (Sunny Slopes, pp. 164–170) James Ward Lee demonstrated that what might be called the "non-folk" folksongs are at least as numerous as the genuine traditional ballads and that they stem of course from cheap print. The problem is intensified also by the fact that both varieties are sentimental and even maudlin. If "Edward" is a tragic ballad, so in a sense is Gussie Davis' 1896 tear-jerker, "The Baggage Coach Ahead."

An entire issue of Northeast Folklore (VIII) was devoted to "Folksongs from Martha's Vineyard." Some twenty-nine songs with music are included as they were sung by the Tilton family and later repeated by Gale Huntington. Among the titles are "Scarlet Town," "Blow the Man Down," "The Boston Burglar," and that ballad dear to logging camps throughout the United States, "The Flying Cloud." The periodical also includes notes and a bibliography.

A two-part study of an isolated section of New York State is "An Ethnomusicological Survey Among the People of the Ramapo Mountains" (*NYFQ*, XXIII, 52–64, 109–131) by Charles H. Kaufman. The author surveyed an anomalous group popularly called the "Jackson Whites" whose origin still seems uncertain but who have occupied a small area some fifty miles north of New York City since the eighteenth century. A low-income, rather maligned group, they have developed a limited interest in music, they own and play guitars and accordions, and they sing such familiar ballads as "The Butcher Boy," "The Farmer and His Wife" (a variant of Child No. 278), and "Springfield Mountain." The ballads reprinted here were collected from various members of a family named Conklin, one of the familiar area names.

A different kind of folksong was studied by Bruce Jackson in "Prison Worksongs: the Composer in Negative" (*WF*, XXVI, 245–268). An inmate of the Ramsey institution of the Texas Prison System, sentenced for murder, composed several songs such as "No More Good Time in the World for Me" and "Too Much Time for the Crime I Done" which showed both musical facility and some adeptness with language. Among the convict's themes were the length of the sentence, the chance of escape, guards and wardens, firearms, and invariably women. Jackson pointed out that although the language was concrete and imagistic, the approach was necessarily negative—unfreedom, unlove, and unvolition.

The Negro bad man Stagolee, hero of a ballad of the same name, induced Richard E. Buehler in "Stacker Lee: A Partial Investigation into the Historicity of a Negro Murder Ballad" (*KFQ*, XII, 187–191) to try to establish the origin of the name. He discovered that there was a Confederate soldier named Stacker Lee who belonged to a steamboat-owning family and that one of the line's boats bore the same name. But the link between the name of the steamboat and the Negro bully remains to be established.

One thing that convicts and soldiers have in common is their penchant for song; both confinement and military duty seem to produce singing. Tom Phillips in "Vietnam Blues" (*NYTM*, Oct. 8, 1967, pp. 12, 32) surveyed some of the protest songs produced by the war in southeast Asia and printed stanzas from "Saigon Bride" (made famous by Joan Baez) and "Waist Deep in the Big Muddy"; he concluded that production of such ditties would continue: "the songs are sometimes satiric, sometimes sorrowful and sometimes indignant, but the tone is always negative." Protest songs in a more limited area stimulated S. Page Stegner's essay, "Protest Songs from the Butte Mines" (*WF*, XXVI, 157–167). George Korson's collection of mining lore from Pennsylvania is well known but less has been done for the copper mining areas of Montana. Stegner's article gives texts of local songs written by a man named Scottie which applied familiar labor chants (such as "Solidarity Forever") to conditions around Butte in 1917 and 1918.

At least two substantial anthologies of American folksongs appeared during the year. Alan Lomax edited *Hard-Hitting Songs for Hard-Hit People*, for which Pete Seeger supplied the musical arrangements (New York: Oak Pubs.). *Songs of the Great American West*, edited by Irwin Silber with arrangements and annotations by Earl Robinson, collected many familiar ballads of the westward movement in a useful if expensive volume. Silber's book has eight sections, including songs about the Mormons, the cowboys, the homesteaders, the gold miners of 1849, and characteristic western outlaws. The final part entitled "Roll On, Columbia" includes appropriately enough two songs by Woody Guthrie and groups together ditties about lumberjacks, bindlestiffs, and the I.W.W. Both music and texts are given and some transcriptions were made from commercial recordings (New York, Macmillan).

The year also saw the appearance of the third volume of Bertrand H. Bronson's monumental work, *The Traditional Tunes of the Child Ballads With Their Texts* (Princeton: Princeton Univ. Press, 1966). The published record now includes Child ballads Nos. 114–242 and supplies full bibliographical information. A fourth volume, yet to appear, will successfully complete a formidable task.

iv. Folk Music

Articles dealing with folk music published during 1967 varied from complex discussions of musical theory to accounts of transcriptions of tunes from hillbilly records. Alan Lomax in "The Good and the

Beautiful in Folksong" (*JAF*, LXXX, 213–235) defined singing as "an act of communication" which consequently could be studied as behavior. His thesis that the traditional transmission of a folksong over the decades could have greater cultural than individual significance led him to explore folksongs in many geographical areas of the world. The performance of a single singer, uninterrupted by the audience, he found to be the dominant pattern in Western Europe and North America but less salient elsewhere. In Africa, on the contrary, dancers or singers rarely perform alone; African performance style is polyphonic and polyrhythmic. Lomax found this kind of singing eminently suitable to a culture of clan lineages armed with hoes and adzes where group action alone could bring about increased production. He then enumerated basic subsistence types and argued that song style in some ways could be said to fit the activity involved. Despite the use of charts and data Lomax's article seems to invite a mild scepticism, although certainly his effort to document human attempts to mold behavior into forms appropriate to man's situation is significant.

In an essay entitled "Folksingers and the Re-Creation of Folksong" (*WF*, XXVI, 101–111) John Quincy Wolf dealt with the problem of alteration of traditional material by American folk singers. A number of vocalists from the White River country of Arkansas provided him with texts and tunes, and of the eleven individuals described only three insisted that they never changed their materials. The majority admittedly improvised when necessary or even substituted or changed lines according to their own artistic judgment. One of the eleven singers interviewed by Wolf was Jimmie Driftwood, a guitarist and singer since boyhood.

Neil V. Rosenberg in "From Sound to Style: the Emergence of Bluegrass" (*JAF*, LXXX, 143–150) traced the history of that branch of country music known as "bluegrass" from the 1930's to the present. Much of the credit for its development is due to a singer and mandolin player named Bill Monroe who performed for a Nashville radio station and subsequently made several famous recordings. His original group included a guitar, a fiddle, a bass, and an accordion. Two of his players, Lester Flatt and Earl Scruggs, later defected and formed their own band. Bluegrass remains a definite musical style, especially in the South, but performers today generally mix it with other forms of country music.

A particularly Negro variety of folk music, notably the "blues,"

is the theme of Mimi Clar Melnick's " 'I Can Peep Through Muddy
Water and Spy Dry Land': Boasts in the Blues" (*Folklore International*, pp. 139–149). More concerned with the subjects and function
of the blues than with language or style, the critic finds the Negro
hero of these songs curiously like the older backwoodsman, a brag-
gart who hides his frustrations under masculine aggressiveness. The
blues hero wants status, and status means fancy clothes, fancy cars,
liquor, and women. The big spender, the big drinker, the good lover
also equate with status. Most of the blues thus deal with male
prowess. Interestingly enough, travel symbols often enter into the
laments or boasts, chiefly the railroad and the length of the train.
But other blues include threats of revenge or violence and even
hoodoo charms. The article quotes from such well-known blues
singers as Muddy Waters, Bill Broonzy, and Bessie Smith.

In "Hillbilly Records and Tune Transcriptions" (*WF*, XXVI,
225–244) Judith McCulloh examined the efforts of various people to
get accurate transcriptions of melodies from early records of hillbilly
music. Defined as "predominantly southern white country music recorded commercially between 1923 and World War II," hillbilly
music was recorded on the Okeh label under the direction of Ralph
Peer and later appeared as sheet music. Carter Family albums were
published in the 1930's and often included fifty songs. One of the first
scholars to tap this cache of material was Guy B. Johnson in his 1929
study of John Henry, but subsequent anthologists such as Alan Lomax, Benjamin Botkin, and Albert Friedman followed suit. Bertrand
Bronson even included hillbilly variants of the Child ballads in his
examination of traditional songs.

Lawrence Cohn in an obituary appreciation of Mississippian
John Hurt (*SatR*, L, Feb. 25, 90) described the career of this Negro
laborer and self-taught guitarist who recorded first at Memphis and
much later in New York City. For a brief time before his death Hurt
enjoyed fame and even a slight prosperity. A competent performer
of the various kinds of Negro music, "blues, religious songs, country-
dance pieces, and bits of suggestive erotica/*double entendre*," Hurt
had as his specialty a "rolling, effervescent, guitar-picking style."

v. Folk Narrative

Various kinds of folk narrative, the tall tale, the ghost story, the
magical episode, still fascinate the collector and continue to appear

in different sections of the country. The narrators may be woodsmen, farmers, or urban immigrants.

David A. Walton contributed two instalments of "Pennsylvania Riverboat Tales" to *KFQ* (XII, 81–93; 177–186), all of them the oral narratives of a retired Pennsylvania riverboat engineer, Louis T. Sesher. Many of his stories are variants of familiar tales or exaggerated events. Thus Sesher's tale of a human being transformed into a frog by magic and then restored to his original condition seems to be a Pennsylvania version of the famous first story in the Grimm collection. Other Sesher tales deal with a rawhide harness which contracts and expands, a hoop snake which can form itself into a ball and roll down a path in pursuit of its victim, flying turtles, enormous mosquitoes, and a genius who herds bees by means of a cub plane. One of the more unusual tales, since it seems to add a dimension to the Paul Bunyan saga, affirms an Irish ancestry for the giant woodsman. According to Sesher, Paul came from Ireland on a stone raft and brought with him a bull measuring five feet between the eyes. When the bull reached New York City, he was so heavy that he broke up the pavement and had to be slaughtered. Eventually the bull's meat fed half the city. The editor pointed out that this is one of the few Paul Bunyan exploits actually collected from oral tradition.

From the Keystone State also came colorful ghost tales. Eugene Utech collected from J. Raymond Bear, a farmer and feed mill operator near Carlisle, a number of stories in which revenants or haunts were prominent (*KFQ*, XII, 211–228). "J. Raymond Bear's Olde Tyme Ghost Tales of Cumberland County" includes a ghostly walker, a wraith attired as a Confederate soldier, ghostly lights, a haunted house, and most curious of all a revenant appearing as a white elephant.

On Minnesota's Iron Range Michael G. Karni found a Finnish miner and woodsman who was notable for his strength and appetite. In "Otto Walta: Finnish Folk Hero of the Iron Range" (*MH*, XL, 391–402) Karni described his hero as a man probably less gigantic than rumor had it (six feet four and a half inches, 240 pounds) but in other ways gargantuan. Walta was too poor to buy dynamite in order to eradicate stumps so he grubbed them out bare-handed or bent a discarded rail which supposedly weighed several hundred pounds into a fish hook to use as a pry. On another occasion he helped a neighbor dress a bear. After consuming several pounds of the raw flesh he shouldered the 450 pound carcass and carried it off. Lacking a team, Walta himself pulled his plow over rugged cut-over land. Although Walta died in a state hospital in 1959, his feats of strength are still recounted by the people of St. Louis County.

In New York Rosemary Agonito collected folktales from immigrant Italians resident in the area around Syracuse. "Il Paisano" (*NYFQ*, XXIII, 52–64) describes a group of impoverished sheep herders and farmers from Guardiaregia in the Abruzzi Mountains who came to central New York state about the turn of the century. They brought with them tales of the marvelous and supernatural, including a story about a speaking snake, another about a woman transformed into a frog who can be restored to human shape only by magic, and an amusing and familiar one about a farm wife who tricked the devil. The woman and the demon agreed to buy farmland together and share the profits. First, they agreed to give the devil all the produce above the ground and the woman all that below (she planted beets). Then the devil chose all the produce below the ground and the woman all that above (she planted corn). Angry and discomfited, the devil finally disappeared.

An older North American Indian tale from the manuscript of C. C. Trowbridge was edited by C. E. Schorer for the *SFQ* (XXXI, 236–243). "The Giants" deals with the quest of man for adventure, a bride, and society. It also includes such familiar motifs as gigantic men and animals, cannibalism, and a magical coal which can melt ice and cause a flood. Trowbridge, the original collector of this and other tales, served as an Indian agent in Detroit in the 1820's.

Two articles in *The Sunny Slopes of Long Ago* deal with individual tales. In "The Hat-in-Mud Tale" (pp. 100–109) Jan H. Brunvand discussed the widely diffused story of the man whose head was barely visible above the roily water of a bog but who claimed to have a horse or mule beneath him. The story goes back at least as far as Paulding's domestic farce, *The Lion of the West* (1830), but was subsequently printed in one form or another by Andy Adams, Vance Randolph, and even Thoreau. James T. Bratcher in "The Baby-Switching Story" (pp. 110–117) took another famous anecdote, given literary kudos by Owen Wister in *The Virginian*, and suggested that the novelist had first heard the tale in Texas. Bratcher added that the story has European analogues and might properly be assigned a motif number (KI923.1).

In a pamphlet entitled *J. Mason Brewer, Negro Folklorist* (SWS, No. 12, Austin, Steck-Vaughn), James W. Byrd traced the career of the most prominent American Negro folklorist and surveyed his work. Brewer, a life-long teacher in Texas and North Carolina, has been an assiduous student of Negro folklore and is particularly well known for his collection of Negro preacher tales, *The Word on the Brazos* (1953), and for *Dog Ghosts and Other Texas Negro Folk Tales* (1958). Byrd supplied a minimum of biographical detail but gave numerous illustrations of the anecdotes and stories that Brewer collected; he emphasized also the authenticity of the material and its linguistic fidelity, despite the fact that Brewer himself has admitted certain revisions and telescopings. The final comparison between Brewer and Joel Chandler Harris is pertinent and convincing.

vi. Folk Speech

Collectors of folk speech, proverbs, and superstitions continued their activities in various parts of the country in 1967 and published their findings. Areas of provenience ranged from the Mammoth Cave region of Kentucky to the redwood country of California.

Gordon Wilson in a series called "Studying Folklore in a Small Region" (*TFSB*, XXXIII, 1–6, 27–35) reported folk beliefs about the weather and the seasons and observed that many of the items showed a mixture of science and superstition. One sentence is succinct and inclusive: "Sunday is no time to *whistle, work, fish,* cut your *nails, sew* with a thimble, burn *brush,* or turn a *grindstone.*" A second section deals with folk grammar and lists both misused parts of speech and verb deviations. Wilson concluded that folk language was alive, picturesque, and incorrect. In another article Wilson and Addie Suggs Hilliard discussed "Folklore in Certain Professions" (*TFSB*, XXXIII, 98–108) and cited figurative expressions from the Mammoth Cave area which had analogies in Shakespeare's plays. Kelsie B. Harder collected "Hay-Making Terms in Perry County" (*TSFB*, XXXIII, 41–48) and commented that hay-making was not only a festive but also a ritualistic occasion. In Tennessee folk colloquialisms replace standard terms in the hay meadows: "frail" for flail, "falfie" for alfalfa, and "patch" for field. George W. Boswell reported on his activities in collecting proverbs from Kentucky college students in "Folk Wisdom in Northeastern Kentucky" (*TFSB*,

XXXIII, 10–17); he gleaned some 313 of which he listed 99. Many
are obvious and familiar, such as "a boiled egg never hatches" and
"there's always a nut on every family tree." Cratis Williams was
concerned mostly with history and description in "Moonshining in
the Mountains" (*NoCF*, XV, 11–17) but included various folk terms
for the essential parts of the distilling process: the mash was called
"beer," fusil oil was known as "bardy grease," and one of the waste
products was termed "singlins."

A different kind of compilation resulted from the investigation of
Ed Cray and Marilyn Herzog of a craze for nonsensical riddles which
swept through the country in the 1960's and was especially current
among high school students. In "The Absurd Elephant: A Recent
Riddle Fad" (*WF*, XXVI, 27–36) they listed elephant jokes under
various captions such as Elephants in Trees and Elephants in Odd
Places. One example in the latter category should suffice: Q. How
can you tell when an elephant is in the bathtub with you? A. You
can smell peanuts on his breath.

In "A Miscellany of Folk Beliefs from the Redwood Country"
(*WF*, XXVI, 169–176) Lynwood Carranco combined beliefs collected from loggers and commercial fishermen in Humboldt County,
California, with items supplied by high school and college students
in the region. Carranco reported that he could find few actual folk
beliefs among the lumbering crews although he was familiar with
both their work and their argot. Of the eight examples cited perhaps
one is worth quoting: "If you want to change your luck, have sexual
intercourse with a colored woman." About 125 beliefs which follow
are tabulated under such obvious headings as the body, death and
funeral practices, animals, sports, marriage, and good and bad luck.

Roger L. Welsch in "American Numskull Tales: the Polack Joke"
(*WF*, XXVI, 183–186) cited some uncomplimentary Polack jokes
which are obvious examples of oral transmission and remarked that
generally in the United States numskull stories have been linked with
various immigrant groups. American stage history would certainly
exemplify this point. Bruce Jackson interested himself in "Prison
Nicknames" (*WF*, XXVI, 48–54) and used as illustrative data his
collection from convicts in the Texas penitentiary system. Slang was
freely used by prisoners, he reported, and nicknames, both descriptive and derisory, were commonly employed. Jackson observed some
distinction between nicknames invented by white prisoners and those

used by Negroes; the nicknames for guards were never used in direct address but those for prisoners were so common that many men did not know the real names of fellow inmates.

The Sunny Slopes of Long Ago includes an article entitled "Cowboy Lingo" by the late John A. Lomax (pp. 12–25), which was partially published in 1920. The essay now appears in its entirety and is a surprisingly fresh account of the routine language of the cowboy in reference to horses and their gear, camp food, animal nomenclature, and range activities in general.

vii. Material and Miscellaneous Folklore

A number of interesting articles dealt with material folklore or with marginal verbal lore. They represent the wide spectrum in which folklore specialists operate.

E. J. Wilhelm, Jr., a professional geographer, studied the ecology of communities in the Shenandoah National Park area and reported his findings in "Folk Settlement Types in the Blue Ridge Mountains" (*KFQ*, XII, 151–174). He was concerned chiefly with the folk in a regional setting and with the geographical importance of settlement types. Deeming cultural isolation more significant than physical isolation, he listed such cultural traits as homogeneity, group solidarity, economic independence, and the continued existence of taboos and traditions. The article enumerates five kinds of physical settlement in the chosen region: the gap or notch, the hollow, the cove (an oval shaped valley), the ridge, and the meadow or plateau.

Austin E. Fife, on the other hand, studied fences that delimit settlements and defined these various obstructions in "Jack Fences of the Intermountain West" (*Folklore International*, pp. 51–54). Fences can be made of wood, stone, metal, or wire and can serve as property lines, corrals, transportational route markers, military zones, or national forest boundaries. The jack fence, simple in construction and generally functional, proved to be a staple form in the western part of the country, equally useful in holding cattle or snow.

The architecture of the prairie sod hut is the subject of Roger L. Welsch's "The Nebraska Soddy" (*NH*, XLVIII, 335–342). Welsch described the construction of the dwelling which was so characteristic of the northern plains and discussed both the materials and the roof types. Incessant rain was the soddy's worst enemy and could

collapse a badly made roof in short order. But the soddy persisted
because it was quickly and cheaply constructed and because it was
warmer than more costly frame houses.

Many people find the practice of dowsing, the location of sub-
terranean water by use of a flexible wand or stick, to have perennial
interest. Thomas G. Lyman, Jr., in "Water Dowsing as a Surviving
Folk Tradition" (KFQ, XII, 133–142) traced the history of the pro-
cedure and showed that it still exists in various parts of the country.
In addition he listed the implements generally used and described
the precise methods. American dowsers, it should be added, have
an annual meeting and demonstration in Danville, Vermont.

The influence of the Negro folk dance stimulated Chadwick
Hansen's article, "Jenny's Toe; Negro Shaking Dances in America"
(AQ, XIX, 554–563). Both title and subject came from a reference
in Fanny Kemble's journal (1838–1839), but the main purpose of the
article was to discuss the evolution of Negro twisting and shaking
dances and their relationship to such terpsichorean steps as the
jitterbug, the hula, the twist, etc. Only lately have white intellectuals
become aware of the long history of Negro erotic dances and their
impact on the dance history of the West.

Arthur A. Berger examined Al Capp's famous comic strip in a
perceptive article entitled "Li'l Abner in American Satire" (NYFQ,
XXIII, 83–98). In the familiar Dogpatch characters he found not
only mythical qualities but also a tradition which he traced back to
William Byrd and the Southwestern humorists. Berger also noted
similarities between the Li'l Abner cartoons and Jewish folklore and
emphasized Capp's reliance on puns, caricature, distortion, and wit.
According to this critic, Li'l Abner is a durable and important American satire.

The current controversy over the deleterious effects of tobacco
gives two articles by J. T. McCullen, Jr., particular salience. "Indian
Myths Concerning the Origin of Tobacco" (NYFQ, XXIII, 264–273)
surveys Indian attitudes toward the use of tobacco and quotes traditions about smoking from such tribes as the Crows, Menominis,
Hurons, Foxes, Winnebagoes, and Navajos. Generally the critic
found that the Indians looked upon tobacco as a beneficent gift of
the gods, designed to give man comfort and solace. A vivid Huron
myth recounts how once in the distant past a nude Indian maid de-
scended from the skies to benefit man; when she left to return to

her celestial abode, corn grew from the spot which her right hand had touched, potatoes from the spot which her left hand had touched, and tobacco sprang from the area where she had sat down. In "Tobacco and Longevity" (*Sunny Slopes*, pp. 128–135) McCullen cited a number of examples of centenarians who attributed their long life to moderate use of tobacco. His illustrations come from the last three centuries and include citizens of England, Cuba, Holland, and Argentina. An addiction to tobacco may induce cancer; apparently it also may bring about longevity.

There is also difference of opinion about the merits of another weed. In a discussion called "Creeping Ignorance of Poke Sallet" (*Sunny Slopes*, pp. 157–163) James W. Byrd cited what he termed Yankee ignorance of the true virtues of pokeweed, claimed by some dictionaries to be poisonous. On the contrary, he affirmed that poke greens (sallet) if properly prepared were not only edible but nutritious and that they had medical support for use as a spring purgative. Moreover, the roots, commonly considered noxious, had value for external use in infections. Folk recipes quoted in the article sustain his point of view but fail to make the dishes sound engaging.

Miscellaneous verbal and material lore is scattered through Folke Hedblom's article, "Research of Swedish Speech and Popular Traditions in America, 1966" (*SPHQ*, XVIII, 76–92). A Swedish recording expedition visited the Scandinavian settlements in northern and western America primarily in quest of Swedish speech and its dialects. Isanti and Chisago counties in Minnesota remain the richest areas for field work.

In an erudite and comprehensive article entitled "Easter Eggs" (*JAF*, LXXX, 3–32) Venetia Newall considered the egg as a symbol of creation or, in Christian ideology, of rebirth, and presented examples from many cultures to prove the importance of the egg in ceremony and ritual. Few American customs are specifically alluded to although reference is made to the common children's belief that eggs are brought by the Easter Rabbit (a confusion with the hare, the original Easter animal).

Alan Dundes in a portmanteau article called "Some Minor Genres of American Folklore" (*SFQ*, XXXI, 20–36) listed with sparse examples some of the less studied but familiar types of American folklore: tongue holders, in which one attempts to hold one's tongue but still enunciate; telephone answers intended to be insulting or smart alecky; initial abbreviations (like the traditional college abridgement, T.G.I.F.); envelope sealers; tag lines frequently inseparable from Wellerisms; rebukes to the greedy ("What do you want, egg in your beer?"); feigned apology; even bodily noises. Dundes concluded that no one of these minor genres has the importance of the proverb but nevertheless "they do represent traditional oral materials in the United States and as such they deserve the attention of folklorists."

viii. Literary Use of Folklore

The intentional use of folklore by literary craftsmen (in poetry and drama, of course, but chiefly in fiction) has always fascinated the reader. Nothing as ambitious and comprehensive as Thistleton Dyer's *Folklore of Shakespeare*, which was reprinted in 1966 eighty years after its first publication, appeared in 1967, but several stimulating articles dealt with various aspects of this major theme.

Martin Light in "Lewis's 'Scarlet Sign': Accommodating to the Popular Market" (*JPC*, I, 106–113) evaluated an early Sinclair Lewis short story, pointed out its inclusion of such folkloristic material as a family curse and a portent, and then stressed the fact that the author in not realizing the potentiality of his theme compromised his artistic success and established a habit of composition which impeded his later artistic development. Lura and Duilio Pedrini examined the figurative language in Cooper's novel *The Pathfinder* (*NYFQ*, XXIII, 99–108) and argued with plausibility if not conviction that the novelist in his approach to his material was more a folklorist than a historian. Characters in the novel like Cap and Jasper, seafarers by profession, employed many nautical locutions and figures while Pathfinder, a man of the woods, utilized analogies involving animals. Of some 160 similes and metaphors noted, over one-third relate to creatures of the forest. Cooper's language seemed especially helpful in distinguishing temperamentally between mariner and frontiersman, white man and red, man and animal.

Several critics observed the use of proverbs and proverbial expressions in various writers. Sylvia Lyons Render in "North Carolina Dialect: Chesnutt Style" (*NoCF*, XV, 67–70) analyzed the dialogue in the fiction of Charles W. Chesnutt, notably *The Conjure Woman*, and commended the Negro author of this regional novel for his accurate use of dialect. Chesnutt had a careful ear for both Negro and poor white speech, and he introduced words ("goopher," "buckra," and "scuppernong") which were natural to the speakers described. To one of his Negro characters a boastful man was "jes a big bladder wid a handful er shot rattlin' roun' in it." Henry Glassie in "The Use of Folklore in *David Harum*" (*NYFQ*, XXIII, 163–185) examined E. N. Westcott's famous novel of a New York State horse trader and demonstrated the faithful use of folk speech. The article lists over seventy proverbs or proverbial expressions which appeared in the novel and provides suitable annotation and analogies. Glassie concluded that in *David Harum* "folklore is used not only to add daubs of local color, but also to emphasize the difference between the culture of the country people and the urban-, education-oriented popular culture." In "The Rhetorical Function of Proverbs in *Walden*" (*JAF*, LXXX, 151–159) Joseph J. Moldenhauer discussed the role of stylistic devices such as paradox, pun, and proverb in Thoreau's writing and emphasized the ingenious way in which Thoreau sometimes employed proverbs to put his audience off guard and sometimes either distorted and altered familiar proverbs or actually devised his own. According to the critic over one hundred proverbial or aphoristic items appear in *Walden* although he does not list them. Thoreau's "a woman's dress . . . is never done," "a goose is a goose still, dress it as you will," and especially the famous dictum, "If a man does not keep pace with his companions, perhaps it is because he hears a different drummer," illustrate vividly the original ways in which the writer employed proverbial language.

But even contemporary writers incorporate proverbs in their work. Mac E. Barrick in "Proverbs and Sayings from Gibbsville, Pa." (*KFQ*, XII, 55–80) showed convincingly that much of the success of John O'Hara's dialogue was due to his use of proverbs and folkloric language in general. O'Hara's people, according to Barrick, use language rich in slang, oaths, backyard or street locutions, and are little indebted to books. Such novels as *Appointment in Samarra* and *The Lockwood Concern*, published thirty-one years apart, suggest that not only did O'Hara employ proverbial material in the beginning of his fictional career but that such use has actually increased in his later novels and stories. *The Lockwood Concern* (1965) contains some 152 proverbial and figurative expressions in its 407 pages, and demonstrates further O'Hara's increasing latitude in the choice of such diction. Barrick arranged his material alphabetically and cited analogues.

Two articles deal with the work of Saul Bellow. Robert Detweiler in "Patterns of Rebirth in *Henderson the Rain King*" (*MFS*, XII, 405–414) pointed out that Bellow's use of grail motifs, womb symbols, and the resurrection myth is already a critical platitude but insisted that the single concept of rebirth is fundamental to the meaning of the novel. This notion is expressed through both language and image, and Bellow is especially adept in utilizing animal imagery to convey his meaning. In "The Devil and Saul Bellow" (*CLS*, III, 197–205) Robert H. Fossum argued that although Bellow is not primarily or conspicuously a religious writer, he is concerned with the state of man's soul in the modern world and that all his heroes are in some way or other in quest of their souls. Bellow's most striking personification of evil, according to this critic, is the character Tamkin in *Seize the Day*, while the pathetic salesman Tommy Wilhelm in the same novel is the Bellow figure who seems closest to selling his soul to the devil. Tamkin is even a Mephistopheles in modern dress, complete with pointed shoulders, clawlike nails, and hypnotic eyes.

One of Melville's most complex stories is the focus of Ray B. Browne's study entitled "The Affirmation of 'Bartleby'" (*Folklore International*, pp. 11–21). Melville's use of folklore and mythology has been recognized for some time, but Browne sees in "Bartleby" additional motifs and themes. The nicknames applied to the copyists in the law office, mediaeval terminology suggestive of the Gawain-Launcelot theme, and the symbolic use of the color green all become important in his reading. Finally the critic identified Bartleby's tragic flaw as his inability to conform and claimed that his death was in keeping with Melville's general notion of the power of the hero and his ultimate resurrection.

In "The Frontiersman in Popular Fiction, 1820–60" (*Frontier Reexamined*, pp. 142–153) Jules Zanger tried to explain the genesis of the typical American frontiersman in nineteenth-century American fiction and reiterated the importance of Daniel Boone and Davy Crockett as archetypes. The heroes of popular novels were indebted to both as they were in other ways to Cooper's Leatherstocking. Crockett in particular epitomized the folk idea of the westerner held by most dwellers on the Atlantic seaboard, the heroic, democratic American. The article is lucid exposition but treads familiar ground.

MacEdward Leach in "Folklore in American Regional Literature" (*JFI*, I [1966], 376–397) asserted that there were five basic regions of folk culture in the United States: New England with Boston as focal center, the New York region, Pennsylvania and Delaware with Philadelphia as center, the Tidewater South, and the Deep South and River country with New Orleans as the nucleus. Later in American history the Middle West and the Far West could be added. Each of these regions Leach found to have its own characteristics and the consensus of the areas has resulted in American folklore. Various writers have enriched their work by employing indigenous material, notably George W. Cable, Washington Irving, Joel Chandler Harris, and particularly William Faulkner. Leach also contended that the large humor segment of American regional literature owed a good deal to the tall tale tradition and to the situational humor which is endemic to regional folklore. But his final note was pessimistic: he felt that regionalism, because of the pressure of industrialism, the pressure to conform, and the ease of communication, was moribund.

In a leisurely article entitled "Shakespeare and Southern Folklore" (*GaR*, XXI, 508–520) George P. Wilson pointed out analogies between the Shakespearian plays and regional folk beliefs or practises. Using such categories as the folklore of celestial bodies, omens, witchcraft beliefs, ghostlore, and superstitions about animals, he recalled folklore familiar to him since childhood and then cited dramatic passages which corroborated the beliefs. Thus the common association of the owl with portents of ill fortune suggested the line from *Macbeth,* "It was the owl that shriek'd, the fatal bellman"; and the tradition that blue lights generally accompanied ghosts brought to mind the ghastly vision of Richard III: "The lights burn blue. It is now dead midnight."

ix. Anthologies[1]

Several substantial volumes of folk material (mostly narrative and expository) appeared during the year, in all cases making available material which is either out of print or difficult of access. A new edition of May Justus' *The Peddler's Pack*, originally published in 1957, was entitled *The Complete Peddler's Pack* (Knoxville, Univ. of Tenn. Press); it added music and the words to nineteen additional

---

1. For a discussion of John Q. Anderson's *With the Bark On*, see p. 296.

songs. Harry Hansen edited *New England Legends and Folklore* (New York, Hastings House), to which Samuel Chamberlain contributed excellent regional photographs. Most of the material in the book was the work of Samuel Adams Drake in 1884, but a paper by Katherine Lee Bates on Cape Cod towns and William Austin's famous short shory, "Peter Rugg, the Missing Man," are also included. Martin Shockley edited *Southwest Writers Anthology* (Austin, Steck-Vaughn), the first two sections of which are devoted to folk songs and folktales. Some of the editorial comments underscore the prefatory statement that the book was designed as a text, but the biographical notes are extremely helpful.

One of the most important gatherings of material to appear in 1967 is Bruce Jackson's *The Negro and His Folklore in Nineteenth-Century Periodicals* (Austin, Univ. of Tex. Press). Some thirty-two articles selected from magazines as different as *Lippincott's* and the *Century* from *Dwight's Journal of Music* and the *Southern Workman* reveal a growing interest in Negro superstitions, idiom, and song. Higginson's well known 1867 account of Negro spirituals is included as well as Cable's description of dancing in Congo Square and Antonin Dvorak's comments on American regional music. The anthology collects a number of obscure articles and proves that after the Civil War folklorists were turning their attention to many aspects of Negro folk life.

x. Obituaries

During the year 1967 three prominent folklorists died and obituary articles not only paid tribute to the deceased but provided useful summaries of their achievements and their contributions to the study of folklore.

MacEdward Leach, Professor of English at the University of Pennsylvania and for a long time the secretary-treasurer of the American Folklore Society, was the subject of a eulogy by Horace Beck (*KFQ*, XII, 193–198). Marshall W. Stearns, chronicler of American Jazz and a close student of popular culture, was given an obituary tribute by William G. Terrell (*NYFQ*, XXIII, 65). George Korson, the indefatigable collector of Pennsylvania mining lore and tales, was memorialized by Benjamin A. Botkin (*NYFQ*, XXIII, 237–239).

A different kind of tribute was paid by William D. Wittliff to J. Frank Dobie, who died in 1964. In "J. Frank Dobie on Folklore" (*The Sunny Slopes*, pp. 89–99) he collected various pronouncements which Dobie had made over the years in many different places— prefaces, articles, books. The fifty-four quotations are neither co-herent nor necessarily consistent, but they reveal admirably the character of Dobie, a folkloristic maverick in the best sense of the term. Dobie often voiced his criticism of the academic folklorists who spent their time in classifying, codifying, and piling up analogies and parallels, each carefully labeled. In 1943 he declared that he cared nothing for the science of folklore and ventured his own defini-tion: "Folklore to me is an expression of folks, the essence of a cultural inheritance."

University of Illinois

18. Themes, Topics, and Criticism

Harry Finestone

i. Literary History: Speculations and Reappraisals

A number of students, friends, and admirers have contributed to *Essays on American Literature in Honor of Jay B. Hubbell*. The contents range from studies in seventeenth-century Puritan literature to contemporary modern poetry and fiction, and the critical and historical level is unusually high. The following essays are of particular interest, however, and illustrate the scope of the collection.

"The Morals of Power: Business Enterprise as a Theme in Mid-Nineteenth Century American Fiction" (pp. 90–107) by Henry Nash Smith shows the attitudes toward the business ethic as illustrated in Hawthorne's *The House of the Seven Gables* and Twain and Warner's *The Gilded Age*. Smith reminds us that the portrait of Beriah Sellers, while destroying the central coherence of the latter novel, is nevertheless its most interesting aspect. He places Sellers clearly in the context of the Civil War and postwar boom which destroyed the innocence of the American Adam, who could exist in his pristine virtue only in an agrarian community. Of course, mid-nineteenth century attitudes toward business survive today, and Smith ironically reminds us that although we may dismiss with a grimace Wilson's famous remark that what was good for General Motors was good for the country, in our hearts we know he was right. We don't believe what all the television ads say, but we are all captivated by the vision of life they seem to hold out. Richard Beale Davis in "Mrs. Stowe's Characters-In-Situations and A Southern Literary Tradition" (pp. 108–125) explores the ramifications of Jay B. Hubbell's early observation that the twentieth-century writer in the South owes much to Harriet Beecher Stowe's plantation novels. He traces the ways in which not only Twain and Cable but Faulkner and Penn Warren have learned from Mrs. Stowe.

James Woodress' "Uncle Tom's Cabin in Italy" (pp. 126–140)

which follows is an examination of the remarkable history of that novel. He records the ironic fact that while the novel has tended to languish in this country, where scant attention has been paid to it since the nineteenth century, in Italy it has always had a wide popular audience and has been an important influence. The essay concludes with a bibliography of the Italian editions of *Uncle Tom's Cabin*. Walter Blair's "Dashiell Hammett: Themes and Techniques" (pp. 295–306) raises the question of whether Hammett's work may qualify not as sub-literature, but as an important form of serious literature. He suggests that Hammett, who has been greatly admired since his first work appeared, has been an important influence on such diverse figures as Robert Graves, André Malraux, and William Faulkner, and he demonstrates by careful examination that the cause for Hammett's influence is the high level of his craft. Also of interest is a provocative essay by Gay Wilson Allen, "The Influence of Space on the American Imagination" (pp. 329–342). He shows the relationship in their attitudes toward space of Whitman, Emily Dickinson, Hart Crane, William Carlos Williams, and even Wallace Stevens.

The first essay in the collection is a general one, Howard Mumford Jones's "American Studies in Higher Education," (pp. 3–20) which raises important issues about the rationale for the study of American literature. Perhaps his attitudes are best summarized in the distinction he makes between the "novel in America" and the "American novel," the latter being, according to Jones, one of our primary concerns. He argues that the study of the American novel can exist only in the context of what responsible writing is supposed to be in this country. The question for Jones is not whether the novel since Freud and Jung is better or worse than it was when Cooper wrote, but rather whether its image of American life endorses, questions, or denies that an enduring republic can be founded on human nature and that the arts in the United States will support and nourish our particular democratic society. Such questions, or questions like these, differentiate for Jones, American studies from other branches of humane learning.

Another work by Professor Jones, *Belief and Disbelief in American Literature* (Chicago, Univ. of Chicago Press), originally formed a series of lectures at the Frank L. Weil Institute for Studies in Religion and the Humanities in Cincinnati. The chapters cover Tom Paine and his religion of Republicanism, the pantheism of the early

Romantics, Irving, Cooper, and Bryant, and the transcendentalism
of Emerson. Whitman and Twain are treated by opposing the cosmic optimism of the former to the profound pessimism of the latter.
The lonely, uncomforting religion of Frost also forms a chapter, and
the book ends with a summarizing postlude. For Professor Jones,
the authors chosen define the movement from 1776 to 1966 toward
some alliance between religious dogma and literature, although religious orthodoxy, he feels, has never been a major concern of most
American writers. The rise of American literature has corresponded
generally with the decline of religious influence and of religious
leaders. It has correspondingly seen the rise of the influence of the
scientist, of the social scientist, and, one suspects to Professor Jones's
regret, of the psychologist. Eliot, of course, has often been cited as
the great exception to this lack of interest in religion, but Professor
Jones reminds us of his early removal to England, where presumably
he found the semblance, at least, of concern for religious authority.
Jones finds it significant, however, that although the classic American
writers are not particularly religious, they are also not atheists, and
he points out that the great themes in literature are still religious
ones. *Herzog* shares with *Pilgrim's Progress* the central problem of
salvation. Accordingly, Jones does not lament the failure of American writers to be drawn to religious orthodoxy, since he feels that all
serious American literary art attempts to grapple with the great
themes of theology: God, man, and the universe.

A study with the same general orientation, *The Cycle of American Literature*, an essay in historical criticism by Robert E. Spiller,
has been reprinted in paperback (New York, The Free Press) with
a special Epilogue. In a preface to this edition, Professor Spiller reminds us that the book, written in 1955, was a distillation of his
experience as editor of the *Literary History of the United States* and
in a sense was a synthesis of the knowledge of the thirty-five contributors to that large work. A re-reading of the preface to the first
edition is a sober reminder of the magnitude of the task which faced
those scholars who were attempting through a theory of cyclic pattern to create a symbolic illumination of the great expanse of literature written in this country from Colonial times to the present. The
final chapter of Spiller's study, "The Uses of Memory: Eliot, Faulkner," had predicted for this country a leadership that would direct
and guide the literature of the Free World into further cycles of

fulfillment. In the Epilogue, Spiller recalls that although that leadership did not immediately appear, the period from 1955–1965, which marked the completion of the careers of most of the major writers of our time, nevertheless provided a new phase or movement in American literary history. He points out that the major creative impulses have come in drama rather than in poetry or fiction, and he emphasizes the remarkable international impact of American literature and the creation of the International Style in art, largely by American influence. This new international style, Spiller feels, is romantic and revolutionary; it is experimental and largely anti-intellectual, often given to the darkly comic and the grotesque. At its core, however, he feels there persists the human will to prevail.

The next three items listed share an interest in Southern themes. *Regionalism and Beyond, Essays of Randall Stewart,* has been edited by George Core with a foreword by Norman Holmes Pearson (Nashville, Vanderbilt Univ. Press, 1968). Part One centers on Hawthorne, Part Two on general aspects of American literature, and Part Three particularly on Southern literature. Stewart's work on Hawthorne is that which is most widely known, but one would like to call attention especially to a penetrating analysis of Faulkner's debt to Hawthorne and a scrupulously scholarly article on the relation of Hawthorne to *The Faerie Queene.* As Pearson points out in his foreword, the essay, "The Old Cost of Human Redemption," from Stewart's most ambitious work, *American Literature and Christian Doctrine,* is the conservative Christian Humanist's answer to Parrington. Many readers, however, will find most interesting the essays on the Fugitives and Agrarians, particularly one on Donald Davidson since, in the final analysis, Stewart's deepest sympathies were with the Southern ideas expressed by this group.

Hunting in the Old South: Original Narratives of the Hunters, selected and edited by Clarence Gohdes (Baton Rouge, La. State Univ. Press) will have a direct appeal on one level to the sportsman who likes a good hunting yarn, and it also provides an historical account of the history of field sports in the ante-bellum South. All the tales in this volume have been previously reprinted in the *Georgia Review,* beginning in the Fall issue of 1964. The material is derived from a number of magazines and books, and the writers are both professional journalists and avid sportsmen representative of the southern gentry and of visitors from the north and Europe.

Professor Gohdes has attempted to cover the methods used to bag game, from bear and deer to wild fowl and varmints. He has written brief and highly informative introductions to each selection. With open frankness, Professor Gohdes admits that he is interested in presenting the Old South as a sportsman's paradise, and the book, as he suggests, is more in the tradition of moonlight and magnolias than in that of *Uncle Tom's Cabin*.

The narratives themselves are, surprisingly, of high quality, and the book with its beautiful illustrations is a pleasure to read. One cannot, however, read these selections without a whole area of Faulkner's work coming to mind. Although the narratives record that world on a totally different level, without the purposefully symbolic and mythic vision which transforms Faulkner's simple hunting tales, the detailed description, for example, of the "blood baptism" of the novice who has killed his first deer cannot fail to remind us of the tradition out of which Faulkner appeared.

John Q. Anderson in *With the Bark On* (Nashville, Vanderbilt Univ. Press) has compiled and edited a collection of popular humor of the Old South illustrated with drawings by Mary Alice Bahler. The material appeared originally in newspapers and magazines between 1835 and 1860, and very little of it has been previously reprinted. The arrangement is by subject matter, and the selections in "Varmints and Hunters" complement the tales in Professor Gohdes' collection. Sections on "The River" and "The Backcountry" are clearly valuable additions to the other collections of early Southern humor. Years ago, Walter Blair began to study this genre in order to indicate important relationships between primitive folk humor and those sophisticated works of Twain and others which evolved from it. This volume is a useful edition to a field of study which has in recent years attracted a number of scholars.

ii. The Thirties

This is a particularly rich year in re-evaluations of the Thirties, perhaps because in increasing numbers both younger scholars and writers who lived through the experience have begun to turn their attention to this important period. It seemed to this reviewer a few years ago that the time would come when interest in the Depression Decade would rival that in the Jazz Age. The works discussed below seem to offer some evidence of the accuracy of that speculation.

Warren French, who has edited *The Thirties*, is because of his particular interests well-qualified to introduce a variety of percep- tive essays. Many of them show how important writers such as Hem- ingway, Fitzgerald, Wolfe, etc., responded to the demands and dislocations of the crisis. David G. Pugh's "Reading the Proletarians —30 Years Later" (pp. 89–95) summarizes with great skill the gen- erally disregarded work of the proletarian writers. Dan Jaffe's "Archibald MacLeish: Mapping the Tradition" (pp. 141–148) dem- onstrates the poet's movement from purely aesthetic concerns to social consciousness with an appropriate estimate of the varying degrees of his success. It could perhaps have placed MacLeish's work in the context of the systematic effort by leftist critics to stigmatize him as an American fascist and the effect that this attack had on his shift in interests. Gerald Rabkin's "The Federal Theater Project" (pp. 201–210) is a good history, and Gene W. Ruoff's "The New Criticism: One Child of the 30s That Grew Up" (pp. 159–174) shows how the new critical movement which was basically antipathetic to the prevailing ideology managed to flourish and even to receive its major impetus in circumstances hostile to it. Jackson R. Bryer (pp. 229–243) has provided an extremely useful checklist of the accumu- lated criticism dealing with the decade.

Years of Protest: A Collection of American Writings of the 1930's, edited by Jack Salzman with the assistance of Barry Wallenstein (New York, Pegasus) is an historical rather than a critical anthology. Its purpose has been to provide pieces intrinsically interesting and significant while at the same time representative of events and atti- tudes of the period. It is not surprising that the weakest selections represent the ephemeral poetry and fiction which were immediate responses to social indignation. We find, however, a great deal of first-rate journalism, especially eye-witness accounts of strikes, the bread lines, hunger marches, etc. Some of the major literary wars are also recorded in part; for example, Michael Gold's vendetta against Thornton Wilder, the ideological struggles surrounding the *Partisan Review*, and James T. Farrell's difficulties once he had run afoul of the Stalinists. Mr. Farrell's influence on the book is clear, and it is also acknowledged by the editor. There are a number of re- productions of photographs, cartoons, and paintings, unfortunately often too small to make a suitable impact.

The Federal Theater, 1935–1939: Plays, Relief, and Politics, by Jane Dehart Mathews (Princeton, N. J., Princeton Univ. Press), traces the origins of this unparalleled venture in federally-sponsored American theater art from its hopeful beginnings to its sad death. It not only chronicles the actual events of the federal theater project but places it in the over-all and important political context of the time and also provides us with portraits of the major figures in the enterprise. That of Hallie Flanagan, the Project's National Director, is both sympathetic and objective. The accounts of the indignation and uproar in the halls of Congress at the Project's radical shenanigans make lively reading and have great relevance. It seems extremely likely that current plays representing vigorous black nationalism, New Left politics, and indeed the whole theater of sexual shock, will be met with the same vigorous retaliation in Congress that the Communist drama of the Thirties had to face. The book contains several admirable illustrations and is a model of accuracy and scrupulous historical objectivity.

Daniel Aaron, who has been a major explorer in the regions of the Thirties, has written in "The American Left: Some Ruins and Monuments" (*UDQ*, I [1966], ii, 5–23) a clear-headed and unsentimental essay which examines and contrasts the radicalism of the Thirties with the present New Left. He argues that the New Left has tended to write off the Old Left as irrelevant to our times, thereby totally disregarding the facts of history. His purpose is to resurrect the salient features of that decade and to place them in some proper perspective. Aaron remarks that we have tended to forget the simple fact of the Terrible Depression with its profound effect not only on the poor and dispossessed but on the upper classes as well, and he records the "litanies of misery" of the young who suddenly found all of their expectations shattered and who responded to the disaster by taking to the road. He points out how social collapse was averted, partially because the crisis was abated by the New Deal and because organized labor was at no time predisposed to revolution. Since there did exist a more cheerful side which seems largely typified in the popular culture, he views the adjectives "tragic," "hopeless," "Red" as inadequate designations of the Thirties. He traces the efforts and subsequent failure of the Communist Party to completely engage and subordinate the intellectuals. Although writers paid a high cost for their involvement with the Party, Aaron denies that the American intelligentsia betrayed themselves or that nothing fruitful emerged from the Thirties.

He concludes that the literature of the time was too diverse, reflective of too many points of view, to lend itself to easy formulation, and he considers, in light of the important output, that it is an impertinence to assert that the Thirties crippled artistic talent. He correctly reminds us that the large majority of critics with leftist tendencies refused to buckle under to the pressures of Marxist aesthetics and avoided most of the pitfalls of the crude and simplistic Marxist apologetics. Aaron concludes that the New Left has a lesson to learn from the manner in which the intellectuals of the Thirties met problems largely similar to those we face today.

Willa Cather was the first important writer to make disparaging remarks about muckrakers. She based these remarks on her experience at *McClure's Magazine,* which was for some time a major center of muckraking journalism. Her objection was that the muckrakers could not decide whether they wanted to be writers or social workers and consequently ended up not being much of either, and her attitudes have had fairly wide currency. Critics largely influenced by conservative new critical positions popular since World War II have tended to dismiss writers of the Progressive Era along with those of the Thirties. The shift to a more favorable critical attitude toward the relationship between sociology and literature may be seen in George L. Groman's decision to edit *Political Literature of the Progressive Era* (East Lansing, Mich. State Univ. Press). The collection deals primarily with muckraking fiction, which has been for the most part ignored. What the most famous muckrakers attempted in their articles, these writers tried to approximate in their imaginative literature. Certain selections reveal the deep moral indignation of the progressives at the corrupt relationship between business and politics. Part One is devoted to little-known pieces by Hamlin Garland, whose work is viewed largely as a Populist influence. Parts Two and Three cover the rural and urban scenes, and Part Four reveals the villains, the large, new, industrial combines, and their victims. In general, the progressives saw the rising trusts as the greatest enemy of democracy. Part Four contrasts Upton Sinclair's indignation over outrageous conditions in the meat trust and Robert Herrick's more thoughtful concerns with the disappearance of moral idealism under the pressures of Big Business. These two authors illustrate two major patterns that sociological literature has taken.

Think Back on Us . . . A Contemporary Chronicle of the 1930's by Malcolm Cowley, edited with an introduction by Henry Dan Piper (Carbondale and Edwardsville, Ill., So. Ill. Univ. Press) is perhaps the most outstanding work on the period to appear so far. Professor Piper has chosen those essays from the *New Republic* which reveal Malcolm Cowley at his best in dealing with both the social and the literary record. In an Epilogue, Mr. Cowley has provided a modest biographical account of what it meant to meet a weekly deadline for the *New Republic*. The first selection, "Angry Professors," (the titles of many of the selections have been especially devised for this edition) is one of many devastating attacks which young radical intellectuals like Cowley and Edmund Wilson were delivering against the staid New Humanist Professors, Babbitt, More, and others. This selection was later expanded and included in *A Critique of Humanism: A Symposium*, edited by C. Hartley Grattan in 1930. This brief account, however, is enough to display the restrained contempt with which the young radicals held the professorial gentility of the American university.

We have, also, a brief exchange between Cowley and MacLeish on the correct attitudes the writer was supposed to assume toward the revolutionary spirit of the time. Cowley's attitude here seems extreme, but interestingly enough this exchange is immediately followed by a review of Granville Hicks's *The Great Tradition*, which demonstrates how deeply Cowley's radicalism was tempered by good sense, or at least by his middle class origins and education.

In addition, there are essays on most of the major poets and novelists, on the People's Theater, and, in light of the violent anti-Trotskyist position then so popular in New York literary circles, an extremely sensitive and cautious review of Trotsky's writings. The whole collection, but particularly an essay on Marxist criticism and its limitations, makes clear that Cowley, though often in deep sympathy with the Left, was never a dogmatist. Probably no work that has appeared so far, with the possible exception of Edmund Wilson's collections which cover the same period, provides a clearer or less prejudiced view. The impact of the book is to send one rushing back to the stacks to examine old files of the *New Republic*.

iii. American Studies

On hand are a number of works which deal at great length with the special field of American Studies, exploring relationships between literature, popular culture, history, politics, and technology. *Ameri-*

can Studies: Essays on Theory and Method, edited by Robert Meredith (Columbus, Ohio, Charles E. Merrill, 1968), attempts to trace the movement over the past ten years toward a coherent, mature methodology in American Studies. There are three parts, the first of which examines issues as they emerged from the Thirties to about 1960. Part Two explores the meanings and uses of "culture" as a central concept of American ideas, and the third part deals with various methodological problems. In Part One, "American Studies as a Discipline" by Roy Harvey Pearce, "'American Studies' in the Doldrums: Or Whistling Up a Breeze" by Edwin H. Cady, and "The Knowledge of Literature: Suggestions for American Studies" by Frederick J. Hoffman are of particular interest. In Part Two, "Art Content and Social Involvement" by Vytautas Kavolis, though written in an opaque style, is especially provocative; and in Part Three, Norman S. Grabo's "The Veiled Vision: The Role of Aesthetics in Early American History" relates the aesthetic theories of Susanne Langer to those of seventeenth century American aesthetics, particularly as revealed in Edward Taylor's poetry.

Two companion volumes which provide additional approaches to the study of the United States are *The American Experience* and *The American Culture,* both edited by Hennig Cohen (Boston, Houghton Mifflin, 1968). *The American Culture,* while not presuming to cover the full range of scholarship in American Studies, does provide a coherent view, particularly when it is paired with its companion volume. All of the articles in both volumes appeared originally in the *American Quarterly,* which itself has played a major role in the development of the field. The essays in *The American Experience,* the first of these two volumes, explore the distinctive qualities of this country, its people, and its historical experience. In attempting to define the national character, it examines the past and its uses, the encounter of innocence and experience, the concept of the hero in the American West, and the relationship of the American culture to that of other nationalities. The four essays which deal with progressivism as a political movement and two methodological essays, Henry Nash Smith's "Can 'American Studies' Develop a Method?" and Richard E. Sykes's "American Studies and the Concept of Culture: A Theory and Method" are all of particular interest. The essays in *American Culture* range from a discussion of images and myths to an examination of important developments in the American intellectual tradition. Included are essays on mass culture from movies to jazz; for example, Parker Tyler's "Hollywood As a Universal Church," a penetrating analysis of the American movies which is almost too excruciating to read. Robert L. Tyler's "The I.W.W. and the West" explores the particular appeal of the "Wobblies" to the American intellectual, and Henry F. May's "The Rebellion of the Intellectuals, 1912–1917," is a subtle historical analysis of the break-up of the genteel tradition.

Three volumes in the Documents in American Civilization Series, of which Hennig Cohen and John William Ward are general editors, illustrate clearly the impressive results that can be achieved when experience, skill, and great sophistication are combined to deal with a wide range of cultural documents. *American Life in the 1840's*, edited by Carl Bode (New York, New York Univ. Press) attempts to acquaint us with what life must have been like in that era. He has brought together documents and pictures, many of which have never before been reproduced, which show perhaps more clearly than any amount of analysis could the amazing relatedness of the 1840's to the present. The introduction by Mr. Bode summarizes with great clarity the predominant feeling of what it meant to be an American at that time.

The American Literary Revolution, 1783–1837, edited by Robert E. Spiller (New York, New York Univ. Press) reprints significant essays which illustrate that groping toward national identity which was finally formulated clearly in Emerson's "The American Scholar." For the first time, perhaps, we are able to get a thorough overview, from the original sources, of the hesitations, the self-doubts, and the feelings of inferiority which led to the quarrel with English literature and the need for the reassurance which literary nationalism attempted to assuage. The final section reprints the Copyright Law of 1790 and provides not only lists of books ordered from England but also those published in America. The section also contains excerpts from the writings of those English literary theorists, such as Lord Kames and Coleridge, who were major influences on the American taste and imagination of the time.

Popular Culture and Industrialism, 1865–1890, edited by Henry Nash Smith (New York, New York Univ. Press), reveals the deep relationship between the development of the steam-powered printing presses, railroads, mass production, and the mass media and their

concomitant, an intensified and enlarged popular culture. Reproduced in this volume are the commonplace and the ordinary rather
than any distinguished achievement. The book deals with beliefs and
attitudes that most Americans took for granted at the time, with
pseudo- or stereotypic ideas rather than with original thinking. According to Professor Smith, this popular culture is primarily important because it embodies an awareness of the transformation of
American society, with its ultimate challenge of all the old beliefs,
which accompanied standardization and the shift from agrarianism.
He has drawn on monthly magazines, widely-read books, and the
columns of the New York *Herald. Harper's Weekly* provides most of
the illustrations. He has, of course, emphasized urban life, and particularly New York, as the focus of the emergent mass culture. The
contents range from accounts of the great, new financial wizards
who had captured the popular imagination to records of the cruel
disparities in big city life between rich and poor and the deep cultural
gaps between natives and immigrants. The plates are brilliantly illuminating, from the sentimental and idealized statue of the American soldier by Carl H. Conrad to the brutally comic political cartoons
of Thomas Nast.

Professor Smith has wisely and of necessity decided to condense
many of the selections. All students of nineteenth century American
Studies are deeply in his debt for his informative introduction and
for his selection of material, which is always fascinating even in its
most alarming revelations. The various scholars who have in recent
years attempted to gloss over the crudities of The Gilded Age will
simply have to face up to the evidence presented here and in a new
collection of the work of Thomas Nast.

The photograph of Nast which comprises the frontispiece of
Thomas Nast, Political Cartoonist by J. Chal Vinson (Athens, Univ.
of Ga. Press) clearly reveals through his piercing eyes and wry smile
the devastating comic wit of the most important and influential political cartoonist of the nineteenth century. This book reproduces over
150 examples of his art, and Professor Vinson has provided a sketch
of his life, useful in its brief discussion of his artistic development
and the relation of his work to the "Ash Can School" of realism in
painting. He does not ignore, however, Nast's major contribution to
the art of the political cartoon, the examples of which are chosen
from *Harper's Weekly*. A study of the plates reveals Nast's develop-

ment from rather simple and traditional satire to the devastating and brutal wit which can be seen, for example, in his major attack on Boss Tweed and Tammany Hall. As one examines the satire of the cartoons, one is also reminded of how clearly the line runs from Nast to such modern cartoonists as Herblock, Haynie, and Conrad, but the high quality of his artistic imagination and reliance on symbol reveal as well his influence on the more serious art of Steinberg.

Another study which examines issues similar to those in Professor Smith's book is *Harvests of Change, American Literature, 1865–1914*, by Jay Martin (Englewood Cliffs, N. J., Prentice Hall). It is concerned, however, not primarily with popular culture but with the ways in which significant artists dealt with the dramatic events taking place. It begins with the assumption that the period under discussion was a time rich in relatedness, when people with common goals attempted to join together to interpret meaningfully the startling changes taking place. In other words, he tends to see it as a more wholesome period than our disjointed present. According to Professor Martin, the writers of the period, noting the growing alienation and loss of social stability, attempted to discover the locus of the change and undertook the task of preserving the old values, of balancing and assessing the preoccupations of their age and creating from them new, complex patterns of understanding and belief. The study deals with a wide range of figures, but perhaps the most interesting portion concerns Henry James and his effort to understand the impact of the events which took place between the two great wars in his lifetime. His story is a tragic one of gradual disillusionment, while refusing to submit to despair. The author has quite aptly chosen for one of his epigraphs to the chapter on James a prophetic quotation from his article on Baudelaire written as early as 1878, "We have passed through the fiery furnace and profited by experience."

Essays on History and Literature, which deserves mention here, deals with the analysis, evaluation, organization, and presentation of historical evidence. The essays are written by historians who use literature as a source of history and whose own style is in turn influenced by literature. Their basic assumption is that literary art, like that of painting, architecture, and sculpture, influences the historian's concept of an age. The importance of literature as historical evidence lies, according to the editor, not only in the quality of the artist's perceptions but in the sensitivity of the historian. These essays ask not whether, but rather how literature should be used to illumine the shape of the past.

The essay by Daniel Aaron, "The Treachery of Recollection: The Inner and the Outer History" raises the question of the great difficulty an historian encounters when he attempts to record a period in which he has participated. Once the historian becomes familiar through interviews and correspondence with the makers and movers of an era, he may find that he is hampered in a way he would not be if he had been dealing with names or abstract figures from some remote time. For example, Aaron examines the complexity of trying to answer a question such as why certain men did or did not join the Communist Party in the Thirties or why writers broke away from the Leftist movement at one time and not another. The question is more complex than it appears on the surface, and a conclusion he reaches, but which he points out he cannot document, is that politics is often simply the vehicle for non-political emotions or compulsions. The attempt to record the present can only produce a reasonably accurate facsimile, but it may also, according to Aaron, succeed in creating what Henry James has called "a palpable imaginable *visitable* past."

All of the remaining essays are illuminating exercises of the historian's art: Edward Lurie's interpretation of nineteenth-century American cultural history, with its examination of Henry James and his circle; Stow Persons' study of the origins of the gentry as seen through nineteenth-century literary eyes; and Russel B. Nye's acute contrast of the ways in which the historian and the poet examine evidence in the social order. There is also a bibliography of books and articles on the use of literature in research in American history, compiled by Margaret E. Kahn and George P. Schoyer. The bibliography itself is an interesting piece of evidence of the difference between the interests of literary history and history. A number of the listings, while obviously of great interest to the historian, could be easily dispensed with by the selective literary historian.

In a year which has seen great cleavages in political parties and in which ideologies have been pitted against each other with rather terrifying frankness and with intimations of retribution and reprisal, one is fortunate to be able to turn to the calm good sense of Allen Guttman's *The Conservative Tradition in America* (New York, Oxford Univ. Press). Guttman points out that the violence of American political rhetoric has been constant from Colonial times to the present and that liberty and equality have always been our watchwords. He argues that the liberal tradition has always dominated American political thought and, to a lesser extent, American political behavior. Liberals have generally been unaccustomed to serious challenge from either left or right, and Guttman asserts that one of the major problems facing liberalism is that it has never had a serious conservative opposition. The people we define as modern conservatives, Guttman reminds us, are in reality those who have retained an attachment to nineteenth-century liberalism, and he has in mind not only Russell Kirk and Friedrich von Hayek, but Barry Goldwater as well. Burkean conservatism as it is commonly understood in England and in Europe, based on a careful and hierarchical separation of classes, is, according to Professor Guttman, clearly not relevant to the American scene. Those politicians of the Early Republic whom we tend to think of as conservatives, John Adams, Alexander Hamilton, even John Calhoun, he feels are in the broad tradition of liberal thought.

It is when one turns to literature that the conservative attitudes are most clearly discovered. Guttman examines writers of fiction from Irving and Cooper to James Gould Cozzens, and he finds in their work, rather than in the utterances of the politicians, the assertions of Burkean conservative thought. The sections on Henry Adams, on the New Humanists, and on the Agrarians, particularly Ransom and Tate and their new critical descendants, are of special interest. What distinguishes all these writers is their sense of the past, and Guttman explores how this sense has served as a corrective influence on liberal thought. It seems clear enough from his closing passages that the author bases his main hope for a sane political and intellectual future in this country on the fusion of liberal thought with those values saved from the past.

Several years ago, Leo Marx published the profoundly provocative *The Machine in the Garden*. One finds it now referred to casually in a footnote in the preface to *Flesh of Steel: Literature and the Machine in American Culture* by Thomas Reed West (Nashville, Vanderbilt Univ. Press), which while treating literary works, is not primarily a study of literature but rather of the machine and machine civilization. The author finds, however, that certain literary temperaments have dealt with the phenomena he wishes to examine more sensitively than sociological studies could have done. The authors he has chosen arbitrarily, for example, Waldo Frank, John Dos Passos, Sinclair Lewis and Carl Sandburg, represent no particular literary movement, nor are they of equal value as writers. It should come as no surprise that the writers he deals with most satisfactorily are Thorstein Veblen and Lewis Mumford. The author is aware, of course, that in the present state of rapid technological change, the word "machine" is perhaps already an anachronism. An Epilogue makes clear that the author's sympathies lie with technological advance, since he believes that machine civilization gains in energy and momentum what it loses in the impersonality of the mechanical technique. This is an interesting study, but it unfortunately does not possess the telling literary and artistic insights which so strongly characterized Leo Marx's more comprehensive work.

iv. Criticism

Why literary criticism is not an exact science (Cambridge, Mass., Harvard Univ. Press) was originally a lecture delivered by Harry Levin at Churchill College, Cambridge, England. With great persuasiveness, Professor Levin attempts to show how every effort to over-systematize in literary criticism is eventually doomed to failure. Coleridge, he points out, was the first modern villain, and the thirteenth chapter of the *Biographia Literaria* has led many important critics up the garden path. I. A. Richards, René Wellek, and Northrop Frye are all seen as having fallen victim to the besetting sin of legalism and schematic over-ingenuity. Professor Levin, however, especially in his remarks on I. A. Richards, is quick to acknowledge the debt all readers owe to the individual brilliant critical insights of all these men. We are finally urged to remember that in comparison with the natural sciences, literary criticism is, as Levin puts it, "still at the stage of botanising or indulging in the hobbies of natural history."

Levin's lecture may be read as an antidote to a rather old-fashioned discussion written in somewhat new-fangled, psychoanalytic-scientific terminology, John V. Hagopian's "Literary Criticism As a Science" in *Topic* (VI [1966], xii, 50–57). Hagopian is astonished by the all-too-frequent misuse of literature—as theology, as philosophy, as propaganda, even as emotional catharsis. He argues that since it is true that the reading of literature is an attempt to perceive a complete human experience embodied in language, it follows that criticism is an inter-disciplinary science, embracing psycho-linguistics. The good critic keeps up with research in the fields of linguistics and psychology, and, as if to illustrate, the author even provides us with a beautifully formed graph which analyzes the neurotic distortion of the creative processes. He concludes that the thrill of reading with "cerebral competence" derives from successful cognition and that catharsis is an obstacle to cognition. As readers, we strive for accurate perceptions, as critics, for a language and methodology to communicate these perceptions. A remark in Chapter Four of Aristotle's *Poetics* is offered to substantiate these remarks. Professor Hagopian needs perhaps to read the *Poetics* again, this time Chapters Six and Fourteen.

A brief essay by Robert O. Evans in the same periodical, "A Prospective for American Novelists" (pp. 58–66), comments on the popular lament about the state of the novel in the United States and suggests that a source of new vigor for American fiction might well lie in the works of three British writers: Sybille Bedford's *The Legacy*, Muriel Sparks's *The Mandelbaum Gate*, and Kingsley Amis' *The Anti-Death League*. All three novels deal with world issues in a fresh, experimental fashion, and Evans offers them as controverting evidence to the current speculations that the novel is dead. He finds it ironic that England, whose world power has waned rapidly since 1945, should be more active creatively than either the United States or Russia, whose great traditions in fiction are currently dormant.

Cleanth Brooks delivered the Sir George Watson lecture at the University of Leicester in April, 1966. Printed by the Leicester University Press under the title, *American Literature: Mirror, Lens, or Prism*, it contains an important restatement of his position on the uses of literature, which he demonstrates by brief readings of various portraits of the Southern poor white by Eudora Welty, William Faulkner, and Robert Penn Warren. In a digression, he shows how closely allied such portraits are to corresponding New England country types by comparing them with Robert Frost's "The Witch of Coos." Literature, he says, provides us "with a special kind of truth about human beings . . . always related to ourselves." It is only incidentally historically, sociologically, or scientifically accurate. It can, however, cover the statistics of sociology with warm flesh, make the dry bones of history live, and turn the alien into a brother whom we can understand. Brooks's remarks are here centered on America, but, as he suggests, his conclusions could easily apply to any other literature in the Western tradition. This essay is distinguished primarily by the fine balance which he maintains between his carefully considered generalizations and the brilliantly lucid analyses which he uses to illustrate them.

Finally, three volumes by critics whose careers have been ended by death. *A Primer of Ignorance* (New York, Harcourt, Brace and World) is a posthumous collection of essays by R. P. Blackmur, chosen and edited by Joseph Frank and based on a long-term project of Blackmur's to write a book which would synthesize America's vigor and momentum and Europe's force of mind. The editor has also included essays which deal with pathological themes in American culture. Mr. Blackmur's range of interests was indeed remarkable, and his admirers are always struck by the startling insights which are imbedded in his essays even when his style is at its most baroque and impenetrable. Probably no other critic of his generation, with the exception of Kenneth Burke, had the power to tease the mind with provocative statements, the meaning of which always appears to lie just beyond the horizon. The third part of this collection, entitled "American Witnesses," deals with two writers for whom Blackmur had remarkably strong affinities, Henry James and Henry Adams. The final essay, "Henry Adams: Three Late Moments," focuses with great poignancy on both Adams and James at the time of the first World War, when they were attempting to come to terms with the distintegration of the world as they knew it.

The four lectures which comprise *The Imagination's New Beginning: Theology and Modern Literature* by Frederick J. Hoffman (Notre Dame, Univ. of Notre Dame Press) were originally given at Notre Dame in May, 1966. Hoffman looked on these essays as a continuation of his work begun in *Samuel Beckett: The Language of Self* and *The Mortal No: Death and the Modern Imagination*. All three deal with a common set of literary and moral phenomena in twentieth-century culture. The writers discussed here have assimilated part or much of a religious system or of religious values and attempt to explore these values in the light of modern attitudes of disillusionment. They either describe the world that exists without religion or they attempt to transform religious values into modern terms. In the first half of the book, which deals with Yeats, Stevens, and Joyce, Hoffman makes a general statement of his position. The second half deals with the modern effort to translate the death of

Christ into relevant mythic terms. The final chapter, which deals with Henry Adams and Faulkner, centers on the relationship between those writers' interests in the religious monuments of the past and their distaste with modern machine civilization. He uses *Mont-Saint-Michel and Chartres* to focus on Adams' efforts to come to terms with these opposing relationships. As usual, there is much of interest to the reader in Professor Hoffman's essays, and here the style, perhaps out of deference to the lecture form, does not impede the reader with the formidable opacities and thick clusters of allusion which are so often a problem in his work.

A moving personal memoir by Allen Tate and a fine introduction by Stanley Edgar Hyman precede the excellent collection of criticism entitled *William Troy: Selected Essays* (Rutgers, N.J., Rutgers Univ. Press). Both Tate and Hyman record William Troy's impossible perfectionism, which prevented him from compiling a collection during his own lifetime, and they both attest to the fact of his reputation as one of the most important critics of our time, which the essays in this volume substantiate. As Hyman recalls, because Troy was slow to rush into print, many of his most brilliant remarks, delivered in his lectures or casually in conversation, found their way into other people's essays. He was a man not only of taste but also of great intellectual range and power and was quite obviously a founder of literary trends. This latter fact is seen most explicitly in his shift in interest from Freud to Jung in 1941. Mistaken as one may believe this shift to have been, it nonetheless served to initiate a whole new interest in myth criticism, which has tended to overpower much of modern critical theory.

The essays on James, Stein, and Fitzgerald will be of interest to students of American fiction, and particularly his 1931 essay on James, "The Lesson of the Master," shows how much he was in the vanguard of the James revival. However, Part One, "Perspectives in Modern Criticism," which includes a previously unpublished essay delivered as a lecture at Bennington College, "Time and Space Conceptions in Modern Literature," and the two brief essays which follow it, "A Note on Myth" and "Myth, Method, and the Future," show most clearly the source of his great influence.

San Fernando Valley State College

Index

The 1967 index, like the preceding *ALS* indexes, gives references to literary and historical figures who are referred to throughout the book, as well as to authors of the literary scholarship therein surveyed. Works are cited only for those authors given chapter coverage (Part I). Literary movements and genres are not indexed as such, since the organization of the book makes pertinent pages clear for most such studies.

Joseph M. Flora

Index